DAILY PRAYER 2006

A BOOK OF PRAYER,
PSALMS, SACRED READING,
AND REFLECTION
IN TUNE WITH THE SEASONS,
FEASTS, AND ORDINARY DAYS OF THE YEAR

BRYAN M. CONES

LTP

LITURGY
TRAINING
PUBLICATIONS

DAILY PRAYER 2006 © 2005 Archdiocese of Chicago: Liturgy Training
Publications, 1800 N. Hermitage Ave., Chicago IL 60622-1101; 1-800-933-1800;
fax 1-800-933-7094; orders@ltp.org. All rights reserved.

Intercessions and prayers for each day are original compositions by
Bryan M. Cones.

The publisher is grateful to the copyright holders who granted permission to
reprint their texts in this book. Sources are listed beginning on page 400.

This book was edited by Danielle A. Knott. Audrey Novak Riley was the
production editor. The design is by Larry Cope. Kari Nicholls typeset it
in Times Roman and Exocet.

Printed in Canada.

ISBN 1-56854-539-8

ADP06

TABLE OF CONTENTS

INTRODUCTION

Daily Prayer 2006 holds within it an order of prayer for each day of the liturgical year. It draws on the long tradition of Christian prayer, especially on the tradition of *lectio divina,* that is, holy reading, and on the ancient daily liturgical prayer of the Church, the Liturgy of the Hours.

Daily Prayer is meant to foster a habit of devotional prayer inspired by the calendar of the Church. The book is intended for individuals or groups, and is appropriate for older students and teachers, catechumens and candidates for full communion, as well as for any Christian who wants to pray in tune with the rhythm of the Church year.

PRAYING DAILY

Jesus gave many instructions about prayer (see Matthew 6:5–13, Luke 11:2–4, and others), and the apostle Paul exhorted those to whom he preached to "pray without ceasing" (see 1 Thessalonians 5:17). Early Christian texts such as the *Didache* encourage Christians to pray the Lord's Prayer three times a day. Later Christian writers such as Tertullian and Origen prescribed prayer as often as six times daily, basing their counsel on the life of the early Church as recorded in the Acts of the Apostles or on examples from the Hebrew scriptures, among others.

Over the course of the first Christian centuries, public liturgies came to be held at certain times of day, especially at sunrise and sunset. These liturgies joined psalms and other scriptural songs with prayers to celebrate the paschal mystery over the course of the day. The monastic movement developed its own style of prayer, focused primarily on praying all 150 psalms over a particular period of time, even all in one day. Along with the praying of the psalms came the practice of *lectio divina,* or holy reading, through which the monks meditated upon God's word revealed in scripture.

Liturgical forms of daily prayer continue to be celebrated in religious communities. Among diocesan clergy and itinerant friars, a form of this prayer for individual use developed and was published in a book called the breviary. These liturgies of the Church endure today in a variety of forms, known under the names "Liturgy of the Hours" or "Divine Office."

At one time these liturgies were celebrated in parishes. Although participation in liturgical morning and evening prayer declined among parishioners, praying daily did not. Other forms of daily prayer nourish the lives of Christians, such as the rosary, litanies, morning offerings, and "little offices." Such devotional prayers were sometimes collected and published in books of hours — prayer books used by Christians for their personal prayer. The practices of meal blessing and bedtime prayers also reflect the long tradition of prayer at certain times of day.

These practices and others all fall under the category of Christian prayer, and indeed they often share characteristics: praise and thanksgiving, psalmody, communal resonance, prayer at specific times of day, holy reading and reflection, and focus on the paschal mystery of Jesus' life, death, and Resurrection.

Drawing from these characteristics and inspired by the religious devotion they express, we offer this book of daily prayer.

THE ORDER OF PRAYER

The order of prayer in *Daily Prayer 2006* is structured primarily as a form of the Liturgy of the Hours, incorporating scripture reading and reflection with the Hours' psalmody and prayers, along with an opening and closing versicle and a brief reflection. Unlike the Liturgy of the Hours, however, *Daily Prayer* uses only a few psalms and follows a different cycle of readings, omitting antiphons, responsories, canticles, and other elements appropriate to monastic or choral celebration of the Hours.

DAILY HEADING

Each page of *Daily Prayer 2006* begins with the date and day of the week, along with the title of the liturgical observance of the day. The day may be kept as a Lord's Day, a weekday, a solemnity or a feast, or as the memorial of a saint.

OPENING AND CLOSING VERSICLE

The prayer begins and ends with the sign of the cross accompanied by a brief verse drawn from the psalm or written in light of the liturgical season. Like the sign of the cross at any liturgy, it is meant to frame the time of prayer and call to mind the triune God in whose name we pray.

PSALMODY

Prayer continues with a psalm. The psalms in *Daily Prayer 2006* have been chosen according to the celebration of the liturgical seasons. Psalms praising God's promises and God's glory have been chosen for Advent, while the psalms for Lent have been chosen from among the biblical songs of lamentation, renewal, and restoration. The Christmas and Easter seasons employ psalms of praise, while the psalms of Ordinary Time focus on thanksgiving, the gift of the law, and our faithfulness to God's will, as well as praise of divine wisdom.

The psalm is meant to help us offer praise and thanksgiving to God, and it also helps us acknowledge our place before God. Sometimes we admit sinfulness, sometimes we are bold in asking for God's faithfulness, sometimes we seek guidance. Always we give thanks for what God has done and will continue to do for us.

An individual psalm generally is repeated for several weeks to help the user learn it by heart.

READING

Each day contains a reading from scripture. These passages are inspired by the Lectionary for daily Mass. As in the Lectionary, the order of readings in *Daily Prayer 2006* is semi-continuous;

longer sections of a book or epistle may be read over the course of several weeks.

In order to introduce a greater variety of God's word, scriptures not proclaimed during the Sunday eucharistic liturgy have been favored in this book of prayer. On Sundays and major feast days one of the Mass readings for the day, or an excerpt, has been chosen, and occasionally, longer Sunday readings have been broken up over several weekdays.

As in the daily Lectionary for Mass, the readings chosen for *Daily Prayer 2006* highlight themes appropriate to the liturgical season. Advent includes passages expressing the early Church's expectation of Christ's return, readings from the Hebrew prophets that envision the future "day of the Lord," and stories of God's promises made and fulfilled. Christmas includes both Gospel stories about the infancy of Jesus and readings from the letters of John about the meaning of the divine Word's coming as a human being.

The readings for Lent draw on the Church's ancient order of Lenten readings, primarily from the Old Testament, which focus on themes of renewal, fidelity, and cleansing. Easter's readings are taken primarily from the Acts of the Apostles, which offers a picture of the first Christians and their experience of the Risen Christ.

Finally, Ordinary Time includes longer courses of readings from both the Old Testament scriptures and the New Testament letters. This winter also provides a series of readings from Mark's Gospel, which is proclaimed on the Sundays of Ordinary Time this year (Year B).

The focus in *Daily Prayer 2006* on holy reading allows the user to become more familiar with the stories and wisdom of our tradition; the format of the prayer encourages extended meditation upon scripture.

REFLECTIONS

Although not a necessary part of the prayer, the reflection is meant to share a portion of the Church's wisdom, some information about the day's saint or the reading, or simply something to contemplate. Reflections are drawn from a variety of sources including the Church's teachers and poets, its hymnody, and its liturgical and catechetical documents.

PRAYERS

The order of prayer closes with brief intercessions, the Lord's Prayer, and a closing prayer.

Intercessory prayer offers an opportunity to voice our needs. The petitions and prayers are written in light of themes suggested by the reading, feast, season, or saint remembered that day. The texts may be adapted or changed according to the needs of the user.

In keeping with tradition, the intercessions given in this book are general in focus and include prayers for the Church, the world, those in need, and those at prayer. Private intentions may be added, of course. The response to each petition may be used in individual or communal celebration.

The Lord's Prayer gathers the intercessions together into the words Jesus gave us. It has long been part of the Church's prayer. In the mind of the

Church's tradition, no Christian prayer is complete without it.

The closing prayer, in keeping with the tradition of other collect prayers, draws upon the imagery of the season and of the day and "collects" our intercessions offered to God the Father through Jesus Christ in the unity of the Holy Spirit.

USING THIS BOOK

PRAYER BY INDIVIDUALS

Although Christian prayer is most fully expressed when the assembly gathers for liturgy, the pace and schedule of daily life can make daily liturgical prayer an impossibility.

Daily Prayer 2006 is first and foremost designed to be used easily by an individual. Each order of prayer fills one page; only the psalm is on another page. In addition, the prayer is completely self-contained; there is no need for other books, such as a Bible. Because each page includes the date, there is also no need for an additional calendar, nor is it necessary to know the week of the liturgical season or the saint of the day. All such information is provided in each day's heading.

Daily Prayer 2006 is meant to be flexible. It can be prayed at any time of day and is meant to be easily carried along to work or on trips. Establishing a habit of daily prayer can be fostered by choosing a particular time of day and even a particular space, such as a corner of the home that is dedicated to prayer. Lighting a candle or burning some incense can also become a habit that helps call the heart and mind and soul to prayer.

The psalm may be recited aloud or prayed in silence, although praying aloud seems best. A psalm is best rendered as poetry that is meant to be sung: Take the lines one at a time, perhaps with a breath between lines. The effect of song can be achieved through measured recitation. Think of the psalm as the opening hymn of the prayer; it is a way of praising God and sets the tone for what follows.

If a part of the psalm draws your attention, feel free to pray only that portion, allowing those few words to draw you into prayer. Allowing periods of silence between stanzas or especially after the psalm can also invite the power and strength and full meaning of the psalm—and what it may mean to you—to develop each day.

Since a single psalm is generally used over the course of several weeks, it may be tempting to skip it altogether. Don't give in to the temptation. Psalms are the heart of prayer, the songs of God's people that catch us up in the spirit of prayer.

Psalms bear the weight of repetition. Like all good poetry, they say different things to us at different times. Learning a psalm by heart makes it possible for the words to come to mind and to give voice to prayer at other moments in a lifetime.

The day's reading follows the psalm. Because the reading may be a prophetic exhortation, a story, or part of a letter or epistle, how you use it in prayer may vary. Reflect on a prophetic reading as you might a good homily; try to apply it to your own life. If the reading is from a narrative, place yourself in the context of the story, perhaps as one of the characters. As with the psalm, one line may attract your attention. Feel free to pause and reflect. There is no rush.

The prayers can be used in a number of ways. Although they are written in light of the reading and the season, the intercessions may or may not reflect your own thoughts and intentions that day; feel free to add to them or replace them with your own. The response to the intercessions may or may not be useful to someone praying privately. If the prayer is for the sick, call to mind those close to you who are ill. If it is for civil leaders, pause to remember your own elected officials.

The Lord's Prayer can be chanted as at Mass or else recited. The collect prayer draws all to a close.

PRAYING WITH OTHERS

Daily Prayer 2006, with a few minor adaptations, can easily be prayed with others. A group may choose a leader who opens the prayer with the sign of the cross, announces the intercessions, invites the group to pray the Lord's Prayer, and prays the final collect. Another person would be chosen to proclaim the reading.

Everyone can recite the psalm together or two parts of the group can take turns reciting the stanzas. A group might alternate stanzas between an individual who sets the pace for recitation and the rest of those gathered.

It's appropriate for others to set aside their books and listen to the reading. For group use, only the leader and reader would need the books; copies of the psalm would be sufficient for everyone else to participate.

Intercessions can be announced by the leader, with everyone responding to each petition using the given response. Members may speak their own intentions. In groups, the Lord's Prayer is appropriately chanted. The collect would be spoken by the leader.

Groups may also want to add music or ritual elements, such as burning incense during the intercessions. Prayer should be adapted to the needs and capacities of the group.

WE'D LIKE TO HEAR FROM YOU

Daily Prayer 2006 is the fifth edition of an annual publication. *Daily Prayer 2007* is already being prepared. Because this book is an annual, it can be changed from year to year to become a better tool for prayer. As you use this book and adapt it for yourself, you may have ideas about how it can be made more useful. Feel free to forward your thoughts to the editor at LTP: Editor, *Daily Prayer,* 1800 N. Hermitage Ave., Chicago IL 60622-1101. You may also e-mail us at DailyPrayer@ltp.org.

ABOUT THE AUTHOR

Bryan M. Cones holds a master's degree in theology from Catholic Theological Union in Chicago. Bryan was trained in the habit of holy reading and daily prayer by the Benedictine monks of Conception Abbey and the faculty of Conception Seminary College in Conception, Missouri. He resides in Chicago, where he writes on topics touching Roman Catholic liturgy and theology.

✦ *Maranatha! Come, Lord Jesus!*

PSALM 85 *page 417*

READING *Mark 13:33–37*

Jesus said to his disciples, "Beware, keep alert; for you do not know when the time will come. It is like a man going on a journey, when he leaves home and puts his slaves in charge, each with his work, and commands the doorkeeper to be on the watch. Therefore, keep awake—for you do not know when the master of the house will come, in the evening, or at midnight, or at cockcrow, or at dawn, or else he may find you asleep when he comes suddenly. And what I say to you I say to all: Keep awake."

REFLECTION

This first day of the liturgical year and beginning of Advent reminds us that this season is not at first about the birth of a baby. The Christ we await is the glorious Judge of the second coming, who may return at any time, without any warning. In the meantime, we live as if he will appear at any minute to demand an account of our faithfulness. We must be busy about the work of God's reign, awake and watchful to Christ's presence, wherever he may be found.

PRAYERS *others may be added*

Awake, watchful, and busy about God's work, we pray:

◆ Come quickly, Lord of glory!

That Christian leaders may guide the baptized in faithfulness, we pray: ◆ *That the promise of Christ's return may bring a new dawn of justice and peace among nations, we pray:* ◆ *That Jesus' disciples may keep busy in the service of the poor, we pray:* ◆ *That the Master's return may bring eternal life to the dead, we pray:* ◆ *That we may be watchful for the coming of glory, we pray:* ◆

Our Father . . .

Lord of glory,
we keep watch for salvation's dawn
and the Son of Man's return.
Awaken us to Christ's presence
revealed in the poor among us,
that we may serve you in them
and so recognize the Christ,
he who was, who is,
and who is to come,
who lives and reigns with you,
in the unity of the Holy Spirit,
one God, forever and ever. Amen.

✦ *Maranatha! Come, Lord Jesus!*

✝ *Maranatha! Come, Lord Jesus!*

PSALM 85 *page 417*

READING *Isaiah 35:1–4*

The wilderness and the dry land
    shall be glad,
  the desert shall rejoice
    and blossom;
like the crocus it shall blossom
    abundantly,
  and rejoice with joy and singing.
The glory of Lebanon shall be
    given to it,
  the majesty of Carmel and Sharon.
They shall see the glory of the LORD,
  the majesty of our God.
Strengthen the weak hands,
  and make firm the feeble knees.
Say to those who are of a fearful heart,
  "Be strong, do not fear!
Here is your God.
  He will come with vengeance,
with terrible recompense.
  He will come and save you."

REFLECTION

*Where Jesus' words about the end times
seem forbidding, Isaiah's words today are
filled with beauty. There will be something
marvelous about judgment day: Creation
will shine as never before because it will
come into its fullness at last. What was
once dead will flower; what is weak will
be made strong. On that day creation itself
will rise up in praise of the Creator.*

PRAYERS *others may be added*

*Ready to behold the majesty of God,
we pray:*

◆ Come quickly, Lord of glory!

*To pour glory on the baptized and
comfort the faithful, we pray: ◆ To bind
up the weak and strengthen the feeble,
we pray: ◆ To encourage the fearful and
comfort the brokenhearted, we pray: ◆
To shelter refugees and restore exiles,
we pray: ◆ To bring beauty to the
wilderness and springs to the desert,
we pray: ◆ To show forth your power
and reveal your heavenly glory, we pray: ◆*

Our Father . . .

Saving God,
you promise a glorious day
when all creation will sing
and all creatures leap for joy.
Strengthen our weak hands
and make firm our feeble knees
that we may rush to welcome
the one whose coming is certain,
whose day draws near,
Jesus Christ our Savior,
who lives and reigns
forever and ever. Amen.

✝ *Maranatha! Come, Lord Jesus!*

✛ *Maranatha! Come, Lord Jesus!*

PSALM 85   *page 417*

READING   *Isaiah 35:5–7*

Then the eyes of the blind shall
    be opened,
  and the ears of the deaf unstopped;
then the lame shall leap like a deer,
  and the tongue of the speechless
    sing for joy.
For waters shall break forth
    in the wilderness,
  and streams in the desert;
the burning sand shall become a pool,
  and the thirsty ground
    springs of water;
the haunt of jackals shall become
    a swamp,
  the grass shall become
    reeds and rushes.

REFLECTION

This continuation of the prophetic song we begin yesterday further unfolds Isaiah's vision of the blooming desert. The inclusion of the "blind," "deaf," and "lame" extends the oracle's promise to the human family as well. The restoration and completion we anticipate in Advent is one in which the entire created order—land, sea, animals, human beings—is restored to right relationship with God. We are waiting for God to complete what was begun on the first day of Creation and to restore what was lost to sin. The mysteries of evil, illness, and desolation will be wiped away on the glorious Day of the Lord.

PRAYERS   *others may be added*

Awaiting the completion of God's creative work, we pray:

◆ Come quickly, Lord of glory!

To deliver the baptized from the desolation of sin and sorrow, we pray: ◆ To show forth your glory in those who cannot see, hear or walk, we pray: ◆ To deliver the earth from abuse and misuse, we pray: ◆ To restore beauty to places destroyed by greed or apathy, we pray: ◆ To bring joy to the sick and those burdened by sadness, we pray: ◆ To reveal to us your saving power, we pray: ◆

Our Father . . .

God of wonder,
you make dry places burst
with springs of water,
and blossom with fragrant flowers.
Open our eyes to the beauty
   Christ brings,
and release us from the shackles of sin,
that we may leap for joy
on the Day of the Lord,
for Christ lives and reigns
forever and ever. Amen.

✛ *Maranatha! Come, Lord Jesus!*

✝ *Maranatha! Come, Lord Jesus!*

PSALM 85 *page 417*

READING *Matthew 4:18–22*

As Jesus walked by the Sea of Galilee, he saw two brothers, Simon, who is called Peter, and Andrew his brother, casting a net into the sea—for they were fishermen. And he said to them, "Follow me, and I will make you fish for people." Immediately they left their nets and followed him. As he went from there, he saw two other brothers, James son of Zebedee and his brother John, in the boat with their father Zebedee, mending their nets, and he called them. Immediately they left the boat and their father, and followed him.

REFLECTION *Augustine of Hippo*

Christ says: Give me this fisherman, this man without education or experience, this man to whom no senator would deign to speak, not even if he were buying fish. Yes, give me him; once I have taken possession of him, it will be obvious that it is I who am at work in him. Although I mean to include senators, orators, and emperors among my recruits, even when I have won over the senator I shall still be surer of the fisherman. The senator can always take pride in what he is; so can the orator and the emperor, but the fisherman can glory in nothing except Christ alone.

PRAYERS *others may be added*

Setting aside all things to follow Jesus, we pray:

◆ Come quickly, Lord of glory!

That the apostles of our time may carry Christ's word to all nations, we pray: ◆ *That the disciples of Jesus may embrace and live his Gospel, we pray:* ◆ *That the power of Christ's Resurrection may prepare the world for its final and glorious destiny, we pray:* ◆ *That those who hear the Good News may respond in faith, we pray:* ◆ *That our faith in Christ's Resurrection may give us hope in the fullness of his glory, we pray:* ◆

Our Father . . .

God of mission,
you send us forth to proclaim the love
poured out in Christ's cross
and made alive in the Resurrection.
Make us heralds of the Savior,
and open the hearts of those
who do not yet believe,
that on the coming day of glory
all the earth may share
new life in Christ,
who is Lord forever and ever. Amen.

✝ *Maranatha! Come, Lord Jesus!*

✦ *Maranatha! Come, Lord Jesus!*

PSALM 85 *page 417*

READING *Isaiah 35:8–10*

A highway shall be there,
and it shall be called the Holy Way;
the unclean shall not travel on it,
but it shall be for God's people;
no traveler, not even fools,
shall go astray.
No lion shall be there,
nor shall any ravenous beast
come up on it;
they shall not be found there,
but the redeemed shall walk there.
And the ransomed of the LORD
shall return,
and come to Zion with singing;
everlasting joy shall be
upon their heads;
they shall obtain joy and gladness,
and sorrow and sighing
shall flee away.

REFLECTION

In our age of interstates and freeways, the image of a highway doesn't seem too exciting as an image of God's coming salvation. To those in the prophet's own time, however, this promise probably sounded too good to be true. The author of this passage addressed Israelites exiled in Babylon, who felt far from their true home, with a great and dangerous wasteland between them and ruined Jerusalem. A "holy way" free of beasts and bandits, a highway just for the holy people, was a wild dream indeed. We Christians understand the highway differently; for us the "Way"—as the path of discipleship was known among the earliest Christians—is the trail we walk in our journey toward the heavenly Jerusalem.

PRAYERS *others may be added*

Faithful to Christ's holy Way,
we cry out:

◆ Come quickly, Lord of glory!

For God's people as they walk the path to glory, we pray: ◆ *For the nations as they seek the highway of peace, we pray:* ◆ *For the poor as they search for paths of justice, we pray:* ◆ *For refugees as they hope for a place of protection, we pray:* ◆ *For exiles as they await their day of return, we pray:* ◆ *For us as we follow the way of Jesus, we pray:* ◆

Our Father . . .

God of our journey,
you prepare a highway before us,
leading us ever closer to you.
Cast out sorrow and fear,
that we may march on with joy
and enter Zion singing with gladness,
praising you always
through the one whose coming is
certain, whose day draws near,
Jesus Christ our Savior,
who is Lord forever and ever. Amen.

✦ *Maranatha! Come, Lord Jesus!*

✛ *Maranatha! Come, Lord Jesus!*

PSALM 85   *page 417*

READING   *Isaiah 40:1–5*

Comfort, O comfort my people,
   says your God,
Speak tenderly to Jerusalem
   and cry to her
that she has served her term,
   that her penalty is paid,
that she has received from
     the LORD's hand
   double for all her sins.
A voice cries out:
"In the wilderness prepare the way
    of the LORD,
   make straight in the desert
    a highway for our God.
Every valley shall be lifted up,
   and every mountain and hill
    be made low;
the uneven ground shall become level,
and the rough places a plain.
Then the glory of the LORD
    shall be revealed,
   and all people shall see it together
   for the mouth of the LORD
    has spoken."

REFLECTION

Making a highway is no easy task. Ground must be leveled, earth moved, and channels and tunnels cut through mountains. Clearing the straight path for the coming of the Just One is no small matter either. The obstacles of prejudice and racism must be thrown aside, imbalances in wealth must be righted, and the tools of war must be destroyed. Yet this great undertaking is part of the Christian vocation, for if we seek the comfort the prophet promises, we must labor with God to see it fulfilled.

PRAYERS   *others may be added*

*Making straight in our hearts a
highway for God, we cry out:*

◆ Come quickly, Lord of glory!

That the Church's ministers may speak words of comfort and hope, we pray: ◆
That God's people may clear a path for the coming of justice and peace, we pray: ◆ *That world leaders may lift up citizens burdened by discrimination and poverty, we pray:* ◆ *That the world's poor may know the compassion of the King of glory, we pray:* ◆ *That all may behold together God's shining radiance, we pray:* ◆

Our Father . . .

God of creation,
you throw down the mountains
and fill in the valleys
to make a straight path
for your Anointed One.
Have mercy on us,
and transform our hearts
to receive your Holy One,
Jesus Christ, who is coming in glory.
Amen.

✛ *Maranatha! Come, Lord Jesus!*

✦ *Maranatha! Come, Lord Jesus!*

PSALM 85   *page 417*

READING   *Isaiah 40:9–11*

Get up to a high mountain,
   O Zion, herald of good tidings;
lift up your voice with strength,
   O Jerusalem, herald of good tidings,
   lift it up, do not fear;
say to the cities of Judah,
   "Here is your God!"
See, the Lord GOD comes with might,
   and his arm rules for him;
his reward is with him,
   and his recompense before him.
He will feed his flock like a shepherd;
   he will gather the lambs in his arms,
and carry them in his bosom,
   and gently lead the mother sheep.

REFLECTION

Toward the end of the book of Isaiah, the prophet envisions a new Jerusalem, in which not only the dispersed people of Israel gather on God's mountain, but people of all nations come to worship the God of Israel as well. Francis Xavier, a member of the first generation of Jesuit priests, sought to make Isaiah's vision a reality, carrying the Gospel beyond the confines of Europe to the peoples of India, Ceylon, the Philippines, and Japan. Today the Asian churches continue to grow, embodying the Gospel in the distinctive genius of the many cultures of Asia and enriching the Church throughout the world.

PRAYERS   *others may be added*

Lifting up our voices with gladness, we pray:

◆ Come quickly, Lord of glory!

That God's people may speak of hope and renewal in a world struggling with violence and despair, we pray: ◆ *That world leaders may model themselves on Israel's gentle shepherd, we pray:* ◆ *That the lost and wounded of God's flock may be led to safety and comfort, we pray:* ◆ *That the fearful and depressed may open their hearts to the glad tidings of God's love, we pray:* ◆ *That we may follow more closely our divine shepherd in the ways of righteousness, we pray:* ◆

Our Father . . .

Shepherd of your people,
the fulfillment of your promised reign
is good news for weary hearts
and comfort to the broken.
By the example of Francis Xavier,
make us heralds of your glad tidings
and signs of your tender care,
that we may be ready to greet
   our Redeemer
when he comes in glory,
for Christ lives and reigns,
forever and ever. Amen.

✦ *Maranatha! Come, Lord Jesus!*

✦ *Maranatha! Come, Lord Jesus!*

PSALM 85   *page 417*

READING   *Mark 1:1–8*

The beginning of the good news of Jesus Christ, the Son of God. As it is written in the prophet Isaiah,
"See, I am sending my messenger
    ahead of you,
  who will prepare your way;
the voice of one crying out in the
    wilderness:
   'Prepare the way of the Lord,
   make his paths straight,'"

John the baptizer appeared in the wilderness, proclaiming a baptism of repentance for the forgiveness of sins. And people from the whole Judean countryside and all the people of Jerusalem were going out to him, and were baptized by him in the river Jordan, confessing their sins. Now John was clothed with camel's hair, with a leather belt around his waist, and he ate locusts and wild honey. He proclaimed, "The one who is more powerful than I is coming after me; I am not worthy to stoop down and untie the thong of his sandals. I have baptized you with water; but he will baptize you with the Holy Spirit."

REFLECTION

We honor in a special way two saints as patrons of Advent: John the Baptist and Mary, the mother of Jesus. This Sunday and next, John appears as an imposing figure, living on the edge of society and drawing crowds to him with his fiery preaching. Yet even this impressive prophet, like all prophets, points beyond himself. John is only the messenger, not the message. Like John, we must point beyond ourselves in our lives of faith and bear witness to the One who gives us life.

PRAYERS   *others may be added*

  *Proclaiming the One who is coming,
  we pray:*

◆ Come quickly, Lord of glory!

For those who preach on the fringes, we pray: ◆ *For those who proclaim a message of repentance, we pray:* ◆ *For those who announce God's promises, we pray:* ◆ *For those who seek prophetic wisdom, we pray:* ◆ *For those who point the way to Christ in service to others, we pray:* ◆

Our Father . . .

O God of power,
we await the One
who will baptize us
with the Holy Spirit.
Give us prophetic words
and true repentance of heart.
May we prepare the way
for the One who comes in your name,
and so rejoice in his advent,
for Christ lives and reigns with you,
in the unity of the Holy Spirit,
one God, forever and ever. Amen.

✦ *Maranatha! Come, Lord Jesus!*

✤ *Maranatha! Come, Lord Jesus!*

PSALM 85 *page 417*

READING *Isaiah 40:27–31*

Why do you say, O Jacob,
  and speak, O Israel,
"My way is hidden from the LORD,
  and my right is disregarded
    by my God"?
Have you not known? Have you
  not heard?
The LORD is the everlasting God,
  the Creator of the ends of the earth.
He does not faint or grow weary;
  his understanding is unsearchable.
He gives power to the faint,
  and strengthens the powerless.
Even youths will faint and be weary,
  and the young will fall exhausted;
but those who wait for the LORD shall
    renew their strength,
  they shall mount up with wings
    like eagles,
they shall run and not be weary,
  they shall walk and not faint.

REFLECTION

*The community addressed by the prophet
was not particularly happy about waiting
for deliverance from exile; no doubt some
were losing hope. In our times we may
sometimes feel the same. Violence continues to plague the world in acts of terrorism, crime, and war. Countless millions
suffer hunger in countries both rich and
poor. Peoples of various races, cultures,
and religions have yet to find harmony.
Isaiah's words can restore us in times
like these.*

PRAYERS *others may be added*

*Confident of our victory in Christ,
we pray:*

◆ Come quickly, Lord of glory!

*That God's people may be sustained
in hope by the example of the saints,
we pray: ◆ That all people may know
the enduring faithfulness of the Most
High, we pray: ◆ That political leaders
may remember that true authority belongs
to God alone, we pray: ◆ That the poor
and oppressed may not give in to despair,
we pray: ◆ That we who wait for the
Lord may be renewed in strength and
hope, we pray: ◆*

Our Father . . .

Source of comfort,
though we weary of waiting
you console us with prophetic words.
Increase our hope in your promise
and renew our strength
  with your presence.
May we joyfully welcome Christ
  when he returns
and soar like eagles
to your dwelling place.
We ask this in Jesus' name. Amen.

✤ *Maranatha! Come, Lord Jesus!*

✦ *Maranatha! Come, Lord Jesus!*

PSALM 85 *page 417*

READING *Isaiah 41:13–14a, 15–16*

I, the LORD your God,
  hold your right hand;
it is I who say to you, "Do not fear,
  I will help you."
I will help you, says the LORD;
  your Redeemer is the Holy One
    of Israel.
Now, I will make of you
  a threshing sledge,
  sharp, new, and having teeth;
you shall thresh the mountains
    and crush them,
  and you shall make the hills
    like chaff.
You shall winnow them and the wind
    shall carry them away,
  and the tempest shall scatter them.
Then you shall rejoice in the LORD;
  in the Holy One of Israel
    you shall glory.

REFLECTION

Isaiah's imagery may be a little strong for our comfort, describing as it does the power God will give to the Chosen People to "crush" and "scatter" their obstacles, most likely the nations that stood in their way. Oracles combining both martial and harvest imagery are part of our tradition, however, and they point toward the full revelation of God's power. At the same time, we must handle these images with care, as such texts have been used in history to give religious justification for violence and oppression.

PRAYERS *others may be added*

Awaiting the fullness of God's power, we pray:

◆ Come quickly, Lord of glory!

To redeem the people who trust in you, we pray: ◆ *To crush the power of oppression and injustice, we pray:* ◆ *To drive out fear and anxiety, we pray:* ◆ *To scatter human vanity and pride, we pray:* ◆ *To bring an end to idolatry, we pray:* ◆ *To gather the dead into the eternal harvest, we pray:* ◆ *To reveal to us your saving power, we pray:* ◆

Our Father . . .

God of power,
in the fullness of time
your Anointed One will return
to bring an end to injustice.
Free us from all anxiety
as we await Christ's day,
that we may trust
in his power to save
and place our hope
in the world to come,
where Christ will live and reign
forever and ever. Amen.

✦ *Maranatha! Come, Lord Jesus!*

✜ *Maranatha! Come, Lord Jesus!*

PSALM 85   *page 417*

READING   *Isaiah 41:17–20*

Thus says the Lord:
When the poor and needy seek water,
   and there is none,
     and their tongue is parched
      with thirst,
I the LORD will answer them,
   I the God of Israel will not
     forsake them.
I will open rivers on the bare heights,
   and fountains in the midst
     of the valleys;
I will make the wilderness a pool
     of water,
   and the dry land springs of water.
I will put in the wilderness the cedar,
   the acacia, the myrtle, and the olive;
I will set in the desert the cypress,
   the plane and the pine together,
so that all may see and know,
   all may consider and understand,
that the hand of the LORD
     has done this,
   the Holy One of Israel has created it.

REFLECTION   *Ambrose of Milan*

What you, rich, give to the needy brings profit to yourself; for yourself too your possession is increased when it is diminished. You yourself are fed by the bread you give to the poor, because whoever has mercy on the poor is sustained by the fruits of compassion. Mercy is sown on the earth and sprouts in heaven; what is planted in the poor produces in front of God. . . . When giving to the poor you are not giving them what is yours; rather you are paying back to them what is theirs.

PRAYERS   *others may be added*

  Joining with all the saints, we pray:

◆ Come quickly, Lord of glory!

That God's people may welcome any who seek the Lord, we pray: ◆ *That those entrusted with the ministry of bishop may be great teachers of the faith, we pray:* ◆ *That those who lead may be servants of all, we pray:* ◆ *That students may search diligently for God's wisdom, we pray:* ◆ *That we who are disciples of Jesus may seek first the righteousness of God's reign, we pray:* ◆

Our Father . . .

God of wisdom,
in Bishop Ambrose you found
an attentive student
and a holy leader for your people.
May we, like Ambrose,
search diligently for you
not only in study and reflection
but in service to the poorest among us.
We ask this through Jesus Christ,
who is coming in glory. Amen.

✜ *Maranatha! Come, Lord Jesus!*

✝ *Maranatha! Come, Lord Jesus!*

PSALM 96 *page 421*

READING *Ephesians 1:3–6, 11–12*

Blessed be the God and Father of our Lord Jesus Christ, who has blessed us in Christ with every spiritual blessing in the heavenly places, just as he chose us in Christ before the foundation of the world to be holy and blameless before him in love. He destined us for adoption as his children through Jesus Christ, according to the good pleasure of his will, to the praise of his glorious grace that he freely bestowed on us in the Beloved.

In Christ we have also obtained an inheritance, having been destined according to the purpose of him who accomplishes all things according to his counsel and will, so that we, who were the first to set our hope on Christ, might live for the praise of his glory.

REFLECTION

As the second of Advent's great patrons, Mary appears as one who, like John the Baptist, prepared the way for Christ by her own openness to God's will. By welcoming God's plan and accepting her own role in it, she made possible our salvation in Christ. It is for this reason that we honor Mary as mother of all the redeemed.

PRAYERS *others may be added*

Chosen in Christ before the world's foundation, we cry out:

◆ Pray for us, favored one!

That the Church may boldly proclaim God's desire that all be saved, we cry out: ◆ That God's people may give thanks for the gifts bestowed on them in Christ, we cry out: ◆ That the poor may know their dignity as God's beloved children, we cry out: ◆ That those who set their hope in Christ may live forever in God's presence, we cry out: ◆ That we may rejoice in the glory we have inherited in Christ, we cry out: ◆

Our Father . . .

Blessed are you,
God and Father of Jesus Christ.
From before time you chose
a daughter of Israel
to bear your eternal Word.
May Mary's example
of openness and humility,
courage and faith,
inspire us to become ever more open
to the grace you offer Jesus Christ,
Son of God and of Mary,
who lives and reigns with you,
in the unity of the Holy Spirit,
one God, forever and ever. Amen.

✝ *Maranatha! Come, Lord Jesus!*

✦ *Maranatha! Come, Lord Jesus!*

PSALM 85 *page 417*

READING *1 Samuel 1:1–3a, 4–8*

There was a certain man of Ramathaim, a Zuphite from the hill country of Ephraim, whose name was Elkanah. He had two wives; the name of the one was Hannah, and the name of the other Peninnah. Peninnah had children, but Hannah had no children.

Now this man used to go up year by year from his town to worship and to sacrifice to the LORD of hosts at Shiloh. On the day when Elkanah sacrificed, he would give portions to his wife Peninnah and to all her sons and daughters; but to Hannah he gave a double portion, because he loved her, though the LORD had closed her womb. Her rival used to provoke her severely, to irritate her, because the LORD had closed her womb. So it went on year by year; as often as she went up to the house of the LORD, she used to provoke her. Therefore Hannah wept and would not eat. Her husband Elkanah said to her, "Hannah, why do you weep? Why do you not eat? Why is your heart sad? Am I not more to you than ten sons?"

REFLECTION

The story of Jesus' conception and birth echoes the birth stories of the Hebrew prophets. The birth of Samuel is one such story, recounting the unlikely birth of a great hero and leader in Israel.

PRAYERS *others may be added*

Remembering our ancestors in faith, we pray:

◆ Come quickly, Lord of glory!

For the baptized, that they may remain faithful in times of barrenness and sadness, we pray: ◆ *For wives and husbands, that their love for one another may bear Christ to those around them, we pray:* ◆ *For those who hope for children, that God may fulfill their longing, we pray:* ◆ *For those who are ridiculed, berated, and provoked, that God may give them justice, we pray:* ◆ *For all who long for the fulfillment of God's promises, that we may support one another in our time of trial, we pray:* ◆

Our Father . . .

Faithful God,
your Son was born
into a chosen and beloved people,
the fulfillment of your promise
    to David.
Fill us in this time
    of pregnant expectation
with the faith of your people Israel.
May all who await
the coming day of redemption
trust in your everlasting covenant.
We ask this in the name
    of Jesus Christ,
Son of God and of Israel,
who lives and reigns
forever and ever. Amen.

✦ *Maranatha! Come, Lord Jesus!*

✦ *Maranatha! Come, Lord Jesus!*

PSALM 85 *page 417*

READING *1 Samuel 1:9–11*

After they had eaten and drunk at Shiloh, Hannah rose and presented herself before the LORD. Now Eli the priest was sitting on the seat beside the doorpost of the temple of the LORD. She was deeply distressed and prayed to the LORD, and wept bitterly. She made this vow: "O LORD of hosts, if only you will look on the misery of your servant, and remember me, and not forget your servant, but will give to your servant a male child, then I will set him before you as a nazirite until the day of his death. He shall drink neither wine nor intoxicants, and no razor shall touch his head."

REFLECTION

Unlike Mary, who was not considering pregnancy before the angel's announcement, Hannah raises an impassioned prayer to God, promising her child to God's service. Her prayer echoes those of many childless men and women, as well the prayers of the thousands of parentless children longing for a loving home.

PRAYERS *others may be added*

With great longing for the coming of our Savior, we pray:

◆ Come quickly, Lord of glory!

For the Church, praying for an end to this time of trial, we pray: ◆ *For the people of the world, weeping for the sins of hunger and hoping for a renewed creation, we pray:* ◆ *For the fearful and anxious, longing for the dawn of hope and salvation, we pray:* ◆ *For the childless and parentless, hoping for a family with whom to share life, we pray:* ◆ *For those who present themselves to the Most High, trusting that our God keeps promises, we pray:* ◆ *For all who await the revelation of Jesus Christ, seeking to live lives worthy of God's coming reign, we pray:* ◆

Our Father . . .

God of the matriarchs,
with your daughter Hannah
we offer tears and great sighs,
trusting in your faithfulness.
Fill our empty hearts with hope,
that we may bear Christ in our time
as we await his day of glory,
for Christ lives and reigns
forever and ever. Amen.

✦ *Maranatha! Come, Lord Jesus!*

✝ *Rejoice, Jerusalem!*
Your Savior will come!
God's promises to David
will be fulfilled!

PSALM 89 *page 419*

READING *1 Thessalonians 5:16–24*

Rejoice always, pray without ceasing, give thanks in all circumstances; for this is the will of God in Christ Jesus for you. Do not quench the Spirit. Do not despise the words of prophets, but test everything; hold fast to what is good; abstain from every form of evil.

May the God of peace himself sanctify you entirely; and may your spirit and soul and body be kept sound and blameless at the coming of our Lord Jesus Christ. The one who calls you is faithful, and he will do this.

REFLECTION

The apostle Paul offers an excellent prescription for keeping Advent: Pray, give thanks, hold fast to good, avoid evil. Yet first and foremost, Paul tells us to rejoice— always. Our Advent preparation is serious business, but we are preparing for a joyous event—the marriage of heaven and earth. As anyone who has planned a wedding knows, getting ready requires piles of work, some of it not very exciting. Couples prepare the liturgy and themselves; families prepare meals; guests choose gifts. Everyone even "fasts" a bit to fit into their best clothes. Yet in every moment there is sweet anticipation that builds toward the day of the wedding—Christmas Day— which in turn begins the joyful honeymoon of the Christmas season.

PRAYERS *others may be added*

Rejoicing always, giving thanks in every circumstance, we pray:

◆ Show us the Promised One!

That the Church may always give thanks for God's grace in Jesus Christ, we pray: ◆ *That the baptized may be sanctified as they await the full revelation of the Savior, we pray:* ◆ *That all people may hold fast to what is good and abstain from every evil, we pray:* ◆ *That the poor and hungry may have cause to rejoice in God's goodness, we pray:* ◆ *That the sick may be strengthened by God's promises, we pray:* ◆ *That the Spirit may dwell within us, preparing the way for our Redeemer, we pray:* ◆

Our Father . . .

We give you thanks,
Fountain of joy,
for you sustain us
while we await the Savior's coming.
Pour out Christ's Spirit upon us,
that we may pray without ceasing
for the coming of your kingdom
and rejoice in the confidence
that your day of glory draws near.
We ask this through our Savior
Jesus Christ,
who lives and reigns with you
in the unity of the Holy Spirit,
one God, forever and ever. Amen.

✝ *Rejoice, Jerusalem!*
Your Savior will come!
God's promises to David
will be fulfilled!

✝ *Maranatha! Come, Lord Jesus!*

PSALM 96 *page 421*

READING *Zechariah 2:10–13*

Sing and rejoice, O daughter Zion! For lo, I will come and dwell in your midst, says the LORD. Many nations shall join themselves to the LORD on that day, and shall be my people; and I will dwell in your midst. And you shall know that the LORD of hosts has sent me to you. The LORD will inherit Judah as his portion in the holy land, and will again choose Jerusalem.

Be silent, all people, before the LORD; for he has roused himself from his holy dwelling.

REFLECTION

This passage from the prophet Zechariah, the first reading for Mass on the feast of Our Lady of Guadalupe, directs us to Mary's role in salvation history and to the significance of her appearance to the Aztec Cuatitloatzin (Juan Diego) in sixteenth-century Mexico. She is God's messenger, sent as the prophets were, to deliver a message of hope. Her appearance is a sign of God's favor to the oppressed and conquered, embodied in Juan Diego. Finally, she is a sign of God's presence, pointing the way to her son, the Savior of all people.

PRAYERS *others may be added*

Awaiting with joy the coming of God among us, we pray:

◆ Show us the Promised One!

For the many races and peoples that make up the household of God, we pray: ◆ *For indigenous peoples throughout the world, we pray:* ◆ *For those who face cultural annihilation or genocide, we pray:* ◆ *For those oppressed by racism and prejudice, we pray:* ◆ *For those who promote equity and peace among nations, we pray:* ◆ *For those who labor for racial justice and unity among cultures, we pray:* ◆

Our Father . . .

God of all peoples,
you sent the mother of your Son
with a message of love and hope
to a people conquered and oppressed.
May her appearance always remind us
that you cast down the proud,
granting justice to the oppressed
and choosing the poor over the rich.
We ask this in the name
    of Jesus Christ,
Son of Mary and your Son,
who is Lord now and forever. Amen.

✝ *Maranatha! Come, Lord Jesus!*

✦ *Maranatha! Come, Lord Jesus!*

PSALM 89   *page 419*

READING   *1 Samuel 1:12–18*

As Hannah continued praying before the LORD, Eli [the priest] observed her mouth. Hannah was praying silently; only her lips moved, but her voice was not heard; therefore Eli thought she was drunk. So Eli said to her, "How long will you make a drunken spectacle of yourself? Put away your wine." But Hannah answered, "No, my lord, I am a woman deeply troubled; I have drunk neither wine nor strong drink, but I have been pouring out my soul before the LORD. Do not regard your servant as a worthless woman, for I have been speaking out of my great anxiety and vexation all this time." Then Eli answered, "Go in peace; the God of Israel grant the petition you have made to him." And she said, "Let your servant find favor in your sight." The woman went to her quarters, ate and drank with her husband, and her countenance was sad no longer.

REFLECTION

Eli presumes Hannah drunk and chides her without really knowing what's going on. Perhaps we all make assumptions about people's religious practices and then jump to judgment as well. It is best to remember the many ways God comes to each of us, and the varied ways we respond, whether in academic pursuits or emotional experiences.

PRAYERS   *others may be added*

Trusting that God will hear our prayers, we pray:

◆ Show us the Promised One!

That ministers and priests may be sources of hope and counsel to those they serve, we pray: ◆ *That the Church may trust in God's promise of salvation, we pray:* ◆ *That the nations of the world may honor and protect the freedom of religion, we pray:* ◆ *That those who petition God with persistence may be rewarded with God's peace, we pray:* ◆ *That the sorrowful may find a measure of joy in the faithfulness of God, we pray:* ◆ *That we may persevere in this time of waiting, confident that we will see the fruits of our hope, we pray:* ◆

Our Father . . .

Faithful God,
your servant Hannah was persistent
    in her prayer
despite misunderstanding
    and opposition.
Embolden us to give voice
to our hope in Christ
and courage in our prayer,
that the Christmas festival
may find us ready to rejoice
in the birth of the long-awaited one,
who lives forever and ever. Amen.

✦ *Maranatha! Come, Lord Jesus!*

✦ *Maranatha! Come, Lord Jesus!*

PSALM 89 *page 419*

READING *1 Samuel 1:19–23*

They rose early in the morning and worshiped before the LORD; then they went back to their house at Ramah. Elkanah knew his wife Hannah, and the LORD remembered her. In due time Hannah conceived and bore a son. She named him Samuel, for she said, "I have asked him of the LORD."

The man Elkanah and all his household went up to offer to the LORD the yearly sacrifice, and to pay his vow. But Hannah did not go up, for she said to her husband, "As soon as the child is weaned, I will bring him, that he may appear in the presence of the LORD, and remain there forever; I will offer him as a nazirite for all time." Her husband Elkanah said to her, "Do what seems best to you, wait until you have weaned him; only—may the LORD establish his word." So the woman remained and nursed her son, until she weaned him.

REFLECTION

In response to God's faithfulness, Hannah keeps her promise to God. In this she is a model of covenant fidelity, a precursor of Mary's own faithful response to God's marvelous invitation.

PRAYERS *others may be added*

Rejoicing in God's faithfulness, we pray:

◆ Show us the Promised One!

For the baptized, who proclaim the coming of your Anointed One in glory, we pray: ◆ For the created world, which reveals God's beauty and mystery, we pray: ◆ For spouses, who live their love for one another, we pray: ◆ For mothers and fathers, who are devoted to their children, we pray: ◆ For answered prayers, which renew our hope in God, we pray: ◆ For a time of patience and expectation to prepare for the coming of your Son, we pray: ◆

Our Father . . .

God of wonder,
through the love of Hannah
   and Elkanah
you blessed your people
   with a mighty prophet.
Grant that our love for you and
   for one another
may create in our hearts
the readiness to accept
the child of Bethlehem,
the king of glory, Jesus Christ,
who lives and reigns
forever and ever. Amen.

✦ *Maranatha! Come, Lord Jesus!*

✝ *Maranatha! Come, Lord Jesus!*

PSALM 89 *page 419*

READING *1 Samuel 1:24–28*

When Hannah had weaned him, she took him up with her, along with a three-year-old bull, an ephah of flour, and a skin of wine. She brought him to the house of the LORD at Shiloh; and the child was young. Then they slaughtered the bull, and they brought the child to Eli. And she said, "Oh, my lord! As you live, my lord, I am the woman who was standing here in your presence, praying to the LORD. For this child I prayed; and the LORD has granted me the petition I made to him. Therefore I have lent him to the LORD; as long as he lives, he is given to the LORD."

She left him there for the LORD.

REFLECTION

The story of Samuel's birth bears many resemblances to the birth stories of both John the Baptist and Jesus in the Gospel of Luke. It is quite likely that the evangelist used Samuel's birth as the model for his telling of John's and Jesus'. As in the announcement of John's birth (Luke 1:5–25), the main action—Hannah's prayer and the appearance of the angel to Zechariah—takes place in the temple. Both John and Samuel are set apart as "nazirites," and both become powerful prophets in Israel. Hannah herself shares many characteristics with Mary. Both are the protagonists of their stories, and both announce God's work on behalf of the poor and outcast, Mary in the Magnificat (Luke 1:46–55) and Hannah in her own song of praise (1 Samuel 2:1–10).

PRAYERS *others may be added*

Ready to fulfill our promises to God, we pray:

◆ Show us the Promised One!

That the Church may bear witness to the coming of the Christ, we pray: ◆ *That the leaders of the earth may prepare for the day of Christ by faithful service to the weak, we pray:* ◆ *That parents may rejoice in the gift of children, we pray:* ◆ *That the poor may know the faithfulness of God in the service of God's people, we pray:* ◆ *That we who have known God's blessings may render him our debt of praise and thanksgiving, we pray:* ◆

Our Father . . .

God of wonder,
we eagerly await the coming
    of your Son
ready to live according to
    the Good News he bears.
Fill our hearts with praise of your name
and make us ready to live
    the Good News
that we may be ready to accept anew
the gift we will celebrate
on the festival of Christ's birth.
We ask this through the same
Christ our Lord. Amen.

✝ *Maranatha! Come, Lord Jesus!*

✛ *Maranatha! Come, Lord Jesus!*

PSALM 89 *page 419*

READING *1 Samuel 2:1–5*

Hannah prayed and said,
"My heart exults in the LORD;
my strength is exalted in my God.
My mouth derides my enemies,
    because I rejoice in my victory.
There is no Holy One like the LORD,
    no one beside you;
    there is no Rock like our God.
Talk no more so very proudly,
    let not arrogance come
        from your mouth;
for the LORD is a God of knowledge,
    and by him actions are weighed.
The bows of the mighty are broken,
    but the feeble gird on strength.
Those who were full have hired
        themselves out for bread,
    but those who were hungry
        are fat with spoil.
The barren has borne seven,
    but she who has many children
        is forlorn."

REFLECTION

Hannah's joyous song sums up what we hope for in this Advent season: the dawn of a new day, the reversal of the current unjust order of things, and the restoration of God's plan for creation. It is a marvelous vision, one Mary repeats and augments in her joyous song of thanksgiving in Luke's Gospel (1:46–55).

PRAYERS *others may be added*

Rejoicing in the Holy One of Israel, we pray:

◆ Show us the Promised One!

To raise the Church in holiness, clothing the baptized in glory, we pray: ◆ To create the world anew, bringing peace to the nations, we pray: ◆ To give food to the hungry, strengthening to the weak, we pray: ◆ To cast down the mighty and arrogant, enthroning the powerless and humble, we pray: ◆ To comfort the sorrowing and give children to the barren, we pray: ◆ To reward our waiting with the fullness of God's reign, we pray: ◆

Our Father . . .

Holy God,
the words of Hannah
proclaim your mighty deeds,
giving hope and strength
to the disheartened and depressed.
May we who await the festival
of the Anointed One's birth
have cause to rejoice in you
and so come to share Christ's glory,
for he lives and reigns
forever and ever. Amen.

✛ *Maranatha! Come, Lord Jesus!*

✝ *Come, O Holy Wisdom of God!*
Teach us the way of salvation!

PSALM 89 *page 419*

READING *Proverbs 8:22, 27–31*

Thus says the Wisdom of God:
The LORD created me
    at the beginning of his work,
the first of his acts of long ago.
When he established the heavens,
    I was there,
when he drew a circle
    on the face of the deep,
when he made firm the skies above,
when he established
    the fountains of the deep,
when he assigned to the sea its limit,
so that the waters might not
    transgress his command,
when he marked out
    the foundations of the earth,
then I was beside him,
    like a master worker;
and I was daily his delight,
    rejoicing before him always,
rejoicing in his inhabited world
    and delighting in the human race.

REFLECTION

*Today begins a turn toward Christmas
with the O Antiphons, short phrases from
the monastic liturgy that call upon Christ
using images from the Old Testament.
Today we acclaim Christ with a feminine
image of God, Holy Wisdom. Lady Wisdom
was imagined to be the consort of God
the Creator and God's special gift to the
Hebrew people. Jewish tradition sees
the embodiment of Wisdom in the Law, the*
*Torah. We Christians see the embodiment
of Wisdom in Jesus, the Word made flesh.*

PRAYERS *others may be added*

*Rejoicing in the gift of God's Word,
we pray:*

◆ Come, O holy Wisdom of God!

*To shower the baptized with insight,
we pray:* ◆ *To inspire leaders to work
for justice, we pray:* ◆ *To delight in
the human race, we pray:* ◆ *To confound
the arrogant and enlighten the simple,
we pray:* ◆ *To renew creation with God's
power, we pray:* ◆ *To show all people
the way to salvation, we pray:* ◆

Our Father . . .

Source of creation,
before the first mote of dust
came into being
you set up your Wisdom
as a gift to your people.
Send us your Wisdom from on high,
that Christ may lead us
in the way of salvation
and all creation
may praise you through him,
who lives and reigns
forever and ever. Amen.

✝ *Come, O Holy Wisdom of God!*
Teach us the way of salvation!

✢ *Come, O Adonai, O Lord of Israel!*
Come to rule your people
with justice!

PSALM 89 *page 419*

READING *Luke 1:28–33, 38*

And the angel of the Lord came to Mary and said, "Greetings, favored one! The Lord is with you." But Mary was much perplexed by his words and pondered what sort of greeting this might be. The angel said to her, "Do not be afraid, Mary, for you have found favor with God. And now, you will conceive in your womb and bear a son, and you will name him Jesus. He will be great, and will be called the Son of the Most High, and the Lord God will give to him the throne of his ancestor David. He will reign over the house of Jacob forever, and of his kingdom there will be no end."

Then Mary said, "Here am I, the servant of the Lord; let it be with me according to your word." Then the angel departed from her.

REFLECTION *Catherine of Siena*

O Mary,
may you be proclaimed blessed
among all women
for endless ages,
for today you have shared with us
your flour.
Today the Godhead
is joined and kneaded into one dough
with our humanity—
so securely
that this union could never be broken.

PRAYERS *others may be added*

Acclaiming Mary, the servant of the Lord, we pray:

◆ Come, O Adonai, O Lord of Israel!

That the Church may lovingly carry God's Word to all people, we pray: ◆ *That nations may favor and protect the poor and lowly, we pray:* ◆ *That single mothers and their children may have aid and support, we pray:* ◆ *That all mothers may be assured medical care and security before and after birth, we pray:* ◆ *That, like Mary, we may open our lives to Emmanuel, we pray:* ◆

Our Father . . .

God Most High,
you highly favored Mary
with the grace to bear
the Word of life.
Give us open hearts:
May we, like Mary,
welcome your invitation
to carry and bear Emmanuel,
    God-with-us,
who lives and reigns with you
in the unity of the Holy Spirit,
one God, forever and ever. Amen.

✢ *Come, O Adonai, O Lord of Israel!*
Come to rule your people
with justice!

✤ *Come, O Flower of Jesse!*
Come and refresh us with the
fragrance of your glory!

PSALM 89   *page 419*

READING   *Jeremiah 23:5–8*

The days are surely coming, says the LORD, when I will raise up for David a righteous Branch, and he shall reign as king and deal wisely, and shall execute justice and righteousness in the land. In his days Judah will be saved and Israel will live in safety. And this is the name by which he will be called: "The LORD is our righteousness."

Therefore, the days are surely coming, says the LORD, when it shall no longer be said, "As the LORD lives who brought the people of Israel up out of the land of Egypt," but "As the LORD lives who brought out and led the offspring of the house of Israel out of the land of the north and out of all the lands where he had driven them." Then they shall live in their own land.

REFLECTION

Jesus is sometimes called Son of David, the great king of Israel; Jesse was David's father. Today we call upon Christ as the Flower of Jesse, royal descendant of royal ancestors. Those who have been adopted in Christ share this royal lineage. Since Christ will come as a ruler of justice and righteousness, we live today as citizens of the rule he will bring. We are born in baptism as children of God's reign, and so are called to be living signs of the kingdom yet to come.

PRAYERS   *others may be added*

Embracing the duties of our royal heritage, we pray:

◆ Come, O Flower of Jesse!

To crown God's people with justice and righteousness, we pray: ◆ To adopt all nations as your royal inheritance, we pray: ◆ To establish equity among the world's peoples, we pray: ◆ To execute judgment for the poor, we pray: ◆ To gather exiles from the corners of the earth, we pray: ◆ To save the lost and deliver to safety those in danger, we pray: ◆ To reveal us as the royal daughters and sons of the Most High, we pray: ◆

Our Father . . .

True Ruler of heaven and earth, you raise up a righteous Branch to lead your people in justice. Send us the Flower of Jesse, the royal Son of Israel, that all people may be gathered into your noble house and so praise you forever through the Son of David, who is Lord forever and ever. Amen.

✤ *Come, O Flower of Jesse!*
Come and refresh us with the
fragrance of your glory!

✜ *Come, O Key of David!*
Come and restore your people!

PSALM 89 *page 419*

READING *Isaiah 22:15, 19–23*

Thus says the Lord GOD of hosts: Come, go to this steward, to Shebna, who is master of the household, and say to him: I will thrust you from your office, and you will be pulled down from your post. On that day I will call my servant Eliakim son of Hilkiah, and will clothe him with your robe and bind your sash on him. I will commit your authority to his hand, and he shall be a father to the inhabitants of Jerusalem and to the house of Judah. I will place on his shoulder the key of the house of David; he shall open, and no one shall shut; he shall shut, and no one shall open. I will fasten him like a peg in a secure place, and he will become a throne of honor to his ancestral house.

REFLECTION

Today's reading may seem out of place as we approach Christmas, but it illuminates Jesus as the Key of David. Keys are symbols of authority; the one who holds them can open doors or close them, permit or deny entrance. Eliakim became the royal steward of Israel, the keeper of the keys. Jesus, too, is a steward of another kind— God's steward who releases the captives and flings open heaven's doors. And what Christ opens, no one can ever close again.

PRAYERS *others may be added*

As those welcomed into the household of God, we pray:

◆ Come, O Key of David!

To make the Church a gateway to everlasting life, we pray: ◆ To invite all nations to the eternal banquet, we pray: ◆ To cast down the powerful, unjust, and proud, we pray: ◆ To pour forth the grace of forgiveness, we pray: ◆ To shatter the dominion of death and sin, we pray: ◆ To share with the poor God's many gifts, we pray: ◆ To open forever the road to the heavenly city, we pray: ◆

Our Father . . .

Ever-faithful God,
you free us from death
and call all people
to be citizens of the holy city.
Send us the Key of David
to shatter death's power
and open wide
the path to salvation,
for Christ is Lord
forever and ever. Amen.

✜ *Come, O Key of David!*
Come and restore your people!

✠ *Come, O radiant Dawn!*
Come and brighten our hearts
with your love!

PSALM 89   *page 419*

READING   *Malachi 4:1–3, 5*

See, the day is coming, burning like an oven, when all the arrogant and all evildoers will be stubble; the day that comes shall burn them up, says the LORD of hosts, so that it will leave them neither root nor branch. But for you who revere my name the sun of righteousness shall rise, with healing in its wings. You shall go out leaping like calves from the stall. And you shall tread down the wicked, for they will be ashes under the soles of your feet, on the day when I act, says the LORD of hosts.

Lo, I will send you the prophet Elijah before the great and terrible day of the LORD comes.

REFLECTION

On this, the shortest day of the year, we pray for the eternal dawn of the light of the world. On the day of Christ's return we will no longer live in the shadow of war, nor shall anyone suffer the cold emptiness of poverty; the warmth and light of the Sun of justice will scatter injustice and violence forever, and the day Christ brings will be eternal.

PRAYERS   *others may be added*

Awaiting the dawn of the Righteous Son, we pray:

◆ Come, O Dawn!

To bathe the faithful ones in healing rays, we pray: ◆ *To drive out from among the nations the evil of war, we pray:* ◆ *To confound the arrogant and cast down the proud, we pray:* ◆ *To bless all people with righteousness and love, we pray:* ◆ *To reduce to ash the works of evildoers, we pray:* ◆ *To restore to the downtrodden what is rightfully theirs, we pray:* ◆ *To bring joy to those who serve God, we pray:* ◆

Our Father . . .

Shine on us, O Dawn!
Give us your healing rays,
Dayspring from on high!
Burn away the shroud of sin,
and reduce injustice to ashes,
that we may rejoice forever
in your eternal day,
leaping in joy before you,
and praising God in your name
unto the endless ages of age. Amen.

✠ *Come, O radiant Dawn!*
Come and brighten our hearts
with your love!

✝ *Come, O Desire of nations!*
Come and bring us peace!

PSALM 89   *page 419*

READING   *Zephaniah 3:14–18*

Sing aloud, O daughter Zion;
   shout, O Israel!
Rejoice and exult with all your heart,
   O daughter Jerusalem!
The LORD has taken away the
     judgments against you,
   he has turned away your enemies.
The king of Israel, the LORD,
   is in your midst;
   you shall fear disaster no more.
On that day it shall be said
   to Jerusalem:
Do not fear, O Zion;
   do not let your hands grow weak.
The LORD, your God, is in your midst,
   a warrior who gives victory;
he will rejoice over you with gladness,
   he will renew you in his love;
he will exult over you
     with loud singing
   as on a day of festival.
I will remove disaster from you,
   so that you will not bear reproach
     for it.

REFLECTION

Today we acclaim Jesus as the fulfillment
of our longings, and the hope of all nations.
At the heart of this desire is the hunger for
peace, which is not the absence of conflict,
but the shalom *that God promises—right*
relationship between God and creation
that makes possible full human life. This
peace is an end to sickness, to injustice, to
anxiety, to violence; this peace will bring
the fullness of what we only dare to hope.

PRAYERS   *others may be added*

Longing for the peace of the Messiah,
we pray:

◆ Come, O Desire of nations!

To rejoice with your spouse, the Church,
we pray: ◆ To renew your covenant
with the Chosen People, we pray: ◆
To embrace with love those who have
turned away from you, we pray: ◆
To remove conflict from among the
nations, we pray: ◆ To strengthen
the hands of those burdened by labor,
we pray: ◆ To cast out sorrow with
a festive song, we pray: ◆ To make your
dwelling place among us, we pray: ◆

Our Father . . .

Faithful God,
we long for the coming
of the Promised One
and the peace he will bring.
Send us the Desire of nations,
the Prince of Peace,
so we may rejoice and exult
with all our hearts
and praise you forever
through your Son Jesus Christ,
who is Lord forever and ever. Amen.

✝ *Come, O Desire of nations!*
Come and bring us peace!

✦ *Come, Emmanuel, God-with-us!*
Come and make your dwelling
among us!

PSALM 89 *page 419*

READING *Isaiah 7:10–14*

Again the LORD spoke to Ahaz, say-ing, Ask a sign of the LORD your God; let it be deep as Sheol or high as heaven. But Ahaz said, I will not ask, and I will not put the LORD to the test. Then Isaiah said: "Hear then, O house of David! Is it too little for you to weary mortals, that you weary my God also? Therefore the Lord himself will give you a sign. Look, the young woman is with child and shall bear a son, and shall name him Immanuel."

REFLECTION

Today the O Antiphons reach their cres-cendo as we call upon Jesus as Emmanuel, "God-with-us." This image not only directs us toward Mary's child but also returns to the beginning of Advent, when we prayed for Christ's glorious return. The name "Emmanuel" evokes the prophetic promise, found both in the Old and New Testaments that God will dwell among us forever.

PRAYERS *others may be added*

Joyfully confident of God's presence, we pray:

◆ Come, O Emmanuel, God-with-us!

That God's people may have courage in times of trial, we pray: ◆ *That prophets may sustain the Church with words of comfort and challenge, we pray:* ◆ *That nations may turn to faith in God, we pray:* ◆ *That world leaders may listen to voices of wisdom, we pray:* ◆ *That all people may recognize in children a sign of hope, we pray:* ◆ *That we may have confidence in our saving God, we pray:* ◆

Our Father . . .

Hope of Israel,
you promise to abide always
with your people.
May we never lose hope
in your abiding care
and find peace in your
    constant presence.
We ask this through Jesus Christ,
our Emmanuel, God-with-us,
who lives and reigns
forever and ever. Amen.

✦ *Come, Emmanuel, God-with-us!*
Come and make your dwelling
among us!

✠ *Come, beloved Bridegroom,*
   heaven's eternal spring!
   Come speak to us your
   eternal Word.

PSALM 89 *page 419*

READING *Song of Solomon 2:8–13*

The voice of my beloved!
  Look, he comes,
leaping upon the mountains,
  bounding over the hills.
My beloved is like a gazelle
  or a young stag.
Look, there he stands behind our wall,
gazing in at the windows,
  looking through the lattice.
My beloved speaks and says to me:
"Arise, my love, my fair one,
  and come away;
for now the winter is past,
  the rain is over and gone.
The flowers appear on the earth;
  the time of singing has come,
and the voice of the turtledove
  is heard in our land.
The fig tree puts forth its figs,
  and the vines are in blossom;
  they give forth fragrance.
Arise, my love, my fair one,
  and come away."

REFLECTION

The words of the Song of Songs, an ancient Hebrew love poem, express well our Christmas faith: God so loves us, so longs to be with us, that Christ leaps the mountains separating human and divine and, like a joyful lover, rushes to gather us in an eternal embrace. Out of love and love
alone, God in Christ plunges into our lives that we might at last be drawn into God's eternal life.*

PRAYERS *others may be added*

Attentive to the voice of the Beloved, we pray:

◆ Come, O Bridegroom!

That the Church may rejoice at the coming of Christ, we pray: ◆ *That the world's people may hear God's voice calling them in love, we pray:* ◆ *That the abandoned and forgotten may be refreshed by God's presence, we pray:* ◆ *That the earth may be renewed by the coming of its maker, we pray:* ◆ *That the coming of the Savior may bring us delight and hope, we pray:* ◆

Our Father . . .

God of love,
over hills and through valleys
you come to meet us,
joyfully calling us by name.
Release us from the winter of our sin,
and restore us to the springtime
  of your love
that we may return to the garden
  of paradise
to rejoice forever at your side,
for you live and reign
forever and ever. Amen.

✠ *Come, beloved Bridegroom,*
   heaven's eternal spring!
   Come speak to us your
   eternal Word.

✠ *Alleluia!*
The Word of God dwells among us!
God is one with humankind!

PSALM 96   *page 421*

READING   *Luke 2:1–7*

In those days a decree went out from Emperor Augustus that all the world should be registered. This was the first registration and was taken while Quirinius was governor of Syria. All went to their own towns to be registered. Joseph also went from the town of Nazareth in Galilee to Judea, to the city of David called Bethlehem, because he was descended from the house and family of David. He went to be registered with Mary, to whom he was engaged and who was expecting a child. While they were there, the time came for her to deliver her child. And she gave birth to her firstborn son and wrapped him in bands of cloth, and laid him in a manger, because there was no place for them in the inn.

REFLECTION

As a wanderer God's Word comes into the world. Though he is of the family of King David, Jesus enters not with royal fanfare but with barely any human comfort. From his humble beginning, Emmanuel chooses his place among the poor and forgotten, even among the maligned. Even in his birth, Jesus foretells the community he will form, an assembly of the broken, the rejected, the hungry, and the forsaken.

PRAYERS   *others may be added*

Acclaiming Emmanuel, we cry out:

◆ May all your works praise you!

That the Church may proclaim boldly the good news that our God is with us, we cry out: ◆ *That all people may come to recognize Christ's presence in the smallest and least of God's children, we cry out:* ◆ *That the homeless and itinerant may have glad tidings proclaimed to them, we cry out:* ◆ *That refugees and travelers may find shelter and protection, we cry out:* ◆ *That we may open our hearts more deeply to receive the child of Bethlehem, we cry out:* ◆

Our Father . . .

God of wonder,
your eternal Word was born
among the poorest of your people,
as a newborn child in a feeding trough.
Fill us anew with the wonder
of your presence among us,
and open our hearts
to hear the glad tidings.
May we who proclaim Jesus
   Messiah and Lord
seek him first among poor of the earth.
This we ask through Jesus Christ,
child of Bethlehem and eternal King,
who lives and reigns with you,
in the unity of the Holy Spirit,
one God, forever and ever. Amen.

✠ *Alleluia!*
The Word of God dwells among us!
God is one with humankind!

✚ *Alleluia!*
The Word of God dwells among us!
God is one with humankind!

PSALM 96 *page 421*

READING *Matthew 10:16–22*

Jesus said to his disciples: "See, I am sending you out like sheep into the midst of wolves; so be wise as serpents and innocent as doves. Beware of them, for they will hand you over to councils and flog you in their synagogues; and you will be dragged before governors and kings because of me, as a testimony to them and the Gentiles. When they hand you over, do not worry about how you are to speak or what you are to say; for what you are to say will be given to you at that time; for it is not you who speak, but the Spirit of your Father speaking through you. Brother will betray brother to death, and a father his child, and children will rise against parents and have them put to death; and you will be hated by all because of my name. But the one who endures to the end will be saved."

REFLECTION

Today we remember the first of the comites Christi, *"the companions of Christ" — Stephen, John the Evangelist, and the Holy Innocents — whose feast days immediately follow Christmas. Today's saint, Stephen, reminds us that we celebrate not just an infant but an adult Christ at Christmas. We do not separate manger from cross in this festival. Mary's firstborn is the one whose* words were so dangerous that the world's powers put him to death — a fate shared by Stephen and many who have followed the Christ.

PRAYERS *others may be added*

Recognizing in the child of Bethlehem the fiery Messiah, we cry out:

◆ May all your works praise you!

For the witness of Stephen, the first martyr, we cry out: ◆ *For the service of deacons to the Church, we cry out:* ◆ *For the courage to profess boldly our faith in Christ, we cry out:* ◆ *For the wisdom to speak words of justice to the powerful, we cry out:* ◆ *For the strength to endure until the day of salvation, we cry out:* ◆ *For your gentle presence in times of trial, we cry out:* ◆

Our Father . . .

God of mystery,
the coming of your Only-begotten Son
    as a human being
brings both joy and division.
May the witness of Stephen
stir up in us the courage
to live in bold witness to Christ,
embracing both his joy and his cross.
We ask this through Jesus Christ,
Child of Bethlehem and
    Suffering Servant,
who lives and reigns now and forever.
Amen.

✚ *Alleluia!*
The Word of God dwells among us!
God is one with humankind!

✦ *Alleluia!*
  The Word of God dwells among us!
  God is one with humankind!

PSALM 96 *page 421*

READING *1 John 1:1–4*

We declare to you what was from the beginning, what we have heard, what we have seen with our eyes, what we have looked at and touched with our hands, concerning the word of life—this life was revealed, and we have seen it and testify to it, and declare to you the eternal life that was with the Father and was revealed to us—we declare to you what we have seen and heard so that you also may have fellowship with us; and truly our fellowship is with the Father and with his Son Jesus Christ. We are writing these things so that our joy may be complete.

REFLECTION

The author of First John describes the goal of our Christmas proclamation: fellowship with one another and with God. The Christmas stories proclaim this: Angels, shepherds, magi—all come to see and touch the Word of life, and in doing so grow in relationship with each other. Because the Word of God has come close to us, becoming one of us, we cannot help but grow closer to one another—or so we hope.

PRAYERS *others may be added*

Gazing with joy on the Word of life, we pray:

◆ May all your works praise you!

That the Church may invite all people to fellowship, we pray: ◆ That all God's people may share what they have seen and heard concerning the Word of life, we pray: ◆ That all people may be drawn into deeper relationship with God, we pray: ◆ That the grieving and sorrowful may experience the complete joy offered in Emmanuel, we pray: ◆ That we may witness to Christ in our homes, communities, schools, and places of work, we pray: ◆

Our Father . . .

God of joy,
in the Word-made-flesh
we see and touch the Giver of life.
Open our eyes to recognize the Christ
in the faces of our sisters
    and brothers,
that we may grow in fellowship
    with them
and so draw nearer to you.
We ask this through the Child
    of Bethlehem,
Son of Mary and your Son,
who lives and reigns with you
forever and ever. Amen.

✦ *Alleluia!*
  The Word of God dwells among us!
  God is one with humankind!

✚ *Alleluia!*
  The Word of God dwells among us!
  God is one with humankind!

PSALM 96   *page 421*

READING   *Jeremiah 31:15–17*

Thus says the LORD:
A voice is heard in Ramah,
  lamentation and bitter weeping.
Rachel is weeping for her children;
  she refuses to be comforted
    for her children,
  because they are no more.
Thus says the LORD:
Keep your voice from weeping,
  and your eyes from tears;
for there is a reward for your work,
    says the LORD:
  they shall come back from the land
    of the enemy;
there is hope for your future,
    says the LORD:
  your children shall come back
    to their own country.

REFLECTION

The story of the last of the comites Christi,
the Holy Innocents (Matthew 2:16–18),
fills us with horror. Whether the story is
historically accurate is beside the point:
We know that such things happen today,
are happening today, to abused and bat-
tered women and children, to refugees, to
the starving, and to countless others. Here
our Christmas faith calls us to look beyond
Bethlehem. If we see in one newborn child
the Word-made-flesh, we cannot fail to see
God's presence in that child's suffering
brothers and sisters. As the same Jesus

Christ tells us over and over, they are first
in the reign of God.

PRAYERS   *others may be added*

  Crying out on behalf of the innocent,
  we pray:

◆ Word of God, abide with us.

When the prophets of peace are silenced,
we pray: ◆ *When rulers oppress the*
people entrusted to their care, we pray: ◆
When the unarmed and defenseless are
caught between the hatred of the mighty,
we pray: ◆ *When refugees are forced*
to flee the terrors of war and natural
disaster, we pray: ◆ *When tribes and*
peoples suffer genocide, we pray: ◆
When children are abused, neglected,
or unloved, we pray: ◆ *When mothers*
and fathers mourn the death of a child,
we pray: ◆ *When we turn our faces from*
the suffering of the innocent, we pray: ◆

Our Father . . .

God of all mothers and fathers,
the forces of greed and evil
sought to destroy the Child of Justice
and even today oppose his reign.
Forgive us for the times
we have failed to protect the lowly:
May we who adore the Christ Child
seek him among the suffering
    innocent of the world.
This we ask in Jesus' name. Amen.

✚ *Alleluia!*
  The Word of God dwells among us!
  God is one with humankind!

✠ *Alleluia!*
The Word of God dwells among us!
God is one with humankind!

PSALM 96 *page 421*

READING *Luke 2:22–28*

When the time came for their purification according to the law of Moses, his parents brought Jesus up to Jerusalem to present him to the Lord (as it is written in the law of the Lord, "Every firstborn male shall be designated as holy to the Lord"), and they offered a sacrifice according to what is stated in the law of the Lord, "a pair of turtledoves or two young pigeons."

Now there was a man in Jerusalem whose name was Simeon; this man was righteous and devout, looking forward to the consolation of Israel, and the Holy Spirit rested on him. It had been revealed to him by the Holy Spirit that he would not see death before he had seen the Lord's Messiah. Guided by the Spirit, Simeon came into the temple; and when the parents brought in the child Jesus, to do for him what was customary under the law, Simeon took him in his arms.

REFLECTION

The author of Luke counts Simeon among the devout and righteous of Israel who recognize Mary's child as the promised Messiah. Simeon lives today in our own elders, who by their example point the way to Christ. Not only are they worthy of our service and prayer, they also deserve our praise, for in their words and lives we have encountered the living God.

PRAYERS *others may be added*

Giving thanks for God's consolation of the righteous, we cry out:

◆ May all your works praise you!

For the witness and example of holy Simeon, we cry out: ◆ *For the obedience of the holy ones of God, we cry out:* ◆ *For the fulfillment of the hopes of the devout and holy, we cry out:* ◆ *For the faithfulness and wisdom of our elders, we cry out:* ◆ *For the guidance of the Spirit in our search for you, we cry out:* ◆ *For the embrace of grandparents and elders, we cry out:* ◆

Our Father . . .

Source of hope and faith,
your devout servant Simeon
kept vigil in old age
for the coming of the Anointed One,
and you rewarded him
with the gift of the Christ child.
Increase our faith
as we journey through life
that death may find us ready
to embrace the risen Christ
   in eternity,
for Christ is Lord
forever and ever. Amen.

✠ *Alleluia!*
The Word of God dwells among us!
God is one with humankind!

✦ *Alleluia!*
The Word of God dwells among us!
God is one with humankind!

PSALM 96   *page 421*

READING   *Luke 28b–35*

And Simeon praised God, saying,
"Master, now you are dismissing
    your servant in peace,
    according to your word;
for my eyes have seen your salvation,
    which you have prepared
        in the presence of all peoples,
a light for revelation to the Gentiles
        and for glory to your people
            Israel."

And the child's father and mother were amazed at what was being said about him. Then Simeon blessed them and said to his mother Mary, "This child is destined for the falling and the rising of many in Israel, and to be a sign that will be opposed so that the inner thoughts of many will be revealed— and a sword will pierce your own soul too."

REFLECTION

Today we read the last of the canticles of Luke's Gospel, the Nunc dimittis. *Taken together, the songs of Mary, Zechariah, and Simeon sum up who this child is to be: the promised Savior who will cast down the mighty and fill the hungry; the light of God's revelation to all people; the son and glory of Israel. Perhaps that is why the Church sings each daily, morning (Bene-dictus), evening (Magnificat), and night*

(Nunc dimittis). *Each in its own way names the Savior, and reminds us whom we follow.*

PRAYERS   *others may be added*

Amazed by the child of Joseph and Mary, we cry out:

◆ May all your works praise you!

For revealing your light among the Gentiles, we cry out: ◆ For bringing glory to your chosen people, we cry out: ◆ For beginning your reign of peace among us, we cry out: ◆ For comforting the elderly and dying, we cry out: ◆ For astounding us with your graciousness, we cry out: ◆ For opening our eyes to the wonders of salvation, we cry out: ◆

Our Father . . .

Glory to you, O Source of Light,
for in Jesus Christ
you reveal salvation to the nations
and bring glory to the chosen people.
Fill our hearts with Simeon's praise,
that we too may bless you
for your faithfulness`
and praise you forever
through Jesus Christ,
Light of nations and Glory of Israel,
Lord forever and ever. Amen.

✦ *Alleluia!*
The Word of God dwells among us!
God is one with humankind!

✛ *Alleluia!*
The Word of God dwells among us!
God is one with humankind!

PSALM 96   *page 421*

READING   *Luke 2:36–40*

There was also a prophet, Anna the daughter of Phanuel, of the tribe of Asher. She was of a great age, having lived with her husband seven years after her marriage, then as a widow to the age of eighty-four. She never left the temple but worshiped there with fasting and prayer night and day. At that moment she came, and began to praise God and to speak about the child to all who were looking for the redemption of Jerusalem.

When they had finished everything required by the law of the Lord, they returned to Galilee, to their own town of Nazareth. The child grew and became strong, filled with wisdom; and the favor of God was upon him.

REFLECTION

On this New Year's Eve, we join the prophetess Anna in her vigil before God. Anna's faithfulness brought her the vision of the child who would bring Jerusalem's redemption. We hope our faithfulness to prayer, tonight and every night, will also bring us the vision of the world's redemption, as we wait in hope for a new beginning of peace tomorrow in the New Year.

PRAYERS   *others may be added*

Joining with holy women of all ages, we cry out:

◆ May all your works praise you!

For the witness of the prophet Anna, we cry out: ◆ *For all faithful and holy prophets, we cry out:* ◆ *For the example of holy women in every age, we cry out:* ◆ *For companions on the journey of faith, we cry out:* ◆ *For women who serve the Church, we cry out:* ◆ *For faithful friends and loving spouses, we cry out:* ◆ *For mothers and grandmothers who have shown us the way to Christ, we cry out:* ◆

Our Father . . .

God of the prophets,
Anna, faithful daughter of Israel,
praised you for the gift of Emmanuel
and spoke to others of the promise
    Christ brings.
Give us Anna's gift of insight
    and prayer,
that we too may recognize the Christ
in children and parents,
in the poor and hungry.
We ask this through Jesus Christ,
God-with-us, who lives and reigns
forever and ever. Amen.

✛ *Alleluia!*
The Word of God dwells among us!
God is one with humankind!

✠ *Alleluia!*
The Word of God dwells among us!
God is one with humankind!

PSALM 96   *page 421*

READING   *Galatians 4:4–7*

When the fullness of time had come, God sent his Son, born of a woman, born under the law, in order to redeem those who were under the law, so that we might receive adoption as children. And because you are children, God has sent the Spirit of his Son into our hearts, crying, "Abba! Father!" So you are no longer a slave but a child, and if a child then also an heir, through God.

REFLECTION

Galatians speaks of our "adoption" as God's children in Christ. Through Mary, Jesus has become one of us to make us one with God. The mystery of Emmanuel, "God-with-us," can be put the other way as well: "us-with-God." Although not nearly as elegant, it is no less true, and is no less a cause for Christmas joy.

PRAYERS   *others may be added*

Crying out in the Spirit, "Abba! Father!" we pray:

◆ Word of God, abide with us.

That Christians may share with joy the good news that God is with us, we pray: ◆ *That God may send the Spirit of the Son into the hearts of all people, we pray:* ◆ *That the fullness of God's time may bring peace to the world, we pray:* ◆ *That those who suffer slavery may be recognized as God's children, we pray:* ◆ *That the poor may receive their rightful inheritance, we pray:* ◆ *That we may rejoice in the mystery of our adoption as God's children, we pray:* ◆

Our Father . . .

Abba, Father,
in the fullness of time
you sent your Son,
born of Mary.
Make us your children,
and fill us with Christ's Spirit,
that we may rejoice in you
   through Mary's Son,
who is Lord with you,
in the unity of the Holy Spirit,
one God, forever and ever. Amen.

✠ *Alleluia!*
The Word of God dwells among us!
God is one with humankind!

✚ *Alleluia!*
The Word of God dwells among us!
God is one with humankind!

PSALM 96 *page 421*

READING *John 1:1–5*

In the beginning was the Word, and the Word was with God, and the Word was God. He was in the beginning with God. All things came into being through him, and without him not one thing came into being. What has come into being in him was life, and the life was the light of all people. The light shines in the darkness, and the darkness did not overcome it.

REFLECTION

In this last week of the Christmas season, we turn to the Gospel of John. Rather than including a story about Jesus' infancy, as Matthew and Luke do, John begins instead at the real "beginning," Creation. Using images of light and life, the Gospel writer offers us a new facet of the Christmas mystery: "God-with-us" has indeed been "with us" all along, for God's Word is the foundation of all creation, as well as the child of Bethlehem.

PRAYERS *others may be added*

Rejoicing in the light, we pray:

◆ Word of God, abide with us.

That the baptized may share the life they have found in the Word of God, we pray: ◆
That all nations may praise the One through whom all things came to be, we pray: ◆ *That the shadow of injustice may be overcome by Christ's light, we pray:* ◆ *That creation may shine with the glory of God Most High, we pray:* ◆
That we may be beacons of the light offered in Jesus Christ, we pray: ◆

Our Father . . .

God of all creation,
in the beginning
you brought forth light and life
by the power of your Word.
Make us shining beacons
of truth and love,
that your light may overcome
all that is darkness
and all people may share your life
through the Word-made-flesh,
who lives and reigns
now and forever. Amen.

✚ *Alleluia!*
The Word of God dwells among us!
God is one with humankind!

✦ *Alleluia!*
The Word of God dwells among us!
God is one with humankind!

PSALM 96   *page 421*

READING   *John 1:6–9*

There was a man sent from God, whose name was John. He came as a witness to testify to the light, so that all might believe through him. He himself was not the light, but he came to testify to the light. The true light, which enlightens everyone, was coming into the world.

REFLECTION

Each of the four Gospels includes material about John the Baptist; scripture scholars suggest that there may have been some conflict between those who thought John was the Messiah and those who believed in Jesus. The writer of John is clear: "[John] was not the light." Yet the mention of John directs us to another Christmas mystery: the baptism of Jesus. The Christmas season may begin with a silent infant in a manger, but it ends with an adult Jesus who has a lot to say! Each moment of the season—the birth at Christmas, the Magi at Epiphany, and Jesus' baptism— further unfolds the Christmas mystery. Each moment invites our attention and prayer.

PRAYERS   *others may be added*

Attentive to the testimony of John, we pray:

◆ Word of God, abide with us.

For Church ministers and preachers, and all who point the way to Christ, we pray: ◆ *For teachers and scholars, and all who enlighten minds, we pray:* ◆ *For prophets and activists, and all who seek justice, we pray:* ◆ *For the poor and lowly, and all who reveal the coming of Christ into the world, we pray:* ◆ *For us, and all sent by God to testify to the light, we pray:* ◆

Our Father . . .

Light of heaven,
you send forth your servants
to lead us to you.
Open our ears
to the prophet's call,
that all hearts may be ready
to receive the One sent from above,
our Savior Jesus Christ,
the Word-made-flesh,
who is Lord now and forever. Amen.

✦ *Alleluia!*
The Word of God dwells among us!
God is one with humankind!

✠ *Alleluia!*
The Word of God dwells among us!
God is one with humankind!

PSALM 96 *page 421*

READING *John 1:10–13*

He was in the world, and the world came into being through him; yet the world did not know him. He came to what was his own, and his own people did not accept him. But to all who received him, who believed in his name, he gave power to become children of God, who were born, not of blood or of the will of the flesh or of the will of man, but of God.

REFLECTION

The Gospel of John continues to expand the Christmas mystery for us: The Word came into the world to make us God's children. Scripture scholars point out that this statement is at the very center of the composition; John's hymn is meant to focus us on our eternal destiny. To be given such an honor, we have only to "receive" God's Word, which of course is the challenge. Where and in whom is the Word of God present to us today? Are we ready to recognize and receive him?

PRAYERS *others may be added*

Watchful for Christ's presence,
we pray:

◆ Word of God, abide with us.

For those who make Christ present in words of truth, we pray: ◆ *For those who make Christ present in deeds of justice, we pray:* ◆ *For those who make Christ present in acts of compassion, we pray:* ◆ *For those who make Christ present in the search for peace, we pray:* ◆ *For those who make Christ present in their suffering, we pray:* ◆ *For those who make Christ present in their weakness, we pray:* ◆ *For those who make Christ present in their humility, we pray:* ◆

Our Father . . .

Eternal God,
you speak your Word
to every nation,
inviting all to faith.
Open our hearts to receive
the Word-made-flesh
in the poor and hungry,
in prophets and preachers,
and in all who do your will,
for Christ lives and reigns
forever and ever. Amen.

✠ *Alleluia!*
The Word of God dwells among us!
God is one with humankind!

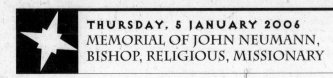
✜ *Alleluia!*
The Word of God dwells among us!
God is one with humankind!

PSALM 96 *page 421*

READING *John 1:14–18*

And the Word became flesh and lived among us, and we have seen his glory, the glory as of a father's only son, full of grace and truth. (John testified to him and cried out, "This was he of whom I said, 'He who comes after me ranks ahead of me because he was before me.'") From his fullness we have all received, grace upon grace. The law indeed was given through Moses; grace and truth came through Jesus Christ. No one has ever seen God. It is God the only Son, who is close to the Father's heart, who has made him known.

REFLECTION

It is important to note that these words of faith and praise come before the Gospel tells the human story of Jesus. John's Gospel, like all the Gospels, is a reflection on the experience of faith in Jesus, not a modern biography or purely historical account. Before telling us anything about Jesus of Nazareth, John's writer reveals who Jesus "really" is, God's Word who lived among us. Before we begin the story, the writer invites us to faith.

PRAYERS *others may be added*

With thanksgiving for the nearness of God, we pray:

◆ Word of God, abide with us.

That the baptized may drink deeply of the fullness of grace, we pray: ◆ *That God's truth may find a home among the nations, we pray:* ◆ *That the living Word of God may be honored and served in the poor and lowly, we pray:* ◆ *That the dead may behold the glory of the Only-begotten Son, we pray:* ◆ *That we may lead others to the Father's heart, we pray:* ◆

Our Father . . .

Father of light,
in Christ Jesus your Son
you pour forth grace upon grace.
Reveal to us the fullness of truth,
that we may at last behold your glory
shining in the Word-made-flesh,
who is Lord forever and ever. Amen.

✜ *Alleluia!*
The Word of God dwells among us!
God is one with humankind!

✠ *Alleluia!*
The Word of God dwells among us!
God is one with humankind!

PSALM 96   *page 421*

READING   *John 1:19–23*

This is the testimony given by John when the Jews sent priests and Levites from Jerusalem to ask him, "Who are you?" He confessed and did not deny it, but confessed, "I am not the Messiah." And they asked him, "What then? Are you Elijah?" He said, "I am not." "Are you the prophet?" He answered, "No." Then they said to him, "Who are you? Let us have an answer for those who sent us. What do you say about yourself?" He said,

"I am the voice of one crying out
in the wilderness,
'Make straight the way
of the Lord,'"
as the prophet Isaiah said.

REFLECTION

The Gospel writer recounts the testimony of the fiery prophet John the Baptist; today we celebrate a witness of another sort, Blessed André Bessette, a Holy Cross brother known for his gift of prayer rather than challenging preaching. Many sick and disabled sought the intercession of this holy handyman and janitor, and many experienced God's healing through his prayer. To this day his shrine in Montreal is filled with tokens of illnesses healed— crutches and canes, among others. Yet healed of physical disabilities or not, peo- ple undoubtedly experienced the presence of God's Word in this humble man. It is said that when he died in 1937, half a mil- lion people filed past his coffin.

PRAYERS   *others may be added*

Attentive to the testimony of Blessed André, we pray:

◆ Word of God, abide with us.

That the baptized may be blessed with people of deep prayer, we pray: ◆
That religious brothers may be strengthened in their ministry to the Church and the world, we pray: ◆
That those who minister to the sick may be inspired by the example of Blessed André, we pray: ◆ *That the work of laborers may be honored and respected, we pray:* ◆ *That all who seek healing may find comfort and support, we pray:* ◆

Our Father . . .

God of the humble,
in Brother André
your Word found a witness
whose testimony was compassion.
Bless us with your healing touch
that we, like André, may share it
with the sick and frightened among us.
We ask this in the name
of Jesus Christ,
your compassion made flesh,
who lives and reigns
forever and ever. Amen.

✠ *Alleluia!*
The Word of God dwells among us!
God is one with humankind!

✛ *Alleluia!*
The Word of God dwells among us!
God is one with humankind!

PSALM 96   *page 421*

READING   *John 1:24–28*

Now the priests and Levites had been sent from the Pharisees. They asked him, "Why then are you baptizing if you are neither the Messiah, nor Elijah, nor the prophet?" John answered them, "I baptize with water. Among you stands one whom you do not know, the one who is coming after me; I am not worthy to untie the thong of his sandal." This took place in Bethany across the Jordan where John was baptizing.

REFLECTION

On Monday, the Christmas season will come to an abrupt end with the feast of the Baptism of the Lord; Christmas usually lasts another week. This last reading from the first chapter of the Gospel of John concludes with the account of Jesus' baptism, which will be proclaimed during Monday's liturgy. The entire Advent-Christmas cycle, then, begins near the end of Jesus' earthly work, with his final warnings about the Second Coming, and ends at the beginning of Jesus' public ministry.

PRAYERS   *others may be added*

Awaiting the one who is greater than the prophets, we pray:

◆ Word of God, abide with us.

That the baptized may announce the coming Christ, we pray: ◆ *That prophets and preachers may be heard and heeded, we pray:* ◆ *That the curious and questioning may find answers, we pray:* ◆ *That those searching for God may find the presence of the one they have yet to know, we pray:* ◆ *That we may lead others to faith in God's Word, we pray:* ◆

Our Father . . .

Faithful God,
in every age
you send your messengers
to clear the way for your reign.
Empower us as prophets
to proclaim the Good News,
leading others to faith in the one
who stands among us,
the Word-made-flesh,
who lives and reigns with you
in the unity of the Holy Spirit,
one God forever and ever. Amen.

✛ *Alleluia!*
The Word of God dwells among us!
God is one with humankind!

✦ *Alleluia!*
   The Word of God dwells among us!
   God is one with humankind!

PSALM 96   *page 421*

READING   *Ephesians 3:2–3a, 5–6*

You have already heard of the commission of God's grace that was given me for you, and how the mystery was made known to me by revelation.

In former generations this mystery was not made known to humankind, as it has now been revealed to his holy apostles and prophets by the Spirit: that is, the Gentiles have become fellow heirs, members of the same body, and sharers in the promise in Christ Jesus through the gospel.

REFLECTION

Ephesians expresses the heart of the Epiphany mystery: The offer of salvation, once restricted to the Jewish people, has now been extended to those who do not share in God's covenant with Israel. In Jesus all are offered membership in the one body. All now claim a share in the glorious inheritance of God's children. God's generosity is revealed in its fullness, a shining gift for all who believe.

PRAYERS   *others may be added*

   Rejoicing in God's generous love,
   we pray:

◆ *Word of God, abide with us.*

That all people may find welcome among the baptized, we pray: ◆ *That the nations may rejoice in the mystery now revealed in its fullness, we pray:* ◆ *That those excluded and cast out may be restored to their rightful place in God's household, we pray:* ◆ *That God's many gifts may be justly shared, we pray:* ◆ *That all who share in the promise of God may live in joy, grace and peace, we pray:* ◆

Our Father . . .

Source of grace,
in Christ you make all people
heirs of your eternal promise.
Open our eyes and hearts
to the mystery of your love,
that we may never fail
to see one another
as members of the one Body,
joined in Jesus Christ,
who lives and reigns with you,
in the unity of the Holy Spirit,
one God, forever and ever. Amen.

✦ *Alleluia!*
   The Word of God dwells among us!
   God is one with humankind!

✙ *Alleluia!*
The Word of God dwells among us!
God is one with humankind!

PSALM 96 page 421

READING Mark 1:4–11

John the baptizer appeared in the wilderness, proclaiming a baptism of repentance for the forgiveness of sins. And people from the whole Judean countryside and all the people of Jerusalem were going out to him, and were baptized by him in the river Jordan, confessing their sins. Now John was clothed with camel's hair, with a leather belt around his waist, and he ate locusts and wild honey. He proclaimed, "The one who is more powerful than I is coming after me; I am not worthy to stoop down and untie the thong of his sandals. I have baptized you with water; but he will baptize you with the Holy Spirit."

In those days Jesus came from Nazareth of Galilee and was baptized by John in the Jordan. And just as he was coming up out of the water, he saw the heavens torn apart and the Spirit descending like a dove on him. And a voice came from heaven, "You are my Son, the Beloved; with you I am well pleased."

REFLECTION

The Christmas season ends with another "epiphany," this time the baptism of the Lord. The heavenly voice confirms the prophecy of John the Baptist: This is God's chosen, the one who brings good news.

We end our Christmas festival ready to follow an adult Christ, ready to attend to the one with whom God is well pleased, who will pour out the Holy Spirit upon us.

PRAYERS others may be added

Christ is revealed as God's Beloved; in hope, we pray:

◆ Word of God, abide with us.

For all who follow the way of God's Beloved, we pray: ◆ *For fiery prophets who challenge us to conversion, we pray:* ◆ *For preachers who proclaim the Good News, we pray:* ◆ *For those who are preparing for baptism, we pray:* ◆ *For all who seek God's forgiveness, we pray:* ◆ *For the full revelation of the Beloved of God, we pray:* ◆

Our Father . . .

God Most High,
your people wait with longing
to see your Anointed One,
    the Beloved.
As we await the salvation
of the Son of God
make us ever attentive to his presence
in our brothers and sisters.
May we too be counted
among those beloved of God.
We ask this in the name of Jesus,
who lives and reigns with you,
in the unity of the Holy Spirit,
one God, forever and ever. Amen.

✙ *Alleluia!*
The Word of God dwells among us!
God is one with humankind!

✝ *To you, O Lord, I lift up my soul.*
All my hope is in you.

PSALM 25   *page 410*

READING   *Mark 1:14–20*

Now after John was arrested, Jesus came to Galilee, proclaiming the good news of God, and saying, "The time is fulfilled, and the kingdom of God has come near; repent, and believe in the good news."

As Jesus passed along the Sea of Galilee, he saw Simon and his brother Andrew casting a net into the sea—for they were fishermen. And Jesus said to them, "Follow me and I will make you fish for people." And immediately they left their nets and followed him. As he went a little farther, he saw James son of Zebedee and his brother John, who were in their boat mending the nets. Immediately he called them; and they left their father Zebedee in the boat with the hired men, and followed him.

REFLECTION

The Sunday Gospel during Ordinary Time is generally taken from one of the three synoptic Gospels: Matthew, Mark, and Luke. ("Synoptic" means "to see together" and describes these three Gospels because they share the same basic order of events and recount many of the same stories. The Gospel of John, on the other hand, is quite different.) Since this year is Mark's year, the weekdays between now and Lent—almost eight weeks—will include readings from this Gospel.

PRAYERS   *others may be added*

Attentive to the call of the Teacher, we pray:

◆ Teach us your ways.

That all the baptized may heed Christ's call to discipleship, we pray: ◆ *That those the Church calls to ministry may respond with generosity, we pray:* ◆ *That the nearness of the reign of God may usher in a new day of peace in the world, we pray:* ◆ *That the proclamation of the Good News may bring justice for the oppressed and downtrodden, we pray:* ◆ *That we may put aside what keeps us from responding generously to the Master's call, we pray:* ◆

Our Father . . .

God of election,
in baptism you choose us in Christ
to be heralds of your Good News.
By your grace expand our hearts
to respond generously to Christ's call,
that all the world may know
that the kingdom of heaven is at hand,
for Christ lives and reigns
forever and ever. Amen.

✝ *To you, O Lord, I lift up my soul.*
All my hope is in you.

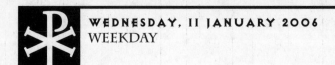
✝ *To you, O Lord, I lift up my soul.*
All my hope is in you.

PSALM 25 page 410

READING Mark 1:21–28

They went to Capernaum; and when the sabbath came, he entered the synagogue and taught. They were astounded at his teaching, for he taught them as one having authority, and not as the scribes. Just then there was in their synagogue a man with an unclean spirit, and he cried out, "What have you to do with us, Jesus of Nazareth? Have you come to destroy us? I know who you are, the Holy One of God." But Jesus rebuked him, saying, "Be silent, and come out of him!" And the unclean spirit, convulsing him and crying with a loud voice, came out of him. They were all amazed, and they kept on asking one another, "What is this? A new teaching—with authority! He commands even the unclean spirits, and they obey him." At once his fame began to spread throughout the surrounding region of Galilee.

REFLECTION

Mark's Gospel is filled with both Jesus' teaching and his deeds of power. These two facets of his ministry are interrelated: Jesus' authority to teach is backed up by his authority over the evil forces of the world, especially those that oppress human beings. Mark's "demons" represent all the powers that oppose Jesus' ministry; the demon's words to Jesus are a hostile challenge, which Jesus meets with equal hostility and greater power.

PRAYERS *others may be added*

Attentive to God's Holy One,
we pray:

◆ Teach us your ways.

For those beset by demons of self-doubt, we pray: ◆ *For those beset by demons of injustice, we pray:* ◆ *For those beset by demons of anger, we pray:* ◆ *For those beset by demons of isolation, we pray:* ◆ *For those beset by demons of addiction, we pray:* ◆ *For those beset by demons of prejudice, we pray:* ◆ *For those beset by demons of despair, we pray:* ◆

Our Father . . .

God of power,
you sent your Holy One
to banish evil's power
and drive out the demons
that oppress your people.
Set us free from what binds us,
that we too may cast out
spirits of division and injustice
and so announce the dawn
of your reign in Jesus Christ,
who is Lord forever and ever. Amen.

✝ *To you, O Lord, I lift up my soul.*
All my hope is in you.

✝ *To you, O Lord, I lift up my soul.*
All my hope is in you.

PSALM 25   *page 410*

READING   *Mark 1:29–34*

As soon as they left the synagogue, they entered the house of Simon and Andrew, with James and John. Now Simon's mother-in-law was in bed with a fever, and they told him about her at once. He came and took her by the hand and lifted her up. Then the fever left her, and she began to serve them.

That evening, at sundown, they brought to him all who were sick or possessed with demons. And the whole city was gathered around the door. And he cured many who were sick with various diseases, and cast out many demons; and he would not permit the demons to speak, because they knew him.

REFLECTION

Some might wonder if Jesus healed Peter's mother-in-law just so she could serve them! But this misses the point: Peter's mother-in-law responds to Jesus' act of mercy with one of her own, relieving his exhaustion with her hospitality. Jesus makes possible her active participation in relationship with him by restoring her health; she responds in kindness by meeting his needs and so restoring him. She is no less a disciple than Simon and Andrew, and no less a model for us in her service.

PRAYERS   *others may be added*

Seeing in Simon's mother-in-law a model of faith and service, we pray:

◆ Teach us your ways.

That the baptized may embrace all who gather around the Church's doors, we pray: ◆ That the baptized may seek out the sick and exhausted, we pray: ◆ That the contribution of women in the Church may be valued and celebrated, we pray: ◆ That the healing touch of Jesus may cast out the demons of addiction and mental illness, we pray: ◆ That the sick may experience Jesus' gentle touch in the ministry of his disciples, we pray: ◆ That we may respond to Christ's call with service to those in need, we pray: ◆

Our Father . . .

God of wholeness,
the brokenness of the world
is restored by Christ's touch,
and the forces of evil flee.
Empower our hands to heal the broken,
and expand our hearts to gather
   the weary,
that the world may be restored
to right relationship,
and Christ's reign of justice
may come to completion.
We ask this in Jesus' name. Amen.

✝ *To you, O Lord, I lift up my soul.*
All my hope is in you.

✝ *To you, O Lord, I lift up my soul.*
All my hope is in you.

PSALM 25 — page 410

READING — *Mark 1:35–39*

In the morning, while it was still very dark, he got up and went out to a deserted place, and there he prayed. And Simon and his companions hunted for him. When they found him, they said to him, "Everyone is searching for you." He answered, "Let us go on to the neighboring towns, so that I may proclaim the message there also; for that is what I came out to do." And he went throughout Galilee, proclaiming the message in their synagogues and casting out demons.

REFLECTION

For those accustomed to worshiping Jesus as the Son of God, it can be hard to imagine his human struggle to understand his mission. Today's passage portrays Jesus retreating in solitude to discern his next step. All the people searching for him were looking for more signs and wonders; even his disciples seem to think he's missing a great opportunity to expand his fame. Jesus, however, leads them away; rather than seeking local fame, he must carry the Gospel message throughout Galilee. Jesus' signs and wonders are not ends in themselves; like all Jesus' actions, they serve the kingdom God sent Jesus to announce.

PRAYERS — *others may be added*

Ready to follow wherever Jesus leads, we pray:

◆ Teach us your ways.

That the baptized may carry the Good News to every town and city, we pray: ◆ That Christian leaders may seek not personal fame but the growth of God's reign, we pray: ◆ That every nation may behold God's saving power, we pray: ◆ That the sick in every place may receive the Good News, we pray: ◆ That we may seek God's will in silence and prayer, we pray: ◆

Our Father . . .

God of discernment,
your Son sought your counsel
and you led him in your way.
Speak to us in our depths,
and call to us in silence,
that we may follow your way
and proclaim the Good News
in every land, among every people.
This we ask in Jesus' name. Amen.

✝ *To you, O Lord, I lift up my soul.*
All my hope is in you.

✙ *To you, O Lord, I lift up my soul.*
All my hope is in you.

PSALM 25 *page 410*

READING *Mark 1:40–45*

A leper came to him begging him, and kneeling he said to him, "If you choose, you can make me clean." Moved with pity, Jesus stretched out his hand and touched him, and said to him, "I do choose. Be made clean!" Immediately the leprosy left him, and he was made clean. After sternly warning him he sent him away at once, saying to him, "See that you say nothing to anyone; but go, show yourself to the priest, and offer for your cleansing what Moses commanded, as a testimony to them." But he went out and began to proclaim it freely, and to spread the word, so that Jesus could no longer go into a town openly, but stayed out in the country; and people came to him from every quarter.

REFLECTION

The boldness of the leper in approaching Jesus was no doubt shocking to the ancient readers of Mark. Coming close enough for Jesus to touch him violated all kinds of rules that kept lepers at a "safe distance." Yet both Jesus and the leper reject the gulf between them, and through the leper's faith, Jesus restores him to full membership in society. While curing debilitating illnesses may be beyond our power, we surely have the ability to leap across the psychological and social gulfs that keep us
from right relationship with all people. Perhaps we only lack the will.

PRAYERS *others may be added*

Crossing all boundaries to preach the Good News, we pray:

◆ Teach us your ways.

That the people of God may reach out to the suffering with mercy, we pray: ◆ That the Church may embrace with open arms people from every quarter, we pray: ◆ That those stigmatized by society may be restored by the cleansing touch of Jesus, we pray: ◆ That the sick may trust in the healing power of God's Anointed One, we pray: ◆ That we may always testify to what God has done for us in Jesus Christ, we pray: ◆

Our Father . . .

God of the outcast,
you sent your Word
to restore unity among us
by removing shame and stigma.
Give us courage
to overcome our fear,
that we may reach out in mercy
to those isolated and forgotten,
and so be counted among those
who are first in your kingdom.
This we ask in Jesus' name. Amen.

✙ *To you, O Lord, I lift up my soul.*
All my hope is in you.

✠ *To you, O Lord, I lift up my soul.*
All my hope is in you.

PSALM 25   page 410

READING   *1 Corinthians 6:13c–15a, 17–20*

The body is meant not for fornication but for the Lord, and the Lord for the body. And God raised the Lord and will also raise us by his power. Do you not know that your bodies are members of Christ?

But anyone united to the Lord becomes one spirit with him. Shun fornication! Every sin that a person commits is outside the body; but the fornicator sins against the body itself. Or do you not know that your body is a temple of the Holy Spirit within you, which you have from God, and that you are not your own? For you were bought with a price; therefore glorify God in your body.

REFLECTION

The second reading for the Sundays of Ordinary Time is taken from a letter of the New Testament, which is read semi-continuously over several Sundays. Today we begin a section from First Corinthians; this passage focuses on the dignity of the human body. Paul seems to be arguing with some Corinthians who say the body has no value; from this principle they reason that it is permissible to do anything one desires, including having sexual relationships with prostitutes. Paul argues to the contrary that the body is indeed holy, a temple of the Spirit, and will be raised
along with the rest of our person in glory. In the meantime, then, we must praise God with our whole selves, bodies included!

PRAYERS   *others may be added*

Praising God with body and spirit, we pray:

◆ Teach us your ways.

That the baptized may honor the holiness of created things, we pray: ◆ That nations may see to the human needs of all citizens, we pray: ◆ That the gift of sexuality may be used wisely, we pray: ◆ That human hands may embody God's love for the poor, we pray: ◆ That the bodies of the sick may be restored through the Holy Spirit, we pray: ◆ That the bodies of the dead may be glorified with Christ, we pray: ◆ That we serve God with our whole selves, we pray: ◆

Our Father . . .

God of spirit and flesh,
you breathed life into clay
that we might praise you
    in our bodies,
and in the Word-made-flesh
you joined yourself to creation.
Open our eyes to the marvel
    of humanity,
that with body and spirit
we may glorify you
through Jesus the Christ,
who lives and reigns with you,
in the unity of the Holy Spirit,
one God, now and forever. Amen.

✠ *To you, O Lord, I lift up my soul.*
All my hope is in you.

✜ *To you, O Lord, I lift up my soul.*
   All my hope is in you.

PSALM 25 · page 410

READING · Romans 8:18–23

I consider that the sufferings of this present time are not worth comparing with the glory about to be revealed to us. For the creation waits with eager longing for the revealing of the children of God; for the creation was subjected to futility, not of its own will but by the will of the one who subjected it, in hope that the creation itself will be set free from its bondage to decay and will obtain the freedom of the glory of the children of God. We know that the whole creation has been groaning in labor pains until now; and not only the creation, but we ourselves, who have the first fruits of the Spirit, groan inwardly while we wait for adoption, the redemption of our bodies.

REFLECTION

Today the United States observes the birthday of Dr. Martin Luther King Jr. Dr. King's ministry and work on behalf of civil rights embodied today's passage. King and his many coworkers—women and men, black and white, Protestant and Catholic—gave voice to creation's groaning, and bore in their bodies, sometimes even to death, the labor pains that will lead to greater justice. King's example reminds us that the redemption we seek is not purely otherworldly; God's reign must break into the here-and-now, lest Christianity be nothing more than pie-in-the-sky, another nice story that has nothing to do with the world today.

PRAYERS · *others may be added*

Groaning inwardly as we await redemption, we pray:

◆ Teach us your ways.

That the baptized may cry out for a new birth of justice and righteousness, we pray: ◆ *That all people may be set free from the bondage of sin and prejudice, we pray:* ◆ *That creation's groaning may hasten the Day of the Lord, we pray:* ◆ *That the suffering of this present time may give way to the fullness of life, we pray:* ◆ *That we who have the first fruits of the Spirit may labor unceasingly for the coming of Christ, we pray:* ◆

Our Father . . .

God of creation,
your Spirit groans within us,
laboring to bring about
the revelation of your children.
By the intercession of your servants,
sustain us in this time of struggle,
that all may share
the freedom and the glory
of the children of God,
through Christ our Redeemer,
who is Lord forever and ever. Amen.

✜ *To you, O Lord, I lift up my soul.*
   All my hope is in you.

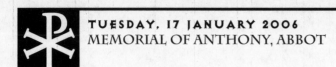
✛ *To you, O Lord, I lift up my soul.*
All my hope is in you.

PSALM 25 *page 410*

READING *Mark 2:1–5*

When Jesus returned to Capernaum after some days, it was reported that he was at home. So many gathered around that there was no longer room for them, not even in front of the door; and he was speaking the word to them. Then some people came, bringing to him a paralyzed man, carried by four of them. And when they could not bring him to Jesus because of the crowd, they removed the roof above him; and after having dug through it, they let down the mat on which the paralytic lay. When Jesus saw their faith, he said to the paralytic, "Son, your sins are forgiven."

REFLECTION

Of the many characters in this wonderful story, the friends of the paralyzed person are perhaps the most endearing. They'll stop at nothing to get their friend to the healer. If only every person in need had such friends! It is the faith of the paralytic's friends—rather than the paralytic's own faith—that calls forth Jesus' response.

PRAYERS *others may be added*

Astounded by Jesus' authority and power, we pray:

◆ Teach us your ways.

For those who share Jesus' ministry of healing and reconciliation, we pray: ◆
For those who seek forgiveness from sin, we pray: ◆ *For those who are suspicious, fearful, or full of scorn, we pray:* ◆
For those who seek healing with trust and faith, we pray: ◆ *For those who care for the needs of the sick, we pray:* ◆
For those with physical or mental disabilities, we pray: ◆ *For those who glorify God through Jesus Christ, we pray:* ◆

Our Father . . .

God of new creation,
in your mercy you forget our sins
and pour out upon us your love.
Fill us with faith in Jesus,
that we may accept forgiveness
and be restored to wholeness
and so praise you through our Lord
   Jesus Christ,
your compassion made flesh,
who lives and reigns
forever and ever. Amen.

✛ *To you, O Lord, I lift up my soul.*
All my hope is in you.

✤ *To you, O Lord, I lift up my soul.*
All my hope is in you.

PSALM 25 *page 410*

READING *Mark 2:6–12*

Now some of the scribes were sitting there, questioning in their hearts, "Why does this fellow speak in this way? It is blasphemy! Who can forgive sins but God alone?" At once Jesus perceived in his spirit that they were discussing these questions among themselves; and he said to them, "Why do you raise such questions in your hearts? Which is easier, to say to the paralytic, 'Your sins are forgiven,' or to say, 'Stand up and take your mat and walk'? But so that you may know that the Son of Man has authority on earth to forgive sins"—he said to the paralytic—"I say to you, stand up, take your mat and go to your home." And he stood up, and immediately took the mat and went out before all of them; so that they were all amazed and glorified God, saying, "We have never seen anything like this!"

REFLECTION

The story of the paralytic's healing is part of a larger section of Mark that focuses on Jesus' conflict with the religious authorities. In this case Jesus claims to forgive sins; his opponents protest that this is blasphemy, since only God can forgive sins. The healing itself, then, acts as a sign giving divine authority to Jesus' claim. The Son of Man—here, merely Jesus' oblique way of referring to himself—can forgive sins, then and now.

PRAYERS *others may be added*

Amazed at God's power in Jesus, we pray:

◆ Teach us your ways.

For those who continue Jesus' healing ministry, we pray: ◆ *For those who speak with divine authority, we pray:* ◆ *For those who promote reconciliation, we pray:* ◆ *For those who seek forgiveness, we pray:* ◆ *For those who seek bodily wholeness, we pray:* ◆ *For those who question in their hearts, we pray:* ◆ *For those who glorify God for wondrous works, we pray:* ◆

Our Father . . .

God of power,
you sent Jesus Christ
to reveal your mercy.
Give us a share of his authority:
May we too be agents
of healing and compassion
and so bring to greater fullness
the kingdom Jesus proclaimed,
for Jesus is Lord
now and forever. Amen.

✤ *To you, O Lord, I lift up my soul.*
All my hope is in you.

✝ *To you, O Lord, I lift up my soul.*
All my hope is in you.

PSALM 25   *page 410*

READING   *Mark 2:13–17*

Jesus went out again beside the sea; the whole crowd gathered around him, and he taught them. As he was walking along, he saw Levi son of Alphaeus sitting at the tax booth, and he said to him, "Follow me." And he got up and followed him.

And as he sat at dinner in Levi's house, many tax collectors and sinners were also sitting with Jesus and his disciples—for there were many who followed him. When the scribes of the Pharisees saw that he was eating with sinners and tax collectors, they said to his disciples, "Why does he eat with tax collectors and sinners?" When Jesus heard this, he said to them, "Those who are well have no need of a physician, but those who are sick; I have come to call not the righteous but sinners."

REFLECTION

Even in print, Jesus' irritation is obvious as he rebukes his detractors. We might also wonder if there was a note of irony in his voice when he mentions the "righteous." Jesus, it seems, preferred the company of sinners, confident that they knew their need for forgiveness; they were clearly hungry for something better. The "righteous," on the other hand, were too self-satisfied to see their need or the gift standing before them.

PRAYERS   *others may be added*

Sinners embraced by God's mercy, we pray:

◆ Teach us your ways.

That the baptized may welcome sinner and saint alike, we pray: ◆ *That the Church's ministers may generously offer God's boundless mercy in Christ, we pray:* ◆ *That the Eucharistic table may join rich and poor, every race and way of life, as one family, we pray:* ◆ *That sinners may know God's healing love, we pray:* ◆ *That we may turn away from self-righteousness and judgment, we pray:* ◆

Our Father . . .

Divine Physician,
you offer healing to the sick,
and compassion to the sinner.
Heal us from the self-righteousness
that afflicts our hearts,
and give us a desire
to seek the lost,
that we may welcome
those in need of your mercy,
recognizing in them
our own wounds and sin.
We ask this through the one
who ate with sinners,
for Christ lives and reigns
forever and ever. Amen.

✝ *To you, O Lord, I lift up my soul.*
All my hope is in you.

✚ *To you, O Lord, I lift up my soul.*
   All my hope is in you.

PSALM 25   *page 410*

READING   *Mark 2:18–22*

Now John's disciples and the Pharisees were fasting; and people came and said to him, "Why do John's disciples and the disciples of the Pharisees fast, but your disciples do not fast?" Jesus said to them, "The wedding guests cannot fast while the bridegroom is with them, can they? As long as they have the bridegroom with them, they cannot fast. The days will come when the bridegroom is taken away from them, and then they will fast on that day.

"No one sews a piece of unshrunk cloth on an old cloak; otherwise, the patch pulls away from it, the new from the old, and a worse tear is made. And no one puts new wine into old wineskins; otherwise, the wine will burst the skins, and the wine is lost, and so are the skins; but one puts new wine into fresh wineskins."

REFLECTION

The long passage that began with the healing of the paralytic comes to its climax today. Jesus reveals himself as the Bridegroom, an allusion to the image of the God of Israel as the husband of the chosen people. As Bridegroom, Jesus brings something new, which requires a new religious response. The old forms—worn-out cloaks and brittle wineskins—are incapable of containing the Good News Jesus brings.

We hear in this passage an echo of the preaching of Paul, which he argued against Gentile Christians accepting circumcision and the Jewish law. Already by the time of Mark (around the year 70), Christianity was beginning to move away from its Jewish roots.

PRAYERS   *others may be added*

In thanksgiving for the presence of the Bridegroom, we pray:

◆ Teach us your ways.

That Christians may share with all people the joy they have in Jesus Christ, we pray: ◆ That the new wine of peace may burst the skins of conflict and division, we pray: ◆ That the cloth of justice may cover those in need, we pray: ◆ That the dead may feast at the eternal wedding banquet, we pray: ◆ That we may recognize the presence of the Bridegroom in all our celebrations, we pray: ◆

Our Father . . .

God of joy,
the Bridegroom brings a new vintage,
the rich wine of the new covenant.
Fill us with Christ's Spirit,
that our feasts may be foretastes
of the celebration to come,
where all people will be gathered
   at one table,
with Christ the Bridegroom
forever and ever. Amen.

✚ *To you, O Lord, I lift up my soul.*
   All my hope is in you.

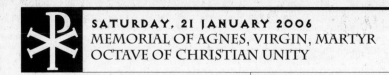
✦ *To you, O Lord, I lift up my soul.*
   All my hope is in you.

PSALM 25   *page 410*

READING   *Mark 2:23–28*

One sabbath he was going through the grainfields; and as they made their way his disciples began to pluck heads of grain. The Pharisees said to him, "Look, why are they doing what is not lawful on the sabbath?" And he said to them, "Have you never read what David did when he and his companions were hungry and in need of food? He entered the house of God, when Abiathar was high priest, and ate the bread of the Presence, which it is not lawful for any but the priests to eat, and he gave some to his companions." Then he said to them, "The sabbath was made for humankind, and not humankind for the sabbath; so the Son of Man is lord even of the sabbath."

REFLECTION

The conflict between Jesus and his opponents continues, this time over Sabbath observance. At the heart of the dispute is whether religious observance alone is more important than human need. Jesus favors the latter; Sabbath rest is a gift to humankind. God did not create humanity for the sake of religious law!

PRAYERS   *others may be added*

Attentive to the needs of humanity,
we pray:

◆ Teach us your ways.

That God's people may treasure mercy over sacrifice, we pray: ◆ That people of faith may set aside empty practices, we pray: ◆ That governments may see first to the needs of their citizens, we pray: ◆ That those cast out because of unjust laws and restrictions may find restoration, we pray: ◆ That our constant hope may be the full human life of our sisters and brothers, we pray: ◆

Our Father . . .

Lord of the sabbath,
you desire mercy rather than sacrifice
and compassion above all.
Cleanse us of empty ritual
and self-serving religion,
that we may serve first
the needs of your children
in whom you are revealed,
for you live and reign
now and forever. Amen.

✦ *To you, O Lord, I lift up my soul.*
   All my hope is in you.

✦ *To you, O Lord, I lift up my soul.*
All my hope is in you.

PSALM 25   *page 410*

READING   *1 Corinthians 7:29b–31*

Brothers and sisters, the appointed time has grown short; from now on, let even those who have wives be as though they had none, and those who mourn as though they were not mourning, and those who rejoice as though they were not rejoicing, and those who buy as though they had no possessions, and those who deal with the world as though they had no dealings with it. For the present form of this world is passing away.

REFLECTION

After insisting in last Sunday's reading of the importance of the human body, and with it all of human life, today Paul seems to argue the opposite. Actually, he is dealing with an argument in the community about marriage. Some in Corinth practiced strict celibacy and abstained from sex even in marriage—and pressured others to do the same. In earlier verses Paul argues that Christians are free to marry and, indeed, should marry if they lack "self-control" (7:9). At the same time, especially in these verses, Paul reminds his readers of the Second Coming, which the early Christians expected at any time. With this in mind, it is more important to concentrate on the world to come than on this world. Christians must always keep their eyes on the future, anticipating the world to come.

PRAYERS   *others may be added*

Eagerly awaiting the fullness of God's reign, we pray:

◆ Teach us your ways.

That the baptized may keep their eyes fixed always on Christ, we pray: ◆
That the appointed time may find believers ready to receive God's reign, we pray: ◆
That those with an abundance of possessions may seek justice, we pray: ◆
That celibates and couples alike may live in faithfulness, we pray: ◆ *That those who mourn may find hope in God's promise, we pray:* ◆

Our Father . . .

God of our future,
you call us to live today
as children of the world to come.
Make us ready for Christ's return,
that we may welcome him in joy
and so enter the glory you promise
in the same Jesus Christ, our Lord,
who lives and reigns with you
in the unity of the Holy Spirit,
one God, forever and ever. Amen.

✦ *To you, O Lord, I lift up my soul.*
All my hope is in you.

✠ *To you, O Lord, I lift up my soul.*
All my hope is in you.

PSALM 25   *page 410*

READING   *Mark 3:1–6*

Again Jesus entered the synagogue, and a man was there who had a withered hand. They watched him to see whether he would cure him on the sabbath, so that they might accuse him. And he said to the man who had the withered hand, "Come forward." Then he said to them, "Is it lawful to do good or to do harm on the sabbath, to save life or to kill?" But they were silent. He looked around at them with anger; he was grieved at their hardness of heart and said to the man, "Stretch out your hand." He stretched it out, and his hand was restored. The Pharisees went out and immediately conspired with the Herodians against him, how to destroy him.

REFLECTION

Today's reading is a call to all Christians as we observe the Octave of Prayer for Christian Unity, which began last Wednesday. Again Jesus challenges a religious practice that would prevent someone's healing, the restoration of full human life. His opponents meet his challenge with silent, stony hearts, and eventually conspire to kill him. Yet are we divided Christians not guilty of the same? Have we not, in our hardness of heart, allowed Christ's body to remain divided? And when we do so, do we not fail in our mission to restore the sick, lift up the lowly, and proclaim the good news to the poor?

PRAYERS   *others may be added*

Repenting of our hard hearts, we pray:

◆ Teach us your ways.

That together, all Christians may set aside all that divides us, uniting in service of the Gospel, we pray: ◆ *That Church leaders may speak with one voice, demanding justice and peace on behalf of the poor, we pray:* ◆ *That nations may attend to the Gospel call, listening to the united voice of believers, we pray:* ◆ *That we may never fail to do good, witnessing to the One who restores all who are bowed down, we pray:* ◆

Our Father . . .

Source of unity,
by our baptism you make us
   one people,
one body in Christ.
Shatter our hard hearts,
and give us your healing grace,
that together all disciples of Christ
may restore what sin has broken
and bring wholeness to the nations.
This we ask in Jesus' name. Amen.

✠ *To you, O Lord, I lift up my soul.*
All my hope is in you.

✢ *To you, O Lord, I lift up my soul.*
  All my hope is in you.

PSALM 25   *page 410*

READING   *Mark 3:13–19*

He went up the mountain and called to him those whom he wanted, and they came to him. And he appointed twelve, whom he also named apostles, to be with him, and to be sent out to proclaim the message, and to have authority to cast out demons. So he appointed the twelve: Simon (to whom he gave the name Peter); James son of Zebedee and John the brother of James (to whom he gave the name Boanerges, that is, Sons of Thunder); and Andrew, and Philip, and Bartholomew, and Matthew, and Thomas, and James son of Alphaeus, and Thaddaeus, and Simon the Cananaean, and Judas Iscariot, who betrayed him. Then he went home.

REFLECTION

Jesus' choice of twelve apostles serves two functions. First, the number twelve alludes to the twelve tribes of Israel; by choosing twelve, Jesus creates the nucleus of a New Israel. Second, the twelve are given a share in Jesus' ministry, with power to proclaim the message and cast out demons. Jesus' ministry, then, is not restricted to him alone but must be shared if it is to endure. At the same time, while they are chosen for a special role, these twelve are not perfect. In fact, the rest of the Gospel is filled with their failures to grasp what Jesus' mission is all about.

PRAYERS   *others may be added*

Ready to share Christ's ministry,
we pray:

◆ Teach us your ways.

For the baptized, coworkers with Christ in his ministry, we pray: ◆ *For bishops, sharers in the apostolic ministry, we pray:* ◆ *For priests, deacons, and parish ministers, workers in building up the people of God, we pray:* ◆ *For preachers and prophets, bearers of Christ's message, we pray:* ◆ *For healers, signs of God's healing grace, we pray:* ◆ *For all who follow Christ's way, guides to others on the path of righteousness, we pray:* ◆

Our Father . . .

God of mission,
you call us to share your work
and proclaim your reign.
Enliven us by the Spirit
to go forth in power,
to cast out demons,
and announce the message
of mercy, hope, and love.
We ask this through Christ,
who sends us with authority,
for he lives and reigns
forever and ever. Amen.

✢ *To you, O Lord, I lift up my soul.*
  All my hope is in you.

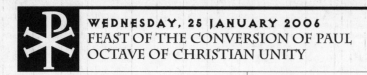
✠ *Alleluia! Christ is risen!*
Christ is risen indeed!
Alleluia, alleluia!

PSALM 34 *page 412*

READING *Acts 9:1–5*

Meanwhile Saul, still breathing threats and murder against the disciples of the Lord, went to the high priest and asked him for letters to the synagogues at Damascus, so that if he found any who belonged to the Way, men or women, he might bring them bound to Jerusalem. Now as he was going along and approaching Damascus, suddenly a light from heaven flashed around him. He fell to the ground and heard a voice saying to him, "Saul, Saul, why do you persecute me?" He asked, "Who are you, Lord?" The reply came, "I am Jesus, whom you are persecuting."

REFLECTION

On this last day of the Octave of Christian Unity, Pope John Paul II encourages ecumenism using the words of Saint Paul, whose conversion we celebrate today: "The Catholic Church embraces with hope the commitment to ecumenism as a duty of the Christian conscience enlightened by faith and guided by love. Here too we can apply the words of Saint Paul to the first Christians of Rome: 'God's love has been poured into our hearts through the Holy Spirit'; thus our 'hope does not disappoint us' (Romans 5:5). This is the hope of Christian unity, which has its divine source in the Trinitarian unity of the Father, the Son, and the Holy Spirit."

PRAYERS *others may be added*

Seeking to share Paul's conversion, we pray:

◆ Turn to us, Lord of life!

That the Church may be transformed by the light of God's glory, we pray: ◆ *That those who are persecuted because of their faith may be consoled and strengthened, we pray:* ◆ *That governments may guarantee the religious freedom of all their citizens, we pray:* ◆ *That those who seek to control others may turn to respect freedom, we pray:* ◆ *That prisoners of conscience may be released, we pray:* ◆ *That we may behold the glory of the Risen One, we pray:* ◆

Our Father . . .

God of conversion,
through the Risen Christ
you called Saul away from violence
and made him your own.
Blind us as well with the light
 of your grace;
burn away all that keeps us
from following Christ's Way
as one body, one people,
that we may glorify you in one voice
through Jesus Christ,
who lives and reigns
with you in the unity of the Holy Spirit,
one God, forever and ever. Amen.

✠ *Alleluia! Christ is risen!*
Christ is risen indeed!
Alleluia, alleluia!

✚ *To you, O Lord, I lift up my soul.*
All my hope is in you.

PSALM 25 *page 410*

READING *Mark 3:31–35*

Then his mother and his brothers came; and standing outside, they sent to him and called him. A crowd was sitting around him; and they said to him, "Your mother and your brothers and sisters are outside, asking for you." And he replied, "Who are my mother and my brothers?" And looking at those who sat around him, he said, "Here are my mother and my brothers! Whoever does the will of God is my brother and sister and mother."

REFLECTION

Jesus' saying about his true family comes at the end of a longer passage about whether or not he was himself possessed by a demon! It seems some of his family members—even his mother in Mark— thought he was a little crazy and came to take him home. Jesus responds to their presence with an astonishing statement: His true family is not the one created by blood and kinship, but the one created by common purpose, doing the will of God. Jesus creates a new community, the family of God, in which family ties and, later, nationality are neither an advantage nor an obstacle to serving God.

PRAYERS *others may be added*

Members of one family, we pray:

◆ Teach us your ways.

That the Church may embrace people of every kind, we pray: ◆ That human families may find strength in the family of faith, we pray: ◆ That the world's people may find unity in the search for peace, we pray: ◆ That the human family may reject prejudice and fear, we pray: ◆ That the poor, outcast, and forgotten may be welcomed as sisters and brothers, we pray: ◆ That we may be one in our struggle to do God's will, we pray: ◆

Our Father . . .

God of all nations,
you are father and mother
to a great multitude,
for in Christ you make us one family.
Strengthen the ties
that bind us as one people,
that we may see in each other
daughters and sons of God,
brothers and sisters in Christ,
who lives and reigns
forever and ever. Amen.

✚ *To you, O Lord, I lift up my soul.*
All my hope is in you.

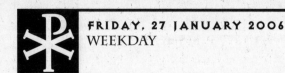

✦ *To you, O Lord, I lift up my soul.*
All my hope is in you.

PSALM 25 *page 410*

READING *Mark 4:1–9*

Again Jesus began to teach beside the sea. Such a very large crowd gathered around him that he got into a boat on the sea and sat there, while the whole crowd was beside the sea on the land. He began to teach them many things in parables, and in his teaching he said to them: "Listen! A sower went out to sow. And as he sowed, some seed fell on the path, and the birds came and ate it up. Other seed fell on rocky ground, where it did not have much soil, and it sprang up quickly, since it had no depth of soil. And when the sun rose, it was scorched; and since it had no root, it withered away. Other seed fell among thorns, and the thorns grew up and choked it, and it yielded no grain. Other seed fell into good soil and brought forth grain, growing up and increasing and yielding thirty and sixty and a hundredfold." And he said, "Let anyone with ears to hear listen!"

REFLECTION

Today begins one of the longer parables of Jesus. As with many of his stories, Jesus' meaning is elusive. Even his own disciples, in tomorrow's passage, need an explanation. What is crucial to grasping a parable is faith. To those without an "ear to hear," the parable is but an entertaining (or irritating) riddle. To those who see in Jesus a teacher and guide, it is a gem revealing many facets of wisdom. Like so many things, it all depends on how you look at it!

PRAYERS *others may be added*

Attentive to Jesus' wisdom,
we pray:

◆ Teach us your ways.

That the baptized may be astute hearers of the Gospel, we pray: ◆ *That preachers and teachers may expand our knowledge of the good news, we pray:* ◆ *That the stories of children, youth, and the elderly may be heard and heeded, we pray:* ◆ *That all ears may be opened to divine wisdom, we pray:* ◆ *That we may find in our human stories the revelation of God, we pray:* ◆

Our Father . . .

God of mystery,
in tales and riddles
your Anointed One
points the way to you.
Open our hearts to receive
the message
and our minds to understand,
that we too may tell the story
of your love for the world.
This we ask in Jesus' name. Amen.

✦ *To you, O Lord, I lift up my soul.*
All my hope is in you.

✠ *To you, O Lord, I lift up my soul.*
   All my hope is in you.

PSALM 25   *page 410*

READING   *Mark 4:10–20*

When he was alone, those who were around him along with the twelve asked him about the parables. And he said to them, "To you has been given the secret of the kingdom of God, but for those outside, everything comes in parables; in order that
'they may indeed look,
      but not perceive,
and may indeed listen,
      but not understand;
so that they may not turn again
      and be forgiven.'"
   And he said to them, "Do you not understand this parable? Then how will you understand all the parables? The sower sows the word. These are the ones on the path where the word is sown: when they hear, Satan immediately comes and takes away the word that is sown in them. And these are the ones sown on rocky ground: when they hear the word, they immediately receive it with joy. But they have no root, and endure only for a while; then, when trouble or persecution arises on account of the word, immediately they fall away. And others are those sown among the thorns: these are the ones who hear the word, but the cares of the world, and the lure of wealth, and the desire for other things come in and choke the word, and it yields nothing. And these are the ones sown on the good soil: they hear the word and accept it and bear fruit, thirty and sixty and a hundredfold."

REFLECTION

Today we celebrate Saint Thomas Aquinas, one who sought to expand our understanding of Jesus' words. Though he wrote one of the greatest theological works of Christian history, he noted at the end of his life that his work was "mere straw" when held before the divine mystery.

PRAYERS   *others may be added*

   Attentive to wisdom, we pray:

◆ Teach us your ways.

For theologians and scripture scholars, we pray: ◆ *For preachers and storytellers, we pray:* ◆ *For philosophers and scientists, we pray:* ◆ *For students and teachers, we pray:* ◆ *For all who seek the wisdom of Jesus, we pray:* ◆

Our Father . . .

God of wonder,
your servant Thomas
sought you in creation's glory
and in scripture's wisdom.
Give us a share of his hunger
   for understanding,
that we too may find you
in the stars of heaven
and in the stories of faith.
We ask this in Jesus' name. Amen.

✠ *To you, O Lord, I lift up my soul.*
   All my hope is in you.

✛ *To you, O Lord, I lift up my soul.*
   All my hope is in you.

PSALM 25   *page 410*

READING   *1 Corinthians 7:32–35*

I want you to be free from anxieties.
The unmarried man is anxious about
the affairs of the Lord, how to please
the Lord; but the married man is anxious about the affairs of the world,
how to please his wife, and his interests are divided. And the unmarried
woman and the virgin are anxious
about the affairs of the Lord, so that
they may be holy in body and spirit;
but the married woman is anxious
about the affairs of the world, how to
please her husband. I say this for your
own benefit, not to put any restraint
upon you, but to promote good order
and unhindered devotion to the Lord.

REFLECTION

Paul desires that his readers be "free from
anxieties," speaking specifically of the
demands of married life. In this season,
however, there are other ways to be "free
of anxieties" in great celebration. Many
Christians keep the time between Christmas
and Lent as Carnival, which is especially
long this year because of Easter's late
date. In parts of Asia, today begins the cele-
bration of the New Year 4704 by the lunar
calendar, a two-week festival filled with
parades and parties. Such "freedom from
anxiety" may not be exactly what Paul had
in mind, of course! At the same time, God
can be glorified in our feasting as well as
our fasting.

PRAYERS   *others may be added*

  Rejoicing in God's many gifts,
  we pray:

◆ Teach us your ways.

For Christian married couples, we pray: ◆
For those overcome with worldly anxiety,
we pray: ◆ *For all who celebrate the*
Lunar New Year, we pray: ◆ *For those*
who keep Carnival, we pray: ◆ *For those*
uninvited and forgotten, we pray: ◆
For those who feast and those who fast,
we pray: ◆ *For all who give thanks for*
the goodness of God, we pray: ◆

Our Father . . .

Source of joy,
our true happiness
lies in you alone.
Free us from anxiety,
and fill us with hope,
that we may rejoice in you.
We ask this through Jesus Christ,
    our Lord,
who lives and reigns with you,
in the unity of the Holy Spirit,
one God, forever and ever. Amen.

✛ *To you, O Lord, I lift up my soul.*
   All my hope is in you.

✚ *To you, O Lord, I lift up my soul.*
All my hope is in you.

PSALM 25 *page 410*

READING *Mark 4:21–25*

Jesus said to his disciples, "Is a lamp brought in to be put under the bushel basket, or under the bed, and not on the lampstand? For there is nothing hidden, except to be disclosed; nor is anything secret, except to come to light. Let anyone with ears to hear listen!" And he said to them, "Pay attention to what you hear; the measure you give will be the measure you get, and still more will be given you. For to those who have, more will be given; and from those who have nothing, even what they have will be taken away."

REFLECTION

As we read more of—and perhaps puzzle over—the wisdom sayings of Jesus, we also remember today another wisdom teacher, Mohandas Gandhi, who was assassinated on this date in 1948. Gandhi as much as enacted Jesus' sayings: By his light, the hidden persecution and oppression of his people by the British was revealed to the whole world. What would the world be like if Christians used their light in the same way, to reveal injustice, and so bring the earth one step closer to the fullness of God's reign?

PRAYERS *others may be added*

Shining before all, we pray:

◆ Teach us your ways.

That the baptized may share the Gospel's light with all who seek it, we pray: ◆
That heavenly insight may open the minds of world leaders, we pray: ◆
That prophets may rise up from among every people, we pray: ◆ *That Gandhi's example may lead others to seek greater justice, we pray:* ◆ *That Jesus' wisdom may enliven all who follow him, we pray:* ◆

Our Father . . .

God of insight,
in Christ your wisdom took flesh,
revealing the fullness of life.
Show us the path of insight,
that we may hear and understand,
and so light the way
for all nations and peoples.
This we ask in Jesus' name. Amen.

✚ *To you, O Lord, I lift up my soul.*
All my hope is in you.

✝ *To you, O Lord, I lift up my soul.*
All my hope is in you.

PSALM 25 *page 410*

READING *Mark 4:26–34*

Jesus also said, "The kingdom of God is as if someone would scatter seed on the ground, and would sleep and rise night and day, and the seed would sprout and grow, he does not know how. The earth produces of itself, first the stalk, then the head, then the full grain in the head. But when the grain is ripe, at once he goes in with his sickle, because the harvest has come."

He also said, "With what can we compare the kingdom of God, or what parable will we use for it? It is like a mustard seed, which, when sown upon the ground, is the smallest of all seeds on earth; yet when it is sown it grows up and becomes the greatest of all shrubs, and puts forth large branches, so that the birds of the air can make nests in its shade."

With many such parables he spoke the word to them, as they were able to hear it; he did not speak to them except in parables, but he explained everything in private to his disciples.

REFLECTION

Perhaps it strikes us as odd that Jesus' parables about God's reign never have "kingly" imagery. Never does Jesus say that God's kingdom comes as a great army to destroy God's opponents. Instead, these sayings point to the mystery of God's action in the world: how it seems to start small, almost invisibly; how it grows in the night, almost imperceptibly; and how suddenly it appears in fullness, ready for harvest. We must ask ourselves, then: Where do we find the seedlings? Where is the mustard seed slowly sprouting?

PRAYERS *others may be added*

Watching for signs of the kingdom, we pray:

◆ Teach us your ways.

For those who scatter the seeds of God's reign, we pray: ◆ *For those who nurture the growth of grace, we pray:* ◆ *For those who watch for God's presence, we pray:* ◆ *For those who prepare to gather the harvest, we pray:* ◆ *For all who seek the mystery of God's coming into the world, we pray:* ◆

Our Father . . .

Divine Sower,
you scatter seed far and wide,
and nurture the plant to harvest,
making ready the heavenly barns.
Rain down upon us
the Word of life,
that we may flourish before you
and bear fruit on the day of salvation,
when the Lord of the harvest
shall live and reign
forever and ever. Amen.

✝ *To you, O Lord, I lift up my soul.*
All my hope is in you.

✝ *To you, O Lord, I lift up my soul.*
All my hope is in you.

PSALM 25   page 410

READING   Mark 4:35–41

On that day, when evening had come, Jesus said to his disciples, "Let us go across to the other side." And leaving the crowd behind, they took him with them in the boat, just as he was. Other boats were with him. A great windstorm arose, and the waves beat into the boat, so that the boat was already being swamped. But he was in the stern, asleep on the cushion; and they woke him up and said to him, "Teacher, do you not care that we are perishing?" He woke up and rebuked the wind, and said to the sea, "Peace! Be still!" Then the wind ceased, and there was a dead calm. He said to them, "Why are you afraid? Have you still no faith?" And they were filled with great awe and said to one another, "Who then is this, that even the wind and the sea obey him?"

REFLECTION

Of the many ways to interpret this story, seeing it from the perspective of the early community Mark was writing for may reveal some of its meaning. In the year 70, the Church was shell-shocked: The temple in Jerusalem had been destroyed by the Romans, and Jesus had not quickly returned. No doubt these early Christians felt storm-tossed and abandoned; perhaps we can hear their desperation in the disciples' outcry, "Do you not care that we are

perishing?" Yet the Gospel writer rebukes their fear: Jesus, who has power to calm storms, has not abandoned them—or us.

PRAYERS   *others may be added*

Seeking shelter in life's storm,
we pray:

◆ Teach us your ways.

For those who offer Christ's peace, we pray: ◆ *For those who seek faith, we pray:* ◆ *For those who comfort the frightened, we pray:* ◆ *For those who suffer natural disaster, we pray:* ◆ *For those who cry out in terror, we pray:* ◆ *For those who feel abandoned, we pray:* ◆ *For those who trust in Christ's presence, we pray:* ◆

Our Father . . .

God of power,
though we are tossed by life's storms
you are always present,
calming our churning hearts.
Give us confidence
in your saving help,
that we may always trust in you,
the God of our salvation,
who lives and reigns
forever and ever. Amen.

✝ *To you, O Lord, I lift up my soul.*
All my hope is in you.

✦ *Alleluia!*
The Word of God dwells among us!
God is one with humankind!

PSALM 96 *page 421*

READING *Malachi 3:1–4*

See, I am sending my messenger to prepare the way before me, and the Lord whom you seek will suddenly come to his temple. The messenger of the covenant in whom you delight—indeed, he is coming, says the LORD of hosts. But who can endure the day of his coming, and who can stand when he appears?

For he is like a refiner's fire and like fullers' soap; he will sit as a refiner and purifier of silver, and he will purify the descendants of Levi and refine them like gold and silver, until they present offerings to the LORD in righteousness. Then the offering of Judah and Jerusalem will be pleasing to the LORD as in the days of old and as in former years.

REFLECTION

Today's feast commemorates an event recounted only in Luke's Gospel (Luke 2:22–38), in which the infant Jesus is brought to the Jerusalem temple. This first reading from Mass today instead imagines the Lord's messenger—definitely not a baby!—entering the temple to purify it. We may find Micah's imagery a bit disturbing: Both refining fire and bleaching soap burn! Yet the image is appropriate. After all, sometimes our "impurities" are as deeply ingrained as a stubborn stain in fabric or worthless minerals in silver ore. Once in a while we need Christ to scour us—even if it hurts!

PRAYERS *others may be added*

Offering a prayer pleasing to the God of hosts, we pray:

◆ Word of God, abide with us.

That the baptized may be purified and refined by Emmanuel's enduring presence, we pray: ◆ *That the world's people may attend to the voice of God's messengers, we pray:* ◆ *That God's power may burn away the impurities of prejudice and fear, we pray:* ◆ *That the poor may delight in the God who loves them, we pray:* ◆ *That the day of salvation may find us ready to greet our glorious Savior, we pray:* ◆

Our Father . . .

God of fiery judgment,
your Anointed One will return
   without warning
to cleanse and purify us
like the refiner's fire
and the fuller's soap.
Strengthen us as we await
the day of our salvation:
May we be watchful and ready
to recognize the Christ
when he returns in glory,
for he lives and reigns
forever and ever. Amen.

✦ *Alleluia!*
The Word of God dwells among us!
God is one with humankind!

✚ *To you, O Lord, I lift up my soul.*
All my hope is in you.

PSALM 25   *page 410*

READING   *Mark 5:1–10*

They came to the other side of the sea, to the country of the Gerasenes. And when he had stepped out of the boat, immediately a man out of the tombs with an unclean spirit met him. He lived among the tombs; and no one could restrain him any more, even with a chain; for he had often been restrained with shackles and chains, but the chains he wrenched apart, and the shackles he broke in pieces; and no one had the strength to subdue him. Night and day among the tombs and on the mountains he was always howling and bruising himself with stones. When he saw Jesus from a distance, he ran and bowed down before him; and he shouted at the top of his voice, "What have you to do with me, Jesus, Son of the Most High God? I adjure you by God, do not torment me." For he had said to him, "Come out of the man, you unclean spirit!" Then Jesus asked him, "What is your name?" He replied, "My name is Legion; for we are many." He begged him earnestly not to send them out of the country.

REFLECTION

The story of the Gerasene demoniac is rich in imagery and vivid detail. Jesus is in Gentile country, and his demonic opponents are on their home turf, "among the tombs." The demons even try to thwart Jesus' *power by revealing his true identity—"Son of the Most High God." Jesus, undeterred, demands and receives the demons' name: "Legion, for we are many." It is hard to deny the legion of evil in our own world: degrading poverty, epidemic illness, unending war, continual violence. Yet in Jesus we have found our hope.*

PRAYERS   *others may be added*

With confidence in the Son of the Most High, we pray:

◆ Teach us your ways.

For those ground down by hunger and poverty, we pray: ◆ *For nations decimated by war and destruction, we pray:* ◆ *For communities wracked by violence and anger, we pray:* ◆ *For peoples laid waste by disease and chronic illness, we pray:* ◆ *For all bound by the forces of evil, we pray:* ◆

Our Father . . .

God Most High,
we are beset by evil,
overwhelmed by suffering,
in need of your help.
Show us your saving power,
that evil may be driven
from the face of the earth,
and your children may live in freedom,
through our Savior Jesus Christ,
who lives and reigns
forever and ever. Amen.

✚ *To you, O Lord, I lift up my soul.*
All my hope is in you.

✦ *To you, O Lord, I lift up my soul.*
  All my hope is in you.

PSALM 25 page 410

READING Mark 5:11–20

Now there on the hillside a great herd of swine was feeding; and the unclean spirits begged him, "Send us into the swine; let us enter them." So he gave them permission. And the unclean spirits came out and entered the swine; and the herd, numbering about two thousand, rushed down the steep bank into the sea, and were drowned in the sea.

The swineherds ran off and told it in the city and in the country. Then people came to see what it was that had happened. They came to Jesus and saw the demoniac sitting there, clothed and in his right mind, the very man who had had the legion; and they were afraid. Those who had seen what had happened to the demoniac and to the swine reported it. Then they began to beg Jesus to leave their neighborhood. As he was getting into the boat, the man who had been possessed by demons begged him that he might be with him. But Jesus refused, and said to him, "Go home to your friends, and tell them how much the Lord has done for you, and what mercy he has shown you." And he went away and began to proclaim in the Decapolis how much Jesus had done for him; and everyone was amazed.

REFLECTION

The people's response to Jesus' powerful deed is to ask him to leave! Jesus charges the former demoniac to share his story with his friends and so he becomes the first "missionary" among them.

PRAYERS others may be added

  Amazed by God's power revealed in
  Jesus, we pray:

◆ Teach us your ways.

That the baptized may wonder at God's action among them, we pray: ◆ *That the nations may welcome the Gospel message, we pray:* ◆ *That demons of oppression and prejudice may be driven from all people, we pray:* ◆ *That those who have found healing in Christ may share their story, we pray:* ◆ *That Jesus may send us forth to announce the message to all we meet, we pray:* ◆

Our Father . . .

God of salvation,
you set us free
and send us forth in joy.
Give us courage to face
all that oppresses humanity,
that by your grace
we may win the victory
and so behold at last
the fullness of your reign,
where Christ is Lord
forever and ever. Amen.

✦ *To you, O Lord, I lift up my soul.*
  All my hope is in you.

✚ *My soul, give thanks to the LORD.*
All my being, bless God's holy name.

PSALM 103   *page 422*

READING *1 Corinthians 9:16–19, 22–23*

If I proclaim the gospel, this gives me no ground for boasting, for an obligation is laid on me, and woe to me if I do not proclaim the gospel! For if I do this of my own will, I have a reward; but if not of my own will, I am entrusted with a commission. What then is my reward? Just this: that in my proclamation I may make the free of charge, so as not to make full use of my rights in the gospel.

For though I am free with respect to all, I have made myself a slave to all, so that I might win more of them.

To the weak I became weak, so that I might win the weak. I have become all things to all people, that I might by all means save some. I do it all for the sake of the gospel, so that I may share in its blessings.

REFLECTION

It's not too often in our society that we can get something for nothing; the wisdom of the world dictates that everything has its price. Yet we are called precisely to offer something for nothing: the Gospel, free of charge. Even more, we are to expend ourselves for its sake and the sake of others, pouring ourselves out in service without expecting payment or reward. No wonder the world calls it foolishness.

PRAYERS   *others may be added*

Sharing the great gift of the Gospel, we pray:

◆ Show us your compassion.

That God's people may embrace their commission to proclaim the Good News, we pray: ◆ *That the Church may be a place of welcome for all people, we pray:* ◆ *That ministers and preachers may offer the Gospel freely and generously, we pray:* ◆ *That all people may share in God's abundant blessing, we pray:* ◆ *That we may do all things for the sake of Christ, we pray:* ◆

Our Father . . .

God of life,
in Christ your Word became flesh
to save those in the flesh.
Give us grace to pour ourselves out
   in service,
that, like the apostle Paul,
we may become all things
   to all people
doing everything for the sake
   of the Gospel
and Christ's eternal glory,
for he is Lord with you,
in the unity of the Holy Spirit,
one God, forever and ever. Amen.

✚ *My soul, give thanks to the LORD.*
All my being, bless God's holy name.

✦ *My soul, give thanks to the LORD.*
All my being, bless God's holy name.

PSALM 103 *page 422*

READING *Mark 5:21–29*

When Jesus had crossed again in the boat to the other side, a great crowd gathered around him; and he was by the sea. Then one of the leaders of the synagogue named Jairus came and, when he saw him, fell at his feet and begged him repeatedly, "My little daughter is at the point of death. Come and lay your hands on her, so that she may be made well, and live." So he went with him.

And a large crowd followed him and pressed in on him. Now there was a woman who had been suffering from hemorrhages for twelve years. She had endured much under many physicians, and had spent all that she had; and she was no better, but rather grew worse. She had heard about Jesus, and came up behind him in the crowd and touched his cloak, for she said, "If I but touch his clothes, I will be made well." Immediately her hemorrhage stopped; and she felt in her body that she was healed of her disease.

REFLECTION

In Mark's Gospel, it is the "little people"—the forgotten, the sick, and the possessed—that often reveal themselves as true followers of Jesus. The woman with the hemorrhage is such a person: a woman (her sex automatically made her "little" in ancient Palestine) made religiously unclean because of her condition. Yet she dares to touch one who is both male and a religious teacher—and receives what she seeks.

PRAYERS *others may be added*

Inspired by the confidence of the lowly, we pray:

◆ Show us your compassion.

That the Church may welcome the forgotten, we pray: ◆ *That there may be no "clean" and "unclean" among Christ's followers, we pray:* ◆ *That women may find true equality in every nation, we pray:* ◆ *That the sick may be restored by Christ's touch, we pray:* ◆ *That we may embody Christ's healing grace, we pray:* ◆

Our Father . . .

God of the lowly,
in Christ you stretch out your hand
to the forgotten and invisible,
restoring them in love.
Give us a share
of Christ's healing grace,
that with a touch we too
may restore those cast out
to the community of believers.
This we ask in Jesus' name. Amen.

✦ *My soul, give thanks to the LORD.*
All my being, bless God's holy name.

✝ *My soul, give thanks to the LORD.*
All my being, bless God's holy name.

PSALM 103 *page 422*

READING *Mark 5:30–36*

Immediately aware that power had gone forth from him, Jesus turned about in the crowd and said, "Who touched my clothes?" And his disciples said to him, "You see the crowd pressing in on you; how can you say, 'Who touched me?'" He looked all around to see who had done it. But the woman, knowing what had happened to her, came in fear and trembling, fell down before him, and told him the whole truth. He said to her, "Daughter, your faith has made you well; go in peace, and be healed of your disease."

While he was still speaking, some people came from the leader's house to say, "Your daughter is dead. Why trouble the teacher any further?" But overhearing what they said, Jesus said to the leader of the synagogue, "Do not fear, only believe."

REFLECTION

It would have been easy for Jesus to let the woman remain invisible in the crowd; his disciples are almost derisive when he asks who touched him. Yet Jesus effects further healing by allowing the woman to tell her story. Though she comes in fear and trembling, Jesus responds by calling her "daughter." Jesus offers not only physical healing but spiritual as well: "Go in peace." What wonders might be worked today if, like Jesus, we were ready to receive the stories of the forgotten?

PRAYERS *others may be added*

With ears open to others,
we pray:

◆ Show us your compassion.

For those forgotten among the baptized, we pray: ◆ *For those shunned in the community of faith, we pray:* ◆ *For those silenced in Church and society, we pray:* ◆ *For those denied a listening ear or a healing touch, we pray:* ◆ *For those refused their rightful place in the human family, we pray:* ◆ *For those still not recognized as children of God, we pray:* ◆

Our Father . . .

Strength of the poor,
in the lowly you show us
the fullness of faith.
Make us humble before others,
that we may be always ready
to welcome as Christ
those who come to us
in search of compassion.
This we ask in Jesus' name. Amen.

✝ *My soul, give thanks to the LORD.*
All my being, bless God's holy name.

✛ *My soul, give thanks to the LORD.*
All my being, bless God's holy name.

PSALM 103 — page 422

READING — Mark 5:37–43

Jesus allowed no one to follow him except Peter, James, and John, the brother of James. When they came to the house of the leader of the synagogue, he saw a commotion, people weeping and wailing loudly. When he had entered, he said to them, "Why do you make a commotion and weep? The child is not dead but sleeping." And they laughed at him. Then he put them all outside, and took the child's father and mother and those who were with him, and went in where the child was. He took her by the hand and said to her, "Talitha cum," which means, "Little girl, get up!" And immediately the girl got up and began to walk about (she was twelve years of age). At this they were overcome with amazement. He strictly ordered them that no one should know this, and told them to give her something to eat.

REFLECTION

Jesus takes only a select few with him into the home of Jairus; these three are also the sole witnesses to the Transfiguration and the agony in the garden. Like those moments, Jesus' raising of the little girl reveals his true identity as the Son of God. At the heart of both this miracle and the healing of the woman with the hemorrhage is faith. It is by faith in the Son that we too will share life—the risen life of Christ.

PRAYERS — *others may be added*

Steadfast in faith, we pray:

◆ Show us your compassion.

For those who trust in God's power, we pray: ◆ *For those who make present Christ's healing touch, we pray:* ◆ *For those who mourn the death of a child, we pray:* ◆ *For those who have lost hope, we pray:* ◆ *For those who care for the sick and dying, we pray:* ◆ *For all who hope in the life Jesus promises, we pray:* ◆

Our Father . . .

Source of life,
in Christ's victory over death
you promise an end to sorrow
and a new day of joy.
Fill us with confident faith
as we await the fullness of life.
May we live today
in the hope of the world to come,
when Christ shall live and reign
forever and ever. Amen.

✛ *My soul, give thanks to the LORD.*
All my being, bless God's holy name.

✝ *My soul, give thanks to the LORD.*
All my being, bless God's holy name.

PSALM 103   *page 422*

READING   *Mark 6:7–13*

He called the twelve and began to send them out two by two, and gave them authority over the unclean spirits. He ordered them to take nothing for their journey except a staff; no bread, no bag, no money in their belts; but to wear sandals and not to put on two tunics. He said to them, "Wherever you enter a house, stay there until you leave the place. If any place will not welcome you and they refuse to hear you, as you leave, shake off the dust that is on your feet as a testimony against them." So they went out and proclaimed that all should repent. They cast out many demons, and anointed with oil many who were sick and cured them.

REFLECTION

By sending his followers out to preach, Jesus transforms those who were disciples into apostles. Having instructed them in his wisdom, Jesus sends them out to share it. Yet they still lack the heart of the Gospel: the saving death and triumphant Resurrection of Jesus. They must return and again be disciples, opening them-selves more and more to God's plan of salvation. Both moments—discipleship and apostleship—are indispensable parts of our Christian lives.

PRAYERS   *others may be added*

Sent by Christ with a message of repentance, we pray:

◆ Show us your compassion.

For those sent in service of the poor and oppressed, we pray: ◆ *For those sent to preach a word of justice and peace, we pray:* ◆ *For those sent to proclaim words of challenge and conversion, we pray:* ◆ *For those sent to anoint the sick with healing grace, we pray:* ◆ *For those sent to cast out the spirits of depression and anxiety, we pray:* ◆ *For those sent to offer a word of hope to the sorrowful, we pray:* ◆ *For those sent to warn the apathetic and unrepentant, we pray:* ◆

Our Father . . .

God of mission,
your Anointed One sends us forth
with a message of both warning
   and comfort,
to challenge the apathetic
and bring mercy to the sick.
By the power of your Spirit
strengthen us in our mission
that the Good News may reach
the ends of the earth.
May all peoples come to praise you,
who live and reign
forever and ever. Amen.

✝ *My soul, give thanks to the LORD.*
All my being, bless God's holy name.

✝ *My soul, give thanks to the LORD.*
All my being, bless God's holy name.

PSALM 103   page 422

READING   Mark 6:34–44

As Jesus went ashore, he saw a great crowd; and he had compassion for them, because they were like sheep without a shepherd; and he began to teach them many things. When it grew late, his disciples came to him and said, "This is a deserted place, and the hour is now very late; send them away so that they may go into the surrounding country and villages and buy something for themselves to eat." But he answered them, "You give them something to eat." They said to him, "Are we to go and buy two hundred denarii worth of bread, and give it to them to eat?" And he said to them, "How many loaves have you? Go and see." When they had found out, they said, "Five, and two fish." Then he ordered them to get all the people to sit down in groups on the green grass. So they sat down in groups of hundreds and of fifties. Taking the five loaves and the two fish, he looked up to heaven, and blessed and broke the loaves, and gave them to his disciples to set before the people; and he divided the two fish among them all. And all ate and were filled; and they took up twelve baskets full of broken pieces and of the fish. Those who had eaten the loaves numbered five thousand men.

REFLECTION

Though we often see the institution of the Eucharist in the Last Supper, there is no denying that the feeding of the multitudes has a Eucharistic character: From simple gifts and prayers of thanksgiving comes a feast for the multitudes.

PRAYERS   others may be added

  In thanksgiving, we pray:

◆ Show us your compassion.

That the celebration of the Eucharist may enliven the Church to serve the hungry, we pray: ◆ *That catechumens may grow in their desire to partake of the Body and Blood of Christ, we pray:* ◆ *That Christians may overcome the divisions that prevent them from gathering at one table, we pray:* ◆ *That the world's hungry may receive their just share of creation's bounty, we pray:* ◆ *That we may invite all people to the Church's table, we pray:* ◆

Our Father . . .

Provident God,
you fed Israel with manna in the desert
and even now you feed us
with the living bread of your Son.
May our sharing in the Eucharist
inspire us to greater service.
May we generously offer
all that we have received
to all the hungry and the poor.
We ask this in Jesus' name. Amen.

✝ *My soul, give thanks to the LORD.*
All my being, bless God's holy name.

✝ *My soul, give thanks to the* LORD.
All my being, bless God's holy name.

PSALM 103   page 422

READING   Mark 7:1–5

Now when the Pharisees and some of the scribes who had come from Jerusalem gathered around him, they noticed that some of his disciples were eating with defiled hands, that is, without washing them. (For the Pharisees, and all the Jews, do not eat unless they thoroughly wash their hands, thus observing the tradition of the elders; and they do not eat anything from the market unless they wash it; and there are also many other traditions that they observe, the washing of cups, pots, and bronze kettles.) So the Pharisees and the scribes asked him, "Why do your disciples not live according to the tradition of the elders, but eat with defiled hands?"

REFLECTION

Mark sets up another series of conflicts between Jesus and the religious authorities, this time about ritual purification. Jesus' harsh response, which we will read next Monday and Tuesday, must be kept in context. The argument is about the authority of halakah, *the oral law, which the Pharisees insisted should be observed by all. The Pharisees' "mistake," which Jesus attacks, is that they elevate mere human tradition—even pious religious tradition— and place it on the same level as divine law. We are no less prone to making the same mistake today.*

PRAYERS   *others may be added*

Seeking God's will above all else, we pray:

◆ Show us your compassion.

That the baptized may welcome people of every culture, race and language, we pray: ◆ *That Christian's may never confuse human law with divine law, we pray:* ◆ *That tolerance may lead to an end to prejudice and injustice, we pray:* ◆ *That we may never confuse human tradition and God's will, we pray:* ◆

Our Father . . .

God of east and west,
you created humankind
    in great variety,
in many cultures and peoples,
with many traditions
and ways of life.
Teach us to honor
the goodness found in every people,
that we may recognize
the divine image that makes us one,
for you live and reign
forever and ever. Amen.

✝ *My soul, give thanks to the* LORD.
All my being, bless God's holy name.

✝ *My soul, give thanks to the LORD.*
All my being, bless God's holy name.

PSALM 103   page 422

READING   *1 Corinthians 10:31—11:1*

Whether you eat or drink, or whatever you do, do everything for the glory of God. Give no offense to Jews or to Greeks or to the church of God, just as I try to please everyone in everything I do, not seeking my own advantage, but that of many, so that they may be saved. Be imitators of me, as I am of Christ.

REFLECTION

In this last reading from First Corinthians, Paul sums up what we have heard over the past several weeks. Eating and drinking, the body and marriage, were all sources of controversy among the Corinthians, dividing the one body of Christ. Paul exhorts them—and us today—not to let these things get in the way of living the Gospel. All that we do must witness to Christ, and so we must avoid giving offense, even if we are "right." In the end, what is most important is bringing others to Christ, and the best way to do that is imitating Christ in all we do.

PRAYERS   *others may be added*

Glorifying God in all that we do,
we pray:

◆ Show us your compassion.

For bishops, priests, and ministers, who lead the Church of God, we pray: ◆
For all Christians, who guide others to Jesus, we pray: ◆ *For politicians and public servants, who seek not their own advantage but the common good, we pray:* ◆ *For negotiators and diplomats, who seek to overcome divisions among nations, we pray:* ◆ *For parents and teachers, who serve as models for the young, we pray:* ◆ *For all servants of God, who praise God with body and spirit, we pray:* ◆

Our Father . . .

God of salvation,
you call all people
to life in you.
Make us imitators of Christ,
that by our lives of faith
we may reveal your grace
and lead others to you,
who lives and reigns
in the unity of the Son and Holy Spirit,
one God, forever and ever. Amen.

✝ *My soul, give thanks to the LORD.*
All my being, bless God's holy name.

✝ *My soul, give thanks to the LORD.*
All my being, bless God's holy name.

PSALM 103 page 422

READING Mark 7:6–13

He said to the Pharisees, "Isaiah prophesied rightly about you hypocrites, as it is written,

'This people honors me with their lips,
    but their hearts are far from me;
in vain do they worship me,
    teaching human precepts
    as doctrines.'

You abandon the commandment of God and hold to human tradition."

Then he said to them, "You have a fine way of rejecting the commandment of God in order to keep your tradition! For Moses said, 'Honor your father and your mother'; and, 'Whoever speaks evil of father or mother must surely die.' But you say that if anyone tells father or mother, 'Whatever support you might have had from me is Corban' (that is, an offering to God)—then you no longer permit doing anything for a father or mother, thus making void the word of God through your tradition that you have handed on. And you do many things like this."

REFLECTION

Jesus criticizes his opponents for using religion to suit their own ends, and his challenge rings true today. How often do we "practice religion" to benefit ourselves? How often are our hearts truly pure, or are we always seeking something in return, whether from God or from human beings?

PRAYERS *others may be added*

*Seeking only what God desires,
we pray:*

◆ Show us your compassion.

For a new birth of faith among all believers, we pray: ◆ *For leaders who seek the reign of God, we pray:* ◆
For an end to atrocities committed in God's name, we pray: ◆ *For true piety expressed in service of others, we pray:* ◆
For good works that expect nothing in return, we pray: ◆ *For prayer that seeks only God's will, we pray:* ◆ *For religion that brings forth the fullness of life for all, we pray:* ◆

Our Father . . .

God of our ancestors,
you show us your path,
yet we follow our own will.
Throw down the idols we worship,
and cleanse our hearts
of self-serving faith,
that we may praise you alone,
the God of all creation,
who lives and reigns
forever and ever. Amen.

✝ *My soul, give thanks to the LORD.*
All my being, bless God's holy name.

✝ *My soul, give thanks to the LORD.*
All my being, bless God's holy name.

PSALM 103   *page 422*

READING   *Mark 7:14–23*

Then he called the crowd again and said to them, "Listen to me, all of you, and understand: there is nothing outside a person that by going in can defile, but the things that come out are what defile."

When he had left the crowd and entered the house, his disciples asked him about the parable. He said to them, "Then do you also fail to understand? Do you not see that whatever goes into a person from outside cannot defile, since it enters, not the heart but the stomach, and goes out into the sewer?" (Thus he declared all foods clean.) And he said, "It is what comes out of a person that defiles. For it is from within, from the human heart, that evil intentions come: fornication, theft, murder, adultery, avarice, wickedness, deceit, licentiousness, envy, slander, pride, folly. All these evil things come from within, and they defile a person."

REFLECTION

Jesus goes straight to the heart of the matter, and his message is critical for all people of faith: True religion comes from the heart and is expressed in acts of virtue, not in empty tradition. Cleanness and uncleanness have to do with how we live—what "comes out" of us—not what we eat.

PRAYERS   *others may be added*

Attentive to the voice of wisdom,
we pray:

◆ Show us your compassion.

That the baptized may offer in the liturgy the sacrifice of service to others, we pray: ◆ That the Church's celebration of the Eucharist may bear fruit in works of justice, we pray: ◆ That people of faith may reject empty acts of piety, we pray: ◆ That all people may turn away from violence, deceit, infidelity, and injustice, we pray: ◆ That we may cleanse our hearts of all that defiles us, we pray: ◆

Our Father . . .

Holy Wisdom,
in Jesus you call to us,
inviting us to true praise.
Cleanse our hearts of all that defiles
and enlighten us with knowledge
that we may serve you
in lives filled with virtue
glorifying you in acts of service.
This we ask in Jesus' name,
who is Lord forever and ever. Amen.

✝ *My soul, give thanks to the LORD.*
All my being, bless God's holy name.

✠ *My soul, give thanks to the LORD.*
All my being, bless God's holy name.

PSALM 103 page 422

READING Mark 7:24–30

Jesus set out and went away to the region of Tyre. He entered a house and did not want anyone to know he was there. Yet he could not escape notice, but a woman whose little daughter had an unclean spirit immediately heard about him, and she came and bowed down at his feet. Now the woman was a Gentile, of Syrophoenician origin. She begged him to cast the demon out of her daughter. He said to her, "Let the children be fed first, for it is not fair to take the children's food and throw it to the dogs." But she answered him, "Sir, even the dogs under the table eat the children's crumbs." Then he said to her, "For saying that, you may go—the demon has left your daughter." So she went home, found the child lying on the bed, and the demon gone.

REFLECTION

Jesus' words to the Syrophoenician woman sound harsh and even spiteful to our ears, yet it seems that even she expected such a response. It was bold of her to speak to him at all, and bolder still to challenge him when he turned away. In some way, she ministered to Jesus, inviting him to broaden his own vision of his mission. She is for us an outstanding model of courage and faith.

PRAYERS *others may be added*

Emboldened by the faith of the Syrophoenician woman, we pray:

◆ Show us your compassion.

For women who bear witness to Christ, we pray: ◆ *For loving mothers, devoted to their children, we pray:* ◆ *For women who are refugees or migrants, we pray:* ◆ *For all who challenge prejudice, we pray:* ◆ *For all who seek healing in Jesus, we pray:* ◆ *For all who boldly ask for God's favor, we pray:* ◆

Our Father . . .

Compassionate God,
the Syrophoenician woman
boldly asked for Jesus' help
and her faith saved her daughter
   from death.
Bless us with her strength,
that we may boldly ask
for what we need,
always confident that you will answer.
We ask this in the name of Jesus,
in whom all find salvation,
for he lives and reigns
forever and ever. Amen.

✠ *My soul, give thanks to the LORD.*
All my being, bless God's holy name.

✚ *My soul, give thanks to the LORD.*
All my being, bless God's holy name.

PSALM 103 *page 422*

READING *Mark 7:31–37*

Then he returned from the region of Tyre, and went by way of Sidon towards the Sea of Galilee, in the region of the Decapolis. They brought to him a deaf man who had an impediment in his speech; and they begged him to lay his hand on him. He took him aside in private, away from the crowd, and put his fingers into his ears, and he spat and touched his tongue. Then looking up to heaven, he sighed and said to him, "Ephphatha," that is, "Be opened." And immediately his ears were opened, his tongue was released, and he spoke plainly. Then Jesus ordered them to tell no one; but the more he ordered them, the more zealously they proclaimed it. They were astounded beyond measure, saying, "He has done everything well; he even makes the deaf to hear and the mute to speak."

REFLECTION

The setting of today's miracle story is important. Jesus is in Gentile country, "Galilee of the Gentiles," and he opens the ears and releases the tongue of a person who is deaf and mute. The symbolism is hard to miss: The Gentiles, who have not heard God's word and so cannot proclaim it, are now offered salvation. The story has baptismal overtones as well: The Rite of Christian Initiation of Adults includes an "Ephphetha" as part of the Holy Saturday preparations for baptism. In it the minister touches the ears of the catechumens and prays, "Ephphetha, that is, be opened, that you may profess the faith you hear, to the praise and glory of God."

PRAYERS *others may be added*

With hearts open to the Good News of salvation, we pray:

◆ Show us your compassion.

That the baptized may announce their faith in Jesus Christ, we pray: ◆ *That the ears of catechumens may be opened to the living Word, we pray:* ◆ *That the gifts of people with disabilities may transform both Church and society, we pray:* ◆ *That the sick may know the healing touch of Christ, we pray:* ◆ *That our tongues may be free to praise the God of salvation, we pray:* ◆

Our Father . . .

Open our ears and free our tongues,
God of wondrous power,
to hear your living Word
and proclaim the salvation
brought forth in Christ.
Astound us beyond measure
with your power
that we may praise you
with joyful songs
through the same Christ your Son,
who is Lord forever and ever. Amen.

✚ *My soul, give thanks to the LORD.*
All my being, bless God's holy name.

✠ *My soul, give thanks to the LORD.*
All my being, bless God's holy name.

PSALM 103   *page 422*

READING   *Mark 8:22–26*

They came to Bethsaida. Some people brought a blind man to him and begged him to touch him. He took the blind man by the hand and led him out of the village; and when he had put saliva on his eyes and laid his hands on him, he asked him, "Can you see anything?" And the man looked up and said, "I can see people, but they look like trees, walking." Then Jesus laid his hands on his eyes again; and he looked intently and his sight was restored, and he saw everything clearly. Then he sent him away to his home, saying, "Do not even go into the village."

REFLECTION

Today's healing of the blind man parallels yesterday's story of the healing of the deaf-mute. Their function in the Gospel is more than merely highlighting Jesus' power to heal; they coincide with the disciples' complete failure to understand Jesus' mission. Jesus has the power to overcome physical disability with a word and a touch; spiritual deafness and blindness, on the other hand, are far more difficult to heal.

PRAYERS   *others may be added*

Longing to see and to hear,
we pray:

◆ Show us your compassion.

That the baptized may seek the Spirit's true vision, we pray: ◆ *That the ears of the world may be open to words of justice, we pray:* ◆ *That those blinded by prejudice and fear may be healed, we pray:* ◆ *That those deaf to the cries of the hungry may hear, we pray:* ◆ *That Jesus may remove all obstacles to the Gospel, we pray:* ◆

Our Father . . .

Gentle God,
with a touch and a word
your Son makes us whole.
Free us from the blindness of sin
and from unhearing apathy
to the needs of others,
that we may mend the broken
and restore the forgotten.
This we ask in Jesus' name. Amen.

✠ *My soul, give thanks to the LORD.*
All my being, bless God's holy name.

✛ *My soul, give thanks to the LORD.*
All my being, bless God's holy name.

PSALM 103   *page 422*

READING   *Mark 8:31–35*

Then Jesus began to teach the disciples that the Son of Man must undergo great suffering, and be rejected by the elders, the chief priests, and the scribes, and be killed, and after three days rise again. He said all this quite openly. And Peter took him aside and began to rebuke him. But turning and looking at his disciples, he rebuked Peter and said, "Get behind me, Satan! For you are setting your mind not on divine things but on human things."

Jesus called the crowd with his disciples, and said to them, "If any want to become my followers, let them deny themselves and take up their cross and follow me. For those who want to save their life will lose it, and those who lose their life for my sake, and for the sake of the gospel, will save it."

REFLECTION

Jesus' rebuke of Peter comes right on the heels of Peter's confession of faith in Jesus as the Messiah (Mark 8:27–30). Though Peter got the words right—Jesus is indeed the Messiah—he failed to understand the Messiah's mission, that he had to suffer rejection and die. Like Peter, we too are often unwilling to accept the paradox of the cross: It is only through death that we receive true life.

PRAYERS   *others may be added*

With eyes fixed on the cross,
we pray:

◆ Show us your compassion.

That the baptized may find strength to bear the cross with Jesus, we pray: ◆
That nations may relieve those weighed down by crosses of poverty and hunger, we pray: ◆ *That those burdened by suffering may find aid and hope, we pray:* ◆ *That those bearing the cross of illness may find life, we pray:* ◆
That we may seek Christ in the downtrodden and weary, we pray: ◆

Our Father . . .

God of the cross,
the fullness of your power
was revealed in weakness,
for in Christ's cross
you have destroyed death's power.
Give us courage
to take up the cross,
that we too may pass
from death to life
and so share the glory
of Christ our Savior,
who lives and reigns
forever and ever. Amen.

✛ *My soul, give thanks to the LORD.*
All my being, bless God's holy name.

✠ *My soul, give thanks to the LORD.*
All my being, bless God's holy name.

PSALM 103   page 422

READING   *2 Corinthians 1:18–22*

As surely as God is faithful, our word to you has not been "Yes and No." For the Son of God, Jesus Christ, whom we proclaimed among you, Silvanus and Timothy and I, was not "Yes and No"; but in him it is always "Yes." For in him every one of God's promises is a "Yes." For this reason it is through him that we say the "Amen," to the glory of God. But it is God who establishes us with you in Christ and has anointed us, by putting his seal on us and giving us his Spirit in our hearts as a first installment.

REFLECTION

The Sunday Lectionary now turns to Second Corinthians, which reveals some of the conflicts among and within the early Christian communities. Even in its infancy, the Church was often torn by disagreement and egotism. In this opening passage, Paul puts all disagreement in its proper context. In Christ, God has spoken an eternal affirmation—an eternal "Yes!"—upon creation, and all people are invited to share in the blessing God offers. God's "yes" in Christ is the heart of the Christian message; petty squabbles and disagreements are unworthy of people who have heard this fundamental proclamation.

PRAYERS   *others may be added*

Proclaiming God's "yes" in Christ, we pray:

◆ Show us your compassion.

That God may raise up in the Church faithful followers, we pray: ◆
That catechists may be enlivened in their ministry by the presence of the Holy Spirit, we pray: ◆ *That coworkers in ministry may work together in harmony and trust, we pray:* ◆ *That disagreements among Christians may be resolved in a spirit of charity, we pray:* ◆ *That we may live as those sealed with the first fruits of the Holy Spirit, we pray:* ◆

Our Father . . .

God of preachers,
the apostle Paul
proclaimed your Word to the Gentiles,
announcing your eternal "yes"
to people of all nations.
Send us forth in the Spirit of power
to be messengers of charity
    and reconciliation,
that all nations may glorify you
through Jesus the Christ,
in whom the world is reconciled,
who lives and reigns with you,
in the unity of the Holy Spirit,
one God, forever and ever. Amen.

✠ *My soul, give thanks to the LORD.*
All my being, bless God's holy name.

✦ *My soul, give thanks to the LORD.*
All my being, bless God's holy name.

PSALM 103 *page 422*

READING *Mark 9:14–22*

When they came to the disciples, they saw a great crowd around them, and some scribes arguing with them. When the whole crowd saw him, they were immediately overcome with awe, and they ran forward to greet him. He asked them, "What are you arguing about with them?" Someone from the crowd answered him, "Teacher, I brought you my son; he has a spirit that makes him unable to speak; and whenever it seizes him, it dashes him down; and he foams and grinds his teeth and becomes rigid; and I asked your disciples to cast it out, but they could not do so." He answered them, "You faithless generation, how much longer must I be among you? How much longer must I put up with you? Bring him to me." And they brought the boy to him. When the spirit saw him, immediately it convulsed the boy, and he fell on the ground and rolled about, foaming at the mouth. Jesus asked the father, "How long has this been happening to him?" And he said, "From childhood. It has often cast him into the fire and into the water, to destroy him; but if you are able to do anything, have pity on us and help us."

REFLECTION

In the father's cry for his son, perhaps we can hear the pleas of many parents: the mother of a sick child without health insurance, the father who cannot support his family on meager wages, the refugee family driven from home by war and violence. How are we to respond to such suffering? How can we fail to respond?

PRAYERS *others may be added*

Attentive to the needs of the world,
we pray:

◆ Show us your compassion.

For parents who have lost all hope,
we pray: ◆ *For families torn apart*
by despair, we pray: ◆ *For children*
abandoned to poverty, we pray: ◆
For adolescents driven from home,
we pray: ◆ *For spouses and children*
oppressed by violence in their own home,
we pray: ◆ *For households overwhelmed*
by addiction, we pray: ◆

Our Father . . .

Fountain of mercy,
in Christ you reach out
    in compassion
to free us from despair.
Hear our cries for help,
and deliver us from evil,
that we may live in joy before you
and praise you always
through Christ Jesus your Son. Amen.

✦ *My soul, give thanks to the LORD.*
All my being, bless God's holy name.

✢ *My soul, give thanks to the LORD.*
All my being, bless God's holy name.

PSALM 103   *page 422*

READING   *Mark 9:23–29*

Jesus said to the father of the boy, "If you are able!—All things can be done for the one who believes." Immediately the father of the child cried out, "I believe; help my unbelief!" When Jesus saw that a crowd came running together, he rebuked the unclean spirit, saying to it, "You spirit that keeps this boy from speaking and hearing, I command you, come out of him, and never enter him again!" After crying out and convulsing him terribly, it came out, and the boy was like a corpse, so that most of them said, "He is dead." But Jesus took him by the hand and lifted him up, and he was able to stand. When he had entered the house, his disciples asked him privately, "Why could we not cast it out?" He said to them, "This kind can come out only through prayer."

REFLECTION

Like the Syrophoenician woman (see February 15), the father of the possessed boy has courage to respond to Jesus' rebuke. Actually, Jesus' hard words are for his disciples; it is their lack of faith, not the father's, that prevents them from freeing the boy. The father's love for his son shines through his cry: "Help my unbelief!" Here again, the outsider, rather than the disciple, shows us the way. He knows he needs help and does not hesitate to ask for it.

PRAYERS   *others may be added*

Longing to believe, we pray:

◆ Show us your compassion.

That the followers of Jesus may have courage to cry out in their need, we pray: ◆ *That all people may behold what is possible through faith, we pray:* ◆ *That the cries of parents for their children may be answered, we pray:* ◆ *That Christ may drive out demons of fear and despair forever, we pray:* ◆ *That we may seek faith in constant prayer, we pray:* ◆

Our Father . . .

We cry out for help,
O God of wondrous love,
and in Jesus you answer with mercy.
Strengthen our faith
in your constant care,
that we may behold
all you make possible
in Jesus your Son,
who is Lord forever and ever. Amen.

✢ *My soul, give thanks to the LORD.*
All my being, bless God's holy name.

✚ *Alleluia! Christ is risen!*
  Christ is risen indeed!
  Alleluia, alleluia!

PSALM 34   page 412

READING   Matthew 16:13–19

Now when Jesus came into the district of Caesarea Philippi, he asked his disciples, "Who do people say that the Son of Man is?" And they said, "Some say John the Baptist, but others Elijah, and still others Jeremiah or one of the prophets." He said to them, "But who do you say that I am?" Simon Peter answered, "You are the Messiah, the Son of the living God." And Jesus answered him, "Blessed are you, Simon son of Jonah! For flesh and blood has not revealed this to you, but my Father in heaven. And I tell you, you are Peter, and on this rock I will build my church, and the gates of Hades will not prevail against it. I will give you the keys of the kingdom of heaven, and whatever you bind on earth will be bound in heaven, and whatever you loose on earth will be loosed in heaven."

REFLECTION

It seems paradoxical that the man who nearly drowned for lack of faith (see February 18) is now to be the Church's foundation, whose "chair" or ministry of leadership we celebrate today! Yet Jesus pronounces such a blessing on Peter, recognizing him as a seer who has received direct revelation from God. Because of his faith, Peter becomes the "rock" (the meaning of his new name) of a new community, one that extends beyond even death, "the gates of Hades." Peter hasn't earned this honor. His faith, as Jesus notes, is God's gift; the authority and leadership conferred upon Peter is God's gift as well—a grace rather than a reward.

PRAYERS   others may be added

  Upheld by Peter's faith, we pray:

◆ Turn to us, Lord of life!

That the Church may prevail against the forces of despair and injustice, we pray: ◆ *That the pope may be a sign and source of unity for all Christians, we pray:* ◆ *That God's people may warmly embrace all who seek salvation, we pray:* ◆ *That God may reveal heavenly wisdom to all people of the earth, we pray:* ◆ *That we may recognize the Son of the living God in all our sisters and brothers, we pray:* ◆

Our Father . . .

Living God,
your Church is built up
on the sure foundation of the apostles.
Strengthen us with Peter's faith,
that we may believe in Jesus,
our Messiah and Lord,
and proclaim him to earth's ends,
for Christ is Lord
forever and ever. Amen.

✚ *Alleluia! Christ is risen!*
  Christ is risen indeed!
  Alleluia, alleluia!

✠ *My soul, give thanks to the LORD.*
All my being, bless God's holy name.

PSALM 103 *page 422*

READING *Mark 10:17–22*

As he was setting out on a journey, a man ran up and knelt before him, and asked him, "Good Teacher, what must I do to inherit eternal life?" Jesus said to him, "Why do you call me good? No one is good but God alone. You know the commandments: 'You shall not murder; You shall not commit adultery; You shall not steal; You shall not bear false witness; You shall not defraud; Honor your father and mother.'" He said to him, "Teacher, I have kept all these since my youth." Jesus, looking at him, loved him and said, "You lack one thing; go, sell what you own, and give the money to the poor, and you will have treasure in heaven; then come, follow me." When he heard this, he was shocked and went away grieving, for he had many possessions.

REFLECTION

At the beginning of the passage, the young man seems ready to please, even ready to brag about his accomplishments: "I have kept all these since my youth." He is thunderstruck by the end of the exchange; he never expected to be asked to give up his comfortable life to follow Jesus. Jesus demands a total commitment from his disciples. What began, then, with much excitement ends in sadness; in all the Gospels,
this is the only time someone declines Jesus' invitation to follow him.

PRAYERS *others may be added*

Seeking treasure for life eternal, we pray:

◆ Show us your compassion.

That God's people may generously offer the divine wisdom entrusted to them in Jesus, we pray: ◆ *That catechumens may seek above all else God who is good, we pray:* ◆ *That those with great wealth may seek first the treasure of God's reign, we pray:* ◆ *That the sick may know the healing gaze of Jesus, we pray:* ◆ *That we may take up the challenge of Jesus to give all we have to the poor, we pray:* ◆

Our Father . . .

Eternal God of heaven and earth,
in your eyes the riches of this world
    are but dust,
yet you offer treasure for eternity.
Inspire us with a greater desire
for heavenly riches,
and renew within us
the gift of your living Word,
Jesus our Savior,
who lives and reigns with you
in the unity of the Holy Spirit,
God forever and ever. Amen.

✠ *My soul, give thanks to the LORD.*
All my being, bless God's holy name.

✚ *My soul, give thanks to the LORD.*
All my being, bless God's holy name.

PSALM 103 *page 422*

READING *Mark 10:23–27*

Then Jesus looked around and said to his disciples, "How hard it will be for those who have wealth to enter the kingdom of God!" And the disciples were perplexed at these words. But Jesus said to them again, "Children, how hard it is to enter the kingdom of God! It is easier for a camel to go through the eye of a needle than for someone who is rich to enter the king-dom of God." They were greatly astounded and said to one another, "Then who can be saved?" Jesus looked at them and said, "For mortals it is impossible, but not for God; for God all things are possible."

REFLECTION

It was common belief in Jesus' day that riches were a sign of God's favor; for Jesus to say that a rich person could not be saved was shocking. Yet Jesus qualifies his statement: Although it is impossible for human beings to achieve salvation for themselves, with God all things are possi-ble. Salvation is God's free gift, not some-thing earned—even by those who give up everything to follow Christ.

PRAYERS *others may be added*

Praising the generosity of God,
we pray:

◆ Show us your compassion.

For those who set aside earthly ambition to follow Christ, we pray: ◆ *For those who choose the side of the poor, we pray:* ◆ *For those who sacrifice their time and their treasure as parents, we pray:* ◆ *For those who trust only in God's saving power, we pray:* ◆ *For those who await the glorious revelation of the Son of Man, we pray:* ◆

Our Father . . .

God of salvation,
alone we can do nothing,
but with you all things are possible.
Give us courage to trust your promise,
that we may set aside
earthly ambition and worldly gain
to follow Christ alone,
for he lives and reigns
forever and ever. Amen.

✚ *My soul, give thanks to the LORD.*
All my being, bless God's holy name.

✛ *My soul, give thanks to the LORD.*
  All my being, bless God's holy name.

PSALM 103   *page 422*

READING   *Mark 10:28–31*

Peter began to say to Jesus, "Look, we have left everything and followed you." Jesus said, "Truly I tell you, there is no one who has left house or brothers or sisters or mother or father or children or fields, for my sake and for the sake of the good news, who will not receive a hundredfold now in this age—houses, brothers and sisters, mothers and children, and fields with persecutions—and in the age to come eternal life. But many who are first will be last, and the last will be first."

REFLECTION

Peter seems to protest; unlike the rich young man, he and the rest have indeed left everything behind to follow Jesus. What reward can they hope for? Jesus in this instance is encouraging: Even in this life, the disciples will be rewarded with the fellowship of believers. In the age to come, Jesus' followers, having been last in the present order of things, will be first in God's kingdom.

PRAYERS   *others may be added*

Seeking the reward of the faithful, we pray:

◆ Show us your compassion.

That the baptized may set their sights on God's reign, we pray: ◆ *That Christians may set aside all that prevents them from following Jesus, we pray:* ◆ *That those persecuted for their faith will find comfort in the fellowship of the Church, we pray:* ◆ *That those with great riches may seek heavenly treasures by sharing their wealth, we pray:* ◆ *That we may remain true to the path of life eternal, we pray:* ◆

Our Father . . .

God of abundance,
you promise a new world
to those who are faithful.
Guide us on our journey:
May we seek out the least
   of this world,
that with them
we may be welcomed in the next,
when Christ shall live and reign
   with you,
in the unity of the Holy Spirit,
one God, forever and ever. Amen.

✛ *My soul, give thanks to the LORD.*
  All my being, bless God's holy name.

✝ *My soul, give thanks to the LORD.*
All my being, bless God's holy name.

PSALM 103 — page 422

READING — 2 Corinthians 3:1b–6

Surely we do not need, as some do, letters of recommendation to you or from you, do we? You yourselves are our letter, written on our hearts, to be known and read by all; and you show that you are a letter of Christ, prepared by us, written not with ink but with the Spirit of the living God, not on tablets of stone but on tablets of human hearts.

Such is the confidence that we have through Christ toward God. Not that we are competent of ourselves to claim anything as coming from us; our competence is from God, who has made us competent to be ministers of a new covenant, not of letter but of spirit; for the letter kills, but the Spirit gives life.

REFLECTION

In the ancient world, it was customary that travelers carry letters of recommendation attesting to their identity and trustworthiness. The letter Paul refers to seems to have been a kind of apostolic credential that would have recounted signs or wonders worked through the bearer. Paul argues that the Corinthian community itself is his letter; the faith they accepted through his preaching is the proof of his apostleship. Indeed, for Paul, a community formed in Christian charity is greater proof of the Spirit's presence than amazing deeds of power.

PRAYERS — others may be added

Enlivened by the Spirit, we pray:

◆ Show us your compassion.

That the people of God may grow in mutual trust and charity, we pray: ◆
That the baptized may testify to the Spirit that lives within them by their Christian works, we pray: ◆ *That communities of faith may be signs of the power and mercy of God to those around them, we pray:* ◆ *That believers may rely on the Spirit of life over the letter of law, we pray:* ◆ *That we have confidence in the salvation God offers in Christ, we pray:* ◆

Our Father . . .

Living God,
your Spirit enlivens the Church,
making it a sign of your power.
Write upon the tablets of our hearts
the living law of love
that we may be your witnesses,
proclaiming the life you offer
and praising you
through Jesus Christ, your Son,
who lives and reigns with you,
in the unity of the Holy Spirit,
one God, forever and ever.
Amen.

✝ *My soul, give thanks to the LORD.*
All my being, bless God's holy name.

✚ *My soul, give thanks to the LORD.*
All my being, bless God's holy name.

PSALM 103 *page 422*

READING *Mark 10:32–34*

The disciples were on the road, going up to Jerusalem, and Jesus was walking ahead of them; they were amazed, and those who followed were afraid. He took the twelve aside again and began to tell them what was to happen to him, saying, "See, we are going up to Jerusalem, and the Son of Man will be handed over to the chief priests and the scribes, and they will condemn him to death; then they will hand him over to the Gentiles; they will mock him, and spit upon him, and flog him, and kill him; and after three days he will rise again."

REFLECTION

According to Mark's account, by this time in Jesus' ministry the conflict between him and his adversaries has intensified. Jesus knows what awaits him and he does not hide this from his disciples. There is no escaping the cross. As we approach the beginning of Lent, we too look to Jerusalem for the final confrontation, when God's power will paradoxically be revealed in the weakness of the cross.

PRAYERS *others may be added*

With eyes set on Jerusalem,
we pray:

◆ Show us your compassion.

That God's people may faithfully follow the path of salvation, we pray: ◆ That Christians may seek Christ's presence in the weak, we pray: ◆ That the sign of the cross may strengthen those who suffer, we pray: ◆ That the derided and ridiculed may find courage in Christ's example, we pray: ◆ That we may have courage to bear our share of Christ's cross, we pray: ◆

Our Father . . .

God of the poor,
you choose the side of the weak
and raise up the powerless.
By the sign of the cross,
strengthen us on our journey,
that we may reach at last
our heavenly dwelling-place,
where you live and reign
forever and ever. Amen.

✚ *My soul, give thanks to the LORD.*
All my being, bless God's holy name.

✢ *My soul, give thanks to the LORD.*
All my being, bless God's holy name.

PSALM 103   *page 422*

READING   *Mark 10:35–38, 41–45*

James and John, the sons of Zebedee, came forward to Jesus and said to him, "Teacher, we want you to do for us whatever we ask of you." And he said to them, "What is it you want me to do for you?" And they said to him, "Grant us to sit, one at your right hand and one at your left, in your glory." But Jesus said to them, "You do not know what you are asking. Are you able to drink the cup that I drink, or be baptized with the baptism that I am baptized with?"

When the ten heard this, they began to be angry with James and John. So Jesus called them and said to them, "You know that among the Gentiles those whom they recognize as their rulers lord it over them, and their great ones are tyrants over them. But it is not so among you; but whoever wishes to become great among you must be your servant, and whoever wishes to be first among you must be slave of all. For the Son of Man came not to be served but to serve, and to give his life a ransom for many."

REFLECTION

On this eve of Lent, as we prepare to take up the disciplines of fasting, almsgiving, and prayer, Mark reminds us once more that the heart of discipleship is to serve as Jesus did.

PRAYERS   *others may be added*

Joyfully accepting Jesus' call to service, we pray:

◆ Give us wisdom!

That the baptized may rejoice in God's life-giving word, we pray: ◆ *That clergy and all who lead God's people may embrace Christ's call to service, we pray:* ◆ *That the Jewish people may rejoice in their dignity as the first to hear God's word, we pray:* ◆ *That mercy and justice may guide heads of state, judges and legislators, we pray:* ◆ *That those who have died in faith may receive the reward of God's faithful servants, we pray:* ◆ *That we may seek not to be served but to serve, we pray:* ◆

Our Father . . .

God of the cross,
your Anointed One
became the servant of all,
offering his life for our salvation.
Give us the courage to follow
    Christ's way.
May our sharing in his cup
    of suffering
make us sharers in his glory as well.
We ask this through our Lord
    Jesus Christ,
who lives and reigns
forever and ever. Amen.

✢ *My soul, give thanks to the LORD.*
All my being, bless God's holy name.

✝ *Create a clean heart for me, O God.*
In compassion wipe away my sin.

PSALM 51 *page 414*

READING *2 Corinthians 5:20—6:2*

We are ambassadors for Christ, since God is making his appeal through us; we entreat you on behalf of Christ, be reconciled to God. For our sake he made him to be sin who knew no sin, so that in him we might become the righteousness of God.

As we work together with him, we urge you also not to accept the grace of God in vain. For he says, "At an acceptable time I have listened to you, and on a day of salvation I have helped you." See, now is the acceptable time; see, now is the day of salvation!

REFLECTION

Today begins, once again, the Lenten springtime—the great season of grace when we remember our identity as those baptized into Christ. Images of washing and cleansing fill the psalm we pray in these first weeks of Lent, and early spring's rains echo our prayer as they wash away winter's accumulated grit and grime. The disciplines of fasting, almsgiving, and prayer serve as our cleansing rain, refreshing and restoring Christ's image in us. By embracing them we commit ourselves anew to serve as ambassadors of Christ— signs of God's reconciliation and beacons of God's righteousness in the world.

PRAYERS *others may be added*

In confidence, we pray:

◆ Have mercy, God, in your kindness.

That the people of God may embrace Lent as a time of repentance and renewal, we pray: ◆ *That those preparing for Baptism may become signs of God's righteousness, we pray:* ◆ *That Christians everywhere may be reconciled to God by seeking forgiveness from one another, we pray:* ◆ *That those who feel sin's isolation may embrace God's offer of grace, we pray:* ◆ *That we may seek to live our baptismal call more fully during this holy season, we pray:* ◆

Our Father . . .

God of boundless mercy,
on this day of salvation
you offer us anew
the grace of forgiveness in Christ.
Renew us in this Lenten season
to live more fully the Baptism
that made us your children.
May Easter find us ready
to celebrate and proclaim
the new life offered in Christ,
who lives and reigns with you,
in the unity of the Holy Spirit,
one God, forever and ever. Amen.

✝ *Create a clean heart for me, O God.*
In compassion wipe away my sin.

✛ *Create a clean heart for me, O God.*
In compassion wipe away my sin.

PSALM 51   *page 414*

READING   *Isaiah 58:1–4*

Shout out, do not hold back!
Lift up your voice like a trumpet!
Announce to my people their rebellion,
   to the house of Jacob their sins.
Yet day after day they seek me
   and delight to know my ways,
as if they were a nation that
     practiced righteousness
   and did not forsake the ordinance
     of their God;
they ask of me righteous judgments,
   they delight to draw near to God.
"Why do we fast, but you do not see?
   Why humble ourselves,
     but you do not notice?"
Look, you serve your own interest
     on your fast day,
   and oppress all your workers.
Look, you fast only to quarrel
     and to fight
   and to strike with a wicked fist.
Such fasting as you do today
     will not make your
   voice heard on high.

REFLECTION

Isaiah's warning about exterior religious practices that lack interior commitment is a good reminder of what our Lenten fast must be about. Fasting is useless if it does not remind us of our duty to the hungry. Almsgiving is meaningless if it does not force us to confront the social structures that keep people poor. Prayer will not draw us closer to God unless we open our hearts both to God's love and to God's challenge.

PRAYERS   *others may be added*

Seeking to offer an acceptable fast,
we pray:

◆ Have mercy, God, in your kindness.

That the Lenten disciplines of the Church may lead to justice and renewal, we pray: ◆ That those preparing for Baptism may become pleasing offerings to God, we pray: ◆ That people of faith may not twist religion for their own benefit, we pray: ◆ That we may be a people who delight in God by practicing righteousness, we pray: ◆

Our Father . . .

Righteous Judge,
our sins overwhelm us
for we have rebelled against you.
Give us a fast pleasing to you,
a fast of righteousness and justice,
of unity and service to others.
May this time of fasting,
almsgiving and prayer
make of us a holy nation,
a people in whom you delight.
This we ask in Jesus' name. Amen.

✛ *Create a clean heart for me, O God.*
In compassion wipe away my sin.

✠ *Create a clean heart for me, O God.*
In compassion wipe away my sin.

PSALM 51 *page 414*

READING *Isaiah 58:6–9a*

Is not this the fast that I choose:
    to loose the bonds of injustice,
    to undo the thongs of the yoke,
to let the oppressed go free,
    and to break every yoke?
Is it not to share your bread
      with the hungry,
    and bring the homeless poor
      into your house;
when you see the naked, to cover them,
    and not to hide yourself
      from your own kin?
Then your light shall break forth
      like the dawn,
    and your healing shall spring up
      quickly;
your vindicator shall go before you,
    the glory of the LORD shall be
      your rear guard.
Then you shall call, and the LORD
      will answer;
    you shall cry for help, and he
      will say, Here I am.

REFLECTION

While the Lenten fast is in some way about
personal spiritual renewal, Isaiah reminds
us that an authentic fast must bear fruit in
justice: Ours is a fast with a mission. Even
more, it is through the service demanded
by our fast that our healing will spring up
within us.

PRAYERS *others may be added*

God will answer us when we call. In
confidence, we pray:

◆ Have mercy, God, in your kindness.

That the disciples of Jesus may model
for the world the fast God desires,
we pray: ◆ *That civil leaders may turn*
to the needs of the poorest of their citizens,
we pray: ◆ *That families broken by*
anger or misunderstanding may not hide
themselves from one another but be
reconciled, we pray: ◆ *That the Lenten*
fast of God's people may shatter the
yokes of poverty, hunger, and homelessness,
we pray: ◆ *That during this time of*
fasting we may shine more brightly as
beacons of God's glory, we pray: ◆

Our Father . . .

God of the poor,
you require of us an offering
    pleasing to you—
a holocaust of justice and service.
In your mercy, renew in us the fast
    that you have chosen.
May our light break forth like
    the dawn,
revealing your glory to all the world.
We ask this in Jesus' name. Amen.

✠ *Create a clean heart for me, O God.*
In compassion wipe away my sin.

✚ *Create a clean heart for me, O God.*
   In compassion wipe away my sin.

PSALM 51   *page 414*

READING   *Isaiah 58:9b–12*

If you remove the yoke
     from among you,
   the pointing of the finger,
     the speaking of evil,
if you offer your food to the hungry
   and satisfy the needs
     of the afflicted,
then your light shall rise
     in the darkness
   and your gloom be
     like the noonday.
The LORD will guide you continually,
   and satisfy your needs
     in parched places,
   and make your bones strong;
and you shall be like a watered garden,
   like a spring of water,
     whose waters never fail.
Your ancient ruins shall be rebuilt;
   you shall raise up the foundations
     of many generations;
you shall be called the repairer
     of the breach,
   the restorer of streets to live in.

REFLECTION   *John XXIII*

Every endeavor to make peace between one person and another, or one nation and another, is worthy of our heartfelt admiration. Every sincere and eager movement toward peace, from whatever quarter it may come, provided that it conceal no deceit and be inspired by pure justice and universal love, any such movement, we repeat, is worthy of our trust and respect. All is forgiven to those who know how to forgive and are willing to do so.

PRAYERS   *others may be added*

God will refresh us in our time of penance. In hope, we pray:

◆ Have mercy, God, in your kindness.

That the people of God may remove from among them the pointing of fingers and speaking of evil, we pray: ◆ That those preparing for baptism may be signs of God's glory to the Church, we pray: ◆ That God may strengthen the spirits and bones of the poor and afflicted, refreshing them in mercy, we pray: ◆ That the sick may be refreshed by God's healing mercy, we pray: ◆ That our Lenten penance may repair the breaches among us, restoring us to one another, we pray: ◆

Our Father . . .

Fountain of grace,
in our time of penance
you renew us with the promise
     of refreshment.
Nourish us anew with your mercy
and make of us a garden
     of righteousness,
that we may bear a harvest of justice
and so come to share
your glory in Christ,
who lives and reigns forever and ever.
Amen.

✚ *Create a clean heart for me, O God.*
   In compassion wipe away my sin.

✦ *Create a clean heart for me, O God.*
In compassion wipe away my sin.

PSALM 51   *page 414*

READING   *Mark 1:12–15*

The Spirit immediately drove Jesus out into the wilderness. He was in the wilderness forty days, tempted by Satan; and he was with the wild beasts; and the angels waited on him.

Now after John was arrested, Jesus came to Galilee, proclaiming the good news of God, and saying, "The time is fulfilled, and the kingdom of God has come near; repent, and believe in the good news."

REFLECTION

In every Gospel, the temptation of Jesus immediately follows his baptism. Although he is God's "Beloved," he is not exempt from the challenges of human life. Jesus had to struggle to be faithful to his mission, just as we, in Lent, must seek greater fidelity to our own baptismal identity. Our journey with Jesus in the desert is not, however, an end in itself. With Jesus, we will emerge from our fast ready to announce that God's kingdom has come near.

PRAYERS   *others may be added*

Seeking fidelity to the Gospel,
we pray:

◆ Have mercy, God, in your kindness.

That God's people may faithfully follow Jesus into the Lenten desert, we pray: ◆
That all the baptized may be renewed in fasting, almsgiving and prayer, we pray: ◆
That all people may resist the Tempter's promise of unjust power and ill-gotten wealth, we pray: ◆ *That those who oppress the poor may repent and believe in the good news, we pray:* ◆ *That we may be bold in our announcement that God's kingdom has come near, we pray:* ◆

Our Father . . .

God of the desert,
Strengthened by the Spirit,
you lead us in Christ
through earthly wilderness.
Make us deaf
to the Evil One's promises
and blind to Satan's vision
    of the world,
that Easter may find us renewed,
ready to announce your kingdom,
which has come near in Christ,
who lives with you,
in the unity of the Holy Spirit,
one God, forever and ever. Amen.

✦ *Create a clean heart for me, O God.*
in compassion wipe away my sin.

✝ *Create a clean heart for me, O God.*
  In compassion wipe away my sin.

PSALM 51   *page 414*

READING   *Genesis 2:4–9*

These are the generations of the heavens and the earth when they were created. In the day that the LORD God made the earth and the heavens, when no plant of the field was yet in the earth and no herb of the field had yet sprung up—for the LORD God had not caused it to rain upon the earth, and there was no one to till the ground; but a stream would rise from the earth, and water the whole face of the ground—then the LORD God formed man from the dust of the ground, and breathed into his nostrils the breath of life; and the man became a living being. And the LORD God planted a garden in Eden, in the east; and there he put the man whom he had formed. Out of the ground the LORD God made to grow every tree that is pleasant to the sight and good for food, the tree of life also in the midst of the garden, and the tree of the knowledge of good and evil.

REFLECTION

Today we begin the second story of Creation found in the book of Genesis. (The first one, Genesis 1:1—2:3, describes the Creation over six days.) This account of Creation eventually leads to a description of the first sin of Adam and Eve, an important Lenten theme. At the same time, it is equally important to start at the beginning, with the description of the original grace given by God. After all, Lent is only secondarily about sin; of primary importance is the restoration we find in Christ, in whom we are created anew through Baptism.

PRAYERS   *others may be added*

Filled with God's own breath,
we pray:

◆ Have mercy, God, in your kindness.

That the breath of God may fill the Church with the divine presence, we pray: ◆ *That the breath of God may inspire the nations to peace, we pray:* ◆ *That the breath of God may enliven the bodies of the sick, we pray:* ◆ *That the breath of God may strengthen the spirits of the anxious and sorrowful, we pray:* ◆ *That the breath of God may renew in us the divine image, we pray:* ◆

Our Father . . .

Divine Artisan,
you fashioned us from the dust
    of the earth
and your breath made us
    living beings.
Mold us in your creative power
and inspire us with holy breath,
that our living may give glory to you,
Source of life and being,
for you live and reign
forever and ever. Amen.

✝ *Create a clean heart for me, O God.*
  In compassion wipe away my sin.

✛ *Create a clean heart for me, O God.*
In compassion wipe away my sin.

PSALM 51 *page 414*

READING *Genesis 2:15–20*

The LORD God took the man and put him in the garden of Eden to till it and keep it. And the LORD God commanded the man, "You may freely eat of every tree of the garden; but of the tree of the knowledge of good and evil you shall not eat, for in the day that you eat of it you shall die." Then the LORD God said, "It is not good that the man should be alone; I will make him a helper as his partner." So out of the ground the LORD God formed every animal of the field and every bird of the air, and brought them to the man to see what he would call them; and whatever the man called every living creature, that was its name. The man gave names to all cattle, and to the birds of the air, and to every animal of the field; but for the man there was not found a helper as his partner.

REFLECTION

This Creation story's author tends to anthropomorphize God—casting God in human likeness. Although such language has its limits, it allows the author to describe God's tender care for the man. The image of the Creator busily fashioning animal after animal to bring to the man as a helper is charming. Indeed, it reveals a great truth about our God—a God who is constantly seeking us and offering the gift of love at every turn.

PRAYERS *others may be added*

With thanksgiving for the loving care of the Creator, we pray:

◆ Have mercy, God, in your kindness.

For pastors and catechists, who teach others to distinguish good from evil, we pray: ◆ *For farmers, who till the soil and harvest earth's fruit, we pray:* ◆ *For gardeners, who work with the earth to produce beauty and sustenance, we pray:* ◆ *For pets, who provide companionship and comfort to their keepers, we pray:* ◆ *For fields and gardens, which provide food and comfort to their keepers, we pray:* ◆

Our Father . . .

Companion of humanity,
in your love you provide us
with animals and plants
that provide for our needs
and bring joy and beauty to our lives.
Bless our plants and pets,
our gardens and fields:
May the joy they give us
bring us to offer thanks to you,
who do not wish us to be alone.
This we ask in Jesus' name. Amen.

✛ *Create a clean heart for me, O God.*
In compassion wipe away my sin.

✛ *Create a clean heart for me, O God.*
   In compassion wipe away my sin.

PSALM 51   *page 414*

READING   *Genesis 2:21–25*

So the LORD God caused a deep sleep to fall upon the man, and he slept; then he took one of his ribs and closed up its place with flesh. And the rib that the LORD God had taken from the man he made into a woman and brought her to the man. Then the man said, "This at last is bone of my bones and flesh of my flesh; this one shall be called Woman, for out of Man this one was taken." Therefore a man leaves his father and his mother and clings to his wife, and they become one flesh. And the man and his wife were both naked, and were not ashamed.

REFLECTION

Many see in today's passage the biblical foundations of marriage, but there is much more going on! Today's story describes the first human relationship—one of mutual help and equality—and the origin of human sexuality—another of God's marvelous gifts. The man is so delighted he shouts with approval! May all our relationships— with spouses, friends, and family alike—be sources of such joy!

PRAYERS   *others may be added*

Rejoicing in the creation of human relationship, we pray:

◆ Have mercy, God, in your kindness.

That the Church may foster and support relationships of equality and love, we pray: ◆ *That spouses may cling to one another faithfully in good times and in bad, we pray:* ◆ *That all nations and races may see in one another bone of bone and flesh of flesh, we pray:* ◆ *That societies may support families in need or danger, we pray:* ◆ *That women and men may seek understanding and right relationship, we pray:* ◆ *That we may be fitting helpers for one another, we pray:* ◆

Our Father . . .

We praise you, God of wonder,
for your gifts of gender and sexuality
which enrich our lives with love
    and joy.
Makes us good stewards
of your marvelous gifts,
that our families may be
schools of justice and
    right relationship,
living together in faithfulness
    and harmony.
We ask this through our Savior,
    Jesus Christ,
who lives and reigns
forever and ever. Amen.

✛ *Create a clean heart for me, O God.*
   In compassion wipe away my sin.

✝ *Create a clean heart for me, O God.*
In compassion wipe away my sin.

PSALM 51 *page 414*

READING *Genesis 3:1–7*

Now the serpent was more crafty than any other wild animal that the LORD God had made. He said to the woman, "Did God say, 'You shall not eat from any tree in the garden'?" The woman said to the serpent, "We may eat of the fruit of the trees in the garden; but God said, 'You shall not eat of the fruit of the tree that is in the middle of the garden, nor shall you touch it, or you shall die.'" But the serpent said to the woman, "You will not die; for God knows that when you eat of it your eyes will be opened, and you will be like God, knowing good and evil." So when the woman saw that the tree was good for food, and that it was a delight to the eyes, and that the tree was to be desired to make one wise, she took of its fruit and ate; and she also gave some to her husband, who was with her, and he ate. Then the eyes of both were opened, and they knew that they were naked; and they sewed fig leaves together and made loincloths for themselves.

REFLECTION

While it may strike us as odd that God wanted to keep the woman and man in ignorance, we have certainly learned the ambiguity of knowledge. In the past century, we have used science both to create horrible weapons and to cure diseases. Today we stand on the brink of a great revolution in genetics, and we are already facing the moral challenges of cloning, genetic engineering, and embryonic tissue research. The Yahwist tradition of Genesis offers a great lesson for our time: The search for knowledge and wisdom must always be pursued with humility—with knowledge of our proper relationship to God and to one another.

PRAYERS *others may be added*

Lamenting the folly of human disobedience, we pray:

◆ Have mercy, God, in your kindness.

That the baptized may find in Christ the remedy to sin and the restoration of life, we pray: ◆ *That the world's people may reject crafty voices offering easy answers to life's problems, we pray:* ◆ *That Holy Wisdom may guide humanity's search for knowledge, we pray:* ◆ *That those burdened by shame may know God's compassion, we pray:* ◆

Our Father . . .

God of wisdom,
we are but dust before you.
Cast out the pride that leads to sin
and fill our hearts with humility.
May we rejoice in our dignity
as your beloved children,
seeking always to become more fully
what you have created us to be.
This we ask in Jesus' name. Amen.

✝ *Create a clean heart for me, O God.*
In compassion wipe away my sin.

✠　*Create a clean heart for me, O God.*
　　In compassion wipe away my sin.

PSALM 51　　　　　　　*page 414*

READING　　　　*Genesis 3:8–13*

They heard the sound of the LORD God walking in the garden at the time of the evening breeze, and the man and his wife hid themselves from the presence of the LORD God among the trees of the garden. But the LORD God called to the man, and said to him, "Where are you?" He said, "I heard the sound of you in the garden, and I was afraid, because I was naked; and I hid myself." He said, "Who told you that you were naked? Have you eaten from the tree of which I commanded you not to eat?" The man said, "The woman whom you gave to be with me, she gave me fruit from the tree, and I ate." Then the LORD God said to the woman, "What is this that you have done?" The woman said, "The serpent tricked me, and I ate."

REFLECTION

The ancient author of this story clearly knew well the human propensity to lay blame rather than accept responsibility. No doubt many parents and teachers have had similar conversations with a child about a broken dish or rule. Events like those described here certainly happen today—and not only among children! All of us, probably adults more than children, are characters in this never-ending drama. Perhaps that is why it deserves the appellation "Word of God."

PRAYERS　　　*others may be added*

With sorrow for our dishonesty and fear, we pray:

◆　Have mercy, God, in your kindness.

That God's people may seek honesty before God and one another, we pray: ◆
That nations may accept responsibility for violence and injustice committed against the poor, we pray: ◆ *That those burdened by fear or shame may know God's loving presence, we pray:* ◆
That fear may not keep those in need from seeking aid, we pray: ◆ *That we may acknowledge our wrongdoing and brokenness before God, we pray:* ◆

Our Father . . .

God of mercy,
we stand naked before you,
trembling with fear,
for you know the depths of our hearts.
Stir up your compassion,
and bathe us in your mercy
that we may be restored to your favor
and live in your presence,
for you live and reign
forever and ever. Amen.

✠　*Create a clean heart for me, O God.*
　　In compassion wipe away my sin.

✝ *Create a clean heart for me, O God.*
In compassion wipe away my sin.

PSALM 51   *page 414*

READING   *Genesis 3:14–19*

The LORD God said to the serpent,
"Because you have done this,
    cursed are you among all animals
    and among all wild creatures;
upon your belly you shall go,
    and dust you shall eat
    all the days of your life.
I will put enmity between you
        and the woman,
    and between your offspring
        and hers;
he will strike your head,
    and you will strike his heel."
To the woman he said,
"I will greatly increase your pangs
        in childbearing;
    in pain you shall bring forth
        children,
yet your desire shall be
        for your husband,
    and he shall rule over you."
And to the man he said,
"Because you have listened
        to the voice of your wife,
    and have eaten of the tree
about which I commanded you,
    'You shall not eat of it,'
cursed is the ground because of you;
    in toil you shall eat of it
        all the days of your life;
thorns and thistles it shall bring forth
        for you;
    and you shall eat the plants
        of the field.

By the sweat of your face
    you shall eat bread
until you return to the ground,
    for out of it you were taken;
you are dust,
    and to dust you shall return."

REFLECTION   Exsultet
O happy fault, O necessary sin of Adam,
which gained for us so great a Redeemer!

PRAYERS   *others may be added*

Sorrowful in sin, we pray:

◆ Have mercy, God, in your kindness.

For all creation, broken by sin, we pray: ◆
For those who live by the sweat of their
faces, we pray: ◆ *For pregnant women*
and those in labor, we pray: ◆ *For those*
who have returned to dust in death,
we pray: ◆ *For all of us, burdened by*
guilt, we pray: ◆

Our Father . . .

God of judgment,
even in our failure we have hope
for your mercy is greater
than your judgment.
Restore to us the divine image
tarnished by our sinfulness
that the divisions caused
by our disobedience
might be restored through Jesus Christ,
who lives and reigns
forever and ever. Amen.

✝ *Create a clean heart for me, O God.*
In compassion wipe away my sin.

✚ *Create a clean heart for me, O God.*
In compassion wipe away my sin.

PSALM 51 *page 414*

READING *Mark 9:2–10*

Six days later, Jesus took with him Peter and James and John, and led them up a high mountain apart, by themselves. And he was transfigured before them, and his clothes became dazzling white, such as no one on earth could bleach them. And there appeared to them Elijah with Moses, who were talking with Jesus. Then Peter said to Jesus, "Rabbi, it is good for us to be here; let us make three dwellings, one for you, one for Moses, and one for Elijah." He did not know what to say, for they were terrified. Then a cloud overshadowed them, and from the cloud there came a voice, "This is my Son, the Beloved; listen to him!" Suddenly when they looked around, they saw no one with them any more, but only Jesus.

As they were coming down the mountain, he ordered them to tell no one about what they had seen, until after the Son of Man had risen from the dead. So they kept the matter to themselves, questioning what this rising from the dead could mean.

REFLECTION

The Gospel for the Second Sunday of Lent always recounts Jesus' Transfiguration, a foretaste of Easter glory. In each Gospel, Jesus immediately reminds his disciples of his rejection and death. For Jesus and for us, the path to glory passes through the cross.

PRAYERS *others may be added*

Longing to see Christ's glory,
we pray:

◆ Have mercy, God, in your kindness.

That the baptized may attentively listen to God's Beloved speaking in their hearts, we pray: ◆ *That all people may know themselves as God's beloved children, we pray:* ◆ *That those who have died may be transfigured in eternal life, we pray:* ◆ *That the disciplines of Lent may transform us into more radiant signs of God's glory, we pray:* ◆

Our Father . . .

God of glory,
in this season of renewal
you give us a foretaste
of the glory that awaits us.
Be with us on our Lenten journey:
May we never forget
that the path leading to Calvary
leads also to the glory
of your new creation,
where Christ lives and reigns with you,
in the unity of the Holy Spirit,
one God, forever and ever. Amen.

✚ *Create a clean heart for me, O God.*
In compassion wipe away my sin.

✛ *Create a clean heart for me, O God.*
In compassion wipe away my sin.

PSALM 51   *page 414*

READING   *Genesis 4:1–7*

Now the man knew his wife Eve, and she conceived and bore Cain, saying, "I have produced a man with the help of the LORD." Next she bore his brother Abel. Now Abel was a keeper of sheep, and Cain a tiller of the ground. In the course of time Cain brought to the LORD an offering of the fruit of the ground, and Abel for his part brought of the firstlings of his flock, their fat portions. And the LORD had regard for Abel and his offering, but for Cain and his offering he had no regard. So Cain was very angry, and his countenance fell. The LORD said to Cain, "Why are you angry, and why has your countenance fallen? If you do well, will you not be accepted? And if you do not do well, sin is lurking at the door; its desire is for you, but you must master it."

REFLECTION

Scripture scholars point out that it was not Cain's fault that his offering was rejected. The fact that God does not accept the offering merely indicates that Cain was not successful as a farmer, while Abel prospered as a herder. Cain's reaction to his misfortune—like our own—is entirely his responsibility.

PRAYERS   *others may be added*

Seeking to offer a pleasing sacrifice to God, we pray:

◆ Have mercy, God, in your kindness.

That the disciplines of Lent may cleanse the baptized of jealousy, we pray: ◆
That the elect may offer a pleasing sacrifice of praise to God, we pray: ◆
That the people of the world may live in peace as sisters and brothers, we pray: ◆
That fields and flocks may flourish in the Lenten spring, we pray: ◆ *That those who suffer failure and misfortune may find comfort and help, we pray:* ◆ *That we may guard against the sins of pride and envy, we pray:* ◆

Our Father . . .

God of salvation,
you do not spurn
the sacrifice of a humble heart
but accept the prayers of the broken.
Bless us with contrite spirits.
May offer you the first fruits
of a Lent well-kept,
that Easter may find us
renewed and ready
to celebrate our life in Christ,
who is Lord forever and ever. Amen.

✛ *Create a clean heart for me, O God.*
In compassion wipe away my sin.

✛ *Create a clean heart for me, O God.*
In compassion wipe away my sin.

PSALM 51 *page 414*

READING *Genesis 4:8–15*

Cain said to his brother Abel, "Let us go out to the field." And when they were in the field, Cain rose up against his brother Abel, and killed him. Then the LORD said to Cain, "Where is your brother Abel?" He said, "I do not know; am I my brother's keeper?" And the LORD said, "What have you done? Listen; your brother's blood is crying out to me from the ground! And now you are cursed from the ground, which has opened its mouth to receive your brother's blood from your hand. When you till the ground, it will no longer yield to you its strength; you will be a fugitive and a wanderer on the earth." Cain said to the LORD, "My punishment is greater than I can bear! Today you have driven me away from the soil, and I shall be hidden from your face; I shall be a fugitive and a wanderer on the earth, and anyone who meets me may kill me." Then the LORD said to him, "Not so! Whoever kills Cain will suffer a sevenfold vengeance." And the LORD put a mark on Cain, so that no one who came upon him would kill him.

REFLECTION

The story of Cain and Abel is another chapter in the spiral of sin that still today threatens to destroy us. Genocide, terrorism, civil war, and the more insidious violence of prejudice still plague us. We can sometimes be so overcome by anger or fear or jealousy that we turn to violence. Lent is the acceptable time to face the lure of violence and be embraced by the healing grace of Christ as a new creation, freed from all that leads to violence.

PRAYERS *others may be added*

Repenting of violence and hatred,
we pray:

◆ Have mercy, God, in your kindness.

That preachers, priests, and ministers may cry out against all violence, we pray: ◆ *That the horrors of war, terrorism, and murder may be blotted from the face of the earth, we pray:* ◆ *That victims of violent crime may know the compassion of God, we pray:* ◆ *That those who have committed acts of violence may repent and seek forgiveness, we pray:* ◆ *That we may fast from violence in thought, word, and deed, we pray:* ◆

Our Father . . .

God of mercy,
the blood of the innocent
cries out to you for justice.
Move in power over us,
and cast out from our hearts
violence born of hatred and envy
that we may live as your children,
brothers and sisters of the Crucified,
who lives and reigns
forever and ever. Amen.

✛ *Create a clean heart for me, O God.*
In compassion wipe away my sin.

✠ *Create a clean heart for me, O God.*
In compassion wipe away my sin.

PSALM 51   *page 414*

READING   *Genesis 6:5–8, 9a–10*

The LORD saw that the wickedness of humankind was great in the earth, and that every inclination of the thoughts of their hearts was only evil continually. And the LORD was sorry that he had made humankind on the earth, and it grieved him to his heart. So the LORD said, "I will blot out from the earth the human beings I have created—people together with animals and creeping things and birds of the air, for I am sorry that I have made them." But Noah found favor in the sight of the LORD.

Noah was a righteous man, blameless in his generation; Noah walked with God. And Noah had three sons, Shem, Ham, and Japheth.

REFLECTION

Christian tradition—especially as found in the writings of the ancient Church Fathers—has long interpreted the story of Noah as a "type" or symbol of the Church's Lenten journey. The connections are easy to make. The 40 days of rain signify the days of Lent. The waters of the flood correspond to the waters of Baptism, which both destroy the old in chaos and renew creation by God's favor. The ark is the Church, which surrounds and protects the righteous, bearing them safely through the treacherous journey to a new relationship with God.

PRAYERS   *others may be added*

Grieved by human wickedness and injustice, we cry:

◆ Have mercy, God, in your kindness.

Despite the failures of the baptized to live as your people, we cry: ◆ *Despite the violence that plagues our homes and communities, we cry:* ◆ *Despite injustices that cause hunger and homelessness, we cry:* ◆ *Despite our abuse of the gift of creation, we cry:* ◆ *Despite the wicked thoughts of our minds and the jealousies of our hearts, we cry:* ◆

Our Father . . .

God of judgment,
our wickedness covers us,
and evil has taken root in our hearts,
yet we trust in your saving mercy.
Give us humble sorrow
for the sins that cause
your heart to grieve.
May we turn to ways of righteousness
and find favor in your sight,
through Christ our Redeemer. Amen.

✠ *Create a clean heart for me, O God.*
In compassion wipe away my sin.

✙ *Create a clean heart for me, O God.*
In compassion wipe away my sin.

PSALM 51 *page 414*

READING *Genesis 6:13–14, 17–22*

And God said to Noah, "I have determined to make an end of all flesh, for the earth is filled with violence because of them; now I am going to destroy them along with the earth. Make yourself an ark of cypress wood; make rooms in the ark, and cover it inside and out with pitch. For my part, I am going to bring a flood of waters on the earth, to destroy from under heaven all flesh in which is the breath of life; everything that is on the earth shall die. But I will establish my covenant with you; and you shall come into the ark, you, your sons, your wife, and your sons' wives with you. And of every living thing, of all flesh, you shall bring two of every kind into the ark, to keep them alive with you; they shall be male and female. Of the birds according to their kinds, and of the animals according to their kinds, of every creeping thing of the ground according to its kind, two of every kind shall come in to you, to keep them alive. Also take with you every kind of food that is eaten, and store it up; and it shall serve as food for you and for them." Noah did this; he did all that God commanded him.

REFLECTION

The story of Noah highlights the radical connection of human beings to the rest of creation. Human violence is God's reason for wiping out all living things; at the same time, a few righteous people are entrusted with the remnant of creation God will preserve. No doubt the same dynamic is at work today. Human violence mars creation with war and pollution, yet we are no less charged with the care of the earth and of one another.

PRAYERS *others may be added*

Obedient to God, we pray:

◆ Have mercy, God, in your kindness.

For all who are sheltered in the ark of the Church, we pray: ◆ *For all who seek to live in righteousness, we pray:* ◆ *For all who mar creation with violence, we pray:* ◆ *For all who care for wildlife and livestock, we pray:* ◆ *For all who obey God's commands with humility, we pray:* ◆

Our Father . . .

God of all living things,
in every age you raise up
righteous women and men
who are obedient to your commands.
Bless us with the faithfulness
of Noah and his family,
that we may be sheltered
by the ark of your mercy
and live as children
of the New Covenant in Christ Jesus,
who lives and reigns
forever and ever. Amen.

✙ *Create a clean heart for me, O God.*
In compassion wipe away my sin.

✤ *Create a clean heart for me, O God.*
In compassion wipe away my sin.

PSALM 51 *page 414*

READING *Genesis 7:1, 11–16*

Then the LORD said to Noah, "Go into the ark, you and all your household, for I have seen that you alone are righteous before me in this generation."

In the six hundredth year of Noah's life, in the second month, on the seventeenth day of the month, on that day all the fountains of the great deep burst forth, and the windows of the heavens were opened. The rain fell on the earth forty days and forty nights. On the very same day Noah with his sons, Shem and Ham and Japheth, and Noah's wife and the three wives of his sons entered the ark, they and every wild animal of every kind, and all domestic animals of every kind, and every creeping thing that creeps on the earth, and every bird of every kind— every bird, every winged creature. They went into the ark with Noah, two and two of all flesh in which there was the breath of life. And those that entered, male and female of all flesh, went in as God had commanded him; and the LORD shut him in.

REFLECTION *Peter Mazar*

Lent's abstinence from meat . . . makes us like travelers aboard Noah's ark. What if one of them had a sudden urge for a hamburger? It would have meant the end of cattle, forever. During Lent's 40 days and 40 nights we refuse to take bites out of one another. Instead, aboard this ark called "earth" we grow hungry together for a fresh harvest.

PRAYERS *others may be added*

Journeying together through the season of Lent, we pray:

◆ Have mercy, God, in your kindness.

For God's people, accompanying one another in Lent's holy fast, we pray: ◆ *For catechumens, preparing to be reborn in the baptismal flood, we pray:* ◆ *For all people, sharing the ark of one planet, we pray:* ◆ *For all living things, filling creation with beauty and wonder, we pray:* ◆ *For us, seeking together righteousness before God, we pray:* ◆

Our Father . . .

God of creation,
in justice you covered the earth
with the waters of chaos;
in mercy you preserved
a living remnant in Noah's ark.
Bless all living things
in this time of birth and growth,
that the springtime fast of Lent
may renew the face of earth
from the scars of human sinfulness.
This we ask in Jesus' name. Amen.

✤ *Create a clean heart for me, O God.*
In compassion wipe away my sin.

✝ *Create a clean heart for me, O God.*
In compassion wipe away my sin.

PSALM 51   *page 414*

READING   *Genesis 7:17–23*

The flood continued forty days on the earth; and the waters increased, and bore up the ark, and it rose high above the earth. The waters swelled and increased greatly on the earth; and the ark floated on the face of the waters. The waters swelled so mightily on the earth that all the high mountains under the whole heaven were covered; the waters swelled above the mountains, covering them fifteen cubits deep. And all flesh died that moved on the earth, birds, domestic animals, wild animals, all swarming creatures that swarm on the earth, and all human beings; everything on dry land in whose nostrils was the breath of life died. God blotted out every living thing that was on the face of the ground, human beings and animals and creeping things and birds of the air; they were blotted out from the earth. Only Noah was left, and those that were with him in the ark.

REFLECTION

Many cultures from around the world tell stories of a great flood, no doubt an indication of the suffering that natural disasters have caused humanity. It is tempting to see, as did the author of this story, divine retribution in these catastrophes, yet our spirits recoil at the thought of such a God. No, natural disaster, like all suffering, is a terrible mystery. What we do know, and what we meditate on during this season, is that in Christ's cross our suffering has been taken up into the life of God—and transformed.

PRAYERS   *others may be added*

Sheltered by the mercy of God,
we pray:

◆ Have mercy, God, in your kindness.

On those made homeless by mighty storms and terrible floods, we pray: ◆ *On those robbed of life by hunger, thirst, and disease, we pray:* ◆ *On fields and farms cracked by drought and ravaged by wind, we pray:* ◆ *On mountains, forests, and prairies spoiled by sprawl and poor stewardship, we pray:* ◆ *On wildlife choked by oil spills and disasters caused by human error, we pray:* ◆ *On sinners seeking your boundless mercy, we pray:* ◆

Our Father . . .

God of the deep,
the waters of chaos
overwhelmed your great work
and still they threaten to destroy us.
Turn your face to the broken earth
and inspire us with compassion,
that we may relieve the suffering
caused by floods, earthquakes,
   and storms
and so contribute to the renewal
begun in Jesus Christ,
who is Lord forever and ever. Amen.

✝ *Create a clean heart for me, O God.*
In compassion wipe away my sin.

✤ *Turn your ear to us, O God.*
Save your people, who trust in you.

PSALM 86 *page 418*

READING *John 2:13–21*

The Passover of the Jews was near, and Jesus went up to Jerusalem. In the temple he found people selling cattle, sheep, and doves, and the money changers seated at their tables. Making a whip of cords, he drove all of them out of the temple, both the sheep and the cattle. He also poured out the coins of the money changers and overturned their tables. He told those who were selling the doves, "Take these things out of here! Stop making my Father's house a marketplace!" His disciples remembered that it was written, "Zeal for your house will consume me." The Jews then said to him, "What sign can you show us for doing this?" Jesus answered them, "Destroy this temple, and in three days I will raise it up." The Jews then said, "This temple has been under construction for forty-six years, and will you raise it up in three days?" But he was speaking of the temple of his body.

REFLECTION

Already in the third week of Lent, we begin to read of the events that will lead to Jesus' death. His rejection of the temple economy—in which moneychangers exchanged Roman coins for currency issued by the temple priests—was a direct challenge to the cozy relationship between the Roman authorities, the temple priesthood, *and the merchants of the time. Those three groups benefited economically from the arrangement, while the faithful poor of Israel—who had no choice but to accept exorbitant exchange rates and prices—suffered. We must ask how Jesus might challenge the connections between religion, power, and wealth in our own day.*

PRAYERS *others may be added*

Filled with zeal for God's house,
we pray:

◆ Give heed, O Lord, to our prayers.

For reformers in Church and society, we pray: ◆ *For prophets who challenge injustice, we pray:* ◆ *For those excluded from the community of faith, we pray:* ◆ *For those at the mercy of others, we pray:* ◆ *For those who suffer social inequity, we pray:* ◆ *For those who stir up renewed zeal for justice, we pray:* ◆

Our Father . . .

Zeal for your house consumes us,
O God of holiness and justice,
and so we seek righteousness.
Drive from our hearts
self-serving religion
and faithless complacency.
May we seek constant renewal
in ourselves and in our communities.
We ask this through the Savior,
who lives and reigns with you,
in the unity of the Holy Spirit,
one God, now and forever. Amen.

✤ *Turn your ear to us, O God.*
Save your people, who trust in you.

✠ *The Word of God dwells among us!*
God is one with humankind!

PSALM 96 *page 421*

READING *Luke 2:41–51a*

Now every year his parents went to Jerusalem for the festival of the Passover. And when he was twelve years old, they went up as usual for the festival. When the festival was ended and they started to return, the boy Jesus stayed behind in Jerusalem, but his parents did not know it. Assuming that he was in the group of travelers, they went a day's journey. Then they started to look for him among their relatives and friends. When they did not find him, they returned to Jerusalem to search for him. After three days they found him in the temple, sitting among the teachers, listening to them and asking them questions. And all who heard him were amazed at his understanding and his answers. When his parents saw him they were astonished; and his mother said to him, "Child, why have you treated us like this? Look, your father and I have been searching for you in great anxiety." He said to them, "Why were you searching for me? Did you not know that I must be in my Father's house?" But they did not understand what he said to them. Then he went down with them and came to Nazareth, and was obedient to them.

REFLECTION

Yesterday we read of an adult Jesus cleansing the temple; today a twelve-year-old Jesus sits among Israel's teachers! Joseph and Mary must have been beside themselves with worry, and so, on this day in Joseph's honor, we pray with and for worried parents and their children. Perhaps it's a small comfort for parents to know that even Jesus was a little smart-alecky at that age!

PRAYERS *others may be added*

With parents of every time and place,
we pray:

◆ Pray for us, Saint Joseph!

For fathers and all who guide and
protect children, we pray: ◆
For families separated by distance
or misunderstanding, we pray: ◆
For lost and runaway children, we pray: ◆
For all who are overcome by anxiety,
we pray: ◆ *For all who look to Saint*
Joseph as patron and protector, we pray: ◆

Our Father . . .

God of anxious parents,
your servant Joseph
faithfully offered your Son
loving care and constant protection.
By his intercession
bind our families in love.
May misunderstanding and hurt
never destroy trust in one another,
that together we may praise you
in the company of the saints
forever and ever. Amen.

✠ *The Word of God dwells among us!*
God is one with humankind!

✠ *Turn your ear to us, O God.*
Save your people, who trust in you.

PSALM 86 *page 418*

READING *Genesis 8:1–5*

But God remembered Noah and all the wild animals and all the domestic animals that were with him in the ark. And God made a wind blow over the earth, and the waters subsided; the fountains of the deep and the windows of the heavens were closed, the rain from the heavens was restrained, and the waters gradually receded from the earth. At the end of one hundred fifty days the waters had abated; and in the seventh month, on the seventeenth day of the month, the ark came to rest on the mountains of Ararat. The waters continued to abate until the tenth month; in the tenth month, on the first day of the month, the tops of the mountains appeared.

REFLECTION

There is something touching about God "remembering" Noah's family and the animals in the ark, and remembering is certainly part of our Lenten journey. More than anything else, during Lent we try to remember who we are as baptized people; of course, that may mean remembering times we haven't lived up to that identity. But we also remember who God is: the Source of mercy, who remembers us as we will be on the day of salvation, who remembers us as we were originally made, even when we have forgotten.

PRAYERS *others may be added*

Trusting that God will remember us, we pray:

◆ Give heed, O Lord, to our prayers.

That the baptized may always remember their call to carry God's mercy to sinners, we pray: ◆ *That catechumens may find encouragement in God's faithfulness, we pray:* ◆ *That nations and peoples may remember their duty to serve the needy, we pray:* ◆ *That people of good will may remember those suffering from droughts and floods, earthquakes and storms, we pray:* ◆ *That God may remember our beloved dead, we pray:* ◆ *That we may find mercy and renewal in this season of fasting, prayer and almsgiving, we pray:* ◆

Our Father . . .

Remember your mercy, Lord,
for we are sorely in need
of your compassion and help.
Look with favor upon us
as we walk the path of Lent.
May we turn from the chaos
   we have embraced
and find restoration
in the cross of Christ,
in whom you have reconciled
   the world,
now and forever. Amen.

✠ *Turn your ear to us, O God.*
Save your people, who trust in you.

✠ *Turn your ear to us, O God.*
Save your people, who trust in you.

PSALM 86 *page 418*

READING *Genesis 8:6–12*

At the end of forty days Noah opened the window of the ark that he had made and sent out the raven; and it went to and fro until the waters were dried up from the earth. Then he sent out the dove from him, to see if the waters had subsided from the face of the ground; but the dove found no place to set its foot, and it returned to him to the ark, for the waters were still on the face of the whole earth. So he put out his hand and took it and brought it into the ark with him. He waited another seven days, and again he sent out the dove from the ark; and the dove came back to him in the evening, and there in its beak was a freshly plucked olive leaf; so Noah knew that the waters had subsided from the earth. Then he waited another seven days, and sent out the dove; and it did not return to him any more.

REFLECTION

After weeks and weeks of being cooped up in the ark, its passengers were probably experiencing the worst bout of cabin fever in history. We can sympathize with them, as we await the end of winter, and the Lenten fast may make our confinement even harder to bear. But wait we must, just as Noah kept vigil for the return of the dove. But we not only await the return of spring; even more, we await the fullness of Easter spring, when our confinement—in sin, injustice, and war—will be over forever.

PRAYERS *others may be added*

Returning to God with humble hearts, we pray:

◆ Give heed, O Lord, to our prayers.

That the baptized may patiently await the fullness of Easter spring, we pray: ◆ *That those preparing for the Easter sacraments may patiently await their re-creation in Christ, we pray:* ◆ *That the nations of the world may patiently await the fullness of peace and justice, we pray:* ◆ *That the sick may patiently await the healing touch of God's grace, we pray:* ◆ *That we may patiently await the revelation of God's presence, we pray:* ◆

Our Father . . .

Faithful God,
with Noah and his companions
we await the day
when all the world will be made new.
Strengthen us with hope,
that this time of purification
may prepare us to enter
into the new creation begun
   in Jesus Christ,
in whose name we pray. Amen.

✠ *Turn your ear to us, O God.*
Save your people, who trust in you.

✚ *Turn your ear to us, O God.*
Save your people, who trust in you.

PSALM 86   *page 418*

READING   *Genesis 8:13, 15–19*

In the six hundred first year, in the first month, the first day of the month, the waters were dried up from the earth; and Noah removed the covering of the ark, and looked, and saw that the face of the ground was drying. Then God said to Noah, "Go out of the ark, you and your wife, and your sons and your sons' wives with you. Bring out with you every living thing that is with you of all flesh—birds and animals and every creeping thing that creeps on the earth—so that they may abound on the earth, and be fruitful and multiply on the earth." So Noah went out with his sons and his wife and his sons' wives. And every animal, every creeping thing, and every bird, everything that moves on the earth, went out of the ark by families.

REFLECTION   *Peter Chrysologus*

When the earth had become hardened in evil, God sent the flood both to punish and to release it. He called Noah to be the father of a new era, urged him with kind words, and showed that he trusted him; he gave him fatherly instruction about the present calamity, and through his grace consoled him with hope for the future. But God did not merely issue commands; rather with Noah sharing the work, he filled the ark with the future seed of the whole world.

PRAYERS   *others may be added*

Confident of God's abiding faithfulness, we pray:

◆ Give heed, O Lord, to our prayers.

That God may form the Church as a sign of new creation, we pray: ◆ *That the elect may keep their eyes on the life that awaits them in the Easter sacraments, we pray:* ◆ *That the races of the earth may embrace one another as members of one family, we pray:* ◆ *That humankind may take seriously the charge to be stewards of the earth, we pray:* ◆ *That the confinement of Lent may prepare us to emerge into risen life, we pray:* ◆

Our Father . . .

God of all creation,
you rewarded Noah's righteousness
with life in a renewed world.
Give us a share of the favor
you showed Noah and his family,
that we too may emerge
from Lent's voyage
ready to live the call
of those who have passed
through the waters
to be remade in the likeness of Christ,
who is Lord forever and ever. Amen.

✚ *Turn your ear to us, O God.*
Save your people, who trust in you.

✙ *Turn your ear to us, O God.*
Save your people, who trust in you.

PSALM 86 *page 418*

READING *Genesis 9:8–16*

Then God said to Noah and to his sons with him, "As for me, I am establishing my covenant with you and your descendants after you, and with every living creature that is with you, the birds, the domestic animals, and every animal of the earth with you, as many as came out of the ark. I establish my covenant with you, that never again shall all flesh be cut off by the waters of a flood, and never again shall there be a flood to destroy the earth." God said, "This is the sign of the covenant that I make between me and you and every living creature that is with you, for all future generations: I have set my bow in the clouds, and it shall be a sign of the covenant between me and the earth. When I bring clouds over the earth and the bow is seen in the clouds, I will remember my covenant that is between me and you and every living creature of all flesh; and the waters shall never again become a flood to destroy all flesh. When the bow is in the clouds, I will see it and remember the everlasting covenant between God and every living creature of all flesh that is on the earth."

REFLECTION

This year, the first readings of the Sundays of Lent recount the many covenants in salvation history. Today's passage, which contains the covenant between God and "every living creature," was read on the first Sunday. This is the basis of what comes in the future: the covenant with Abraham and the rest of the patriarchs and matriarchs, with the Hebrew people in the Exodus, and finally the new covenant in Christ. Key to all of these is that God makes the first move.

PRAYERS *others may be added*

Seeking greater friendship with our God, we pray:

◆ Give heed, O Lord, to our prayers.

That Church ministers may lead God's people into a deeper relationship with the Most High, we pray: ◆ *That catechumens may hear God's voice calling them to the waters of the new covenant, we pray:* ◆ *That all the earth's people may seek the God of heaven and earth, we pray:* ◆ *That humankind may honor its relationship with all created things, we pray:* ◆

Our Father . . .

God of the covenant,
you invite all people
to friendship with you.
Remember your promises of old,
that with Noah and his family,
Abraham and Sarah,
    Moses and Miriam,
and all our ancestors in faith,
we may praise you forever
in the new covenant in Jesus Christ,
who is Lord forever and ever. Amen.

✙ *Turn your ear to us, O God.*
Save your people, who trust in you.

✦ *The Word of God dwells among us!*
God is one with humankind!

PSALM 96   page 421

READING   Isaiah 7:10–14

Again the LORD spoke to Ahaz, saying, Ask a sign of the LORD your God; let it be deep as Sheol or high as heaven. But Ahaz said, I will not ask, and I will not put the LORD to the test. Then Isaiah said: "Hear then, O house of David! Is it too little for you to weary mortals, that you weary my God also? Therefore the Lord himself will give you a sign. Look, the young woman is with child and shall bear a son, and shall name him Immanuel."

REFLECTION

The solemnity of the Annunciation perhaps reminds us more of Advent and Christmas than Lent, and we keep today's feast by suspending Lent's austerity. At the same time, the Annunciation can certainly contribute to our Lenten meditation. Mary's willingness to take part in God's plan, as many Christians throughout history have pointed out, was the first step in the journey that ended at Calvary. Without Mary's generosity, we could still be waiting for the greatest sign of God's generosity—Christ's death for our sakes. Lent gives us the opportunity to cultivate within ourselves openness to God's grace, which Mary willingly received in abundance.

PRAYERS   others may be added

God shows a sign of favor; in joy, we pray:

◆ Word of God, abide with us!

That God's people may have courage in times of trial, we pray: ◆ *That prophets may sustain the Church with words of comfort and challenge, we pray:* ◆ *That the elect may respond to God's call with generosity, we pray:* ◆ *That nations may turn to faith in God, we pray:* ◆ *That world leaders may listen to voices of wisdom, we pray:* ◆ *That all people may recognize in children a sign of hope, we pray:* ◆ *That we may have confidence in our saving God, we pray:* ◆

Our Father . . .

Hope of Israel,
you promise to abide always
   with your people,
supporting them in times of trial.
Instill in us confidence
   in your promise
to be present among us.
May we never fail to recognize you
in the least of your children.
We ask this in the name
   of Jesus Christ,
Emmanuel, God-with-us,
who lives and reigns with you,
in the unity of the Holy Spirit,
one God, forever and ever. Amen.

✦ *The Word of God dwells among us!*
God is one with humankind!

✝ *Turn your ear to us, O God.*
Save your people, who trust in you.

PSALM 86   page 418

READING   *John 3:14–17*

Jesus said to Nicodemus, "Just as Moses lifted up the serpent in the wilderness, so must the Son of Man be lifted up, that whoever believes in him may have eternal life.

"For God so loved the world that he gave his only Son, so that everyone who believes in him may not perish but may have eternal life.

"Indeed, God did not send the Son into the world to condemn the world, but in order that the world might be saved through him."

REFLECTION

As we continue our Lenten journey, we may ask ourselves why we seek such renewal. Do we fear God's punishment? Are we afraid of condemnation? To such fears Jesus offers a comforting answer: Because of God's love, the Son came into the world not to condemn it but to save it. This is a great comfort, and a great invitation. God's offer in Jesus extends to all people without exception, and we are messengers of that good news.

PRAYERS   *others may be added*

In thanksgiving for God's love in Christ, we pray:

◆ Give heed, O Lord, to our prayers!

That Christians may never fail to announce God's great love for the world, we pray: ◆ *That Christian leaders may invite all people into relationship with God in Christ, we pray:* ◆ *That the world may embrace and live the love God offers, we pray:* ◆ *That nations may set aside condemnation for reconciliation and peace, we pray:* ◆ *That we who find salvation in Christ may be faithful messengers of the good news, we pray:* ◆

Our Father . . .

God of salvation,
so great was your love
that you sent your Only-begotten Son
to bring salvation to all.
Free us from fear
and the desire to condemn,
that we may be your witnesses,
announcing your endless mercy
and boundless compassion
revealed in Jesus Christ, your Son,
    who lives and reigns with you,
in the unity of the Holy Spirit,
one God, forever and ever. Amen.

✝ *Turn your ear to us, O God.*
Save your people, who trust in you.

✙ *Turn your ear to us, O God.*
Save your people, who trust in you.

PSALM 86   *page 418*

READING   *Genesis 18:1–8*

The LORD appeared to Abraham by the oaks of Mamre, as he sat at the entrance of his tent in the heat of the day. He looked up and saw three men standing near him. When he saw them, he ran from the tent entrance to meet them, and bowed down to the ground. He said, "My lord, if I find favor with you, do not pass by your servant. Let a little water be brought, and wash your feet, and rest yourselves under the tree. Let me bring a little bread, that you may refresh yourselves, and after that you may pass on—since you have come to your servant." So they said, "Do as you have said." And Abraham hastened into the tent to Sarah, and said, "Make ready quickly three measures of choice flour, knead it, and make cakes." Abraham ran to the herd, and took a calf, tender and good, and gave it to the servant, who hastened to prepare it. Then he took curds and milk and the calf that he had prepared, and set it before them; and he stood by them under the tree while they ate.

REFLECTION

The appearance of the three guests at Abraham's tent demands the hospitality of the entire clan. In the ancient Near East, the survival of travelers relied on the hospitality and good will of those they met on the way. In a time before mass communication, strangers brought news and information. All parties benefited, and in this instance, Abraham serves God, perhaps without knowing it. We do no less when we offer hospitality to others.

PRAYERS   *others may be added*

Inspired by the hospitality of Sarah and Abraham, we pray:

◆ Give heed, O Lord, to our prayers!

For ushers and ministers of hospitality in the Christian assembly, we pray: ◆
For catechumens and all on a spiritual journey, we pray: ◆ *For relief workers and those who serve the needs of the displaced, we pray:* ◆ *For those who provide hospitality for the weary, we pray:* ◆ *For table servers and cooks, we pray:* ◆ *For all who open their homes to guests, we pray:* ◆

Our Father . . .

Divine Visitor,
you come among us
in the hungry and weary,
asking for attention and care.
Inspire us by the example
of our mothers and fathers in faith,
that we too may welcome you
whenever you appear
and so be welcomed as well
into your dwelling-place
when our earthly journey is over.
This we ask in Jesus' name. Amen.

✙ *Turn your ear to us, O God.*
Save your people, who trust in you.

✠ *Turn your ear to us, O God.*
Save your people, who trust in you.

PSALM 86   *page 418*

READING   *Genesis 18:9–15*

The visitors said to Abraham, "Where is your wife Sarah?" And he said, "There, in the tent." Then one said, "I will surely return to you in due season, and your wife Sarah shall have a son." And Sarah was listening at the tent entrance behind him. Now Abraham and Sarah were old, advanced in age; it had ceased to be with Sarah after the manner of women. So Sarah laughed to herself, saying, "After I have grown old, and my husband is old, shall I have pleasure?" The LORD said to Abraham, "Why did Sarah laugh, and say, 'Shall I indeed bear a child, now that I am old?' Is anything too wonderful for the LORD? At the set time I will return to you, in due season, and Sarah shall have a son." But Sarah denied it, saying, "I did not laugh"; for she was afraid. He said, "Oh yes, you did laugh."

REFLECTION

As we remember the covenant with Abraham during this Lenten season, we must never forget that his wife, Sarah, also received God's promise. Sarah's laughter suggests that she thinks the promise is a little too good to be true! Indeed, it seems too much to hope for, but the messenger reveals that he is from God ("Is anything too wonderful for the LORD?"). Still, Sarah's laughter endures in the name of her child—"Isaac" is a play on the Hebrew word for laughter—and so today we share Sarah's chuckle, even in Lent.

PRAYERS   *others may be added*

Filled with wonder, we pray:

◆ Give heed, O Lord, to our prayers!

That the Church may have faith in all God has promised in Christ, we pray: ◆
That the elderly may have cause to rejoice in God's abundant gifts, we pray: ◆
That mothers may have cause to laugh with delight in their children, we pray: ◆
That God may bring light-heartedness to the depressed and anxious, we pray: ◆
That God may fill our lives with laughter and joy, we pray: ◆

Our Father . . .

God of Sarah,
with a mother's tender care
you fill us with laughter
    and happiness.
Lift from our hearts
the burdens of doubt and fear,
that we may trust in your mercy
and rejoice in your grace,
praising you with unending joy
through your Son, Jesus Christ,
who lives and reigns
forever and ever. Amen.

✠ *Turn your ear to us, O God.*
Save your people, who trust in you.

✦ *Turn your ear to us, O God.*
Save your people, who trust in you.

PSALM 86 — *page 418*

READING — *Genesis 21:1–7*

The LORD dealt with Sarah as he had said, and the LORD did for Sarah as he had promised. Sarah conceived and bore Abraham a son in his old age, at the time of which God had spoken to him. Abraham gave the name Isaac to his son whom Sarah bore him. And Abraham circumcised his son Isaac when he was eight days old, as God had commanded him. Abraham was a hundred years old when his son Isaac was born to him. Now Sarah said, "God has brought laughter for me; everyone who hears will laugh with me." And she said, "Who would ever have said to Abraham that Sarah would nurse children? Yet I have borne him a son in his old age."

REFLECTION

The Lenten disciplines of fasting, alms-giving, and prayer are meant to do more than merely purify us; they also direct us outward—challenging us to remember the hungry, the poor, and the forgotten. The story of Sarah and Abraham—elderly people already at the birth of their son—calls to mind many grandparents who still do the work of parents. Their needs, and those of their charges, call for our Lenten prayer, charity, and service.

PRAYERS — *others may be added*

With mothers and fathers,
grandmothers and grandfathers,
we pray:

◆ Give heed, O Lord, to our prayers!

That the baptized may celebrate the fidelity of their elders, we pray: ◆
That the gifts and wisdom of the old may be honored and treasured, we pray: ◆
That senior citizens may have adequate health care, we pray: ◆ *That children may cherish the treasure of parents, we pray:* ◆ *That families estranged from one another may be touched by God's reconciling grace, we pray:* ◆

Our Father . . .

God of young and old,
in the stories of our faith
you call us to care
for those in need.
Make us ready to reach out
to the elderly and the infant,
offering companionship and comfort,
kindness, charity, and rest.
This we ask in Jesus' name. Amen.

✦ *Turn your ear to us, O God.*
Save your people, who trust in you.

✙ *Turn your ear to us, O God.*
Save your people, who trust in you.

PSALM 86 *page 418*

READING *Genesis 22:1–3a, 4–6a, 7–8a*

After these things God tested Abraham. He said to him, "Abraham!" And he said, "Here I am." He said, "Take your son, your only son Isaac, whom you love, and go to the land of Moriah, and offer him there as a burnt offering on one of the mountains that I shall show you." So Abraham rose early in the morning, saddled his donkey, and took two of his young men with him, and his son Isaac. On the third day Abraham looked up and saw the place far away. Then Abraham said to his young men, "Stay here with the donkey; the boy and I will go over there; we will worship, and then we will come back to you." Abraham took the wood of the burnt offering and laid it on his son Isaac, and he himself carried the fire and the knife. Abraham took the wood of the burnt offering and laid it on his son Isaac, and he himself carried the fire and the knife. So the two of them walked on together. Isaac said to his father Abraham, "Father!" And he said, "Here I am, my son." He said, "The fire and the wood are here, but where is the lamb for a burnt offering?" Abraham said, "God himself will provide the lamb for a burnt offering, my son."

REFLECTION

Today we begin the chilling account of the "binding of Isaac." The story comes from a time when the Israelites had rejected human sacrifice. Still, the idea that God would "test" Abraham in such a way is troubling. With stories such as these, it is helpful to remember that our scriptures come from a culture and time quite different from our own.

PRAYERS *others may be added*

Attentive to God, we pray:

◆ Give heed, O Lord, to our prayers!

That the people of God may defend the rights of the innocent and voiceless, we pray: ◆ *That religious leaders may speak with one voice against atrocities committed in the name of religion, we pray:* ◆ *That world leaders may protect the rights of children and families, we pray:* ◆ *That parents and children may grow in mutual love and trust, we pray:* ◆ *That we may trust God to provide all we need, we pray:* ◆

Our Father . . .

God of mystery,
you look with love
on all your children
and do not will their suffering.
Open our eyes to your will,
that we may discern true from false
and so serve you faithfully.
This we ask in Jesus' name. Amen.

✙ *Turn your ear to us, O God.*
Save your people, who trust in you.

✝ *Turn your ear to us, O God.*
Save your people, who trust in you.

PSALM 86 *page 418*

READING *Genesis 22:9–14*

When they came to the place that God had shown him, Abraham built an altar there and laid the wood in order. He bound his son Isaac, and laid him on the altar, on top of the wood. Then Abraham reached out his hand and took the knife to kill his son. But the angel of the LORD called to him from heaven, and said, "Abraham, Abraham!" And he said, "Here I am." He said, "Do not lay your hand on the boy or do anything to him; for now I know that you fear God, since you have not withheld your son, your only son, from me." And Abraham looked up and saw a ram, caught in a thicket by its horns. Abraham went and took the ram and offered it up as a burnt offering instead of his son. So Abraham called that place "The LORD will provide"; as it is said to this day, "On the mount of the LORD it shall be provided."

REFLECTION *Cyprian of Carthage*

The ancient Fathers of the Church saw in the sacrifice of Isaac a prefiguring of Christ's passion: "We discover that the patriarchs, prophets and all the just who in anticipation exhibited the form of Christ paid attention to nothing in the glory of their virtues more than to maintaining patience with brave and constant serenity. . . . When Abraham, who trusted in God and planted the root and foundation of our faith, was tried through his son, he did not hesitate or delay, but obeyed the Lord's commands with the totality of devoted patience. Isaac, too, who, when offered up by his father to be sacrificed, prefigures the Lord as victim, was found to be patient."

PRAYERS *others may be added*

Trusting in God, we pray:

◆ Give heed, O Lord, to our prayers!

That the Church may offer the pleasing sacrifice of faithful service, we pray: ◆
That the baptized may have faith in the abiding presence of the Most High, we pray: ◆ *That catechumens may explore more deeply the riches and mystery of scripture, we pray:* ◆
That those in need may have a sign of God's providence in the service of Christ's disciples, we pray: ◆ *That our hearts may trust more deeply in the enduring love of God, we pray:* ◆

Our Father . . .

Loving Provider,
you stretch out your hand
to protect the innocent
and see to the needs
of your faithful ones.
Fill us with patience in times of trial
that we may praise you
for your fidelity.
We ask this through Jesus the Christ.
Amen.

✝ *Turn your ear to us, O God.*
Save your people, who trust in you.

✝ *Turn your ear to us, O God.*
Save your people, who trust in you.

PSALM 86 — page 418

READING — Genesis 22:15–19

The angel of the LORD called to Abraham a second time from heaven, and said, "By myself I have sworn, says the LORD: Because you have done this, and have not withheld your son, your only son, I will indeed bless you, and I will make your offspring as numerous as the stars of heaven and as the sand that is on the seashore. And your offspring shall possess the gate of their enemies, and by your offspring shall all the nations of the earth gain blessing for themselves, because you have obeyed my voice." So Abraham returned to his young men, and they arose and went together to Beer-sheba; and Abraham lived at Beer-sheba.

REFLECTION

The story of Isaac's near-sacrifice is proclaimed at the Easter Vigil on Holy Saturday night. Isaac, an only son, has long been considered an image of Jesus, also an only Son, offered as a sacrifice to God. The difference of course is that, true to his mission, Jesus offered himself. During this holy season, like Jesus, we too prepare to offer ourselves more completely to God.

PRAYERS — *others may be added*

Spiritual children of our ancestors in faith, we pray:

◆ Give heed, O Lord, to our prayers:

That the faithfulness of God's people may bring blessing to all nations, we pray: ◆
That God may bless people of faith in every nation, we pray: ◆ *That the children of Abraham and Sarah may overcome fear and distrust, we pray:* ◆
That we may be obedient to the voice of God speaking in our hearts, we pray: ◆
That the dead may be gathered among the countless descendents of Abraham in eternity, we pray: ◆

Our Father . . .

God of blessing,
your love extends to a vast multitude,
more numerous than the stars
    of the sky
or the sands of the seashore.
Gather us into the great company
of those blessed in Abraham
    and Sarah,
that together we may rejoice
in the heavenly city,
where Jesus Christ lives and reigns
forever and ever. Amen.

✝ *Turn your ear to us, O God.*
Save your people, who trust in you.

✦ *Turn your ear to us, O God.*
Save your people, who trust in you.

PSALM 86 page 418

READING John 12:20–26

Now among those who went up to worship at the festival were some Greeks. They came to Philip, who was from Bethsaida in Galilee, and said to him, "Sir, we wish to see Jesus." Philip went and told Andrew; then Andrew and Philip went and told Jesus. Jesus answered them, "The hour has come for the Son of Man to be glorified. Very truly, I tell you, unless a grain of wheat falls into the earth and dies, it remains just a single grain; but if it dies, it bears much fruit. Those who love their life lose it, and those who hate their life in this world will keep it for eternal life. Whoever serves me must follow me, and where I am, there will my servant be also. Whoever serves me, the Father will honor."

REFLECTION

The Greeks who wanted to see Jesus must have gone away a little puzzled! Jesus' answer to Philip and Andrew seems to come from nowhere. Of course, the Gospel writer has a purpose here: Jesus is pointing out that the progress of the Gospel beyond Israel will flow from his death and resurrection. The "grain of wheat," the teacher they know and love, must be buried so that he can grow beyond the people of Israel. For the plant to sprout and flourish, the seed must first die.

PRAYERS *others may be added*

Seeking to bear much fruit,
we pray:

◆ Give heed, O Lord, to our prayers.

For those who offer their whole being in the service of the Gospel, we pray: ◆
For those who have shed their blood in faithfulness to Jesus, we pray: ◆
For those who scatter the word among the nations of the earth, we pray: ◆
For those who pour out their lives in the search for justice, we pray: ◆ *For all who willingly give themselves to make way for the reign of God, we pray:* ◆

Our Father . . .

God of life,
through the cross of Christ
you provide a rich harvest
     of salvation.
Give us courage to follow
in Christ's footsteps,
that our lives may yield
     a hundredfold
in the kingdom of God.
We ask this through Jesus Christ,
the crucified and risen Lord,
who lives and reigns with you
in the unity of the Holy Spirit,
one God, forever and ever. Amen.

✦ *Turn your ear to us, O God.*
Save your people, who trust in you.

✚ *Turn your ear to us, O God.*
Save your people, who trust in you.

PSALM 86   *page 418*

READING   *Deuteronomy 26:4–10*

Moses spoke to the people, saying, "When the priest takes the basket from your hand and sets it down before the altar of the LORD your God, you shall make this response before the LORD your God: 'A wandering Aramean was my ancestor; he went down into Egypt and lived there as an alien, few in number, and there he became a great nation, mighty and populous. When the Egyptians treated us harshly and afflicted us, by imposing hard labor on us, we cried to the LORD, the God of our ancestors; the LORD heard our voice and saw our affliction, our toil, and our oppression. The LORD brought us out of Egypt with a mighty hand and an outstretched arm, with a terrifying display of power, and with signs and wonders; and he brought us into this place and gave us this land, a land flowing with milk and honey. So now I bring the first of the fruit of the ground that you, O LORD, have given me.' You shall set it down before the LORD your God and bow down before the LORD your God."

REFLECTION

This reading from Deuteronomy contains within it the basic Hebrew profession of faith: "A wandering Aramean [Abraham] was my ancestor. . . ." Like any act of faith, it contains within it both a statement of identity and a proclamation of praise. Reciting it reminded the speaker of his or her identity before God. Our own baptismal profession of faith in God who is Father, Son, and Holy Spirit, does the same for us. In this Lenten season, we renew that faith in works of fasting, almsgiving, and prayer, that we might profess it confidently with Easter joy.

PRAYERS   *others may be added*

Praising God for our salvation in Christ, we pray:

◆ Give heed, O Lord, to our prayers!

For those who profess faith in Jesus Christ, we pray: ◆ For those preparing for the waters of Baptism, we pray: ◆ For those who share the faith of Abraham and Sarah, we pray: ◆ For those who wander from place to place in search of safety, we pray: ◆ For those who praise God in lives of charity, justice, and peace, we pray: ◆

Our Father . . .

Hear us, O God of our ancestors.
May this holy season renew in us
the image we received in baptism,
that when Easter comes
we may praise you with joy
and serve you with faith renewed
through Jesus Christ, our Savior.
Amen.

✚ *Turn your ear to us, O God.*
Save your people, who trust in you.

✦ *Turn your ear to us, O God.*
  Save your people, who trust in you.

PSALM 86   *page 418*

READING   *Deuteronomy 26:16–19*

This very day the LORD your God is commanding you to observe these statutes and ordinances; so observe them diligently with all your heart and with all your soul. Today you have obtained the LORD's agreement: to be your God; and for you to walk in his ways, to keep his statutes, his commandments, and his ordinances, and to obey him. Today the LORD has obtained your agreement: to be his treasured people, as he promised you, and to keep his commandments; for him to set you high above all nations that he has made, in praise and in fame and in honor; and for you to be a people holy to the LORD your God, as he promised.

REFLECTION

The disciplines of Lent, especially of late, may seem tedious and burdensome, but today's scripture reminds us of the beauty and privilege of our relationship with God. As those baptized, we are named and welcomed as God's treasured people, joined to God in a covenant of love just as are the Jewish people, the "first to hear the Word of God." The privilege of this relationship brings duties as well: We are to be a sign of God's own holiness, justice, and love to all people. No wonder we must devote a lengthy season to remembering who we are!

PRAYERS   *others may be added*

As God's treasured people,
we pray:

◆ Give heed, O Lord, to our prayers!

For the baptized: may they find honor in their obedience to God's will, we pray: ◆
For those preparing for baptism: May they diligently seek God's desire with all their heart and soul, we pray: ◆
For the Jewish people: May they behold the fulfillment of God's promises to them, we pray: ◆ *For all who seek God: May believers be a sign to all of God's saving love, we pray:* ◆ *For all who have forsaken the way of God: May they hear God's voice calling them to faith and hope:* ◆ *For us: May we live in faithfulness to God's commands in Christ, we pray:* ◆

Our Father . . .

Source of life,
you are our God,
and we are your treasured people.
Renew within us your covenant
   of love,
and write your law on our hearts,
that your statutes may live in us
and reveal themselves
in acts of justice,
transforming all creation
through Jesus the Christ,
who is Lord forever and ever. Amen.

✦ *Turn your ear to us, O God.*
  Save your people, who trust in you.

✚ *Turn your ear to us, O God.*
Save your people, who trust in you.

PSALM 86   *page 418*

READING   *Deuteronomy 30:15–20*

See, I have set before you today life and prosperity, death and adversity. If you obey the commandments of the LORD your God that I am commanding you today, by loving the LORD your God, walking in his ways, and observing his commandments, decrees, and ordinances, then you shall live and become numerous, and the LORD your God will bless you in the land that your are entering to possess. But if your heart turns away and you do not hear, but are led astray to bow down to other gods and serve them, I declare to you today that you shall perish; you shall not live long in the land that you are crossing the Jordan to enter and possess. I call heaven and earth to witness against you today that I have set before you life and death. Choose life so that you and your descendants may live, loving the LORD your God, obeying him, and holding fast to him; for that means life to you and length of days, so that you may live in the land that the LORD swore to give to your ancestors, to Abraham, to Isaac, and to Jacob.

REFLECTION   *Dorothy Day*

As you come to know the seriousness of our situation—the war, the racism, the poverty in the world—you come to realize it is not going to be changed just by words or demonstrations. It's a question of risk-ing your life. It's a question of living your life in drastically different ways.*

PRAYERS   *others may be added*

Choosing life, we pray:

◆ Give heed, O Lord, to our prayers!

That the Church may proclaim the Gospel of life, opposing death in all its forms, we pray: ◆ *That governments may protect the full human life of their citizens, opposing the death of poverty and oppression, we pray:* ◆ *That the world's people may not be led astray by the idols of wealth and power, serving instead the God of justice, we pray:* ◆ *That those overshadowed by death and fear may hold fast to God, hoping in God's promises, we pray:* ◆ *That we may walk always in the ways of God's reign, living in divine love, we pray:* ◆

Our Father . . .

God of Israel,
you set before us life,
yet we often turn away
and choose the path of destruction.
Call us back to your service,
that we may enjoy your grace
and be counted among the saved
in the New Jerusalem,
where Christ lives and reigns
forever and ever. Amen.

✚ *Turn your ear to us, O God.*
Save your people, who trust in you.

✚ *Turn your ear to us, O God.*
Save your people, who trust in you.

PSALM 86   *page 418*

READING   *Leviticus 19:1–4, 9–14*

The LORD spoke to Moses, saying:

Speak to all the congregation of the people of Israel and say to them: You shall be holy, for I the LORD your God am holy. You shall each revere your mother and father, and you shall keep my sabbaths: I am the LORD your God. Do not turn to idols or make cast images for yourselves: I am the LORD your God.

When you reap the harvest of your land, you shall not reap to the very edges of your field, or gather the gleanings of your harvest. You shall not strip your vineyard bare, or gather the fallen grapes of your vineyard; you shall leave them for the poor and the alien: I am the LORD your God.

You shall not steal; you shall not deal falsely; and you shall not lie to one another. And you shall not swear falsely by my name, profaning the name of your God: I am the LORD.

You shall not defraud your neighbor; you shall not steal; and you shall not keep for yourself the wages of a laborer until morning. You shall not revile the deaf or put a stumbling block before the blind; you shall fear your God: I am the LORD.

REFLECTION   *Jacques-Benigne Bossuet*

Ours is a Church where God decrees that abundance supply lack, that excess and opulence purchase provisions for the poor. Enter the Church, my friends, with this in mind. If you do not bear the burden of the poor, your own excess will suffocate you; the sheer weight of your unshared riches will drag you into the pit.

PRAYERS   *others may be added*

Ready to offer all that we have received, we pray:

◆ Give heed, O Lord, to our prayers!

That Christian churches may be signs of service to the world, we pray: ◆
That those elected for Baptism may embrace their duty to the poor, we pray: ◆
That the Jewish people may live in faithfulness to the law God has given them, we pray: ◆ *That the goods of the earth may be justly distributed, we pray:* ◆
That immigrants and refugees may be welcomed as God's children, we pray: ◆
That God's law of love and justice may be inscribed in our hearts, we pray: ◆

Our Father . . .

Giver of all good things,
the gift of the law
binds Israel to you
as your chosen people.
Plant in our hearts
your law of justice,
that we may also be counted
among your chosen people,
holy and beloved.
We ask this in Jesus' name. Amen.

✚ *Turn your ear to us, O God.*
Save your people, who trust in you.

✚ *Turn your ear to us, O God.*
Save your people, who trust in you.

PSALM 86 *page 418*

READING *Leviticus 19:15–18*

You shall not render an unjust judgment; you shall not be partial to the poor or defer to the great: with justice you shall judge your neighbor. You shall not go around as a slanderer among your people, and you shall not profit by the blood of your neighbor: I am the LORD.

You shall not hate in your heart anyone of your kin; you shall reprove your neighbor, or you will incur guilt yourself. You shall not take vengeance or bear a grudge against any of your people, but you shall love your neighbor as yourself: I am the LORD.

REFLECTION

These words from Leviticus are timely reminders of the relevance of even the most ancient scriptural wisdom to our modern lives. Injustice, slander, ill-gotten profit, hatred, and vengeance are no less human realities today than they were 2,500 years ago, when the ancient laws of Israel began to be codified. It is a great tragedy that we seem so slow to overcome our ancient failings, which cause suffering for so many. But it is our belief, which we renew during Lent, that Christ's sacrifice has undone the power of death and sin, bringing to fullness at last the reign of justice and love begun in the covenant with Israel.

PRAYERS *others may be added*

Seeking the ways of justice, we pray:

◆ Give heed, O Lord, to our prayers!

For nations torn by religious violence or racial hatred, we pray: ◆
For communities divided by false accusations and slander, we pray: ◆
For families wounded by infidelity or violence, we pray: ◆ *For victims of injustice and corruption, we pray:* ◆
For those who suffer economic exploitation or slavery, we pray: ◆
For those bound by jealousy or the desire for revenge, we pray: ◆

Our Father . . .

Father of justice,
your law lights our path
leading us in ways of righteousness.
Bless us with strength
to obey your commands,
to seek fairness and reconciliation,
and so to grow in love of neighbor
and in love of you,
who live and reign
forever and ever. Amen.

✚ *Turn your ear to us, O God.*
Save your people, who trust in you.

✝ *Turn your ear to us, O God.*
Save your people, who trust in you.

PSALM 86   *page 418*

READING   *Deuteronomy 4:1, 5–9*

So now, Israel, give heed to the statutes and ordinances that I am teaching you to observe, so that you may live to enter and occupy the land that the LORD, the God of your ancestors, is giving you.

See, just as the LORD my God has charged me, I now teach you statutes and ordinances for you to observe in the land that you are about to enter and occupy. You must observe them diligently, for this will show your wisdom and discernment to the peoples, who, when they hear all these statutes, will say, "Surely this great nation is a wise and discerning people!" For what other great nation has a god so near to it as the LORD our God is whenever we call to him? And what other great nation has statutes and ordinances as just as this entire law that I am setting before you today? But take care and watch yourselves closely, so as neither to forget the things that your eyes have seen nor to let them slip from your mind all the days of your life; make them known to your children and your children's children.

REFLECTION

There is always a danger in religion of becoming self-absorbed, too focused on our personal growth or salvation. This is no less so during Lent, when we are more attentive to our lives of faith. Today's passage offers a corrective, a reminder that what we do is not just for our sake but for the sake of the whole world. Like Israel, we are to be signs to others of what God has done for us. After all, we have done nothing to merit salvation; it is God's gift, offered to all people.

PRAYERS   *others may be added*

Reaching out in love to others,
we pray:

◆ Give heed, O Lord, to our prayers!

That the baptized may be signs of God's wisdom, we pray: ◆ *That the elect and candidates may take to heart God's law of love, we pray:* ◆ *That the nations may rejoice in God's statutes, we pray:* ◆ *That all people may find hope in the peoples of the covenant, we pray:* ◆ *That we may share what we have seen and heard with our children and children's children, we pray:* ◆

Our Father . . .

Light to the nations,
you make of your people
a beacon of wisdom
and a sign of hope.
Renew within us love's law,
that we may never forget
what we have seen and heard
in our Savior Jesus Christ,
your saving Word enfleshed,
who lives and reigns,
forever and ever. Amen.

✝ *Turn your ear to us, O God.*
Save your people, who trust in you.

✠ *O God, do not forsake us.*
We place all our trust in you.

PSALM 22 *page 409*

READING *Mark 11:2–10*

Jesus said to two of his disciples, "Go into the village ahead of you, and immediately as you enter it, you will find tied there a colt that has never been ridden; untie it and bring it. If anyone says to you, 'Why are you doing this?' just say this, 'The Lord needs it and will send it back here immediately.'" They went away and found a colt tied near a door, outside in the street. As they were untying it, some of the bystanders said to them, "What are you doing, untying the colt?" They told them what Jesus had said; and they allowed them to take it. Then they brought the colt to Jesus and threw their cloaks on it; and he sat on it. Many people spread their cloaks on the road, and others spread leafy branches that they had cut in the fields. Then those who went ahead and those who followed were shouting,
"Hosanna!
Blessed is the one who comes
in the name of the Lord!
Blessed is the coming kingdom
of our ancestor David!
Hosanna in the highest heaven!"

REFLECTION

Cinematic depictions of the triumphal entry into Jerusalem portray a grand spectacle of singing throngs of people. Scripture scholars point out that there were probably only a few followers accompanying the backwater prophet into Jerusalem. It is only with the eyes of faith that we recognize Jesus as king. He is, after all, nothing like the kings of earth.

PRAYERS *others may be added*

Shouting for joy before our king,
we pray:

◆ Make haste to help us!

That the baptized may acclaim their humble Savior, we pray: ◆ *That the elect may rejoice in the one who comes in the name of the Lord, we pray:* ◆ *That leaders of nations may embrace the lowly kingship of Jesus, we pray:* ◆ *That the poor may find hope in King David's son, we pray:* ◆ *That we who acclaim Jesus as king may also embrace the throne of the cross, we pray:* ◆

Our Father . . .

Strength of King David,
how blessed the one
who comes in your name!
Loose our tongues
to proclaim Christ's coming
and praise you in his name.
May we see the return in glory
of the king who was enthroned
on the cross, Jesus Christ,
who lives and reigns with you,
in the unity of the Holy Spirit,
one God, forever and ever. Amen.

✠ *O God, do not forsake us.*
We place all our trust in you.

✠ *O God, do not forsake us.*
We place all our trust in you.

PSALM 22 *page 409*

READING *Isaiah 53:1–4*

Who has believed what we have heard?
  And to whom has the arm
    of the LORD been revealed?
For God's servant grew up before him
    like a young plant,
  and like a root out of dry ground;
he had no form or majesty
    that we should look at him,
  nothing in his appearance
    that we should desire him.
He was despised and rejected
    by others;
  a man of suffering and acquainted
    with infirmity;
and as one from whom others
    hide their faces
  he was despised, and we held him
    of no account.
Surely he has borne our infirmities
  and carried our diseases;
yet we accounted him stricken,
  struck down by God, and afflicted.

REFLECTION

*Today we begin the first reading from
Good Friday's celebration of the Lord's
Passion, taken from one of the prophet
Isaiah's Songs of the Suffering Servant.
The language is poignant, regretful: We
have ignored God's servant, missed the
point, failed to recognize what he has done
for us. Isaiah's song is a lament, yet filled
with praise for what God has done, and
continues to do, in Jesus.*

PRAYERS *others may be added*

Struck with awe, we pray:

◆ Make haste to help us!

*That the Church may announce all that
God has done through the Suffering
Servant, we pray:* ◆ *That nations may
turn away from earthly majesty and
embrace the beauty of God's servant,
we pray:* ◆ *That the despised and afflicted
of the world may be lifted up, we pray:* ◆
*That the rejected and abused may call
us to faithfulness, we pray:* ◆ *That God
may reveal to us the glory of the Crucified
One, we pray:* ◆

Our Father . . .

God of mystery,
you reveal great power
in the despised and rejected.
Open our eyes to Christ's presence
in the afflicted and condemned,
the forgotten and struck down,
that they may show us
your majestic glory,
for you live and reign
forever and ever. Amen.

✠ *O God, do not forsake us.*
We place all our trust in you.

✝ *O God, do not forsake us.*
We place all our trust in you.

PSALM 22 *page 409*

READING *Isaiah 53:7–9*

God's servant was oppressed,
    and he was afflicted,
yet he did not open his mouth;
like a lamb that is led to the slaughter,
    and like a sheep that
        before its shearers is silent,
    so he did not open his mouth.
By a perversion of justice
        he was taken away.
    Who could have imagined
        his future?
For he was cut off from the land
        of the living,
    stricken for the transgression
        of my people.
They made his grave with the wicked
    and his tomb with the rich,
although he had done no violence,
    and there was no deceit
        in his mouth.

REFLECTION *Gregory the Great*

Christ was made flesh that we might be made to possess the Spirit. He was humiliated in goodness to raise us up. He came from God to lead us to God. He appeared visibly to our eyes to show us that which is invisible. He endured blows to heal us. He sustained outrage and mockery to deliver us from eternal opprobrium. He died to give us life.

PRAYERS *others may be added*

Lamenting injustice, we pray:

◆ Make haste to help us!

For those cast out of the community of faith, we pray: ◆ *For those rejected by family and friends, we pray:* ◆ *For those condemned by perversions of justice, we pray:* ◆ *For those unable to offer protest, we pray:* ◆ *For those who speak no deceit, we pray:* ◆ *For those cut off from among the living, we pray:* ◆ *For those forgotten among the dead, we pray:* ◆

Our Father . . .

Shepherd of Israel,
like a sheep before the shearers,
and a lamb before the slaughter,
your Anointed One was silent,
accepting death for our sake.
Open our ears to the cries of those
in whom Christ suffers,
that their oppressors may be
    cast down
and your life may triumph,
for you live and reign
forever and ever. Amen.

✝ *O God, do not forsake us.*
We place all our trust in you.

✠ *O God, do not forsake us.*
We place all our trust in you.

PSALM 22   *page 409*

READING   *Isaiah 53:10–12*

Yet it was the will of the LORD
    to crush him with pain.
When you make his life an offering
    for sin,
    he shall see his offspring,
      and shall prolong his days;
through him the will of the LORD
    shall prosper.
    Out of his anguish he shall see light;
he shall find satisfaction through
    his knowledge.
    The righteous one, my servant,
      shall make many righteous,
    and he shall bear their iniquities.
Therefore I will allot him a portion
    with the great,
    and he shall divide the spoil
      with the strong;
because he poured out himself
    to death,
    and was numbered
      with the transgressors;
yet he bore the sin of many,
    and made intercession
      for the transgressors.

REFLECTION

The opening line of today's reading is disturbing: Why would God crush anyone with pain? Yet we Christians proclaim that the death of Jesus was "for us," that it destroys the power of sin and restores us to God. Does that mean we have a bloodthirsty God who demands a gruesome death to "make up" for human sinfulness? The answer is no. God desires our salvation, and in Jesus, God has come to save us. We cannot escape the mystery of the cross: When Jesus announces the kingdom of God, the powers of earth crucify him. Yet through the cross, God, in Christ, wins the final victory over death.

PRAYERS   *others may be added*

    Awestruck at God's love for us in Christ, we pray:

◆   Make haste to help us!

That those who suffer in God's service may be lifted up, we pray: ◆ *That those in anguish may be delivered, we pray:* ◆ *That those crushed in pain may find restoration, we pray:* ◆ *That those condemned may share Christ's victory, we pray:* ◆ *That we may offer our lives in obedience to God, we pray:* ◆

Our Father . . .

God of mercy,
in Christ the Righteous One,
you have restored us in grace.
Give us strength
to join ourselves to Christ's offering.
May we too intercede
for the transgressions of the world
and so come to share
    Christ's exaltation,
for he lives and reigns
for ever and ever. Amen.

✠   *O God, do not forsake us.*
    We place all our trust in you.

✦ *O God, do not forsake us.*
We place all our trust in you.

PSALM 22   *page 409*

READING   *John 13:3–9*

Jesus, knowing that the Father had given all things into his hands, and that he had come from God and was going to God, got up from the table, took off his outer robe, and tied a towel around himself. Then he poured water into a basin and began to wash the disciples' feet and to wipe them with the towel that was tied around him. He came to Simon Peter, who said to him, "Lord, are you going to wash my feet?" Jesus answered, "You do not know now what I am doing, but later you will understand." Peter said to him, "You will never wash my feet." Jesus answered, "Unless I wash you, you have no share with me." Simon Peter said to him, "Lord, not my feet only but also my hands and my head!"

REFLECTION

The Gospel of John, unlike the other three Gospels, contains no account of Jesus taking and blessing bread and wine as the celebration of the new covenant. Instead, John's author recounts the washing of feet. While the Johannine community certainly celebrated Eucharist, perhaps this passage was included as a reminder that service lies as the heart of the celebration. We who sit at table with Christ must do as he does.

PRAYERS   *others may be added*

Remembering Christ's paschal mystery, we pray:

◆ Make haste to help us!

That the Church may remain faithful to the breaking of the bread and the sharing of the cup, we pray: ◆ *That those who approach the table of the Church may take on the service it requires, we pray:* ◆ *That all people may embrace service to others, washing the feet of the lowliest among them, we pray:* ◆ *That the Church's table of charity may be a source of nourishment for the hungry and poor, we pray:* ◆ *That we may boldly proclaim the death of the Lord Jesus until he comes in glory, we pray:* ◆

Our Father . . .

God of the new covenant,
Christ's sacrifice of praise on the cross
has restored us to your mercy,
and we proclaim his death
in the breaking of the bread.
May we pour out our lives
in service to the world
and so offer you a fitting sacrifice
through Jesus Christ,
who lives and reigns with you,
in the unity of the Holy Spirit,
one God, forever and ever. Amen.

✦ *O God, do not forsake us.*
We place all our trust in you.

✠ *Holy is God, holy and strong!*
Holy immortal One,
have mercy on us!

PSALM 22   *page 409*

READING   *Hebrews 4:14–16; 5:7–9*

Since we have a great high priest who has passed through the heavens, Jesus, the Son of God, let us hold fast to our confession. For we do not have a high priest who is unable to sympathize with our weaknesses, but we have one who in every respect has been tested as we are, yet without sin. Let us therefore approach the throne of grace with boldness, so that we may receive mercy and find grace to help in time of need.

In the days of his flesh, Jesus offered up prayers and supplications, with loud cries and tears, to the one who was able to save him from death, and he was heard because of his reverent submission. Although he was a Son, he learned obedience through what he suffered; and having been made perfect, he became the source of eternal salvation for all who obey him.

REFLECTION   *Byzantine liturgy*

A dread and marvelous mystery we see come to pass this day. He whom none may touch is seized; he who looses Adam from the curse is bound. He who tries our hearts and inner thoughts is unjustly brought to trial. He who closed the abyss is shut in prison. He before whom the powers of heaven stand with trembling, stands before Pilate; the Creator is struck by the hand of a creature. He who comes to judge the living and the dead is condemned to the cross; the Destroyer of hell is enclosed in a tomb.

PRAYERS   *others may be added*

With loud cries and tears, we pray:

◆ Make haste to help us!

For all who confess the cross of Christ, we pray: ◆ *For all who will pass through Christ's cross in Baptism, we pray:* ◆ *For all who have poured out their lives in service to God, we pray:* ◆ *For all who have endured torture, we pray:* ◆ *For all who suffer anxiety and dread, we pray:* ◆ *For all who live in reverent submission to God, we pray:* ◆

Our Father . . .

God of mystery,
the horror of the cross overwhelms us,
yet when you seem profoundly absent
your love for us is most fully revealed.
Open our hearts to your mercy,
made known in the death of your Son.
May we who stand in awe
approach and embrace the cross
   of Christ,
in whom our shattered lives
have been made whole.
We ask through Jesus Christ,
   our healer,
who lives and reigns with you,
in the unity of the Holy Spirit,
one God, forever and ever. Amen.

✠ *Holy is God, holy and strong!*
Holy immortal One,
have mercy on us!

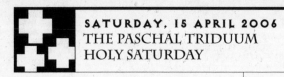
✠ *Holy is God, holy and strong!*
Holy immortal One,
have mercy on us!

PSALM 22 · page 409

READING · Romans 6:3–8

Do you not know that all of us who have been baptized into Christ Jesus were baptized into his death? Therefore we have been buried with him by baptism into death, so that, just as Christ was raised from the dead by the glory of the Father, so we too might walk in newness of life.

For if we have been united with him in a death like his, we will certainly be united with him in a resurrection like his. We know that our old self was crucified with him so that the body of sin might be destroyed, and we might no longer be enslaved to sin. For whoever has died is freed from sin. But if we have died with Christ, we believe that we will also live with him.

REFLECTION · Gregory of Nyssa

Behold the blessed Sabbath of the first creation of the world, and in that Sabbath recognize this Sabbath, the day of the Repose, which God has blessed above the other days. For on this day the only-begotten God truly rested from all his works, keeping Sabbath in the flesh by means of his death; and, returning to what he was before through his resurrection, he raised up with himself all that lay prostrate, having become Life and Resurrection and East and Dawn and Day "for those in darkness and the shadow of death."

PRAYERS · others may be added

Sharing the silence of Christ's tomb, we pray:

◆ Make haste to help us!

That the baptized may seek Christ in watchful silence, we pray: ◆ That those who will be baptized this night into Christ's death may rise to his glory, we pray: ◆ That those enslaved to sin may be liberated by Christ's saving death, we pray: ◆ That all who have shared Christ's death may share his resurrection, we pray: ◆ That we who have been baptized into Christ's death may walk in newness of life, we pray: ◆

Our Father . . .

God of stillness,
in the darkness of the tomb
we await the revelation of your glory.
Raise us up with Christ,
that we may live out our baptism
    into his death
by proclaiming the new life
you offer in him,
who lives and reigns with you,
in the unity of the Holy Spirit,
one God, forever and ever. Amen.

✠ *Holy is God, holy and strong!*
Holy immortal One,
have mercy on us!

✚ *Alleluia! Christ is risen!*
Christ is risen indeed!
Alleluia! Alleluia!

PSALM 66   page 415

READING   John 20:1–7

Early on the first day of the week, while it was still dark, Mary Magdalene came to the tomb and saw that the stone had been removed from the tomb. So she ran and went to Simon Peter and the other disciple, the one whom Jesus loved, and said to them, "They have taken the Lord out of the tomb, and we do not know where they have laid him." Then Peter and the other disciple set out and went toward the tomb. The two were running together, but the other disciple outran Peter and reached the tomb first. He bent down to look in and saw the linen wrappings lying there, but he did not go in. Then Simon Peter came, following him, and went into the tomb. He saw the linen wrappings lying there, and the cloth that had been on Jesus' head, not lying with the linen wrappings but rolled up in a place by itself.

REFLECTION

No Gospel offers an account of the Resurrection itself—only empty tombs and heavenly messengers. It seems that confusion was the first Easter experience of Jesus' disciples: a missing body and an empty hole in the ground. Yet in the ambiguity of such moments, God's glory in the Risen Christ shined through, and the world has never been the same. Perhaps that transformation can give us hope as well when we face our own times of emptiness and ambiguity.

PRAYERS   *others may be added*

Awestruck by God's wondrous deeds, we exclaim:

◆ Alleluia, alleluia!

Risen Christ, your empty tomb gives hope to your disciples, and so we exclaim: ◆ *Risen Christ, you give the neophytes new life in the waters of Baptism, and so we exclaim:* ◆ *Risen Christ, your Resurrection opens the path to life, and so we exclaim:* ◆ *Risen Christ, you transform suffering by your victory over death, and so we exclaim:* ◆ *Risen Christ, you free the dead from the bonds of mortality, and so we exclaim:* ◆ *Risen Christ, you reveal yourself among us, and so we exclaim:* ◆

Our Father . . .

Powerful and glorious God,
your love endures forever.
Raise us in joy with Christ,
that we may marvel
    at your life-giving power
and proclaim to the world
that Christ is risen indeed,
for he lives and reigns with you
in the unity of the Holy Spirit,
one God forever and ever. Amen.

✚ *Alleluia! Christ is risen!*
Christ is risen indeed!
Alleluia! Alleluia!

✤ *Alleluia! Christ is risen!*
Christ is risen indeed!
Alleluia! Alleluia!

PSALM 66   *page 415*

READING   *John 20:11–14*

But Mary stood weeping outside the tomb. As she wept, she bent over to look into the tomb; and she saw two angels in white, sitting where the body of Jesus had been lying, one at the head and the other at the feet. They said to her, "Woman, why are you weeping?" She said to them, "They have taken away my Lord, and I do not know where they have laid him." When she had said this, she turned around and saw Jesus standing there, but she did not know that it was Jesus.

REFLECTION

Perhaps we wonder why Mary couldn't recognize Jesus when he appeared before her. The Gospel of John isn't the only one that "disguises" the risen Jesus; in the Gospel of Luke, the disciples on the road to Emmaus are also constrained from recognizing Christ. Perhaps the Gospels are reminding us that there is something both new and elusive in resurrection; something that is not easy to understand or recognize. The Risen One may be standing before us when we are unaware, inviting us to faith and joy.

PRAYERS   *others may be added*

The Risen One breaks through our confusion and fear. In joy, we cry:

◆ Alleluia, alleluia!

Risen Christ, you are present to your people in their fear and uncertainty, and so we cry: ◆ *Risen Christ, you reveal the source of life to the newly baptized, and so we cry:* ◆ *Risen Christ, you show God's glory to all the world, and so we cry:* ◆ *Risen Christ, you reassure the sorrowful with your hidden presence, and so we cry:* ◆ *Risen Christ, you dry our tears with the light of your love, and so we cry:* ◆

Our Father . . .

Surprising God,
your generosity overwhelms us,
and we dare not believe
what we see with our eyes.
Give us courage to embrace
the great gift you offer us
in Christ's resurrection.
May we dare to hope
that we will share his glory,
for Christ lives and reigns with you,
in the unity of the Holy Spirit,
one God, forever and ever. Amen.

✤ *Alleluia! Christ is risen!*
Christ is risen indeed!
Alleluia! Alleluia!

✤ *Alleluia! Christ is risen!*
Christ is risen indeed!
Alleluia! Alleluia!

PSALM 66   *page 415*

READING   *John 20:15–18*

Jesus said to Mary, "Woman, why are you weeping? Whom are you looking for?" Supposing him to be the gardener, she said to him, "Sir, if you have carried him away, tell me where you have laid him, and I will take him away." Jesus said to her, "Mary!" She turned and said to him in Hebrew, *"Rabbouni!"* (which means Teacher). Jesus said to her, "Do not hold on to me, because I have not yet ascended to the Father. But go to my brothers and say to them, 'I am ascending to my Father and your Father, to my God and your God.'" Mary Magdalene went and announced to the disciples, "I have seen the Lord"; and she told them that he had said these things to her.

REFLECTION

Mary's encounter with the risen Jesus reminds us that his Resurrection is an experience of faith, an encounter with God's undefeatable love and Christ's victory over death. The disciples did not proclaim Jesus was alive because his body was missing; they announced his Resurrection because they experienced him alive and present to them. That experience was not limited to those first believers; we too must experience the living Jesus if we are to truly proclaim him raised from the dead.

PRAYERS   *others may be added*

Our joy overwhelms our sorrow, and we proclaim:

◆ Alleluia, alleluia!

Risen Christ, you astound your Church with your glory, and so we proclaim: ◆
Risen Christ, you invite the baptized to experience your life, and so we proclaim: ◆
Risen Christ, you defeat the forces of sin and death, and so we proclaim: ◆
Risen Christ, you comfort the grieving with your everlasting joy, and so we proclaim: ◆ *Risen Christ, you inspire the sick with hope, and so we proclaim:* ◆
Risen Christ, you send us out to announce your Good News, and so we proclaim: ◆

Our Father . . .

God of boundless joy,
you overcame Mary's sorrow,
and she rejoiced in the risen Lord.
Reveal to us your Risen One
that we too may proclaim with joy,
"We have seen the Lord,"
for Christ lives and reigns with you,
in the unity of the Holy Spirit,
one God, forever and ever. Amen.

✤ *Alleluia! Christ is risen!*
Christ is risen indeed!
Alleluia! Alleluia!

✦ *Alleluia! Christ is risen!*
Christ is risen indeed!
Alleluia! Alleluia!

PSALM 66   page 415

READING   John 21:1–7

After these things Jesus showed himself again to the disciples by the Sea of Tiberias; and he showed himself in this way. Gathered there together were Simon Peter, Thomas called the Twin, Nathanael of Cana in Galilee, the sons of Zebedee, and two others of his disciples. Simon Peter said to them, "I am going fishing." They said to him, "We will go with you." They went out and got into the boat, but that night they caught nothing.

Just after daybreak, Jesus stood on the beach; but the disciples did not know that it was Jesus. Jesus said to them, "Children, you have no fish, have you?" They answered him, "No." He said to them, "Cast the net to the right side of the boat, and you will find some." So they cast it, and now they were not able to haul it in because there were so many fish. That disciple whom Jesus loved said to Peter, "It is the Lord!" When Simon Peter heard that it was the Lord, he put on some clothes, for he was naked, and jumped into the sea.

REFLECTION

The Gospel writer's remark about Peter's nakedness may seem out of place; who cares what Peter was wearing (or wasn't wearing) when Jesus appeared? Maybe even more puzzling is why Peter put his clothes back on before he jumped in the water! Perhaps the remark is merely practical, but there might be something deeper as well. Back in Genesis, after Adam and Eve had eaten the forbidden fruit, they covered themselves out of guilt. Peter, too, whose betrayal Jesus is now exposed, also covers himself before the risen Christ.

PRAYERS   *others may be added*

Praising God, we cry:

◆ Alleluia, alleluia!

Risen Christ, you call to your people with love, and so we cry: ◆ *Risen Christ, you offer abundance of God's grace, and so we cry:* ◆ *Risen Christ, you catch the attention of the distracted and self-absorbed, and so we cry:* ◆ *Risen Christ, you surprise us with your presence, and so we cry:* ◆ *Risen Christ, you fill our hearts with joy, and so we cry:* ◆

Our Father . . .

God of wonder,
the Risen One walks among us,
revealing himself to those he loves.
Inspire us with eagerness
that we may greet with joy
the presence of the Living One
in our brothers and sisters,
for Christ lives and reigns with you,
in the unity of the Holy Spirit,
one God, forever and ever. Amen.

✦ *Alleluia! Christ is risen!*
Christ is risen indeed!
Alleluia! Alleluia!

✠ *Alleluia! Christ is risen!*
Christ is risen indeed!
Alleluia! Alleluia!

PSALM 66 *page 415*

READING *John 21:8–14*

The other disciples came in the boat, dragging the net full of fish, for they were not far from the land, only about a hundred yards off. When they had gone ashore, they saw a charcoal fire there, with fish on it, and bread. Jesus said to them, "Bring some of the fish that you have just caught." So Simon Peter went aboard and hauled the net ashore, full of large fish, a hundred fifty-three of them; and though there were so many, the net was not torn. Jesus said to them, "Come and have breakfast." Now none of the disciples dared to ask him, "Who are you?" because they knew it was the Lord. Jesus came and took the bread and gave it to them, and did the same with the fish. This was now the third time that Jesus appeared to the disciples after he was raised from the dead.

REFLECTION

Today's passage from the Gospel of John is an allusion to the Easter mystery of the Eucharist. At Christ's table, all nations are gathered, perhaps symbolized in the abundance of fish gathered in the unbroken net. The net itself is a fruitful symbol of the Church: large enough to gather a great multitude and strong enough to hold a great diversity.

PRAYERS *others may be added*

We know the Risen One in the sharing of food: In joy, we cry:

◆ Alleluia, alleluia!

Risen Christ, you sustain your Church with a holy meal, and so we cry: ◆
Risen Christ, you invite the newly baptized to come to salvation's table, and so we cry: ◆ *Risen Christ, you gather all nations around one table, and so we cry:* ◆
Risen Christ, you sustain the hungry with food for eternal life, and so we cry: ◆
Risen Christ, you offer us the gift of yourself, and so we cry: ◆

Our Father . . .

God of nourishment,
you provide for us
rich fare for life eternal.
Make known to us the Risen One
in our sharing of food,
that we may in turn
give generously
to all in need.
We ask this through the Risen Christ,
the bread for our journey,
who lives and reigns with you,
in the unity of the Holy Spirit,
one God, forever and ever. Amen.

✠ *Alleluia! Christ is risen!*
Christ is risen indeed!
Alleluia! Alleluia!

✙ *Alleluia! Christ is risen!*
Christ is risen indeed!
Alleluia! Alleluia!

PSALM 66   page 415

READING   *John 21:15–18*

When they had finished breakfast, Jesus said to Simon Peter, "Simon son of John, do you love me more than these?" He said to him, "Yes, Lord; you know that I love you." Jesus said to him, "Feed my lambs." A second time he said to him, "Simon son of John, do you love me?" He said to him, "Yes, Lord; you know that I love you." Jesus said to him, "Tend my sheep." He said to him the third time, "Simon son of John, do you love me?" Peter felt hurt because he said to him the third time, "Do you love me?" And he said to him, "Lord, you know everything; you know that I love you." Jesus said to him, "Feed my sheep. Very truly, I tell you, when you were younger, you used to fasten your own belt and to go wherever you wished. But when you grow old, you will stretch out your hands, and someone else will fasten a belt around you and take you where you do not wish to go."

REFLECTION

Again the Gospel passage breaks opens the meaning of Eucharist. Even before Peter has the opportunity to reconcile with Jesus, Jesus invites Peter to share his meal. The shared meal has reconciling power; even though Peter's betrayal was great, the power of the meal is greater, and it paves the way to this poignant encounter. For the Gospel writer, one does not have to be worthy to share a meal with Jesus, only invited. The meal itself, and the relationship with Christ it fosters, restores what has been broken.

PRAYERS   *others may be added*

Embracing the reconciliation offered by Christ, we proclaim:

◆ Alleluia, alleluia!

Risen Christ, you restore fellowship broken by infidelity, and so we proclaim: ◆
Risen Christ, you ask love and faithfulness of the baptized, and so we proclaim: ◆
Risen Christ, you see to the needs of those entrusted to your care, and so we proclaim: ◆ *Risen Christ, you offer your glory to those who share your cross, and so we proclaim:* ◆ *Risen Christ, you forgive us for the times we deny you, and so we proclaim:* ◆

Our Father . . .

God of gentle mercy,
three times Peter denied Christ,
yet three times professed his love.
Extend to us your saving mercy,
that we too may offer forgiveness
to all those in need.
We ask this through Christ,
who lives and reigns with you,
in the unity of the Holy Spirit,
one God, forever and ever. Amen.

✙ *Alleluia! Christ is risen!*
Christ is risen indeed!
Alleluia! Alleluia!

✠ *Alleluia! Christ is risen!*
Christ is risen indeed!
Alleluia! Alleluia!

PSALM 66   page 415

READING   John 20:19–23

When it was evening on that day, the first day of the week, and the doors of the house where the disciples had met were locked for fear of the Jews, Jesus came and stood among them and said, "Peace be with you." After he said this, he showed them his hands and his side. Then the disciples rejoiced when they saw the Lord. Jesus said to them again, "Peace be with you. As the Father has sent me, so I send you." When he had said this, he breathed on them and said to them, "Receive the Holy Spirit. If you forgive the sins of any, they are forgiven them; if you retain the sins of any, they are retained."

REFLECTION

Jesus' commissioning of the frightened disciples "on that day" offers some guidance into the purpose and meaning of the Resurrection. Risen life is not something we keep to ourselves; it is not the destiny of a chosen few. Instead, those who know the living Christ are sent just as he was: to proclaim peace, to reconcile, and to spread the Good News in the Spirit's power. We can no more remain behind the walls of our parishes or homes than those first followers could stay locked in the upper room. We too are sent to offer what we have received.

PRAYERS   others may be added

Embracing the Spirit of Christ's peace, we exclaim:

◆ Alleluia, alleluia!

Risen Christ, you empower your Church to forgive sins, and so we exclaim: ◆
Risen Christ, you fill the neophytes with the gift of your Spirit, and so we exclaim: ◆
Risen Christ, you offer God's mercy to the world, and so we exclaim: ◆
Risen Christ, you comfort the fearful and anxious, and so we exclaim: ◆
Risen Christ, you send us forth in your service, and so we exclaim: ◆

Our Father . . .

God of lasting peace,
though anxiety surrounds us,
the Risen Christ appears,
offering peace in the Spirit.
Break down the walls
of fear and exclusion
that keep us from proclaiming
your gift of forgiveness:
May we carry to all the world
the life you offer in Jesus Christ,
who is risen indeed,
and lives and reigns with you,
in the unity of the Holy Spirit,
one God, forever and ever. Amen.

✠ *Alleluia! Christ is risen!*
Christ is risen indeed!
Alleluia! Alleluia!

✝ *Alleluia! Christ is risen!*
Christ is risen indeed!
Alleluia! Alleluia!

PSALM 66 page 415

READING *John 20:24–29*

But Thomas (who was called the Twin), one of the twelve, was not with them when Jesus came. So the other disciples told him, "We have seen the Lord." But he said to them, "Unless I see the mark of the nails in his hands, and put my finger in the mark of the nails and my hand in his side, I will not believe."

A week later his disciples were again in the house, and Thomas was with them. Although the doors were shut, Jesus came and stood among them and said, "Peace be with you." Then he said to Thomas, "Put your finger here and see my hands. Reach out your hand and put it in my side. Do not doubt but believe." Thomas answered him, "My Lord and my God!" Jesus said to him, "Have you believed because you have seen me? Blessed are those who have not seen and yet have come to believe."

REFLECTION

During this octave of Easter the Gospel speaks of us directly, those who "have not seen and yet have come to believe." Although we were not present to see the Risen One, in our forebears in faith we were there. Christ's Resurrection and the Church's experience of it stretch through and beyond time, joining into one great multitude those who share faith in Christ. We who have been baptized are one, not because we occupy the same place in history, but because we share the same destiny: eternal life forever in the Resurrection.

PRAYERS *others may be added*

The glory of God overcomes our doubt; joyfully, we exclaim:

◆ Alleluia, alleluia!

Risen Christ, you strengthen your Church with confidence in your presence, and so we exclaim: ◆ *Risen Christ, you bless the neophytes, who have not seen but believe, and so we exclaim:* ◆ *Risen Christ, you call the world's people to faith, and so we exclaim:* ◆ *Risen Christ, you transform in your wounds the suffering of the poor and oppressed, and so we exclaim:* ◆ *Risen Christ, you dispel our doubt, and give us faith, and so we exclaim:* ◆

Our Father . . .

God of our future,
you join as one all who share
the hope of life eternal.
Bind together in charity
all those baptized in Christ
that people of every nation and race
may proclaim Christ as Lord and God,
for he lives and reigns with you
in the unity of the Holy Spirit,
one God forever and ever. Amen.

✝ *Alleluia! Christ is risen!*
Christ is risen indeed!
Alleluia! Alleluia!

✠ *Alleluia! Christ is risen!*
Christ is risen indeed!
Alleluia! Alleluia!

PSALM 66 *page 415*

READING *Acts 2:14a, 22–27*

Peter, standing with the eleven, raised his voice and addressed the crowd, "You that are Israelites, listen to what I have to say: Jesus of Nazareth, a man attested to you by God with deeds of power, wonders, and signs that God did through him among you, as you yourselves know—this man, handed over to you according to the definite plan and foreknowledge of God, you crucified and killed by the hands of those outside the law. But God raised him up, having freed him from death, because it was impossible for him to be held in its power. For David says concerning him, 'I saw the Lord always before me, for he is at my right hand so that I will not be shaken; therefore my heart was glad, and my tongue rejoiced; moreover my flesh will live in hope. For you will not abandon my soul to Hades, or let your Holy One experience corruption.'"

REFLECTION

Throughout the Easter season we will be reading the early Church's proclamation of faith in Jesus Christ as recounted in the Acts of the Apostles. Acts was probably written between the years 80 and 90 AD, and like the Gospel accounts, it is a combination of history and theology. The book tells us how a particular Christian community existed in a particular time and place, and how its author hoped the Church might one day be in every time and place: a community of charity and mission, formed by faith in the risen Christ.

PRAYERS *others may be added*

Ready to proclaim God's deeds in Christ, we pray:

♦ Hear our prayer, God our joy.

That the Church may boldly announce the new life offered in Christ, we pray: ♦ *That the nations may open their hearts to God's messengers, we pray:* ♦ *That all people may behold God's work in Jesus, we pray:* ♦ *That those who work for justice may have confidence in God's presence, we pray:* ♦ *That we may courageously profess our faith in Christ's resurrection, we pray:* ♦

Our Father . . .

Faithful God,
you inspired the apostles
to share their faith in the Risen One.
Give us courage to be witnesses
to the life you offer in Christ
that we too may fearlessly proclaim
the One who has reconciled the world
    to you,
who lives and reigns
forever and ever. Amen.

✠ *Alleluia! Christ is risen!*
Christ is risen indeed!
Alleluia! Alleluia!

✠ *Alleluia! Christ is risen!*
  Christ is risen indeed!
  Alleluia! Alleluia!

PSALM 66   page 415

READING   Mark 16:15–20

And Jesus said to the eleven, "Go into all the world and proclaim the good news to the whole creation. The one who believes and is baptized will be saved; but the one who does not believe will be condemned. And these signs will accompany those who believe: by using my name they will cast out demons; they will speak in new tongues; they will pick up snakes in their hands, and if they drink any deadly thing, it will not hurt them; they will lay their hands on the sick, and they will recover."

So then the Lord Jesus, after he had spoken to them, was taken up into heaven and sat down at the right hand of God. And they went out and proclaimed the good news everywhere, while the Lord worked with them and confirmed the message by the signs that accompanied it.

REFLECTION

On this feast of Saint Mark the evangelist, we hear the Risen One's fundamental charge: Go into all the world and proclaim the Good News in both word and deed. Today, Yom HaShoah or Holocaust Memorial Day, we recall a great failure to do just that. Though the greater burden of guilt for the Holocaust lies with those who formulated and carried out Hitler's "final solution," the deafening silence of many Christians cannot be overlooked. Especially in times of violent insanity, the Gospel must be proclaimed more insistently, even though its dangerous message may bring death to the messenger.

PRAYERS   others may be added

Accepting the command of Jesus to proclaim the Good News, we pray:

◆ Hear our prayer, God our joy.

That all God's people may embrace Christ's charge to proclaim the Gospel, we pray: ◆ *That Christ may fill the neophytes with courage to bear witness to the good news, we pray:* ◆ *That the sick may be healed in body and spirit through the ministry of Jesus' disciples, we pray:* ◆ *That our proclamation of the Gospel may cast out the demons of injustice, prejudice, and hatred, we pray:* ◆

Our Father . . .

God of mission,
you send us forth
to proclaim your word,
and confirm your message within us.
Embolden us to shout the Good News
when evil threatens to take hold,
that in both word and deed
we may be faithful to the One
who was crucified and raised,
Jesus Christ, who lives and reigns
forever and ever. Amen.

✠ *Alleluia! Christ is risen!*
  Christ is risen indeed!
  Alleluia! Alleluia!

✝ *Alleluia! Christ is risen!*
  Christ is risen indeed!
  Alleluia! Alleluia!

PSALM 66   *page 415*

READING   *Acts 2:32–36*

Peter continued, saying, "This Jesus God raised up, and of that all of us are witnesses. Being therefore exalted at the right hand of God, and having received from the Father the promise of the Holy Spirit, he has poured out this that you both see and hear. For David did not ascend into the heavens, but he himself says, 'The Lord said to my Lord, "Sit at my right hand, until I make your enemies your footstool."' Therefore let the entire house of Israel know with certainty that God has made him both Lord and Messiah, this Jesus whom you crucified."

REFLECTION

Today's selection from Acts continues Monday's reading of Peter's speech to those gathered on Pentecost. Jews from all over the world had witnessed the apostles' strange behavior after they received the Holy Spirit (Acts 2:–12), and Peter seeks to explain what has happened: The Jesus who was crucified is now exalted, and the Holy Spirit testifies through the apostles to God's action in him. That same Spirit testifies in us today, and we are called to proclaim our faith as well.

PRAYERS   *others may be added*

Professing our faith in Jesus as Lord and Messiah, we pray:

◆ Hear our prayer, God our joy.

For all God's people, witnesses to the exaltation of the crucified Christ, we pray: ◆ *For preachers and missionaries, fearless prophets of God's work in Jesus, we pray:* ◆ *For neophytes, vessels of God's abundant Spirit, we pray:* ◆ *For those beaten down by poverty, living signs of Christ's suffering, we pray:* ◆ *For us, disciples of the one made Lord and Messiah, we pray:* ◆

Our Father . . .

God of glory,
you have made Jesus Christ,
    the crucified,
both Lord and Messiah.
Fill us with hope in the resurrection,
that we may be your witnesses
to all those in need
    of your Good News.
We ask this in the name
    of Jesus Christ,
hope of the hopeless,
who lives and reigns
forever and ever. Amen.

✝ *Alleluia! Christ is risen!*
  Christ is risen indeed!
  Alleluia! Alleluia!

✝ *Alleluia! Christ is risen!*
Christ is risen indeed!
Alleluia! Alleluia!

PSALM 66 page 415

READING Acts 2:37–42

Now when those gathered heard this, they were cut to the heart and said to Peter and to the other apostles, "Brothers, what should we do?" Peter said to them, "Repent, and be baptized every one of you in the name of Jesus Christ so that your sins may be forgiven; and you will receive the gift of the Holy Spirit. For the promise is for you, for your children, and for all who are far away, everyone whom the Lord our God calls to him." And he testified with many other arguments and exhorted them, saying, "Save yourselves from this corrupt generation." So those who welcomed his message were baptized, and that day about three thousand persons were added. They devoted themselves to the apostles' teaching and fellowship, to the breaking of bread and the prayers.

REFLECTION

Acts has "the Jews" who hear Peter admit their guilt and repent. It is important to remember that Acts was written after most Jewish Christians had left the synagogue. Indeed, in some places Jewish Christians had been cast out with a great deal of acrimony. Relationships between Jews and Christians have developed over the centuries, however, and today the Church rejects the belief that the Jewish people are responsible for the death of Jesus. It is the Catholic belief that God's covenant with the Jewish people still endures today.

PRAYERS others may be added

Ready to welcome others into the Body of Christ, we pray:

◆ Hear our prayer, God our joy.

That the Church may welcome people of all races and nations to the waters of salvation, we pray: ◆ *That those newly born into Christ may draw ever more closely to the Risen One, we pray:* ◆ *That the Jewish people may remain faithful to God's covenant with them, we pray:* ◆ *That nations in conflict may seek forgiveness and reconciliation, we pray:* ◆ *That we may open our hearts to correction, always ready to be reconciled to God, we pray:* ◆

Our Father . . .

God of mercy,
the words of your messengers
cut us to the heart
and leave us in need of your mercy.
Forgive us for our failure to live
as children of the Resurrection.
May our celebration of Easter
make us more faithful citizens
of the New Jerusalem,
where Christ lives and reigns
forever and ever. Amen.

✝ *Alleluia! Christ is risen!*
Christ is risen indeed!
Alleluia! Alleluia!

✤ *Alleluia! Christ is risen!*
  Christ is risen indeed!
  Alleluia! Alleluia!

PSALM 66   *page 415*

READING   *Acts 2:43–47*

Awe came upon everyone, because many wonders and signs were being done by the apostles. All who believed were together and had all things in common; they would sell their possessions and goods and distribute the proceeds to all, as any had need. Day by day, as they spent much time together in the temple, they broke bread at home and ate their food with glad and generous hearts, praising God and having the goodwill of all the people. And day by day the Lord added to their number those who were being saved.

REFLECTION

In today's reading, the picture of the early Christian community sounds almost too good to be true! How often do we hear of such generosity in our society? Regardless of whether this is an accurate portrait of the first Christians, Acts offers us a vision of what the Church and the world could be.

PRAYERS   *others may be added*

As good stewards of God's abundant gifts, we pray:

◆ Hear our prayer, God our joy.

That God's people may teach the nations how to be good stewards of creation, we pray: ◆ *That the newly baptized may have cause to wonder at God's grace in their lives, we pray:* ◆ *That the wealthy of the world may become rich in generosity, we pray:* ◆ *That any in need may receive what is justly theirs, we pray:* ◆ *That we may praise God joyfully in our homes, churches, and places of work, we pray:* ◆

Our Father . . .

Creator of heaven and earth,
through the hands of your servants
you work mighty deeds,
and new members are added
to the Body of your Son.
Work within us great deeds of justice,
that we may glorify you
in lives of service and stewardship,
and so bring others to praise you
through the Risen Christ,
who lives and reigns
forever and ever. Amen.

✤ *Alleluia! Christ is risen!*
  Christ is risen indeed!
  Alleluia! Alleluia!

✝ *Alleluia! Christ is risen!*
Christ is risen indeed!
Alleluia! Alleluia!

PSALM 66 *page 415*

READING *Acts 4:32–35*

Now the whole group of those who believed were of one heart and soul, and no one claimed private ownership of any possessions, but everything they owned was held in common. With great power the apostles gave their testimony to the resurrection of the Lord Jesus, and great grace was upon them all. There was not a needy person among them, for as many as owned lands or houses sold them and brought the proceeds of what was sold. They laid it at the apostles' feet, and it was distributed to each as any had need.

REFLECTION *Catherine of Siena*

Eternal Trinity, you are the Creator, I the creature. I have come to know, the new creation you made of me in the blood of your Son, that you are in love with the beauty of your creature.

O eternal Trinity, God, you are an abyss, a deep sea; you have given yourself to me—what greater could you give? You are a fire, ever burning and never consumed, consuming in your heat all the self-love of the soul, taking away all coldness. By your light you enlighten our minds, as by your light you have brought me to know your truth.

PRAYERS *others may be added*

Inspired by holy Catherine, we pray:

◆ Hear our prayer, God our joy.

For theologians who break open the mystery of salvation, we pray: ◆
For counselors who guide leaders in making good decisions, we pray: ◆
For spiritual directors who walk with others on their journey to God, we pray: ◆
For lay ministers who serve the Church with dedication, we pray: ◆ *For all who seek to follow Christ more closely in prayer and service, we pray:* ◆

Our Father . . .

Wisdom of the saints,
in Saint Catherine
your Church found a holy model
and its shepherds
a wise and faithful counselor.
By her prayers
give us insight into your mystery,
that we may grow in love of you
and in service of our neighbor.
This we ask in Jesus' name,
Gentle First Truth,
now and forever. Amen.

✝ *Alleluia! Christ is risen!*
Christ is risen indeed!
Alleluia! Alleluia!

✛ *Alleluia! Christ is risen!*
Christ is risen indeed!
Alleluia! Alleluia!

PSALM 66   page 415

READING   Luke 24:35–43

Then the disciples told what had happened on the road, and how he had been made known to them in the breaking of the bread. While they were talking about this, Jesus himself stood among them and said to them, "Peace be with you." They were startled and terrified, and thought that they were seeing a ghost. He said to them, "Why are you frightened, and why do doubts arise in your hearts? Look at my hands and my feet; see that it is I myself. Touch me and see; for a ghost does not have flesh and bones as you see that I have." And when he had said this, he showed them his hands and his feet. While in their joy they were disbelieving and still wondering, he said to them, "Have you anything here to eat?" They gave him a piece of broiled fish, and he took it and ate in their presence.

REFLECTION

Eating a piece of broiled fish seems a little underwhelming as a sign of risen life, but there's a point to it. The exalted and resurrected Jesus is the same Jesus who died on the cross. Even in Resurrection, Christ still has a human, though exalted, body; he is not some disembodied spirit but a real living person. We Christians don't separate "soul" and "body"; we aren't dualists who value one over the other. We are created as enfleshed spirits and ensouled bodies, and our final destiny includes both body and spirit.

PRAYERS   others may be added

Startled by God's glory shining in the Risen One, we pray:

◆ Hear our prayer, God our joy.

That the baptized may share the peace they have found in the Risen One, we pray: ◆ *That fear and doubt may be cast from the hearts of the neophytes, we pray:* ◆ *That all nations may find cause to rejoice in the God of salvation, we pray:* ◆ *That we may be startled by the presence of Christ shining in the needy, we pray:* ◆ *That we may find hope and joy in the presence of Christ among us, we pray:* ◆

Our Father . . .

We praise you, God of wonder,
for in Christ you have
startled us with joy
and cast out our fear.
Give us courage to proclaim
    our Easter faith:
May we recognize and serve the Christ
in the poor and oppressed
and so one day come to touch and see
the Risen One face to face,
for Christ lives and reigns with you,
in the unity of the Holy Spirit,
one God, forever and ever. Amen.

✛ *Alleluia! Christ is risen!*
Christ is risen indeed!
Alleluia! Alleluia!

✠ *Alleluia! Christ is risen!*
Christ is risen indeed!
Alleluia! Alleluia!

PSALM 66 — page 415

READING — Acts 3:1–2a, 3–8

One day Peter and John were going up to the temple at the hour of prayer, at three o'clock in the afternoon. And a man lame from birth was being carried in. When he saw Peter and John about to go into the temple, he asked them for alms. Peter looked intently at him, as did John, and said, "Look at us." And he fixed his attention on them, expecting to receive something from them. But Peter said, "I have no silver or gold, but what I have I give you; in the name of Jesus Christ of Nazareth, stand up and walk." And he took him by the right hand and raised him up; and immediately his feet and ankles were made strong. Jumping up, he stood and began to walk, and he entered the temple with them, walking and leaping and praising God.

REFLECTION

We might dismiss the miracles of scripture as either fantastic stories meant to attract believers or works of power made possible only by the great Spirit-driven faith of the apostles. To do so misses the point. We are no less Spirit-inspired today, and no less called to free our brothers and sisters from disease and the isolation that comes with it. What great works might be accomplished if we dared enter nursing homes, hospices, or mental health wards? Might we too find God's power to restore relationships, heal bodies and spirits, and make people whole once more?

PRAYERS — others may be added

Rejoicing in Christ's power to make whole, we pray:

◆ Hear our prayer, God our joy.

That God's people may proclaim the healing offered in Christ, we pray: ◆
That ministers of care may bring God's compassion to the sick, we pray: ◆
That persons with disabilities may offer their gifts to Church and society, we pray: ◆ *That those who beg may receive mercy and help, we pray:* ◆
That we may generously offer what we have received in Christ Jesus, we pray: ◆

Our Father . . .

God of freedom,
in Christ's Resurrection
you promise release
from our brokenness.
Give us courage to embrace
the weakness that makes us human,
that through it we may be made whole
and so glorify you through
    the Risen One
who lives and reigns
forever and ever. Amen.

✠ *Alleluia! Christ is risen!*
Christ is risen indeed!
Alleluia! Alleluia!

✚ *Alleluia! Christ is risen!*
Christ is risen indeed!
Alleluia! Alleluia!

PSALM 66   *page 415*

READING   *Acts 3:11–16*

While the man who was crippled clung to Peter and John, all the people ran together to them in the portico called Solomon's Portico, utterly astonished. When Peter saw it, he addressed the people, "You Israelites, why do you wonder at this, or why do you stare at us, as though by our own power or piety we had made him walk? The God of Abraham, the God of Isaac, and the God of Jacob, the God of our ancestors has glorified his servant Jesus, whom you handed over and rejected in the presence of Pilate, though he had decided to release him. But you rejected the Holy and Righteous One and asked to have a murderer given to you, and you killed the Author of life, whom God raised from the dead. To this we are witnesses. And by faith in his name, his name itself has made this man strong, whom you see and know; and the faith that is through Jesus has given him this perfect health in the presence of all of you."

REFLECTION

Looking past Peter's harsh words to the crowds, we find a belief that lies at the heart of being Christian. As Peter points out, it is not his or John's power or piety that healed "the man who was crippled"; rather, it was God's power joined with human faith that restored him. When we join ourselves to God's plan for humanity, not only will we be restored, we will behold the fullness of the Resurrection, when creation itself will be transformed, when God will be "all in all" (1 Corinthians 15:28).

PRAYERS   *others may be added*

Trusting in the power of God's Holy and Righteous One, we pray:

◆ Hear our prayer, God our joy.

That God's people may be signs of faith in the name of Jesus, we pray: ◆ *That the neophytes may wonder at what God has done in Jesus, we pray:* ◆ *That the world's people may serve the Author of Life in all that they do, we pray:* ◆ *That the sick may find in Jesus, health in body and spirit, we pray:* ◆ *That we may embrace more closely our faith in the one God raised to life, we pray:* ◆

Our Father . . .

God of our ancestors,
you raised Christ to be
the source of our salvation.
Bless us with faith in your Anointed,
that in his name
we may be made strong
as witnesses of his life,
for he lives and reigns
forever and ever. Amen.

✚ *Alleluia! Christ is risen!*
Christ is risen indeed!
Alleluia! Alleluia!

✠ *Alleluia! Christ is risen!*
Christ is risen indeed!
Alleluia! Alleluia!

PSALM 66   *page 415*

READING   *1 Corinthians 15:1–8*

Now I would remind you, brothers and sisters, of the good news that I proclaimed to you, which you in turn received, in which also you stand, through which also you are being saved, if you hold firmly to the message that I proclaimed to you—unless you have come to believe in vain. For I handed on to you as of first importance what I in turn had received: that Christ died for our sins in accordance with the scriptures, and that he was buried, and that he was raised on the third day in accordance with the scriptures, and that he appeared to Cephas, then to the twelve. Then he appeared to more than five hundred brothers and sisters at one time, most of whom are still alive, though some have died. Then he appeared to James, then to all the apostles. Last of all, as to one untimely born, he appeared also to me.

REFLECTION

Today we celebrate two of the twelve apostles. Yet as Paul points out, the apostolic ministry is not restricted to the Twelve. For Paul and the ancient Church, being an apostle meant being a witness to the Resurrection of Christ. For us, some 2,000 years later, the Good News continues to be evangelized through the apostolic ministry of our bishops, and the discipleship of the
clergy, religious, and lay faithful who bear witness to the great faith "that Christ died . . . was buried . . . was raised on the third day."

PRAYERS   *others may be added*

Accepting the testimony of the apostles to the Resurrection, we pray:

◆ Hear our prayer, God our joy.

For bishops and all who share the apostolic ministry, we pray: ◆
For pastors, preachers, catechists, and all who pass on the Christian message, we pray: ◆ *For all who hand on the Good News among the poor and those in need, we pray:* ◆ *For neophytes and all who have embraced the Gospel, we pray:* ◆ *For all those called to hand on the faith they have received, we pray:* ◆

Our Father . . .

God of life,
in every age you bless your Church
with ministers to hand on
the Gospel of Jesus Christ.
May all share the Good News to the
     ends of the earth.
We ask this in the name of
     Jesus Christ,
who lives and reigns
     forever and ever. Amen.

✠ *Alleluia! Christ is risen!*
Christ is risen indeed!
Alleluia! Alleluia!

✚ *Alleluia! Christ is risen!*
Christ is risen indeed!
Alleluia! Alleluia!

PSALM 66 page 415

READING Acts 6:8–9a, 9c–12

Stephen, full of grace and power, did great wonders and signs among the people. Then some of those who belonged to the synagogue of the Freedmen (as it was called), stood up and argued with Stephen. But they could not withstand the wisdom and the Spirit with which he spoke. Then they secretly instigated some men to say, "We have heard him speak blasphemous words against Moses and God." They stirred up the people as well as the elders and the scribes; then they suddenly confronted him, seized him, and brought him before the council.

REFLECTION Leo the Great

It is not only the martyrs who share in Christ's passion by glorious courage. All who have been born again in baptism share in Christ's passion and death. This is why we are to celebrate the Lord's paschal sacrifice with the unleavened bread of sincerity and truth. . . . For sharing the body and blood of Christ changes us into what we receive. And we have died with him, and have been buried with him, and raised to life with him, so we bear him within us, both in body and in spirit, and in everything we do.

PRAYERS others may be added

Longing to be filled with God's Spirit of wisdom, we pray:

◆ Hear our prayer, God our joy.

For God's people, bringing others to faith by their words and deeds, we pray: ◆
For deacons, standing as great signs of service to the Church, we pray: ◆
For those who are slandered, witnessing to the truth, we pray: ◆ *For those persecuted for the name of Jesus, relying on the strength of God's Spirit, we pray:* ◆
For us, in need of the grace that inspired Stephen, we pray: ◆

Our Father . . .

God of wisdom,
you worked great deeds
through your servant Stephen,
and gave him insight to confound
those who opposed him.
Bless us as well
with the gift of your Spirit:
May our lives give witness
to your great work in Jesus Christ
who lives and reigns forever and ever.
Amen.

✚ *Alleluia! Christ is risen!*
Christ is risen indeed!
Alleluia! Alleluia!

✠ *Alleluia! Christ is risen!*
Christ is risen indeed!
Alleluia! Alleluia!

PSALM 66 page 415

READING Acts 6:13–14; 7:1–2a, 51–53

They set up false witnesses against Stephen who said, "This man never stops saying things against this holy place and the law; for we have heard him say that this Jesus of Nazareth will destroy this place and will change the customs that Moses handed on to us."

Then the high priest asked him, "Are these things so?" And Stephen replied: "You stiff-necked people, uncircumcised in heart and ears, you are forever opposing the Holy Spirit, just as your ancestors used to do. Which of the prophets did your ancestors not persecute? They killed those who foretold the coming of the Righteous One, and now you have become his betrayers and murderers. You are the ones that received the law as ordained by angels, and yet you have not kept it."

REFLECTION

Stephen's testimony before the Sanhedrin (Acts 7:2–53), is a remarkable example of how the early Church interpreted the history of Israel. That interpretation was brand new, and it isn't surprising that many disagreed with it. It is important to keep such passages in their historical context. In this case, a small group of Jews believed in Jesus and the majority did not, resulting in no small amount of conflict.

But let us hope that over the course of the centuries, we have learned to manage our disagreements with greater charity, both within our own community of faith and among the world's religions.

PRAYERS others may be added

Embracing Stephen's boldness, we pray:

◆ Hear our prayer, God our joy.

That God's people may never oppose the Holy Spirit's works, we pray: ◆ *That religious leaders may be open to the voices of prophets calling them to faithfulness, we pray:* ◆ *That the neophytes may recognize the voice of the Righteous One in their brothers and sisters, we pray:* ◆ *That the stiff-necked and stubborn may open themselves to God's work in their lives, we pray:* ◆ *That we may seek to keep the law of Jesus, loving generously and freely, we pray:* ◆

Our Father . . .

Fiery God,
you inspire great preachers
with words that cut to the heart,
compelling us to conversion
and change.
Open our hearts and ears
to embrace the challenge you offer,
that we may keep the law of love
revealed in Jesus,
who lives and reigns forever and ever.
Amen.

✠ *Alleluia! Christ is risen!*
Christ is risen indeed!
Alleluia! Alleluia!

✙ *Alleluia! Christ is risen!*
Christ is risen indeed!
Alleluia! Alleluia!

PSALM 66   page 415

READING   Acts 7:54–58a, 59–60

When they heard these things, they became enraged and ground their teeth at Stephen. But filled with the Holy Spirit, he gazed into heaven and saw the glory of God and Jesus standing at the right hand of God. "Look," he said, "I see the heavens opened and the Son of Man standing at the right hand of God!" But they covered their ears, and with a loud shout all rushed together against him. Then they dragged him out of the city and began to stone him. While they were stoning Stephen, he prayed, "Lord Jesus, receive my spirit." Then he knelt down and cried out in a loud voice, "Lord, do not hold this sin against them." When he had said this, he died.

REFLECTION   Fulgentius

The love that brought Christ from heaven to earth raised Stephen from earth to heaven; shown first in the king, it later shone forth in his soldier. His love of God kept him from yielding to the ferocious mob; his love for his neighbor made him pray for those who were stoning him. Love inspired him to reprove those who erred, to make them amend; love led him to pray for those who stoned him, to save them from punishment.

PRAYERS   *others may be added*

Seeking to share Stephen's witness, we pray:

◆ Hear our prayer, God our joy.

That disciples of Jesus may speak out against violence in all its forms, we pray: ◆ *That the law may protect the rights of all, we pray:* ◆ *That violence motivated by religion may cease, we pray:* ◆ *That those who suffer discrimination because of their beliefs may know God's comfort, we pray:* ◆ *That those who witnessed to Christ in life may share his glory in eternity, we pray:* ◆

Our Father . . .

God of martyrs,
in every age you raise up
witnesses to your name
and fill them with courage.
Inflame in us the desire
to proclaim your word,
that we may one day
be received into your glory,
where Christ lives and reigns
forever and ever. Amen.

✙ *Alleluia! Christ is risen!*
Christ is risen indeed!
Alleluia! Alleluia!

✠ *Alleluia! Christ is risen!*
Christ is risen indeed!
Alleluia! Alleluia!

PSALM 34   *page 412*

READING   *John 10:11–16*

"I am the good shepherd. The good shepherd lays down his life for the sheep. The hired hand, who is not the shepherd and does not own the sheep, sees the wolf coming and leaves the sheep and runs away—and the wolf snatches them and scatters them. The hired hand runs away because a hired hand does not care for the sheep. I am the good shepherd. I know my own and my own know me, just as the Father knows me and I know the Father. And I lay down my life for the sheep. I have other sheep that do not belong to this fold. I must bring them also, and they will listen to my voice. So there will be one flock, one shepherd."

REFLECTION

The Fourth Sunday of Easter is commonly referred to as "Good Shepherd Sunday" because the Gospel always comes from the tenth chapter of John, in which Jesus speaks of himself as the Good Shepherd who lays down his life for the sheep. This particular section offers a sweeping picture of the flock, a vision of many nations, cultures, languages, and ways of life gathered as one people with one shepherd.

PRAYERS   *others may be added*

With the Good Shepherd as our model and protector, we pray:

◆ Turn to us, Lord of life!

For the shepherds of God's people: May they faithfully defend the most vulnerable of Christ's flock, we pray: ◆ For those newly reborn as God's children: May their faith in the Risen One grow and deepen, we pray: ◆ For government officials: May they take as their model the Good Shepherd, who lays down his life for those in his care, we pray: ◆ For all who listen to the Shepherd's voice: May all people be gathered as one flock, we pray: ◆ For the poor, the marginalized, and the forgotten: May they know their own dignity as God's children, we pray: ◆ For us: May we be prepared to offer our lives in service of one another, we pray: ◆

Our Father . . .

Eternal Shepherd,
in Christ you have gathered
many nations into one flock.
May the example of Jesus,
    the Good Shepherd,
inspire us to serve the weakest
    among us,
that we may come to share your glory
revealed in Jesus Christ,
who lives and reigns with you
in the unity of the Holy Spirit,
one God, forever and ever. Amen.

✠ *Alleluia! Christ is risen!*
Christ is risen indeed!
Alleluia! Alleluia!

✦ *Alleluia! Christ is risen!*
Christ is risen indeed!
Alleluia! Alleluia!

PSALM 34   *page 412*

READING   *Acts 8:1b–8*

A severe persecution began against the church in Jerusalem, and all except the apostles were scattered throughout the countryside of Judea and Samaria. Devout men buried Stephen and made loud lamentation over him. But Saul was ravaging the church by entering house after house; dragging off both men and women, he committed them to prison.

Now those who were scattered went from place to place, proclaiming the word. Philip went down to the city of Samaria and proclaimed the Messiah to them. The crowds with one accord listened eagerly to what was said by Philip, hearing and seeing the signs that he did, for unclean spirits, crying with loud shrieks, came out of many who were possessed; and many others who were paralyzed or lame were cured. So there was great joy in that city.

REFLECTION

The Acts of the Apostles portrays Stephen's death as the beginning of a great persecution that resulted in the flight of many Christians from Jerusalem. This allows the Gospel to spread beyond the Jewish people. The preaching of the apostle Philip begins this movement, as he goes forth among the Samaritans, considered heretics by the Jews of the time—and probably by some Christians as well.

PRAYERS   *others may be added*

Ready to proclaim the Good News in every place, we pray:

◆ Turn to us, Lord of life!

That missionaries may find hearts open to the Gospel message, we pray: ◆ *That the neophytes' Christian faith may be a source of courage, we pray:* ◆ *That the world may find cause for great joy, we pray:* ◆ *That all people may welcome God's messengers with open hearts, we pray:* ◆ *That the Good News may bring healing to the sick and liberation to the oppressed, we pray:* ◆ *That we may listen eagerly to the news of our salvation, we pray:* ◆

Our Father . . .

God of joy,
the Gospel's power heals the sick
and drives out unclean spirits,
setting us free to praise you.
Release Christ's power among us,
that we may with one accord
proclaim Jesus raised from the dead
and so bring joy and hope
to all we meet.
We ask this through the Exalted One,
   Jesus Christ,
who lives and reigns
forever and ever. Amen.

✦ *Alleluia! Christ is risen!*
Christ is risen indeed!
Alleluia! Alleluia!

✜ *Alleluia! Christ is risen!*
Christ is risen indeed!
Alleluia! Alleluia!

PSALM 34   page 412

READING   Acts 8:9–13

Now a certain man named Simon had previously practiced magic in the city and amazed the people of Samaria, saying that he was someone great. All of them, from the least to the greatest, listened to him eagerly, saying, "This man is the power of God that is called Great." And they listened eagerly to him because for a long time he had amazed them with his magic. But when they believed Philip, who was proclaiming the good news about the kingdom of God and the name of Jesus Christ, they were baptized, both men and women. Even Simon himself believed. After being baptized, he stayed constantly with Philip and was amazed when he saw the signs and great miracles that took place.

REFLECTION

When faith wavers, we sometimes look for signs of God's power to encourage us. Indeed, recognizing God at work in a loved one's return to health, in the promise of a new friendship, in reconciliation among nations, and in many other "signs" can give us confidence when we stumble on the way. The Acts of the Apostles reminds us, however, that not all "signs and great miracles" point to the truth. Both Simon and Philip worked deeds of power, yet it was Philip who brought the truth. The people accepted his message, setting aside their hunger for signs and opening themselves to the message that spoke to their hearts.

PRAYERS   others may be added

   Seeking only Gospel truth, we pray:

◆ Turn to us, Lord of life!

That the faith of God's people may be confirmed by fidelity to the Gospel message, we pray: ◆ *That the neophytes may be amazed at the gift of faith planted within them, we pray:* ◆ *That the world may find joy in great signs of peace, justice and righteousness, we pray:* ◆ *That those seeking faith may receive the Good News with joy, we pray:* ◆ *That we may recognize God's saving work wherever it is revealed, we pray:* ◆

Our Father . . .

Great Wonderworker,
source of hope and joy,
reveal to us your power
and amaze us with your presence,
that we may receive in thanksgiving
your great work in Jesus Christ
and so praise you through him,
risen and exalted,
now and forever. Amen.

✜ *Alleluia! Christ is risen!*
Christ is risen indeed!
Alleluia! Alleluia!

✠ *Alleluia! Christ is risen!*
Christ is risen indeed!
Alleluia! Alleluia!

PSALM 34 *page 412*

READING *Acts 8:14–19*

Now when the apostles at Jerusalem heard that Samaria had accepted the word of God, they sent Peter and John to them. The two went down and prayed for them that they might receive the Holy Spirit (for as yet the Spirit had not come upon any of them; they had only been baptized in the name of the Lord Jesus). Then Peter and John laid their hands on them, and they received the Holy Spirit. Now when Simon saw that the Spirit was given through the laying on of the apostles' hands, he offered them money, saying, "Give me also this power so that anyone on whom I lay my hands may receive the Holy Spirit."

REFLECTION

Today we remember a saint who, like Philip before him, ministered to the outcast. Father Damien of Moloka'i (1840–89) worked at a leper colony in Hawaii. Since there was then no cure for the disease, anyone with leprosy was permanently quarantined to prevent further infection. Father Damien reached out to restore those who were isolated, even after he contracted the disease himself. He reflected, "As for me, I make myself a leper with the lepers, to gain all to Jesus Christ. That is why, in preaching, I say 'we lepers.'"

PRAYERS *others may be added*

Longing to draw all people into Christ's body, we pray:

◆ Turn to us, Lord of life!

That Church leaders may be quick to welcome all people into Christ's fold, we pray: ◆ *That neophytes may be filled with the gift of the Holy Spirit, we pray:* ◆ *That those preparing for full communion with the Catholic Church may be encouraged and welcomed, we pray:* ◆ *That Christian communities may reach out to those isolated by illness or prejudice, we pray:* ◆ *That the sick may be sustained and comforted, we pray:* ◆ *That we may promote greater charity among believers, we pray:* ◆

Our Father . . .

Source of unity,
your Spirit binds together
the strong and weak,
the sick and well,
as one people in Jesus Christ.
May the Easter festival
build up within us
a greater desire for communion
    with all Christians,
that the Church may proclaim
    with one voice
our salvation in Jesus Christ,
risen and exalted,
now and forever. Amen.

✠ *Alleluia! Christ is risen!*
Christ is risen indeed!
Alleluia! Alleluia!

✦ *Alleluia! Christ is risen!*
Christ is risen indeed!
Alleluia! Alleluia!

PSALM 34 *page 412*

READING *Acts 8:20–25*

But Peter said to Simon, "May your silver perish with you, because you thought you could obtain God's gift with money! You have no part or share in this, for your heart is not right before God. Repent therefore of this wickedness of yours, and pray to the Lord that, if possible, the intent of your heart may be forgiven you. For I see that you are in the gall of bitterness and the chains of wickedness." Simon answered, "Pray for me to the Lord, that nothing of what you have said may happen to me."

Now after Peter and John had testified and spoken the word of the Lord, they returned to Jerusalem, proclaiming the good news to many villages of the Samaritans.

REFLECTION

Simon Magus was associated with the heresy of buying and selling holy things, "simony." His sin is more serious than offering the apostles a bribe; he wants power—religiously sanctioned power at that. This is a great temptation and a great danger for all Christians. The gifts of the Spirit, including the charism of authority, are meant for the building up the Church, not the glorification of those who exercise them.

PRAYERS *others may be added*

Longing for hearts set right before God, we pray:

◆ Turn to us, Lord of life!

For bishops and pastors, entrusted with the charism of leadership, we pray: ◆ For neophytes, blessed with the Spirit's gifts for the sake of Christ's body, we pray: ◆ For Christians in public service, charged to exercise their gifts for the sake of all people, we pray: ◆ For those who seek power for its own sake, challenged to seek God's glory alone, we pray: ◆ For us, called to offer without cost the life we have in Jesus Christ, we pray: ◆

Our Father . . .

Power from on high,
in Christ you teach us
that the first among us
must serve the rest,
for authority lies with you alone.
Inspire us by Christ's example
that we may seek not our glory
   but yours
and so come to share
your life in the Risen One,
who lives and reigns
forever and ever. Amen.

✦ *Alleluia! Christ is risen!*
Christ is risen indeed!
Alleluia! Alleluia!

✠ *Alleluia! Christ is risen!*
Christ is risen indeed!
Alleluia! Alleluia!

PSALM 66   *page 415*

READING   *Acts 8:26–31*

Then an angel of the Lord said to Philip, "Get up and go toward the south to the road that goes down from Jerusalem to Gaza." (This is a wilderness road.) So he got up and went. Now there was an Ethiopian eunuch, a court official of the Candace, queen of the Ethiopians, in charge of her entire treasury. He had come to Jerusalem to worship and was returning home; seated in his chariot, he was reading the prophet Isaiah. Then the Spirit said to Philip, "Go over to this chariot and join it." So Philip ran up to it and heard him reading the prophet Isaiah. He asked, "Do you understand what you are reading?" He replied, "How can I, unless someone guides me?" And he invited Philip to get in and sit beside him.

REFLECTION

We tend to think that "evangelization"—a fancy word for proclaiming the Good News—is something reserved to "official" Christians: priests and bishops, missionary orders of men and women, and so on. We must keep reminding ourselves that all the baptized are "official" Christians, each charged to proclaim the Gospel. Philip can be our model for evangelization: He offers to share his faith with the official, and God brings the official to faith in Christ. What other wonders might God work if we were so open with our Christian faith?

PRAYERS   *others may be added*

Ready to share the faith that gives us life, we pray:

◆ Hear our prayer, God our joy.

That all God's people may take up the task of evangelization, we pray: ◆
That the neophytes may readily share their journey to Christ, we pray: ◆
That Church leaders may guide the faithful in mission to the world, we pray: ◆
That God's invitation to faith may find welcome among all people, we pray: ◆
That we may go forth in the wilderness searching for those hungry for faith, we pray: ◆

Our Father . . .

God of all people,
your Son sends us
to every corner of the earth
with Good News for hungry hearts.
Open us to the Spirit's urgings,
that every road may lead us
to another sister or brother
ready to welcome life in Christ,
who lives and reigns
forever and ever. Amen.

✠ *Alleluia! Christ is risen!*
Christ is risen indeed!
Alleluia! Alleluia!

✠ *Alleluia! Christ is risen!*
Christ is risen indeed!
Alleluia! Alleluia!

PSALM 34 *page 412*

READING *Acts 8:32–35*

Now the passage of the scripture that the eunuch was reading was this:
"Like a sheep he was led
    to the slaughter,
and like a lamb silent before its shearer,
    so he does not open his mouth.
In his humiliation justice
    was denied him.
Who can describe his generation?
For his life is taken away
    from the earth."
The eunuch asked Philip, "About whom, may I ask you, does the prophet say this, about himself or about someone else?" Then Philip began to speak, and starting with this scripture, he proclaimed to him the good news about Jesus.

REFLECTION

We resume the story of Philip's proclamation to the Ethiopian official. Like the Samaritans, the official was excluded from the First Covenant; in his case because he was a eunuch and so unable to father children. The Spirit of God, however, directs Philip to reach out to him. Philip is much like Jesus in the Emmaus story: He opens the scriptures to the official, interpreting the passage from Isaiah through the lens of Jesus' death. The household of God expands again, and the Gospel continues its movement toward the ends of the earth.

PRAYERS *others may be added*

Eager to share our faith in Christ, we pray:

◆ Turn to us, Lord of life!

For apostles and prophets: May they be ready to proclaim God's word to the curious, we pray: ◆ *For neophytes: May they joyfully share their baptismal faith, we pray:* ◆ *For catechumens: May they continue their journey toward life in Christ, we pray:* ◆ *For searchers and inquirers: May they find their hearts' desire, we pray:* ◆ *For all Christians: May we be living signs of the Good News about Jesus, we pray:* ◆

Our Father . . .

God of all nations,
you desire to gather
all people to yourself.
Inflame our minds and hearts
to know you more fully,
that we may proclaim the Good News
    of Jesus
to all we meet,
for Jesus Christ is exalted
now and forever. Amen.

✠ *Alleluia! Christ is risen!*
Christ is risen indeed!
Alleluia! Alleluia!

✠ *Alleluia! Christ is risen!*
Christ is risen indeed!
Alleluia! Alleluia!

PSALM 34 *page 412*

READING *John 15:1–5, 7–8*

"I am the true vine, and my Father is the vinegrower. He removes every branch in me that bears no fruit. Every branch that bears fruit he prunes to make it bear more fruit. You have already been cleansed by the word that I have spoken to you. Abide in me as I abide in you. Just as the branch cannot bear fruit by itself unless it abides in the vine, neither can you unless you abide in me. I am the vine, you are the branches. Those who abide in me and I in them bear much fruit, because apart from me you can do nothing. If you abide in me, and my words abide in you, ask for whatever you wish, and it will be done for you. My Father is glorified by this, that you bear much fruit and become my disciples."

REFLECTION *Second Vatican Council*

The Church is God's farm or field. In this field the ancient olive tree grown whose holy root were the patriarchs and in which the reconciliation of Jews and Gentiles has been achieved and will continue to be achieved. The Church has been planted by the heavenly farmer as a choice vineyard. The true vine is Christ who gives life and fruitfulness to the branches, that is, to us, who through the Church abide in Christ without whom we can do nothing.

PRAYERS *others may be added*

Abiding in Christ, confident before God, we pray:

◆ Turn to us, Lord of life!

For the people of God: May the Good News planted in us take root and produce abundant fruit, we pray: ◆ *For the neophytes and those received into full communion: May they draw strength and nourishment from Christ, the True Vine, we pray:* ◆ *For those withered by illness of body or spirit: May the Vinegrower heal and restore them, we pray:* ◆ *For mothers on this Mother's Day: May they and their children draw strength from one another, we pray:* ◆ *For the faithful dead: Having borne much fruit in life, may they be gathered into the rich harvest of God's reign, we pray:* ◆

Our Father . . .

God of the vineyard,
your servant Jesus nourishes us,
building us up to bear a harvest
worthy of your name.
Gently prune us of all
that keeps us from you
and bind us ever more closely
to Christ, the True Vine,
who lives and reigns with you
in the unity of the Holy Spirit,
one God, forever and ever. Amen.

✠ *Alleluia! Christ is risen!*
Christ is risen indeed!
Alleluia! Alleluia!

✦ *Alleluia! Christ is risen!*
Christ is risen indeed!
Alleluia! Alleluia!

PSALM 34   page 412

READING   Acts 8:36–40

As they were going along the road, they came to some water; and the eunuch said, "Look, here is water! What is to prevent me from being baptized?" He commanded the chariot to stop, and both of them, Philip and the eunuch, went down into the water, and Philip baptized him. When they came up out of the water, the Spirit of the Lord snatched Philip away; the eunuch saw him no more, and went on his way rejoicing. But Philip found himself at Azotus, and as he was passing through the region, he proclaimed the good news to all the towns until he came to Caesarea.

REFLECTION

In the United States, today is the memorial of Saints Isidore and Maria, the patrons of farmers and their families. The U.S. bishops have spoken of the importance of preserving family farms: "Both Catholic social teaching and the traditions of our country have emphasized the importance of maintaining the rich plurality of social institutions that enhances personal freedom and increases opportunity for participation in community life. . . . By contributing to the vitality of rural communities, full-time residential farmers enrich the social and political life of the nation as a whole. Cities, too, benefit soundly and economically from a vibrant rural economy based on family farms."

PRAYERS   *others may be added*

Praying fervently for the needs of the world, we pray:

◆ Turn toward us, Lord of life!

That the Church may boldly proclaim the challenge of Gospel justice, we pray: ◆ *That world governments may support the just distribution of land and its produce, we pray:* ◆ *That rural and urban communities may be enriched by each other's gifts, we pray:* ◆ *That those who rely on the land for their livelihood may have good weather and abundant crops, we pray:* ◆ *That we may embrace the call to stewardship of the soil, water, and air, we pray:* ◆

Our Father . . .

God of farms and fields,
you made of creation a rich garden
to supply give us food and beauty.
Fill us with reverence
for the natural world,
and bless those who nurture its growth,
that all people may benefit
from creation's bounty
and see in it the renewal
you have begun in Jesus Christ,
first fruits of the new creation,
who is Lord forever and ever. Amen.

✦ *Alleluia! Christ is risen!*
Christ is risen indeed!
Alleluia! Alleluia!

✦ *Alleluia! Christ is risen!*
Christ is risen indeed!
Alleluia! Alleluia!

PSALM 34 *page 412*

READING *Acts 10:1–8*

In Caesarea there was a man named Cornelius, a centurion of the Italian Cohort, as it was called. He was a devout man who feared God with all his household; he gave alms generously to the people and prayed constantly to God. One afternoon at about three o'clock he had a vision in which he clearly saw an angel of God coming in and saying to him, "Cornelius." He stared at him in terror and said, "What is it, Lord?" He answered, "Your prayers and your alms have ascended as a memorial before God. Now send men to Joppa for a certain Simon who is called Peter; he is lodging with Simon, a tanner, whose house is by the seaside." When the angel who spoke to him had left, he called two of his slaves and a devout soldier from the ranks of those who served him, and after telling them everything, he sent them to Joppa.

REFLECTION *Second Vatican Council*

Those who, through no fault of their own, do not know the Gospel of Christ or his Church, but who nevertheless seek God with a sincere heart, and, moved by grace, try in their actions to do his will as they know it through the dictates of their conscience—these too may attain eternal salvation. Nor will divine providence deny the assistance necessary for salvation to those who, without any fault of theirs, have not yet arrived at an explicit knowledge of God, and who, not without grace, strive to lead a good life. Whatever of good or truth is found amongst them is considered by the Church to be a preparation for the Gospel.

PRAYERS *others may be added*

Offering our prayers as a memorial to God, we pray:

◆ Turn to us, Lord of life!

That the prayers and works of God's people may be a pleasing offering, we pray: ◆ *That pastors and ministers may welcome all who come in search of God, we pray:* ◆ *That the world's people may know God's favor, we pray:* ◆ *That the poor may benefit from the generosity of those who honor God, we pray:* ◆ *That we may seek to be people of constant prayer, we pray:* ◆

Our Father . . .

God of the nations,
you accept the offerings
of all who approach you in integrity.
Bless us with your generosity,
that we too may welcome
all who come to us
in search of you.
We ask this through the Risen Christ,
who lives and reigns
forever and ever. Amen.

✦ *Alleluia! Christ is risen!*
Christ is risen indeed!
Alleluia! Alleluia!

✦ *Alleluia! Christ is risen!*
Christ is risen indeed!
Alleluia! Alleluia!

PSALM 34   page 412

READING   Acts 10:9–15

About noon the next day, as they were on their journey and approaching the city, Peter went up on the roof to pray. He became hungry and wanted something to eat; and while it was being prepared, he fell into a trance. He saw the heaven opened and something like a large sheet coming down, being lowered to the ground by its four corners. In it were all kinds of four-footed creatures and reptiles and birds of the air. Then he heard a voice saying, "Get up, Peter; kill and eat." But Peter said, "By no means, Lord; for I have never eaten anything that is profane or unclean." The voice said to him again, a second time, "What God has made clean, you must not call profane."

REFLECTION

Acts' story of the Gentile Cornelius, of which Peter's vision is a part, presents him as the first non-Jewish convert to the early Church. Cornelius was not a stranger to Judaism; he was a "God-fearer," one who respected and worshiped the God of Israel. God's favor to him might have shocked the early Christians: He was a Roman and a centurion, part of the force that occupied Palestine, the very force that participated in Jesus' execution—an "unclean" human being par excellence. *Peter's vision, then, has as much to do with the distinctions between "clean" and "unclean" people as it does with animals.*

PRAYERS   others may be added

Opening ourselves to the freedom of God's children, we pray:

◆ Turn to us, Lord of life!

That God's people may never allow prejudice to prevent the proclamation of the Gospel, we pray: ◆ *That the neophytes may never confuse human convention with divine command, we pray:* ◆ *That the nations of the world may respect all of God's creation, we pray:* ◆ *That all people may carefully and lovingly steward plants and animals used for food, we pray:* ◆ *That there may be no clean and unclean among us, we pray:* ◆

Our Father . . .

Source of creation,
all the earth is filled with your beauty,
for you have made all things
    and called them good.
Remove from among us distinctions
between clean and unclean,
the chosen and rejected,
that we may be one in Christ,
who lives and reigns forever and ever.
Amen.

✦ *Alleluia! Christ is risen!*
Christ is risen indeed!
Alleluia! Alleluia!

✜ *Alleluia! Christ is risen!*
Christ is risen indeed!
Alleluia! Alleluia!

PSALM 34 page 412

READING Acts 10:17–23a

Now while Peter was greatly puzzled about what to make of the vision that he had seen, suddenly the men sent by Cornelius appeared. They were asking for Simon's house and were standing by the gate. They called out to ask whether Simon, who was called Peter, was staying there. While Peter was still thinking about the vision, the Spirit said to him, "Look, three men are searching for you. Now get up, go down, and go with them without hesitation; for I have sent them." So Peter went down to the men and said, "I am the one you are looking for; what is the reason for your coming?" They answered, "Cornelius, a centurion, an upright and God-fearing man, who is well spoken of by the whole Jewish nation, was directed by a holy angel to send for you to come to his house and to hear what you have to say." So Peter invited them in and gave them lodging.

REFLECTION

The scriptures are filled with stories of hospitality, from Abraham and Sarah to Jesus' table ministry to early Christian practice, to Peter in today's reading. Many religious traditions suggest that when one offers hospitality, one welcomes the presence of God. Perhaps the Letter to the Hebrews says it best: "Do not neglect to show hospitality to strangers, for by doing that some have entertained angels without knowing it" (Hebrews 13:2).

PRAYERS others may be added

Ready to proclaim the good news to all people, we pray:

◆ Turn to us, Lord of life!

For Church leaders, pastors, and all charged with proclaiming the Gospel, we pray: ◆ *For Christian assemblies and all who offer God's hospitality, we pray:* ◆ *For missionaries, catechists, teachers, and all who share the light of truth, we pray:* ◆ *For all those who seek God with open hearts, we pray:* ◆ *For all who listen to the voice of God's Spirit in their lives, we pray:* ◆

Our Father . . .

God of apostles and prophets,
you stir up in your servants
a spirit of welcome and hospitality.
May we, like Peter, listen carefully
to the voice of the Spirit within us,
that all who seek you in Jesus
may find among his disciples
hospitality and care.
We ask this through the Risen Christ
who lives and reigns forever and ever.
Amen.

✜ *Alleluia! Christ is risen!*
Christ is risen indeed!
Alleluia! Alleluia!

✠ *Alleluia! Christ is risen!*
Christ is risen indeed!
Alleluia! Alleluia!

PSALM 34   *page 412*

READING   *Acts 10:23b, 25–26, 28–32*

The next day Peter got up and went with them, and some of the believers from Joppa accompanied him. On Peter's arrival Cornelius met him, and falling at his feet, worshiped him. But Peter made him get up, saying, "Stand up; I am only a mortal." And he said to them, "You yourselves know that it is unlawful for a Jew to associate with or to visit a Gentile; but God has shown me that I should not call anyone profane or unclean. So when I was sent for, I came without objection. Now may I ask why you sent for me?"

Cornelius replied, "Four days ago at this very hour, at three o'clock, I was praying in my house when suddenly a man in dazzling clothes stood before me. He said, 'Cornelius, your prayer has been heard and your alms have been remembered before God. Send therefore to Joppa and ask for Simon, who is called Peter; he is staying in the home of Simon, a tanner, by the sea.'"

REFLECTION

It can be easy to confuse the message with the messenger, as Cornelius does today. Peter quickly redirects Cornelius to the worship of God alone. There are many less honest than Peter, who would manipulate the religious faith and moral values of others to gain power or prestige. We must be careful to discern whether one who appeals to faith in the service of politics of any sort—civic, religious, economic—is pointing us to God or themselves.

PRAYERS   *others may be added*

Ready to recognize God's presence wherever we may find it, we pray:

◆ Turn to us, Lord of life!

That the people of God may share their faith with one another, we pray: ◆ *That the neophytes may witness to the experience of God that led them to Baptism, we pray:* ◆ *That people of faith may worship the God of heaven and earth alone, we pray:* ◆ *That all people may recognize God's presence among them, we pray:* ◆ *That we may listen carefully to God's voice speaking within us, we pray:* ◆

Our Father . . .

God of unity,
you command us to set aside
anything that keeps us
from recognizing your work
in our brothers and sisters.
Open us to acknowledge and embrace
your movement among all nations
    and peoples:
May we in turn always be ready
to share our faith in Christ,
who lives and reigns forever and ever.
Amen.

✠ *Alleluia! Christ is risen!*
Christ is risen indeed!
Alleluia! Alleluia!

✦ *Alleluia! Christ is risen!*
Christ is risen indeed!
Alleluia! Alleluia!

PSALM 34   *page 412*

READING   *Acts 10:34–35, 44–47*

Then Peter began to speak to them: "I truly understand that God shows no partiality, but in every nation anyone who fears him and does what is right is acceptable to him."

While Peter was still speaking, the Holy Spirit fell upon all who heard the word. The circumcised believers who had come with Peter were astounded that the gift of the Holy Spirit had been poured out even on the Gentiles, for they heard them speaking in tongues and extolling God. Then Peter said, "Can anyone withhold the water for baptizing these people who have received the Holy Spirit just as we have?"

REFLECTION

The climax of the story of Cornelius' conversion comes when God chooses to send the Spirit upon the Gentiles before the Church—embodied in Peter and the apostles—is ready to accept them. Faced with God's action, Peter can do nothing but have Cornelius and his household baptized. We, too, must be ready to acknowledge God's presence where we find it, especially when it means overcoming our prejudices and preconceptions.

PRAYERS   *others may be added*

Astounded by God's generosity,
we pray:

◆ Turn to us, Lord of life!

That God's people may show no partiality, welcoming all those chosen by God, we pray: ◆ *That the neophytes may grow in fear and knowledge of God, we pray:* ◆ *That the world's cultures may praise God with their many voices, we pray:* ◆ *That all people may be found acceptable to God, we pray:* ◆ *That we may recognize the work of the Holy Spirit where we least expect it, we pray:* ◆

Our Father . . .

Generous and loving God,
your Spirit moves where it wills
revealing your presence
    throughout creation.
Move in power within us, your people,
that we too may praise you
in our many voices,
extolling you through Christ,
who lives and reigns
forever and ever. Amen.

✦ *Alleluia! Christ is risen!*
Christ is risen indeed!
Alleluia! Alleluia!

✝ *Alleluia! Christ is risen!*
Christ is risen indeed!
Alleluia! Alleluia!

PSALM 34 page 412

READING John 15:9–15

Jesus said, "As the Father has loved me, so I have loved you; abide in my love. If you keep my commandments, you will abide in my love, just as I have kept my Father's commandments and abide in his love. I have said these things to you so that my joy may be in you, and that your joy may be complete.

"This is my commandment, that you love one another as I have loved you. No one has greater love than this, to lay down one's life for one's friends. You are my friends if you do what I command you. I do not call you servants any longer, because the servant does not know what the master is doing; but I have called you friends, because I have made known to you everything that I have heard from my Father."

REFLECTION

Love is the core of our lives as Christians, and the command to love is the first law that sums up the rest. Everything that Christians do—liturgy, good works, fasting, private prayer—is meaningless if not rooted in and motivated by the love that Christ commands. It is in and through this abiding love that we are friends of God, coworkers with Christ, and sisters and brothers to one another.

PRAYERS *others may be added*

Abiding in the love of God, we pray:

◆ Turn toward us, Lord of life!

For the Church: May the baptized grow more fully into a communion of charity, we pray: ◆ *For all God's people: May they grow in friendship with God and one another, we pray:* ◆ *For the neophytes and those received into full communion: May they be filled with complete joy of Christ, we pray:* ◆ *For those in need: May they know the abiding love of God in the service of Jesus' disciples and friends, we pray:* ◆ *For us: May we be a sign to all people of the abiding love of God in Christ, we pray:* ◆

Our Father . . .

Friend and Lover of all,
you command only that we love
    one another.
May our proclamation of your love
bring others to friendship with Christ,
bearing fruit in the renewal
    of your Church.
We ask this in the name
    of Jesus Christ,
who lives and reigns with you
in the unity of the Holy Spirit,
one God, forever and ever. Amen.

✝ *Alleluia! Christ is risen!*
Christ is risen indeed!
Alleluia! Alleluia!

✚ *Alleluia! Christ is risen!*
Christ is risen indeed!
Alleluia! Alleluia!

PSALM 34   *page 412*

READING   *Acts 15:1–5*

Then certain individuals came down from Judea and were teaching the brothers, "Unless you are circumcised according to the custom of Moses, you cannot be saved." And after Paul and Barnabas had no small dissension and debate with them, Paul and Barnabas and some of the others were appointed to go up to Jerusalem to discuss this question with the apostles and the elders. So they were sent on their way by the church, and as they passed through both Phoenicia and Samaria, they reported the conversion of the Gentiles, and brought great joy to all the believers. When they came to Jerusalem, they were welcomed by the church and the apostles and the elders, and they reported all that God had done with them. But some believers who belonged to the sect of the Pharisees stood up and said, "It is necessary for them to be circumcised and ordered to keep the law of Moses."

REFLECTION

We leap ahead in Acts to the first major crisis faced by the Christian community, one occasioned by the inclusion of people like Cornelius and his household, as well as the missionary activity of Paul and Barnabas among the Greeks. The focus of the dispute was whether non-Jews who wanted to be baptized had to first be circumcised and so become Jews as well as disciples. The debate became so heated that Paul, in his letter to the Galatians (2:11), reports that he opposed Peter "to his face." So much for the picture of unity painted in the earlier chapters of Acts!

PRAYERS   *others may be added*

Opening ourselves to the Spirit's wisdom, we pray:

◆ Turn to us, Lord of life!

For those charged with nurturing unity among God's people, we pray: ◆
For Christian communities crippled by division and discord, we pray: ◆
For mediators and all who seek peace and reconciliation, we pray: ◆ *For those in conflict with one another, we pray:* ◆
For those who promote charity among us, we pray: ◆

Our Father . . .

Source of unity,
you wish all your children
to be joined in charity and peace.
Increase in us the desire
to live in harmony with all people,
that we may overcome
what divides us and so signal
the unity of your kingdom,
where Christ is Lord
forever and ever. Amen.

✚ *Alleluia! Christ is risen!*
Christ is risen indeed!
Alleluia! Alleluia!

✝ *Alleluia! Christ is risen!*
Christ is risen indeed!
Alleluia! Alleluia!

PSALM 34 page 412

READING Acts 15:6–11

The apostles and the elders met together to consider this matter. After there had been much debate, Peter stood up and said to them, "My brothers, you know that in the early days God made a choice among you, that I should be the one through whom the Gentiles would hear the message of the good news and become believers. And God, who knows the human heart, testified to them by giving them the Holy Spirit, just as he did to us; and in cleansing their hearts by faith he has made no distinction between them and us. Now therefore why are you putting God to the test by placing on the neck of the disciples a yoke that neither our ancestors nor we have been able to bear? On the contrary, we believe that we will be saved through the grace of the Lord Jesus, just as they will."

REFLECTION

Throughout the Church's history, from this first gathering to the Second Vatican Council, "the elders and apostles" of God's people have come together to make major decisions affecting all the baptized. Councils have often come at times of great controversy, and each time those gathered have relied on the Holy Spirit to guide the Church to a good decision. These councils express the collegial character of Church authority; as the Second Vatican Council put it, this "collegial" character "is shown in the holding of councils in order to reach agreement on questions of major importance, a balanced decision being made possible thanks to the number of those giving counsel" (Lumen gentium, 22).

PRAYERS *others may be added*

Open to the Spirit, we pray:

◆ Turn to us, Lord of life!

For the Church, guided by God's Spirit, we pray: ◆ For preachers and missionaries, through whom the Gospel is announced to the world, we pray: ◆ For the neophytes, in whom God works wonders of faith, we pray: ◆ For the nations, among whom God makes no distinctions, we pray: ◆ For all of us, saved through the grace of the Lord Jesus, we pray: ◆

Our Father . . .

Saving God,
you desire humanity's redemption
and offer your Spirit of faith to all.
Bless us with your generosity,
that we may welcome all people
to the way of salvation
in Jesus the Christ,
for he lives and reigns
forever and ever. Amen.

✝ *Alleluia! Christ is risen!*
Christ is risen indeed!
Alleluia! Alleluia!

✝ *Alleluia! Christ is risen!*
Christi is risen indeed!
Alleluia! Alleluia!

PSALM 34   *page 412*

READING   *Acts 15:22–25a, 28–29*

Then the apostles and the elders, with the consent of the whole church, decided to choose men from among their members and to send them to Antioch with Paul and Barnabas. They sent Judas called Barsabbas, and Silas, leaders among the brothers, with the following letter: "The brothers, both the apostles and the elders, to the believers of Gentile origin in Antioch and Syria and Cilicia, greetings. Since we have heard that certain persons who have gone out from us, though with no instructions from us, have said things to disturb you and have unsettled your minds, we have decided unanimously to choose representatives and send them to you. For it has seemed good to the Holy Spirit and to us to impose on you no further burden than these essentials: that you abstain from what has been sacrificed to idols and from blood and from what is strangled and from fornication. If you keep yourselves from these, you will do well. Farewell."

REFLECTION

The decision of the Jerusalem church to free Gentile Christians from the observance of the Mosaic law was perhaps the single most important decision made by the early community. Had they imposed that law on Christians, the disciples of Jesus would probably have remained a sect within Judaism. Instead, Christianity was able to become a religion open to all people, regardless of ancestry, ethnicity or culture.

PRAYERS   *others may be added*

Trusting in the work of the Holy Spirit, we pray:

◆ Turn to us, Lord of life.

For the people of God, called to live in holiness, we pray: ◆ *For local church communities, called to welcome people of every culture, race, and language, we pray:* ◆ *For church leaders, called to lift burdens and inspire peace, we pray:* ◆ *For synods and councils, called to discern the movement of the Spirit, we pray:* ◆ *For all of us, called to live the freedom of God's children, we pray:* ◆

Our Father . . .

God of freedom,
you desire that we live in holiness,
embracing your law of love.
Give us courage to live
as your children,
that we may choose the path
that leads to you
and so inspire others to the freedom
you offer in Jesus Christ,
who lives and reigns
forever and ever. Amen.

✝ *Alleluia! Christ is risen!*
Christ is risen indeed!
Alleluia! Alleluia!

THURSDAY, 25 MAY 2006
SOLEMNITY OF THE ASCENSION OF THE LORD
In some places, the solemnity is observed next Sunday.

✦ *Alleluia! Christ is risen!*
Christ is risen indeed!
Alleluia! Alleluia!

PSALM 66 page 415

READING Ephesians 4:1–7, 11–13

I therefore, the prisoner in the Lord, beg you to lead a life worthy of the calling to which you have been called, with all humility and gentleness, with patience, bearing with one another in love, making every effort to maintain the unity of the Spirit in the bond of peace. There is one body and one Spirit, just as you were called to the one hope of your calling, one Lord, one faith, one baptism, one God and Father of all, who is above all and through all and in all. But each of us was given grace according to the measure of Christ's gift.

The gifts he gave were that some would be apostles, some prophets, some evangelists, some pastors and teachers, to equip the saints for the work of ministry, for building up the body of Christ, until all of us come to the unity of the faith and of the knowledge of the Son of God, to maturity, to the measure of the full stature of Christ.

REFLECTION Roman Missal

Christ has passed beyond our sight, not to abandon us but to be our hope. Christ is the beginning, the head of the Church; where he has gone, we hope to follow.

PRAYERS others may be added

Christ has ascended in glory to the Father, and so in joy we cry:

◆ Alleluia, alleluia!

Exalted Christ, you make your people one body with one Spirit, and so we cry: ◆
Exalted Christ, you build up your Church with manifold gifts, and so we cry: ◆
Exalted Christ, you gather the nations in an eternal bond of peace, and so we cry: ◆
Exalted Christ, you call all people to an everlasting hope, and so we cry: ◆
Exalted Christ, you heal the sick by your power, and so we cry: ◆ *Exalted Christ, you gather the dead in glory among the saints, and so we cry:* ◆ *Exalted Christ, you intercede for us at God's right hand, and so we cry:* ◆

Our Father . . .

Father of glory,
how great is the calling of those
   baptized
into Christ your Son!
Build up Christ's body
with humility and gentleness,
   patience and love,
that in the Spirit's power
we may grow at last
to the full stature of Christ,
   exalted in glory,
in the unity of the Father
   and the Holy Spirit,
one God, forever and ever. Amen.

✦ *Alleluia! Christ is risen!*
Christ is risen indeed!
Alleluia! Alleluia!

✙ *Lord, send out your Spirit, alleluia!*
And renew the face of the earth,
alleluia, alleluia!

PSALM 104   *page 423*

READING   *Genesis 11:1–4*

Now the whole earth had one language and the same words. And as they migrated from the east, they came upon a plain in the land of Shinar and settled there. And they said to one another, "Come, let us make bricks, and burn them thoroughly." And they had brick for stone, and bitumen for mortar. Then they said, "Come, let us build ourselves a city, and a tower with its top in the heavens, and let us make a name for ourselves; otherwise we shall be scattered abroad upon the face of the whole earth."

REFLECTION

"Making a name" for oneself in the world of the scriptures was something reserved to kings and gods; it was not something common people set out to do. Often, however, people "make a name" for themselves when they don't intend to. This was certainly the case with Jane Addams, an early twentieth-century activist who was a pioneer in the field of social work. Her conviction that those who serve the poor should live and work among them led to the foundation of Hull House in Chicago, where that city's poor found opportunities for education and development. No doubt the Spirit we pray for in these days before Pentecost inspired Jane to great works of justice and service.

PRAYERS   *others may be added*

Longing for the gifts of the Spirit, we pray:

◆ Come, Holy Spirit!

To those who proclaim the Resurrection of Christ, we pray: ◆ *To those baptized in the Easter waters, we pray:* ◆ *To nations torn by war and injustice, we pray:* ◆ *To those who struggle for an end to division, we pray:* ◆ *To those who labor among the poor and forgotten, we pray:* ◆ *To your creation that longs for redemption, we pray:* ◆ *To us as we continue life's journey, we pray:* ◆

Our Father . . .

God of wind and fire,
you sustain all creation
with your living breath.
Pour out your Spirit upon us
that we may be filled
with the joy of your presence
and so praise you through Christ,
seated at your right hand,
who lives and reigns
forever and ever. Amen.

✙ *Lord, send out your Spirit, alleluia!*
And renew the face of the earth,
alleluia, alleluia!

✤ *Lord, send out your Spirit, alleluia!*
And renew the face of the earth,
alleluia, alleluia!

PSALM 104 *page 423*

READING *Genesis 11:5–9*

The LORD came down to see the city and the tower, which mortals had built. And the LORD said, "Look, they are one people, and they have all one language; and this is only the beginning of what they will do; nothing that they propose to do will now be impossible for them. Come, let us go down, and confuse their language there, so that they will not understand one another's speech." So the LORD scattered them abroad from there over the face of all the earth, and they left off building the city. Therefore it was called Babel, because there the LORD confused the language of all the earth; and from there the LORD scattered them abroad over the face of all the earth.

REFLECTION

We may find Genesis' account of why there are so many human languages odd; God seems jealous of what an organized humanity might accomplish! On one level, the story's purpose is simple enough—to explain the variety of human languages—but it has a deeper meaning as well. The tower's builders were driven by pride, and well-organized human pride has led to great tragedies in human history: nationalism leading to war and genocide; economic systems that serve only the wealthy; *philosophical and religious systems that persecute and condemn those who do not agree.*

PRAYERS *others may be added*

Longing for an end to human division, we pray:

◆ Come, Holy Spirit!

To restore the unity of the baptized, we pray: ◆ *To overcome divisions caused by language, culture, and religion, we pray:* ◆ *To bring an end to conflict and violence among nations, we pray:* ◆ *To overturn the effects of pride and desire for fame, we pray:* ◆ *To restore us to unity with one another, we pray:* ◆

Our Father . . .

God of heaven and earth,
your Spirit overcomes the pride
that causes division among us.
Fill us with your Spirit of unity,
that we may overcome the barriers
which separate us from one another
and so live as one human family.
We ask this in the name
    of Jesus Christ,
who intercedes for us
at your right hand,
and who lives and reigns
forever and ever. Amen.

✤ *Lord, send out your Spirit, alleluia!*
And renew the face of the earth,
alleluia, alleluia!

✦ *Lord, send out your Spirit, alleluia!*
And renew the face of the earth,
alleluia, alleluia!

PSALM 104   *page 423*

READING   *John 17:1b, 11b–14, 17–19*

Jesus looked up to heaven and said, "Father, the hour has come; glorify your Son so that the Son may glorify you. Holy Father, protect them in your name that you have given me, so that they may be one, as we are one. While I was with them, I protected them in your name that you have given me. I guarded them, and not one of them was lost except the one destined to be lost, so that the scripture might be fulfilled. But now I am coming to you, and I speak these things in the world so that they may have my joy made complete in themselves. I have given them your word, and the world has hated them because they do not belong to the world, just as I do not belong to the world. Sanctify them in the truth; your word is truth. As you have sent me into the world, so I have sent them into the world. And for their sakes I sanctify myself, so that they also may be sanctified in truth.

REFLECTION

Today's reading comes from Jesus' high priestly prayer in the Gospel of John—his great prayer for his disciples just before his arrest and crucifixion. Jesus prays especially for unity among his disciples, for their protection and for their sanctification. In a sense, the coming of the Holy Spirit "answers" that prayer, for it is in and through the Holy Spirit that we are joined to God the Father through Jesus Christ, made holy and preserved forever in the power and love of God.

PRAYERS   *others may be added*

Gathered by Christ into divine life,
we pray:

◆ Come, Holy Spirit!

To unify and preserve the Church of Christ, we pray: ◆ To sanctify the neophytes in truth, we pray: ◆ To reveal to the nations the glory of God's Word, we pray: ◆ To bring love to a world torn by fear, we pray: ◆ To guard and protect the poor and defenseless, we pray: ◆ To fill us with joy and confidence in the risen Son of God, we pray: ◆

Our Father . . .

God of eternal glory,
before time began
your Word shared your majesty,
which we have seen in Christ.
Send out your Spirit upon us,
that we may be sanctified in truth
and join your Son in glorifying you
by the power of the Holy Spirit,
one God, now and forever. Amen.

✦ *Lord, send out your Spirit, alleluia!*
And renew the face of the earth,
alleluia, alleluia!

✠ *Lord, send out your Spirit, alleluia!*
And renew the face of the earth,
alleluia, alleluia!

PSALM 104   *page 423*

READING   *Ezekiel 37:1–6*

The hand of the LORD came upon me, and he brought me out by the spirit of the LORD and set me down in the middle of a valley; it was full of bones. He led me all around them; there were very many lying in the valley, and they were very dry. He said to me, "Mortal, can these bones live?" I answered, "O Lord GOD, you know." Then he said to me, "Prophesy to these bones, and say to them: O dry bones, hear the word of the LORD. Thus says the Lord GOD to these bones: I will cause breath to enter you, and you shall live. I will lay sinews on you, and will cause flesh to come upon you, and cover you with skin, and put breath in you, and you shall live; and you shall know that I am the LORD."

REFLECTION   *Gertrude the Great*

O ardent fire of my God, which contains, produces, and imprints those living ardours which attract the humid waters of my soul, and dry up the torrents of earthly delights, and afterwards soften my hard self-opinionatedness, which time has hardened so exceedingly! O consuming fire, which even amid ardent flames imparts sweetness and peace to the soul! In thee, and in none other, do we receive this grace of being reformed to the image and likeness in which we were created. O burning furnace, in which we enjoy the true vision of peace, which tries and purifies the gold of the elect, and leads the soul to seek eagerly for its highest good, even thyself, in thy eternal truth.

PRAYERS   *others may be added*

Hoping that our dry bones and hearts might be renewed, we pray:

◆ Come, Holy Spirit!

To those who have lost their faith and hope, we pray: ◆ *To those whose hearts are dry of compassion, we pray:* ◆ *To those who lack food and shelter, we pray:* ◆ *To those oppressed by violence and fear, we pray:* ◆ *To those dead in addiction or despair, we pray:* ◆ *To those awaiting the fullness of resurrection, we pray:* ◆

Our Father . . .

Living God,
without you we languish
in death's wilderness.
Send forth your Spirit
to renew our tired bodies,
that we may rise up anew
and proclaim to the nations
that you are our God,
the source of life,
who has made all things new
in our Savior Jesus Christ,
now and forever. Amen.

✠ *Lord, send out your Spirit, alleluia!*
And renew the face of the earth,
alleluia, alleluia!

✠ *Lord, send out your Spirit, alleluia!*
And renew the face of the earth,
alleluia, alleluia!

PSALM 104 — page 423

READING — *Ezekiel 37:7–10*

So I prophesied as I had been commanded; and as I prophesied, suddenly there was a noise, a rattling, and the bones came together, bone to its bone. I looked, and there were sinews on them, and flesh had come upon them, and skin had covered them; but there was no breath in them. Then he said to me, "Prophesy to the breath, prophesy, mortal, and say to the breath: Thus says the Lord GOD: Come from the four winds, O breath, and breathe upon these slain, that they may live." I prophesied as he commanded me, and the breath came into them, and they lived, and stood on their feet, a vast multitude.

REFLECTION

It is sometimes easy to forget the Holy Spirit; even theologians often overlook the third person of the Trinity. Yet, like the air we breathe, the Spirit surrounds and permeates us, and is indeed the very breath of divine life within us. Without the Spirit, we are but bones and dust; with the Spirit, not only do we live, but we live as children of God.

PRAYERS — *others may be added*

Longing to breathe God's own breath,
we pray:

◆ Come, Holy Spirit!

To infuse new energy into your people, we pray: ◆ To send the neophytes forth in service, we pray: ◆ To give nourishment to the starving, we pray: ◆ To heal those on the threshold of death, we pray: ◆ To restore the fallen, we pray: ◆ To comfort the sorrowing, we pray: ◆ To raise up the dead to life eternal, we pray: ◆

Our Father . . .

Source of creation,
without your breath
we lie in the dust,
but in love you lift us up,
giving us new life
for your service.
Renew in us the Spirit's gifts,
that we may go forth
in mission to the world,
praising your name
   through the Risen Christ,
who is seated at your right hand
and who lives and reigns
forever and ever. Amen.

✠ *Lord, send out your Spirit, alleluia!*
And renew the face of the earth,
alleluia, alleluia!

✝ *Alleluia!*
The Word of God dwells among us!
God is one with humankind!

PSALM 96   *page 421*

READING   *Zephaniah 3:14–18a*

Sing aloud, O daughter Zion;
    shout, O Israel!
Rejoice and exult with all your heart,
    O daughter Jerusalem!
The LORD has taken away
        the judgments against you,
    he has turned away your enemies.
The king of Israel, the LORD,
        is in your midst;
    you shall fear disaster no more.
On that day it shall be said
        to Jerusalem:
Do not fear, O Zion;
    do not let your hands grow weak.
The LORD, your God, is in your midst,
    a warrior who gives victory;
he will rejoice over you with gladness,
    he will renew you in his love;
he will exult over you
        with loud singing
        as on a day of festival.

REFLECTION

*Today we celebrate the Visitation, when
Mary and Elizabeth rejoiced together in
what God had done for them. Two women
who by all rights shouldn't be pregnant—
one "barren," the other a virgin—were
expecting the greatest of Israel's prophets,
John the Baptist and the Messiah. Although
the Gospel story recounts only bare details
and solemn prayers (Luke 1:39–56), there
had to have been a lot of laughter as well;*
*after all, the world looks funny turned
upside down.*

PRAYERS   *others may be added*

*Rejoicing that God dwells among us,
we pray:*

◆ Word of God, abide with us.

*That the people of God may always
announce God's love for humankind,
we pray:* ◆ *That the nations may
praise God with shouts of joy, we pray:* ◆
*That the weary and fearful may find
comfort in the coming of God, we pray:* ◆
*That we may know the presence of God
among us, we pray:* ◆

Our Father . . .

Hope of Jerusalem,
with Mary and Elizabeth,
the daughters of Israel,
we rejoice in Christ's coming.
Renew our faith
    in the Word-made-flesh,
that our fear may be replaced
with praise of your name.
We ask this in the name of Jesus,
son of Mary and your Son,
who lives and reigns forever and ever.
Amen.

✝ *Alleluia!*
The Word of God dwells among us!
God is one with humankind!

✛ *Lord, send out your Spirit, alleluia!*
And renew the face of the earth,
alleluia, alleluia!

PSALM 104 *page 423*

READING *Ezekiel 37:11–14*

Then he said to me, "Mortal, these bones are the whole house of Israel. They say, 'Our bones are dried up, and our hope is lost; we are cut off completely.' Therefore prophesy, and say to them, Thus says the Lord GOD: I am going to open your graves, and bring you up from your graves, O my people; and I will bring you back to the land of Israel. And you shall know that I am the LORD, when I open your graves, and bring you up from your graves, O my people. I will put my spirit within you, and you shall live, and I will place you on your own soil; then you shall know that I, the LORD, have spoken and will act," says the LORD.

REFLECTION *Hildegard of Bingen*

The Holy Spirit is life that gives life,
Moving all things.
It is the root in every creature
And purifies all things,
Wiping away sins,
Anointing wounds.
It is radiant life, worthy of praise,
Awakening and enlivening
All things.

PRAYERS *others may be added*

God will open our graves and give us life; in hope, we pray:

◆ Come, Holy Spirit!

To those who long to live as your people, we pray: ◆ *To the children of the house of Israel, we pray:* ◆ *To all people of good will, we pray:* ◆ *To those cut off from their faith, we pray:* ◆ *To those without hope, we pray:* ◆ *To those who lie in the grave, we pray:* ◆ *To all who await the fullness of life:* ◆

Our Father . . .

God of refreshment,
though we are exhausted
you restore us to life,
by opening our graves
and making us your people.
Bring us back, God of salvation,
and place within us
your Spirit of life,
that we may live as your people,
glorifying you, our God,
through Jesus Christ
forever and ever. Amen.

✛ *Lord, send out your Spirit, alleluia!*
And renew the face of the earth,
alleluia, alleluia!

✝ *Lord, send out your Spirit, alleluia!*
And renew the face of the earth,
alleluia, alleluia!

PSALM 104 page 423

READING *Joel 2:28–32*

Then afterward I will pour out my spirit on all flesh; your sons and your daughters shall prophesy, your old men shall dream dreams, and your young men shall see visions. Even on the male and female slaves, in those days, I will pour out my spirit. I will show portents in the heavens and on the earth, blood and fire and columns of smoke. The sun shall be turned to darkness, and the moon to blood, before the great and terrible day of the LORD comes. Then everyone who calls on the name of the LORD shall be saved; for in Mount Zion and in Jerusalem there shall be those who escape, as the LORD has said, and among the survivors shall be those whom the LORD calls.

REFLECTION

The coming of God's Spirit in the Old Testament writings was often associated with the Day of the Lord, the time of final judgment. On Pentecost, Peter quotes this passage to explain the apostles' ability to preach in the many languages of the earth (Acts 2:17). For Peter and the early Church, the outpouring of the Spirit meant the beginning of the end times, when all people would be brought into relationship with God. Though these "end times" have lasted far longer than the early Church expected, we too wait in hope for the final revelation of the Spirit, when all people will share God's dream and vision for creation.

PRAYERS *others may be added*

Awaiting the day of the Lord and the outpouring of the Spirit, we pray:

◆ Come, Holy Spirit!

To fill the people of God with wisdom, we pray: ◆ *To make disciples of the neophytes, we pray:* ◆ *To fulfill the visions of Israel's prophets, we pray:* ◆ *To give insight to humankind, we pray:* ◆ *To astound the proud with signs of your power, we pray:* ◆ *To renew creation, we pray:* ◆ *To bring salvation to all who call on God, we pray:* ◆

Our Father . . .

God of new creation,
the coming of your Spirit
ushers in a new age
of prophecy and vision.
Clothe us in the Spirit's power
that we may share the salvation
offered in Christ,
who lives and reigns
forever and ever. Amen.

✝ *Lord, send out your Spirit, alleluia!*
And renew the face of the earth,
alleluia, alleluia!

✚ *Lord, send out your Spirit, alleluia!*
And renew the face of the earth,
alleluia, alleluia!

PSALM 104   page 423

READING   *Romans 8:14–17*

All who are led by the Spirit of God are children of God. For you did not receive a spirit of slavery to fall back into fear, but you have received a spirit of adoption. When we cry, "Abba! Father!" it is that very Spirit bearing witness with our spirit that we are children of God, and if children, then heirs, heirs of God and joint heirs with Christ—if, in fact, we suffer with him so that we may also be glorified with him.

REFLECTION

Though the gift of the Spirit is meant to console us as we await the full revelation of Christ, it transforms us as well. In the Spirit's power, we have become God's children, formed anew in the image of Christ. This power within us will always push us forward toward greater unity with and in Christ, making us heirs both of his suffering and his glory.

PRAYERS   *others may be added*

Joint heirs with Christ, we pray:

◆ Come, Holy Spirit!

To lead the baptized in praising God through Jesus Christ, we pray: ◆ *To make the neophytes shining witnesses of the Gospel, we pray:* ◆ *To pour out a spirit of adoption on all earth's people, we pray:* ◆ *To drive from the world the spirit of slavery and fear, we pray:* ◆ *To transform the suffering of the poor into glory, we pray:* ◆ *To make of us worthy heirs of God's promises, we pray:* ◆

Our Father . . .

Father of every nation,
your Holy Spirit fills the baptized,
making us your adopted children.
Pour out your Spirit upon us,
that we may lead all people
in crying out, "Abba, Father."
May fear be cast out at last
and all the earth inherit
the glory you offer
in the risen Christ,
in whose name we pray. Amen.

✚ *Lord, send out your Spirit, alleluia!*
And renew the face of the earth,
alleluia, alleluia!

✝ *Lord, send out your Spirit, alleluia!*
And renew the face of the earth,
alleluia, alleluia!

PSALM 104   page 423

READING   Acts 2:1–11

When the day of Pentecost had come, they were all together in one place. And suddenly from heaven there came a sound like the rush of a violent wind, and it filled the entire house where they were sitting. Divided tongues, as of fire, appeared among them, and a tongue rested on each of them. All of them were filled with the Holy Spirit and began to speak in other languages, as the Spirit gave them ability.

Now there were devout Jews from every nation under heaven living in Jerusalem. And at this sound the crowd gathered and was bewildered, because each one heard them speaking in the native language of each. Amazed and astonished, they asked, "Are not all these who are speaking Galileans? And how is it that we hear, each of us, in our own native language? Parthians, Medes, Elamites, and residents of Mesopotamia, Judea and Cappadocia, Pontus and Asia, Phrygia and Pamphylia, Egypt and the parts of Libya belonging to Cyrene, and visitors from Rome, both Jews and proselytes, Cretans and Arabs—in our own languages we hear them speaking about God's deeds of power."

REFLECTION   Ambrosian liturgy

Through many gifts that differ the Spirit works a wonderful unity; in the variety of what is bestowed the Spirit imparts all things in wisdom; indeed, it is the selfsame Spirit who creates the many tongues that proclaim your word and yet bestows the faith that brings them into one.

PRAYERS   others may be added

Filled with holy breath, we cry:

◆ Alleluia, alleluia!

O Spirit of God, you empower your Church to proclaim the Gospel, and so we cry: ◆ *O Spirit of God, you fill the baptized with your sevenfold gifts, and so we cry:* ◆ *O Spirit of God, you fill the earth with joy, and so we cry:* ◆ *O Spirit of God, you comfort to the sorrowful, and so we cry:* ◆ *O Spirit of God, you breathe new life into the dead, and so we cry:* ◆

Our Father . . .

God of glory,
you inspire us with holy Breath
as ambassadors of your peace
and heralds of your mercy.
Stir up in us the power of your Spirit
that we may go forth,
offering the forgiveness
    we have received
and the life you offer in Christ,
who lives and reigns with you
in the unity of the Holy Spirit
one God, forever and ever. Amen.

✝ *Lord, send out your Spirit, alleluia!*
And renew the face of the earth,
alleluia, alleluia!

✝ *To you, O LORD, I lift up my soul.*
All my hope is in you.

PSALM 27
page 411

READING
1 Kings 17:1–6

Now Elijah the Tishbite, of Tishbe in Gilead, said to Ahab, "As the LORD the God of Israel lives, before whom I stand, there shall be neither dew nor rain these years, except by my word." The word of the LORD came to him, saying, "Go from here and turn eastward, and hide yourself by the Wadi Cherith, which is east of the Jordan. You shall drink from the wadi, and I have commanded the ravens to feed you there." So he went and did according to the word of the LORD; he went and lived by the Wadi Cherith, which is east of the Jordan. The ravens brought him bread and meat in the morning, and bread and meat in the evening; and he drank from the wadi.

REFLECTION

As we begin the summer stretch of Ordinary Time, we both begin the story of the prophet Elijah and celebrate Saint Boniface, the apostle to Germany. Though separated by nearly 1600 years, the prophet and the bishop had similar missions. Elijah was sent by God to lead Israel, especially its king, Ahab, away from idolatry. Boniface made it his mission to proclaim the Gospel among the Germanic tribes. Both suffered for their persistence: Elijah spent much of his ministry on the run, and Boniface eventually met a martyr's fate. Even in adversity, both remained faithful to their mission.

PRAYERS
others may be added

Trusting in the word of God,
we pray:

◆ Hear us, O God our help.

For prophets who proclaim God's word, we pray: ◆ For bishops who lead God's people with care, we pray: ◆ For martyrs who trust in God's help, we pray: ◆ For civil leaders who guide nations to justice and peace, we pray: ◆ For those who suffer famine and drought, who rely on the aid of the righteous, we pray: ◆ For farmers and agricultural workers who rely on the land for their living: ◆

Our Father . . .

Help of prophets,
you gave your servant Elijah
courage to rebuke a king
and sustained him in times of trouble.
Sustain us with the spirit that
   empowered Elijah
that we may have courage to proclaim
   your word
to whomever you send us.
We ask this in Jesus' name. Amen.

✝ *To you, O LORD, I lift up my soul.*
All my hope is in you.

✚ *To you, O LORD, I lift up my soul.*
All my hope is in you.

PSALM 27 *page 411*

READING *1 Kings 17:7–12*

But after a while the wadi dried up, because there was no rain in the land. Then the word of the LORD came to Elijah, saying, "Go now to Zarephath, which belongs to Sidon, and live there; for I have commanded a widow there to feed you." So he set out and went to Zarephath. When he came to the gate of the town, a widow was there gathering sticks; he called to her and said, "Bring me a little water in a vessel, so that I may drink." As she was going to bring it, he called to her and said, "Bring me a morsel of bread in your hand." But she said, "As the LORD your God lives, I have nothing baked, only a handful of meal in a jar, and a little oil in a jug; I am now gathering a couple of sticks, so that I may go home and prepare it for myself and my son, that we may eat it, and die."

REFLECTION

The famine Elijah announced to King Ahab of Israel was a punishment for the king's marriage to the infamous Jezebel and his subsequent worship of Baal, the god of her people. Since the king was the symbol of the nation, God punished the whole people for his apostasy. As always, the vulnerable suffer the most in times of drought, and the widow of Zarephath is no exception. Her suffering compels us to ask: Does God really send plagues and droughts upon people, or willfully and indiscriminately punish? Does God punish at all? These questions are difficult, but we cannot leave them unanswered.

PRAYERS *others may be added*

Lifting our voices for the sake of the poor, we pray:

◆ Hear us, O God our help.

For widows, widowers, and those who mourn, we pray: ◆ *For orphans and all children in need of love and care, we pray:* ◆ *For the starving and those who lack clean water, we pray:* ◆ *For those driven from their homes by war or natural disaster, we pray:* ◆ *For those who offer help to the needy, we pray:* ◆

Our Father . . .

Comfort of the sorrowing,
your servant Elijah relied
    on the hospitality
of the widow of Zarephath,
who gave willingly
    despite her poverty.
Inspire us with her generosity,
that we may greet all in need
as a sign of the presence of Christ
    among us,
for he lives and reigns forever
    and ever. Amen.

✚ *To you, O LORD, I lift up my soul.*
All my hope is in you.

✝ *To you, O LORD, I lift up my soul.*
All my hope is in you.

PSALM 27   *page 411*

READING   *1 Kings 17:13–16*

Elijah said to her, "Do not be afraid; go and do as you have said; but first make me a little cake of it and bring it to me, and afterwards make something for yourself and your son. For thus says the LORD the God of Israel: The jar of meal will not be emptied and the jug of oil will not fail until the day that the LORD sends rain on the earth." She went and did as Elijah said, so that she as well as he and her household ate for many days. The jar of meal was not emptied, neither did the jug of oil fail, according to the word of the LORD that he spoke by Elijah.

REFLECTION

Although the widow of Zarephath had no proof that God would provide for the needs of her family, she gave generously of the little she had. She stands as a counterpoint to our own culture's tendency to hoard against a rainy day. The rainy day for her had come, yet she did not let someone else starve so she could eat. How many of us would do the same? Would we accept hunger to prevent someone else from starving?

PRAYERS   *others may be added*

Ready to share all we have according to God's word, we pray:

◆ Hear us, O God our help.

That God's people may share not only in times of abundance but in times of want as well, we pray: ◆ *That governments and churches may see first to the needs of the most vulnerable, we pray:* ◆ *That no one may lack for food, we pray:* ◆ *That the poor may show the world true generosity, we pray:* ◆ *That we may always seek the common good, we pray:* ◆

Our Father . . .

God of Israel,
you choose the side
of the hungry and poor
and never fail to hear
their cries for justice.
Bless us with your generosity
May we share willingly with
    those in need
and so assure that none
    of your children
suffer want or hunger.
We ask this in the name
    of Jesus Christ,
who lives and reigns forever and ever.
Amen.

✝ *To you, O LORD, I lift up my soul.*
All my hope is in you.

✜ *To you, O LORD, I lift up my soul.*
All my hope is in you.

PSALM 27 *page 411*

READING *1 Kings 17:17–22*

After this the son of the woman, the mistress of the house, became ill; his illness was so severe that there was no breath left in him. She then said to Elijah, "What have you against me, O man of God? You have come to me to bring my sin to remembrance, and to cause the death of my son!" But he said to her, "Give me your son." He took him from her bosom, carried him up into the upper chamber where he was lodging, and laid him on his own bed. He cried out to the LORD, "O LORD my God, have you brought calamity even upon the widow with whom I am staying, by killing her son?" Then he stretched himself upon the child three times, and cried out to the LORD, "O LORD my God, let this child's life come into him again." The LORD listened to the voice of Elijah; the life of the child came into him again, and he revived.

REFLECTION *Second Vatican Council*

"It is when faced with death that the enigma of the human condition is most evident. People are tormented not only by pain and by the gradual diminution of their bodily powers but also, and even more, by the dread of forever ceasing to be. But a deep instinct leads them rightly to shrink from and to reject the utter ruin and total loss of their personality. . . .

"For God has called men and women, and still calls them, to attach themselves with all their being to him in sharing for ever a life that is divine and free from all decay."

PRAYERS *others may be added*

Longing for the life of God's Spirit, we pray:

◆ Hear us, O God our help.

For those who cry out to God on behalf of others, we pray: ◆ *For those who minister to the sick or sorrowful, we pray:* ◆ *For grieving parents and spouses, we pray:* ◆ *For children suffering terrible illness, we pray:* ◆ *For the dead awaiting resurrection, we pray:* ◆ *For all who hope in the God of life, we pray:* ◆

Our Father . . .

God of the living and the dead,
in the resurrection of Jesus
you offer us a hope stronger than death.
Be with us in times of death
    and sorrow,
that we may never lose faith
in your promise of eternal life
through Jesus Christ,
the resurrection and the life,
who lives and reigns forever and ever.
Amen.

✜ *To you, O LORD, I lift up my soul.*
All my hope is in you.

✙ *To you, O LORD, I lift up my soul.*
All my hope is in you.

PSALM 27 *page 411*

READING *1 Kings 18:1, 17–20*

After many days the word of the LORD came to Elijah, in the third year of the drought, saying, "Go, present yourself to Ahab; I will send rain on the earth." When Ahab saw Elijah, Ahab said to him, "Is it you, you troubler of Israel?" He answered, "I have not troubled Israel; but you have, and your father's house, because you have forsaken the commandments of the LORD and followed the Baals. Now therefore have all Israel assemble for me at Mount Carmel, with the four hundred fifty prophets of Baal and the four hundred prophets of Asherah, who eat at Jezebel's table." So Ahab sent to all the Israelites, and assembled the prophets at Mount Carmel.

REFLECTION

Today begins the story of Elijah's show-down with the king of Israel and the prophets of the god Baal. Before the drought could end, Elijah had to demonstrate which deity was the true God of Israel. The cult and prophets of Baal were supported by the king's own treasury ("Jezebel's table"). To uproot them, Elijah had to discredit Baal in front of the whole people of Israel.

PRAYERS *others may be added*

Faithful to our God of compassion, we pray:

◆ Hear us, O God our help.

That the disciples of Jesus may be single-hearted in their devotion to the Gospel, we pray: ◆ *That God's people may be wary of false prophets, we pray:* ◆ *That the Church's ministers may serve God in integrity, we pray:* ◆ *That the world's leaders may resist the idols of power and wealth, we pray:* ◆ *That all false gods may be cast down, we pray:* ◆ *That we may seek the face of the living God, we pray:* ◆

Our Father . . .

All-holy God,
you rule creation with a mighty hand
and there is no other god besides you.
Cast out from within us
the worship of idols,
that we may serve only you
and so give glory to your name,
for you live and reign
forever and ever. Amen.

✙ *To you, O LORD, I lift up my soul.*
All my hope is in you.

✛ *To you, O LORD, I lift up my soul.*
All my hope is in you.

PSALM 27 *page 411*

READING *1 Kings 18:21–24*

Elijah then came near to all the people, and said, "How long will you go limping with two different opinions? If the LORD is God, follow him; but if Baal, then follow him." The people did not answer him a word. Then Elijah said to the people, "I, even I only, am left a prophet of the LORD; but Baal's prophets number four hundred fifty. Let two bulls be given to us; let them choose one bull for themselves, cut it in pieces, and lay it on the wood, but put no fire to it; I will prepare the other bull and lay it on the wood, but put no fire to it. Then you call on the name of your god and I will call on the name of the LORD; the god who answers by fire is indeed God." All the people answered, "Well spoken!"

REFLECTION

It seems that all things human are capable of being transformed into idols of one form or another. Money is an obvious one, along with free markets, central economic planning, and the ideologies that accompany them. Religion, too, can become an idol, especially when it leads to violence. Nationalism, militarism, guns, missiles, freedom for its own sake, the individual: The list goes on and on. We each have our own private idols, too, and we do well to pay attention to them from time to time, lest they become our masters.

PRAYERS *others may be added*

Single-hearted in our worship,
we pray:

◆ Hear us, O God our help.

For the disciples of Jesus, called to place the Gospel before all else, we pray: ◆
For believers of all faiths, called to dialogue in trust and good will, we pray: ◆
For those imprisoned by worship of money or power, called to turn from idolatry, we pray: ◆ *For all oppressed by the idols of others, called to struggle for their freedom, we pray:* ◆ *For all who are lukewarm in faith, called to seek God with their whole being, we pray:* ◆

Our Father . . .

God of Israel,
you allow no rivals
but demand complete commitment
    to your service.
Free us from all that prevents us
from serving you
    with our whole selves:
May we be a people
filled with zeal for your justice,
dedicated citizens of your kingdom,
where Christ lives and reigns
forever and ever. Amen.

✛ *To you, O LORD, I lift up my soul.*
All my hope is in you.

✠ *To you, O LORD, I lift up my soul.*
All my hope is in you.

PSALM 27 *page 411*

READING *Deuteronomy 4:32–34, 39–40*

For ask now about former ages, long before your own, ever since the day that God created human beings on the earth; ask from one end of heaven to the other: has anything so great as this ever happened or has its like ever been heard of? Has any people ever heard the voice of a god speaking out of a fire, as you have heard, and lived? Or has any god ever attempted to go and take a nation for himself from the midst of another nation, by trials, by signs and wonders, by war, by a mighty hand and an outstretched arm, and by terrifying displays of power, as the LORD your God did for you in Egypt before your very eyes? So acknowledge today and take to heart that the LORD is God in heaven above and on the earth beneath; there is no other. Keep his statutes and his commandments, which I am commanding you today for your own well-being and that of your descendants after you, so that you may long remain in the land that the LORD your God is giving you for all time.

REFLECTION

Preachers throughout the ages have sought metaphors to describe the mystery of the Trinity; the triangle and the shamrock are among them. The mystery of the Trinity is much more dynamic than these, however.

One metaphor from Eastern Christianity is the perichoresis, *the "circle dance," which imagines an eternal circular movement of love and grace. The love of the Dancers is so great that it spills out as creation, which in Jesus Christ is taken up again to share in the eternal movement of God.*

PRAYERS *others may be added*

Praising God, we pray:

◆ Hear us, O God our help.

That God's people may invite all nations to share its life in the triune God, we pray: ◆ *That the Jewish people may live in fidelity to the God who called them, we pray:* ◆ *That the love of God may spill out upon the earth, reconciling nations to one another, we pray:* ◆ *That the dead may join the eternal dance of divine life, we pray:* ◆ *That we may strive to be signs of the Trinity's perfect love, we pray:* ◆

Our Father . . .

All-holy God,
Creator of all that is,
Source of salvation and life,
we praise you who reveal yourself
as Father, Son, and Holy Spirit,
one God of three persons.
Draw us into the dance of your life,
that we may share your boundless love
and glorify you through eternity,
who live and reign forever and ever.
Amen.

✠ *To you, O LORD, I lift up my soul.*
All my hope is in you.

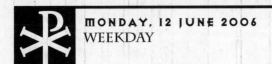
✢ *To you, O LORD, I lift up my soul.*
All my hope is in you.

PSALM 27   *page 411*

READING   *1 Kings 18:25–29*

Then Elijah said to the prophets of Baal, "Choose for yourselves one bull and prepare it first, for you are many; then call on the name of your god, but put no fire to it." So they took the bull that was given them, prepared it, and called on the name of Baal from morning until noon, crying, "O Baal, answer us!" But there was no voice, and no answer. They limped about the altar that they had made. At noon Elijah mocked them, saying, "Cry aloud! Surely he is a god; either he is meditating, or he has wandered away, or he is on a journey, or perhaps he is asleep and must be awakened." Then they cried aloud and, as was their custom, they cut themselves with swords and lances until the blood gushed out over them. As midday passed, they raved on until the time of the offering of the oblation, but there was no voice, no answer, and no response.

REFLECTION

Though the author of First Kings uses the silence of Baal as an indictment of Baal's worshipers, perhaps we too have experienced the apparent silence of God. Though we cry out, even "rave," we don't receive the answer we hope for. Though we long for an end to suffering—our own or that of the poor or sick—we still await God's healing touch. Some may be tempted to point out that we, like the prophets of Baal, are calling out to a God that doesn't exist, or perhaps we blame ourselves for not being faithful enough. Both of these miss the mark, of course. We have no choice but to wait, as our ancestors before us, trusting that in the fullness of time God's power will be revealed.

PRAYERS   *others may be added*

With hope in God's promise,
we pray:

◆ Hear us, O God our help.

That the disciples of Jesus may seek only the face of the one true God, we pray: ◆
That the Church may be blessed with bold and powerful prophets, we pray: ◆
That all people of faith may follow paths of righteousness and peace together, we pray: ◆ *That those who seek God in prayer may find God's presence, we pray:* ◆ *That we may boldly call on the name of our God in hope, we pray:* ◆

Our Father . . .

Strong and faithful God,
you raised up Elijah
to bring your people back to you.
Bless your Church today
with bold and faithful prophets,
that your people may be renewed
    in faithfulness
to the Gospel of Jesus Christ,
who lives and reigns
forever and ever. Amen.

✢ *To you, O LORD, I lift up my soul.*
All my hope is in you.

✚ *To you, O LORD, I lift up my soul.*
All my hope is in you.

PSALM 27   *page 411*

READING   *1 Kings 18:30–35*

Then Elijah said to all the people, "Come closer to me"; and all the people came closer to him. First he repaired the altar of the LORD that had been thrown down; Elijah took twelve stones, according to the number of the tribes of the sons of Jacob, to whom the word of the LORD came, saying, "Israel shall be your name"; with the stones he built an altar in the name of the LORD. Then he made a trench around the altar, large enough to contain two measures of seed. Next he put the wood in order, cut the bull in pieces, and laid it on the wood. He said, "Fill four jars with water and pour it on the burnt offering and on the wood." Then he said, "Do it a second time"; and they did it a second time. Again he said, "Do it a third time"; and they did it a third time, so that the water ran all around the altar, and filled the trench also with water.

REFLECTION

After taunting the prophets of Baal and goading them into a prophetic frenzy, Elijah calls the people of Israel close. Although he seems to be merely taunting the Baalist prophets by drenching the sacrifice with water, he is really mimicking the sacrifice offered by Moses after the Israelites had worshiped the golden calf (Exodus 24:4– 8). Elijah's sacrifice is about renewal, the restoration of the people to their God.

PRAYERS   *others may be added*

Seeking the renewal of our faith,
we pray:

◆ Hear us, O God our help.

For all who guide the baptized in faithfulness to their call, we pray: ◆ For all who seek the renewal of the Church, we pray: ◆ For those who witness to their faith in dangerous times and places, we pray: ◆ For those who seek God's boundless mercy, we pray: ◆ For those who long to see the power of God, we pray: ◆

Our Father . . .

Faithful One of Israel,
too often we stray
from our faith in you
and stand in need of renewal.
Bless us with a spirit
of wisdom and discernment:
May we cast aside
   whatever prevents us
from faithfully following Jesus,
the light of the world,
Lord forever and ever. Amen.

✚ *To you, O LORD, I lift up my soul.*
All my hope is in you.

✦ *To you, O LORD, I lift up my soul.*
  All my hope is in you.

PSALM 27   *page 411*

READING   *1 Kings 18:36–39*

At the time of the offering of the oblation, the prophet Elijah came near and said, "O LORD, God of Abraham, Isaac, and Israel, let it be known this day that you are God in Israel, that I am your servant, and that I have done all these things at your bidding. Answer me, O LORD, answer me, so that this people may know that you, O LORD, are God, and that you have turned their hearts back." Then the fire of the LORD fell and consumed the burnt offering, the wood, the stones, and the dust, and even licked up the water that was in the trench. When all the people saw it, they fell on their faces and said, "The LORD indeed is God; the LORD indeed is God."

REFLECTION

It takes a spectacular sign to finally convince the Israelites of God's power, and perhaps we are tempted to ask why we see no great signs among us today. Could it be that we are unwilling to let God's power shine in us? Perhaps our signs will not include fire from heaven, but what about the fire of love? Are not hands outstretched in service and words of blessing and forgiveness certain signs of God's power among us? Such acts would surely lead others to faith.

PRAYERS   *others may be added*

Professing our faith in the God of our ancestors, we pray:

◆ Hear us, O God our help.

That the fire of God's Spirit may consume the Church, we pray: ◆ *That the works of Jesus' disciples may give glory to God before all people, we pray:* ◆ *That the prayers of those who trust in God may be answered, we pray:* ◆ *That idols of greed and power may be cast down, we pray:* ◆ *That we may always remain faithful to our God of salvation, we pray:* ◆

Our Father . . .

God of Abraham, Isaac, and Israel,
with mighty deeds
you reveal yourself
as the one God of heaven and earth.
Show forth your power among us,
that we may be confident
of your abiding presence,
the God and Father of Jesus Christ,
who lives and reigns forever and ever.
Amen.

✦ *To you, O LORD, I lift up my soul.*
  All my hope is in you.

✝ *To you, O LORD, I lift up my soul.*
All my hope is in you.

PSALM 27   *page 411*

READING   *1 Kings 19:9a, 11–13a*

Elijah came to a cave, and spent the night there. Then the word of the LORD came to him, saying, "Go out and stand on the mountain before the LORD, for the LORD is about to pass by." Now there was a great wind, so strong that it was splitting mountains and breaking rocks in pieces before the LORD, but the LORD was not in the wind; and after the wind an earthquake, but the LORD was not in the earthquake; and after the earthquake a fire, but the LORD was not in the fire; and after the fire a sound of sheer silence. When Elijah heard it, he wrapped his face in his mantle and went out and stood at the entrance of the cave.

REFLECTION

For many of us, "sheer silence" is practically impossible to imagine, much less experience. If we all had to wait for that kind of silence, we would be waiting a long time for prayer. Yet our God seeks us out, desires to know us and to have us know the divine mystery. We need only be attentive to the times and places and people in which God may be found. In church? We hope! But we must also seek God in our spouses, children, and friends, and any number of other expected and unexpected places and people.

PRAYERS   *others may be added*

Always seeking the presence of God, we pray:

◆ Hear us, O God our help.

For the baptized, always attentive to God's voice, we pray: ◆ *For all who seek God, searching in nature, in silence, in others, we pray:* ◆ *For the hungry and poor, awaiting the revelation of God's justice, we pray:* ◆ *For those who feel forsaken, beloved of and sought out by God, we pray:* ◆ *For all of us, seeking God in the silence of our hearts, we pray:* ◆

Our Father . . .

God of mystery,
we search for you
   in marvelous deeds,
but you come to us in sheer silence.
Make us more attentive
to your loving presence:
May we never fail to recognize you
When you make yourself known.
We ask this in Jesus' name. Amen.

✝ *To you, O LORD, I lift up my soul.*
All my hope is in you.

✠ *To you, O LORD, I lift up my soul.*
   All my hope is in you.

PSALM 27   *page 411*

READING   *1 Kings 19:13b,*
                              15b, 16b, 19–21

Then there came a voice to him that said, "Go, return on your way to the wilderness of Damascus; you shall anoint Elisha son of Shaphat of Abel-meholah as prophet in your place.

So he set out from there, and found Elisha son of Shaphat, who was plowing. There were twelve yoke of oxen ahead of him, and he was with the twelfth. Elijah passed by him and threw his mantle over him. He left the oxen, ran after Elijah, and said, "Let me kiss my father and my mother, and then I will follow you." Then Elijah said to him, "Go back again; for what have I done to you?" He returned from following him, took the yoke of oxen, and slaughtered them; using the equipment from the oxen, he boiled their flesh, and gave it to the people, and they ate. Then he set out and followed Elijah, and became his servant.

REFLECTION

When Elijah calls Elisha to be his successor, Elisha makes a radical break from his former life. He slaughters his oxen and roasts them with the wood from his plow, effectively destroying his livelihood. While discipleship may not always require such a change of course, it may indeed mean breaking with the way we used to live. We may find that our job is in conflict with our Christian commitment, or we may feel drawn to simpler living. Of course, may not happen all in one day. For many, discipleship is a gradual process, a slow makeover into the likeness of Christ.

PRAYERS

Ready to serve as ministers of the Gospel, we pray:

◆ Hear us, O God our help.

For those who have inherited the work of the prophets, we pray: ◆ *For those discerning a call to ministry in the Church, we pray:* ◆ *For those who train presbyters, deacons, and lay ministers, we pray:* ◆ *For those who model total commitment to the Gospel, we pray:* ◆ *For those who nurture faith in others, we pray:* ◆ *For those who feed the hungry, we pray:* ◆ *For all who seek to follow God's way, we pray:* ◆

Our Father . . .

God of election,
in every age you send your prophets
to call your people to faithfulness.
Draw out from among us
prophets for our time:
May we be ready to listen
when they preach your word,
ready to serve you
more faithfully through Jesus Christ,
who lives and reigns
forever and ever. Amen.

✠ *To you, O LORD, I lift up my soul.*
   All my hope is in you.

✠ *To you, O LORD, I lift up my soul.*
   All my hope is in you.

PSALM 27   page 411

READING   *2 Kings 2:1b, 6, 9–11*

Elijah and Elisha were on their way from Gilgal. Elijah said to Elisha, "Stay here; for the LORD has sent me to the Jordan." But he said, "As the LORD lives, and as you yourself live, I will not leave you."

When they had crossed the Jordan, Elijah said to Elisha, "Tell me what I may do for you, before I am taken from you." Elisha said, "Please let me inherit a double share of your spirit." He responded, "You have asked a hard thing; yet, if you see me as I am being taken from you, it will be granted you; if not, it will not." As they continued walking and talking, a chariot of fire and horses of fire separated the two of them, and Elijah ascended in a whirlwind into heaven.

REFLECTION

Before assuming Elijah's prophetic mantle, Elisha spent time as an apprentice, absorbing the wisdom and experience of his predecessor. This time of mentoring was crucial for Elisha's success; he didn't begin "from scratch" but could build upon what had already been accomplished by Elijah. The prophets' relationship reminds us of the value of learning from our elders: parents, grandparents, teachers, and mentors. By embracing their wisdom and listening to their experience, we not only honor them but profit from their insight.

PRAYERS   *others may be added*

Awestruck by God's favor to those who serve, we pray:

◆ Hear us, O God our help.

That the Church's ministers may receive a double portion of God's spirit of prophecy, we pray: ◆ *That students may find faithful mentors in their teachers and counselors, we pray:* ◆ *That the young may seek the wisdom of those who have gone before them, we pray:* ◆ *That the experience of seniors may be welcomed and treasured, we pray:* ◆ *That we may recognize God's glory when it is revealed among us, we pray:* ◆

Our Father . . .

All-powerful God,
your servant Elijah
served you in adversity,
and you blessed him
with shining glory.
Pour out upon us a double portion
   of your spirit of prophecy,
that we too may serve you
in good times and bad,
fearlessly proclaiming
your message of justice
   and faithfulness,
for you live and reign
forever and ever. Amen.

✠ *To you, O LORD, I lift up my soul.*
   All my hope is in you.

✛ *To you, O LORD, I lift up my soul.*
  All my hope is in you.

PSALM 27   *page 411*

READING   *Exodus 24:3–8*

Moses came and told the people all the words of the LORD and all the ordinances; and all the people answered with one voice, and said, "All the words that the LORD has spoken we will do." And Moses wrote down all the words of the LORD. He rose early in the morning, and built an altar at the foot of the mountain, and set up twelve pillars, corresponding to the twelve tribes of Israel. He sent young men of the people of Israel, who offered burnt offerings and sacrificed oxen as offerings of well-being to the LORD. Moses took half of the blood and put it in basins, and half of the blood he dashed against the altar. Then he took the book of the covenant, and read it in the hearing of the people; and they said, "All that the LORD has spoken we will do, and we will be obedient." Moses took the blood and dashed it on the people, and said, "See the blood of the covenant that the LORD has made with you in accordance with all these words."

REFLECTION   *Lauda Sion*

Truth the ancient types fulfilling,
Isaac bound, a victim willing,
  Paschal lamb, its lifeblood spilling,
  manna to the fathers sent.
Very bread, good shepherd, tend us,

Jesu, of your love befriend us,
  You refresh us, you defend us,
  Your eternal goodness send us
In the land of life to see.

PRAYERS   *others may be added*

Faithful to the promise of salvation
revealed in the body and blood of
Christ, we pray:

◆ Hear us, O God our help.

For the baptized, commanded to
give thanks in remembrance of Jesus,
we pray: ◆ *For catechumens, who long*
for a place at the Lord's table, we pray: ◆
For the imprisoned, who hunger for the
bread of freedom, we pray: ◆ *For people*
harried by war, who thirst for the wine
of peace, we pray: ◆ *For the dead,*
who await the joy of the Lamb's wedding
banquet, we pray: ◆

Our Father . . .

God of the covenant,
over gifts of bread and wine
we offer you Christ's sacrifice of
  praise.
Through the gift of the Eucharist,
may we become more fully
the mystery we celebrate:
bodies broken in love,
lives poured out in service,
through Christ our Savior,
who lives and reigns with you,
in the unity of the Holy Spirit,
one God, now and forever. Amen.

✛ *To you, O LORD, I lift up my soul.*
  All my hope is in you.

✝ *To you, O LORD, I lift up my soul.*
All my hope is in you.

PSALM 27 *page 411*

READING *Isaiah 6:1–4*

In the year that King Uzziah died, I saw the Lord sitting on a throne, high and lofty; and the hem of his robe filled the temple. Seraphs were in attendance above him; each had six wings: with two they covered their faces, and with two they covered their feet, and with two they flew. And one called to another and said:

"Holy, holy, holy is the LORD of hosts;

the whole earth is full of his glory." The pivots on the thresholds shook at the voices of those who called, and the house filled with smoke.

REFLECTION

While our knowledge of the prophet Elijah comes only through third-person accounts—Elijah apparently left no writings—the prophet Isaiah provides an account of his ministry in his own hand. Like Elijah, Isaiah was sent to the kings of Israel, offering both hope and challenge. The original prophet's influence was so great that the Book of Isaiah in our Bible actually has at least three writers. The second and third invoked the prophet's name and authority to lend credence to their message.

PRAYERS *others may be added*

With eyes open to God's glory,
we pray:

◆ Hear us, O God our help.

That Church leaders may offer words of both hope and challenge, we pray: ◆ *That God's people may become like incense offered to the glory of the Most High, we pray:* ◆ *That the world's people may honor God's glory shining in creation, we pray:* ◆ *That God's holiness may cleanse the earth of injustice, we pray:* ◆ *That the dead may join the heavenly beings who worship before the Holy One, we pray:* ◆

Our Father . . .

Holy, holy, holy God,
creation shines with your glory
for you make the earth your footstool.
Wrap us in the hem of your garment,
and raise us to high places,
that we may sing your praise
with all the angels and saints,
for you live and reign
forever and ever. Amen.

✝ *To you, O LORD, I lift up my soul.*
All my hope is in you.

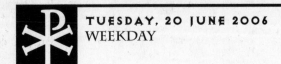
✠ *To you, O L*ORD*, I lift up my soul.*
All my hope is in you.

PSALM 27   *page 411*

READING   *Isaiah 6:5–8*

And I said: "Woe is me! I am lost, for I am a man of unclean lips, and I live among a people of unclean lips; yet my eyes have seen the King, the LORD of hosts!"

Then one of the seraphs flew to me, holding a live coal that had been taken from the altar with a pair of tongs. The seraph touched my mouth with it and said: "Now that this has touched your lips, your guilt has departed and your sin is blotted out." Then I heard the voice of the Lord saying, "Whom shall I send, and who will go for us?" And I said, "Here am I; send me!"

REFLECTION

The call of Isaiah mirrors the story of other biblical figures: God's call, initial protest, God's response, and the some-times reluctant acceptance of mission. Isaiah, too, protests his sinfulness but then eagerly accepts the mission God offers. Rather than dwelling on his unworthiness, Isaiah trusts in God's power to overcome failure. Faced with Isaiah's trust and openness, perhaps we must ask ourselves if our own sense of unworthiness has pre-vented us from accepting both the chal-lenge and the joy of serving God.

PRAYERS   *others may be added*

Ready to answer God's call,
we pray:

◆ Hear us, O God our help.

For those called in baptism to lives
of holiness and service, we pray: ◆
For those called in ordination to service
among God's people, we pray: ◆
For those called in elections to lead and
govern the world's nations, we pray: ◆
For those called in their consciences to
seek justice and transformation, we pray: ◆
For those called in reconciliation
to forgiveness and self-acceptance,
we pray: ◆ *For all called by God to lives*
of authenticity and love, we pray: ◆

Our Father . . .

God of election,
you make all things clean
by the power of your mercy.
Cast aside the stumbling blocks
that prevent us from answering
    your call,
that with the prophets of old
we may announce your message
to every people and nation,
for you live and reign
forever and ever. Amen.

✠ *To you, O L*ORD*, I lift up my soul.*
All my hope is in you.

✤ *To you, O LORD, I lift up my soul.*
All my hope is in you.

PSALM 27 *page 411*

READING *Isaiah 1:10–15*

Hear the word of the LORD,
 you rulers of Sodom!
Listen to the teaching of our God,
 you people of Gomorrah!
What to me is the multitude
 of your sacrifices?
 says the LORD;
I have had enough of burnt offerings
 of rams
 and the fat of fed beasts;
I do not delight in the blood of bulls,
 or of lambs, or of goats.
When you come to appear before me,
 who asked this from your hand?
 Trample my courts no more;
bringing offerings is futile;
 incense is an abomination to me.
New moon and sabbath and calling
 of convocation—
 I cannot endure solemn assemblies
 with iniquity.
Your new moons and your
 appointed festivals
 my soul hates;
they have become a burden to me,
 I am weary of bearing them.
When you stretch out your hands,
 I will hide my eyes from you;
even though you make many prayers,
 I will not listen;
 your hands are full of blood.

REFLECTION

The Hebrew prophets were above all else
great preachers who constantly called
Israel to faithfulness and to a just and
pleasing offering. Their words are filled
with warning—as in today's reading—but
also, eventually, hope as well.

PRAYERS *others may be added*

Putting aside empty fasts and empty
sacrifices, we pray:

◆ Hear us, O God our help.

For ears and hearts open to the word of
the Lord, we pray: ◆ *For attention to God's*
teaching, we pray: ◆ *For the incense*
of prayers humbly offered, we pray: ◆
For hands cleansed of injustice and
oppression, we pray: ◆ *For a sacrifice*
pleasing to the God of hosts, we pray: ◆

Our Father . . .

Lord God,
you turn away from prayers
unaccompanied by acts of justice
and from sacrifices that lack humility.
Give us an offering pleasing to you:
hands cleansed of wrongdoing,
hearts ready to receive your word,
and mouths filled with your praise.
We ask this in the name of Jesus,
who lives and reigns
forever and ever. Amen.

✤ *To you, O LORD, I lift up my soul.*
All my hope is in you.

✛ *To you, O LORD, I lift up my soul.*
All my hope is in you.

PSALM 27   *page 411*

READING   *Isaiah 1:16–20*

Wash yourselves;
   make yourselves clean;
  remove the evil of your doings
   from before my eyes;
cease to do evil,
   learn to do good;
seek justice,
   rescue the oppressed,
defend the orphan,
   plead for the widow.
Come now, let us argue it out,
   says the LORD:
though your sins are like scarlet,
   they shall be like snow;
though they are red like crimson,
   they shall become like wool.
If you are willing and obedient,
   you shall eat the good of the land;
but if you refuse and rebel,
   you shall be devoured
    by the sword;
   for the mouth of the LORD
    has spoken.

REFLECTION

The words of God could not be clearer:
Seek justice; learn to do good; rescue the
oppressed. We know who God calls us to
be; often, we simply lack the will to accept
the consequences. Now is the time to
renew our commitment to living our bap-
tismal vocation, which is nothing less than
living as if God's reign of justice was
already fully revealed.

PRAYERS   *others may be added*

Willing and obedient students of God's
word, we pray:

◆ Hear us, O God our help.

That the baptized may wash themselves
of all that separates them from God,
we pray: ◆ *That catechumens may set*
aside evil acts in the waters of baptism,
we pray: ◆ *That God may cleanse the*
sins of all people, we pray: ◆ *That our*
worship may bear good fruit for the
sake of the oppressed, the widow, and
the orphan, we pray: ◆ *That we may*
learn anew the ways of justice, we pray: ◆

Our Father . . .

God of mercy,
though our sins are like scarlet
you make us white as snow.
May this season of renewal
give us strength to cease doing evil
and learn to do good,
to seek justice
and defend the widow and orphan.
We ask this through Jesus Christ,
in whom we are made clean,
who is Lord forever and ever. Amen.

✛ *To you, O LORD, I lift up my soul.*
All my hope is in you.

✛ *To you, O LORD, I lift up my soul.*
All my hope is in you.

PSALM 27 *page 411*

READING *Hosea 11:1, 3–4, 8c–9*

When Israel was a child, I loved him,
   and out of Egypt I called my son.
It was I who taught Ephraim to walk,
   I took them up in my arms;
     but they did not know that
      I healed them.
I led them with cords
     of human kindness,
   with bands of love.
I was to them like those
   who lift infants to their cheeks.
   I bent down to them and fed them.
My heart recoils within me;
   my compassion grows warm
     and tender.
I will not execute my fierce anger;
   I will not again destroy Ephraim;
for I am God and no mortal,
   the Holy One in your midst,
   and I will not come in wrath.

REFLECTION

The solemnity of the Sacred Heart is a cele-
bration of the overflowing mercy of God.
In response to those who say that human
sinfulness is so great that no one can be
saved, today's solemnity proclaims that the
mercy offered in Christ's paschal mystery
can overcome the most grievous wounds
caused by human sinfulness—both our own
individual acts of fear or malice and our
common ones of injustice, racism, and apa-
thy toward the poor. Our task as Christians
is to live as those who know God's mercy,
freely offering what we have received
without cost. No one can earn the mercy
of God, but God gives it in abundance.

PRAYERS *others may be added*

Sheltered by the compassion of Jesus,
we pray:

◆ Hear us, O God our help.

That the Church may be a sign to all
people of God's great love for the world,
we pray: ◆ *That service of the one God*
may overcome divisions among people of
faith, we pray: ◆ *That the world's races*
and cultures may embrace one another
in mutual love, we pray: ◆ *That mercy*
may triumph over the desire for revenge,
we pray: ◆ *That we may love God more*
deeply by loving our sisters and brothers,
we pray: ◆

Our Father . . .

Source of compassion,
the heart of Jesus overflows
with love for humankind,
for in Christ your mercy is made flesh.
Bathe us in his mercy,
that the wounds of our sinfulness
   may be healed
and your love may shine forth in us,
bearing witness to the same
   Jesus Christ,
who lives and reigns with you,
in the unity of the Holy Spirit,
one God, forever and ever. Amen.

✛ *To you, O LORD, I lift up my soul.*
All my hope is in you.

✦ *Alleluia!*
The Word of God dwells among us!
God is one with humankind!

PSALM 96 *page 421*

READING *Isaiah 49:1–3, 5a, 6b*

Listen to me, O coastlands,
    pay attention, you peoples
        from far away!
The LORD called me before I was born,
    while I was in my mother's womb
        he named me.
He made my mouth like a sharp sword,
    in the shadow of his hand he hid me;
he made me a polished arrow,
    in his quiver he hid me away.
And he said to me, "You are
        my servant,
    Israel, in whom I will be glorified."
And now the LORD says,
"It is too light a thing that you should
        be my servant
    to raise up the tribes of Jacob
    and to restore the survivors of Israel;
I will give you as a light to the nations,
    that my salvation may reach to the
        end of the earth."

REFLECTION *Paul of Apulia*

Hair of the camel furnished
  a coarse raiment
To your blessed members;
  leather your girdle;
You drink the cold spring,
  food for you wild honey
Mingled with locusts.
None has arisen in the mighty spaces
Of round earth's borders holier
  than John was:

Great was his grace who poured
  the mystic waters
O'er the Redeemer.

PRAYERS *others may be added*

God's salvation stretches to the ends
of the earth; in joy, we pray:

◆ Word of God, abide with us.

For the Church, pointing the way to the
Lamb of God, we pray: ◆ *For preachers*
and prophets, inspired by the example of
the Baptist, we pray: ◆ *For catechumens,*
open to the words of God's messenger,
we pray: ◆ *For the world, in need of a*
message of salvation and hope, we pray: ◆
For us, called before birth to God's
service, we pray: ◆

Our Father . . .

God of the prophets,
you made of John the Baptist
a polished arrow in your quiver,
a fiery prophet to your people,
and the forerunner of the Christ.
Open our ears to his sharp words
that our hearts may be cleaved
of darkness and sin.
May we too be a light to the nations,
a sign of the salvation
you offer in Jesus Christ,
who is Lord with you
in the unity of the Holy Spirit,
one God, forever and ever. Amen.

✦ *Alleluia!*
The Word of God dwells among us!
God is one with humankind!

✝ *To you, O LORD, I lift up my soul.*
  All my hope is in you.

PSALM 27   *page 411*

READING   *2 Corinthians 5:14–17*

The love of Christ urges us on, because we are convinced that one has died for all; therefore all have died. And he died for all, so that those who live might live no longer for themselves, but for him who died and was raised for them.

From now on, therefore, we regard no one from a human point of view; even though we once knew Christ from a human point of view, we know him no longer in that way. So if anyone is in Christ, there is a new creation: everything old has passed away; see, everything has become new!

REFLECTION

In the Sundays in Ordinary Time, the second reading is a semi-continuous reading of one of the New Testament letters; for the next several Sundays we read from Second Corinthians. Today, Paul summarizes our mission as Christians: to be ambassadors of God's mercy in the world. Wherever Christians are, the reconciling power of God should be evident, at least if we are doing our job. The mercy is God's, of course, but we are its living signs, pointing the way to God's new creation, where all are reconciled to God and to one another as well. It is a mammoth task, and many resist it, but in the end God's mercy will overcome the divisions that keep us from God and each other.

PRAYERS   *others may be added*

Reconciled to God, new creations in Christ, we pray:

◆ Hear us, O God our help.

That the baptized may proclaim God's new work in Jesus Christ, we pray: ◆
That believers may be ambassadors of reconciliation among all people, we pray: ◆ *That God's creative power may fashion peace among nations, we pray:* ◆ *That the righteousness of God may overcome the decay of injustice and poverty, we pray:* ◆ *That we may live as children of the new creation in Christ, we pray:* ◆

Our Father . . .

God of all people,
in Christ you have made all things new.
Stir up in us your Spirit
   of reconciliation,
that we may be ambassadors
of the reign to come,
living signs of the mercy you offer
in Jesus Christ, our Savior,
who lives and reigns with you,
in the unity of the Holy Spirit,
one God, forever and ever. Amen.

✝ *To you, O LORD, I lift up my soul.*
  All my hope is in you.

✝ *To you, O LORD, I lift up my soul.*
  All my hope is in you.

PSALM 27   *page 411*

READING   *Isaiah 26:7–9, 12*

The way of the righteous is level;
  O Just One, you make smooth
    the path of the righteous.
In the path of your judgments,
  O LORD, we wait for you;
your name and your renown
    are the soul's desire.
My soul yearns for you in the night,
  my spirit within me earnestly
    seeks you.
For when your judgments are
    in the earth,
  the inhabitants of the world
    learn righteousness.
O LORD, you will ordain peace for us,
  for indeed, all that we have done,
    you have done for us.

REFLECTION

The prophet connects righteousness and peace; in other words, if we follow God's law—seeking justice and mercy, remembering the needs of the poor—we will know the peace of God's reign. In a world set on edge by terrorism, in which great masses still starve and suffer wars of all kinds, we must ask ourselves if we have heeded the prophet's wisdom. If together we sought the righteousness Isaiah speaks of, would we not at last have peace? As Pope Paul VI put it, "If you want peace, work for justice."

PRAYERS   *others may be added*

Seeking the path of righteousness, we pray:

◆ Hear us, O God our help.

That Christians together may seek the justice of God's reign, we pray: ◆ *That those with power and influence may lead the world in acts of generosity, we pray:* ◆ *That nations harried by violence and want may find relief and aid, we pray:* ◆ *That prophets of peace may dissuade proponents of war, we pray:* ◆ *That our spirits may yearn for God's righteous judgment, we pray:* ◆

Our Father . . .

God of the nations,
you make smooth the just path
and beckon us to follow.
Guide us in righteousness,
that our souls may yearn
for your promise of peace
and all people may live in justice.
We make our prayer
  through the Just One,
the Prince of Peace,
Jesus our Savior,
now and forever. Amen.

✝ *To you, O LORD, I lift up my soul.*
  All my hope is in you.

✦ *To you, O LORD, I lift up my soul.*
All my hope is in you.

PSALM 27 *page 411*

READING *Isaiah 26:16–19*

O LORD, in distress they sought you,
    they poured out a prayer
    when your chastening was on them.
Like a woman with child,
    who writhes and cries out
      in her pangs
    when she is near her time,
so were we because of you, O LORD;
    we were with child, we writhed,
    but we gave birth only to wind.
We have won no victories on earth,
    and no one is born to inhabit
      the world.
Your dead shall live, their corpses
      shall rise.
    O dwellers in the dust, awake
      and sing for joy!
For your dew is a radiant dew,
    and the earth will give birth
      to those long dead.

REFLECTION

*Isaiah includes two "confessions" in his
oracle. The first is the kind we're most
familiar with: Speaking for Israel, Isaiah
acknowledges that the people failed to follow God, and so "gave birth only to wind."
The second "confession" is different: It is
a confession of God's power and a profession of hope, an acknowledgment that even
now God is able to restore the dead. The
purpose of the first confession is always to
lead us to the second. We never stop with*
*confessing our failures but instead con-
tinue with praise of God, who will save us.*

PRAYERS *others may be added*

Confessing the power of God,
we pray:

◆ Hear us, O God our help.

*For those who hope in the God of life,
we pray:* ◆ *For those who sing in praise,
we pray:* ◆ *For those who call out to
God in distress, we pray:* ◆ *For those who
writhe in pain and suffering, we pray:* ◆
*For those who have lost hope in God's
promise, we pray:* ◆ *For those who
dwell in the dust of the earth, we pray:* ◆
*For those who await the victory of God
Most High, we pray:* ◆

Our Father . . .

God of new creation,
with refreshing dew
you soften our hearts
and give us lasting hope.
Awake us from our sleep,
and make us radiant in praise
    before you,
that we may bring to full birth
the reign you promise
in Jesus the Christ,
who lives and reigns
forever and ever. Amen.

✦ *To you, O LORD, I lift up my soul.*
All my hope is in you.

✛ *To you, O LORD, I lift up my soul.*
All my hope is in you.

PSALM 27 *page 411*

READING *Micah 6:1–4*

Hear what the LORD says:
Rise, plead your case
    before the mountains,
  and let the hills hear your voice.
Hear, you mountains, the controversy
    of the LORD,
  and you enduring foundations
    of the earth;
for the LORD has a controversy
    with his people,
  and he will contend with Israel.
"O my people, what have I done
    to you?
  In what have I wearied you?
    Answer me!
For I brought you up from the land
    of Egypt,
  and redeemed you from the house
    of slavery;
and I sent before you Moses, Aaron,
    and Miriam."

REFLECTION

The message of the prophet Micah is similar to Isaiah's: Israel must return to true worship of the Most High and to the justice that marked Israel's early days. Micah begins, though, by putting Israel in the dock as the defendant, with God arguing the side of the plaintiff. It is not God who has forsaken the people but the people who have turned aside from the covenant. God calls all creation as witnesses to the people's unfaithfulness.

PRAYERS *others may be added*

*Recalling God's wondrous deeds,
we pray:*

◆ Hear us, O God our help.

That the baptized may never forget their salvation in Christ, we pray: ◆ *That God may raise up strong and faithful leaders in the Church, we pray:* ◆ *That all believers may respond to God's challenge with repentance, we pray:* ◆ *That the nations may behold God's saving power, we pray:* ◆ *That we may answer God with humble, contrite hearts, we pray:* ◆

Our Father . . .

O God, just and merciful,
the mountains are your witnesses
and the hills your jury,
for we have failed
to live in faithfulness.
Let your face shine on us,
that we may answer you
    with repentance
and so enjoy your mercy,
you who are gracious and forgiving
in every generation,
and who live and reign
forever and ever. Amen.

✛ *To you, O LORD, I lift up my soul.*
All my hope is in you.

✛ *Alleluia! Christ is risen!*
Christ is risen indeed!
Alleluia! Alleluia!

PSALM 34   *page 412*

READING   *John 21:15–19*

When they had finished breakfast, Jesus said to Simon Peter, "Simon son of John, do you love me more than these?" He said to him, "Yes, Lord; you know that I love you." Jesus said to him, "Feed my lambs." A second time he said to him, "Simon son of John, do you love me?" He said to him, "Yes, Lord; you know that I love you." Jesus said to him, "Tend my sheep." He said to him the third time, "Simon son of John, do you love me?" Peter felt hurt because he said to him the third time, "Do you love me?" And he said to him, "Lord, you know everything; you know that I love you." Jesus said to him, "Feed my sheep. Very truly, I tell you, when you were younger, you used to fasten your own belt and to go wherever you wished. But when you grow old, you will stretch out your hands, and someone else will fasten a belt around you and take you where you do not wish to go." (He said this to indicate the kind of death by which he would glorify God.) After this he said to him, "Follow me."

REFLECTION

Today we commemorate Saints Peter and Paul, two great founders of the Church. Each of these saints has a feast of his own, but it is appropriate that we celebrate them together. Peter, as leader of the Twelve, represents the Jewish roots of Christianity; Paul, as the apostle to the Gentiles, represents the Gospel's spread to the entire world.

PRAYERS   *others may be added*

Committed to love and service,
we pray:

◆ Turn to us, Lord of life!

For the Church, built on the rock of Peter's faith, we pray: ◆ *For the pope, the vicar of Peter, we pray:* ◆ *For bishops and all who shepherd God's people, we pray:* ◆ *For ministers of care and those who serve the neediest of God's flock, we pray:* ◆ *For missionaries and all who share the ministry of Paul, we pray:* ◆ *For all who profess faith in Christ, we pray:* ◆

Our Father . . .

God of the apostles,
in Peter and Paul you give us
models of faith and witness
   to the Gospel.
Through their intercession
confirm your people in their mission
and heal the divisions that hinder them.
May the Church become
a greater sign of unity
proclaiming with one voice
the Gospel of Jesus Christ,
in whose name we pray. Amen.

✛ *Alleluia! Christ is risen!*
Christ is risen indeed!
Alleluia! Alleluia!

✦ *To you, O LORD, I lift up my soul.*
All my hope is in you.

PSALM 27   *page 411*

READING   *Micah 6:6–8*

"With what shall I come before
   the LORD,
  and bow myself before God
   on high?
Shall I come before him
   with burnt offerings,
  with calves a year old?
Will the LORD be pleased with
   thousands of rams,
  with ten thousands of rivers of oil?
Shall I give my firstborn
   for my transgression,
  the fruit of my body for the sin
   of my soul?"
He has told you, O mortal,
   what is good;
  and what does the LORD require
   of you
but to do justice, and to love kindness,
  and to walk humbly with your God?

REFLECTION

It can be a challenge to know if we are
truly serving God; many rival visions of
what God desires from human beings
compete for loyalty. Micah boils it down
into what must be one of the most beautiful
passages in all of scripture. God requires
only that we do justice, that we love kind-
ness, and that we walk in humility.
Imagine the world where such virtues were
valued above all else!

PRAYERS   *others may be added*

Walking humbly with our God,
we pray:

◆ Hear us, O God our help.

That the baptized may adorn themselves
with works of justice, we pray: ◆
That catechumens and inquirers may find
joy in God's way, we pray: ◆ *That love*
of kindness may overcome fear, hatred
and prejudice among earth's people,
we pray: ◆ *That the powerful may nurture*
within themselves humility before God,
we pray: ◆ *That we may be single-hearted*
in our service of God, we pray: ◆

Our Father . . .

You have told us, O God,
what is good,
that we should do justice,
love kindness,
and walk humbly before you.
Make us single-hearted
in our pursuit of virtue,
that kindness may overflow,
justice reign over all,
and humility carry us
to your presence,
for you live and reign
now and forever. Amen.

✦ *O Shepherd of Israel, hear us!*
O Lord, come to our help!

✠ *To you, O LORD, I lift up my soul.*
All my hope is in you.

PSALM 27   *page 411*

READING   *Micah 7:14–15, 18–20*

Shepherd your people with your staff,
   the flock that belongs to you,
which lives alone in a forest
   in the midst of a garden land;
let them feed in Bashan and Gilead
   as in the days of old.
As in the days when you came out
    of the land of Egypt,
   show us marvelous things.
Who is a God like you,
    pardoning iniquity
   and passing over the transgression
   of the remnant of your possession?
He does not retain his anger forever,
   because he delights
    in showing clemency.
He will again have compassion
    upon us;
   he will tread our iniquities
    under foot.
You will cast all our sins
   into the depths of the sea.
You will show faithfulness to Jacob
   and unswerving loyalty to Abraham,
as you have sworn to our ancestors
   from the days of old.

REFLECTION

As much as the Hebrew prophets warned their hearers against failing to follow God's law, they also reminded Israel of God's boundless compassion and faithfulness, mercy and steadfast love. This is our Shepherd, our God, the one who "delights in showing clemency, in whom we find comfort and hope."

PRAYERS   *others may be added*

Trusting in our divine Shepherd,
we pray:

◆ Hear us, O God our help.

That the leaders of God's people
may guide the baptized gently in love,
we pray: ◆ *That Christians may delight*
in showing clemency, we pray: ◆
That world leaders may assure the health
and well-being of citizens, we pray: ◆
That anger may give way to mercy and
vengeance to forgiveness, we pray: ◆
That we may be faithful to one another
as God is faithful to us, we pray: ◆

Our Father . . .

Shepherd of your people,
you guide us to rich pasture,
filling our need with care.
Show us your faithfulness,
and cast our transgressions
   into the sea,
that we may come before you
   in confidence
and delight in showing mercy,
for you live and reign
forever and ever. Amen.

✠ *To you, O LORD, I lift up my soul.*
All my hope is in you.

✚ *Let us see, O LORD, your mercy.*
Give us your saving help.

PSALM 85   *page 417*

READING   *2 Corinthians 8:7, 9, 13–15*

Now as you excel in everything—in faith, in speech, in knowledge, in utmost eagerness, and in our love for you—so we want you to excel also in this generous undertaking. For you know the generous act of our Lord Jesus Christ, that though he was rich, yet for your sakes he became poor, so that by his poverty you might become rich.

I do not mean that there should be relief for others and pressure on you, but it is a question of a fair balance between your present abundance and their need, so that their abundance may be for your need, in order that there may be a fair balance. As it is written, "The one who had much did not have too much, and the one who had little did not have too little."

REFLECTION

The "generous undertaking" Paul speaks of requires a little explanation. At the time, the church in Jerusalem was suffering from famine, and Paul and Titus were raising money to meet their needs; today's passage is similar to "mission appeals" conducted in parishes today. While we may grow tired of being asked for contributions, almsgiving, along with prayer and fasting, it is indeed one of the privileges of the baptized. When we offer our help to those in need, we are living today as if the reign of God was already fully revealed. Our works of justice and mercy reveal us to be the first fruits of the age to come.

PRAYERS   *others may be added*

With generous hearts, we pray:

◆ Revive us, O God our help!

That the disciples of Jesus may rejoice in the privilege of giving to those in need, we pray: ◆ *That Christian communities may be living signs of the justice of the world to come, we pray:* ◆ *That those blessed with abundant goods of this world may share them with the poor, we pray:* ◆ *That the homeless, destitute, and hungry may receive a just share of what is rightfully theirs, we pray:* ◆ *That we may offer what we have eagerly and so excel in generosity and service, we pray:* ◆

Our Father . . .

Bounteous God,
the goods of creation
surpass our need,
yet still your children go hungry.
Fill us with zeal
for the privilege of service,
that we may excel in works
of justice and mercy
and so anticipate the world to come,
where the poor are first
at the banquet of the Lamb,
who is Lord forever and ever. Amen.

✚ *Let us see, O LORD, your mercy.*
Give us your saving help.

✚ *Alleluia! Christ is risen!*
Christ is risen indeed!
Alleluia! Alleluia!

PSALM 34   *page 412*

READING   *Ephesians 2:19–22*

So then you are no longer strangers and aliens, but you are citizens with the saints and also members of the household of God, built upon the foundation of the apostles and prophets, with Christ Jesus himself as the cornerstone. In him the whole structure is joined together and grows into a holy temple in the Lord; in whom you also are built together spiritually into a dwelling place for God.

REFLECTION

Today we celebrate the feast of Saint Thomas the apostle, who refused to believe unless he saw the Risen Christ with his own eyes. When he finally witnessed the Risen One, he had the good sense to believe and worship! Although he is often remembered as "doubting Thomas," the apostle's desire to see for himself isn't a bad one. No one wants to be tricked or deluded, nor is it impossible to see the Risen Christ. The key is knowing where to look, and to prepare ourselves to welcome Christ's presence when we find it.

PRAYERS   *others may be added*

Temples of the Holy Spirit, dwelling places of God, we pray:

◆ Turn to us, Lord of life!

That all the baptized may be gathered together into one household of faith, we pray: ◆ *That the people of God may continue the work of the apostles, we pray:* ◆ *That catechumens and candidates may be made fitting dwelling places for the Spirit of God, we pray:* ◆ *That all people may come to accept one another as brothers and sisters, we pray:* ◆ *That we may live as citizens of the age to come, we pray:* ◆

Our Father . . .

God of life,
the wounds of the Risen One
brought Thomas to faith,
and with him we are members
   of your household.
Strengthen us in the faith
that makes us one.
May the Church grow in unity
and so become a more fitting
dwelling place for your Spirit,
a holy and living temple
built on the foundation stone
   of Jesus Christ,
who lives and reigns forever and ever.
Amen.

✚ *Alleluia! Christ is risen!*
Christ is risen indeed!
Alleluia! Alleluia!

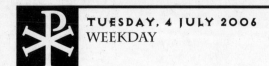

✠ *Let us see, O LORD, your mercy.*
Give us your saving help.

PSALM 85 *page 417*

READING *2 Kings 22:1a, 2–5a, 6b*

Josiah was eight years old when he began to reign; he reigned thirty-one years in Jerusalem. He did what was right in the sight of the LORD, and walked in all the way of his father David; he did not turn aside to the right or to the left. In the eighteenth year of King Josiah, the king sent Shaphan son of Azaliah, son of Meshullam, the secretary, to the house of the LORD, saying, "Go up to the high priest Hilkiah, and have him count the entire sum of the money that has been brought into the house of the LORD, which the keepers of the threshold have collected from the people; let it be given into the hand of the workers who have the oversight of the house of the LORD; and let them use it to buy timber and quarried stone to repair the house."

REFLECTION

In 2000, U.N. Secretary-General Kofi Annan offered a challenge to the United States worth hearing again on this Independence Day: "It is particularly shameful that the United States, the most prosperous and successful country in the history of the world, should be one of the least generous in terms of the share of its gross national product it devotes to helping the world's poor. I am sure many of you share my feeling that this is unworthy of the traditions of this great country."

PRAYERS *others may be added*

Sowing righteousness to reap a harvest of love, we pray:

◆ Revive us, O God our helper!

For the people of God in the United States and all of North America, we pray: ◆ *For the president, legislators, and members of the judiciary, we pray:* ◆ *For those who suffer discrimination in the land of the free, we pray:* ◆ *For factory employees, farm laborers, workers of all types, we pray:* ◆ *For the forgotten poor, sick, and homeless, we pray:* ◆ *For those who celebrate July 4 as a day of freedom, we pray:* ◆

Our Father . . .

Just and loving God,
you warn the prosperous
   against relying on money
and counsel us
to be rich in righteousness.
Bless the United States
   and all countries
with a hunger for justice
and a thirst for peace,
that all the world's citizens
may share in creation's abundance
to the glory of your name,
who live and reign
forever and ever. Amen.

✠ *Let us see, O LORD, your mercy.*
Give us your saving help.

✦ *Let us see, O LORD, your mercy.*
Give us your saving help.

PSALM 85 *page 417*

READING *2 Kings 22:8, 10–13a*

The high priest Hilkiah said to Shaphan the secretary, "I have found the book of the law in the house of the LORD." When Hilkiah gave the book to Shaphan, he read it. Shaphan the secretary informed the king, "The priest Hilkiah has given me a book." Shaphan then read it aloud to the king. When the king heard the words of the book of the law, he tore his clothes. Then the king commanded the priest Hilkiah, Ahikam son of Shaphan, Achbor son of Micaiah, Shaphan the secretary, and the king's servant Asaiah, saying, "Go, inquire of the LORD for me, for the people, and for all Judah, concerning the words of this book that has been found; for great is the wrath of the LORD that is kindled against us, because our ancestors did not obey the words of this book."

REFLECTION

Prophets like Elijah, Isaiah, and others rarely had success in persuading Israel's kings to serve their God alone. King Josiah of Judah is an exception; during his reign, there was a brief reform before the final destruction of Jerusalem. There are some scholars who believe that the book found by Hilkiah was planted there for the king's servants to find. The temple and its worship had fallen into such disrepair that Israel had forgotten who it was—God's chosen people. Yet Josiah acknowledges his guilt the second he realizes it. Who among us would be so quick to admit being wrong?

PRAYERS *others may be added*

Confessing our sin before God,
we pray:

◆ Revive us, O God our helper!

To be faithful to the Gospel, we pray: ◆
To turn aside from false worship,
we pray: ◆ *To reject self-righteousness,*
we pray: ◆ *To be mindful of the needs*
of the poor, we pray: ◆ *To grow in*
knowledge of your will, we pray: ◆
To reject sin in all its forms, we pray: ◆

Our Father . . .

God of mercy,
our sins cover us
for we have forgotten
your way of salvation.
Plant within us knowledge
   of your will,
that we may never fail
to do what pleases you,
who live and reign
forever and ever. Amen.

✦ *Let us see, O LORD, your mercy.*
Give us your saving help.

✠ *Let us see, O LORD, your mercy.*
  Give us your saving help.

PSALM 85   *page 417*

READING   *2 Kings 22:14a,*
15a, 16–19a, 19c–20a

So the priest Hilkiah, Ahikam, Achbor, Shaphan, and Asaiah went to the prophetess Huldah. She declared to them, "Thus says the LORD, I will indeed bring disaster on this place and on its inhabitants—all the words of the book that the king of Judah has read. Because they have abandoned me and have made offerings to other gods, so that they have provoked me to anger with all the work of their hands, therefore my wrath will be kindled against this place, and it will not be quenched. But as to the king of Judah, who sent you to inquire of the LORD, thus shall you say to him, Thus says the LORD, the God of Israel: Regarding the words that you have heard, because your heart was penitent, and you humbled yourself before the LORD, and because you have torn your clothes and wept before me, I also have heard you, says the LORD. Therefore, I will gather you to your ancestors, and you shall be gathered to your grave in peace.

REFLECTION

The examination of conscience was once a common spiritual discipline among Catholics, and the ritual is still helpful today. One way to practice it is to simply go through the day and ask, "Was I kind to others? Was I generous to anyone in need? Did I turn away from someone who asked my help? Did I say something cruel in anger?" It is a simple practice, but one that can bear fruit in greater awareness of both our sinfulness and our goodness.

PRAYERS   *others may be added*

Hoping for God's mercy,
we pray:

♦ Revive us, O God our helper!

That the baptized may always be ready to admit their sins, we pray: ♦
That penitents may know God's mercy through the Church's ministry, we pray: ♦
That the nations may repent of war and struggles for power, we pray: ♦ *That God may accept our contrite hearts, we pray:* ♦
That we may be quick to welcome God's mercy, we pray: ♦

Our Father . . .

God of righteous anger,
our guilt lies open before you,
yet we remain hopeful in your love.
Turn your anger away from us
and replace it with your
    boundless mercy,
that we may offer forgiveness
to those who have wronged us.
We ask this in Jesus' name. Amen.

✠ *Let us see, O LORD, your mercy.*
  Give us your saving help.

✝ *Let us see, O LORD, your mercy.*
   Give us your saving help.

PSALM 85   *page 417*

READING   *2 Kings 23:2–3ac, 21–23*

The king went up to the house of the LORD, and with him went all the people of Judah, all the inhabitants of Jerusalem, the priests, the prophets, and all the people, both small and great; he read in their hearing all the words of the book of the covenant that had been found in the house of the LORD. The king stood by the pillar and made a covenant before the LORD. All the people joined in the covenant. The king commanded all the people, "Keep the passover to the LORD your God as prescribed in this book of the covenant." No such passover had been kept since the days of the judges who judged Israel, or during all the days of the kings of Israel or of the kings of Judah; but in the eighteenth year of King Josiah this passover was kept to the LORD in Jerusalem.

REFLECTION

By forgetting to keep the Passover, the people of Israel had basically forgotten their Jewish identity. The Exodus, which Passover commemorates, was the defining moment in the history of Israel; celebrating the Passover liturgy renewed the people in that story and in their relationship with God. It is for this reason that our Sunday celebration of the Eucharist is so crucial; in it, we who are baptized are rejuvenated in the paschal mystery. When we fail to celebrate the Sunday Eucharist, we risk forgetting who we have become in Christ's death and Resurrection: children of God, brothers and sisters to Christ and one another.

PRAYERS   *others may be added*

Faithful to the mystery of faith,
we pray:

◆ Revive us, O God our helper!

For all who minister in the Eucharistic assembly, we pray: ◆ *For all who keep alive the memory of Jesus, we pray:* ◆ *For all who tell the story of the God made flesh in Christ, we pray:* ◆ *For all who seek new faithfulness to Christ, we pray:* ◆ *For all who remain faithful to the First Covenant, we pray:* ◆ *For all who keep the commandments of God, we pray:* ◆

Our Father . . .

God of Israel,
Father of Jesus Christ,
by the power of your Spirit
you renew within us
the mystery of salvation.
Keep us faithful to our mission:
May we never forget
our destiny in Christ Jesus,
in whom we have become
   a new creation,
praising you always
through the same Christ our Lord
now and forever. Amen.

✝ *Let us see, O LORD, your mercy.*
   Give us your saving help.

✠ *Let us see, O LORD, your mercy.*
Give us your saving help.

PSALM 85 — page 417

READING — 2 Kings 23:26a, 27, 28b–30

Still the LORD did not turn from the fierceness of his great wrath, by which his anger was kindled against Judah. The LORD said, "I will remove Judah also out of my sight, as I have removed Israel; and I will reject this city that I have chosen, Jerusalem, and the house of which I said, My name shall be there." In his days Pharaoh Neco king of Egypt went up to the king of Assyria to the river Euphrates. King Josiah went to meet him; but when Pharaoh Neco met him at Megiddo, he killed him. His servants carried him dead in a chariot from Megiddo, brought him to Jerusalem, and buried him in his own tomb. The people of the land took Jehoahaz son of Josiah, anointed him, and made him king in place of his father.

REFLECTION

Although the author of the second Book of Kings interpreted Josiah's defeat as a sign that God had abandoned Judah, in some ways Judah was doomed from the start as a small country wedged between great powers. Egypt and Assyria were vying for dominance, and those between them felt the brunt of their competition. It is no different today. Nations like Afghanistan, Vietnam, Nicaragua, Guatemala, and others were caught between the Cold War superpowers. Today the struggle among wealthy nations for economic superiority often causes poor nations to suffer currency devaluations, the destruction of local economies, and the corruption of governments.

PRAYERS — *others may be added*

Saddened by the destruction of war, we pray:

◆ Revive us, O God our helper!

For peace activists and conscientious objectors, we pray: ◆ For soldiers and military leaders, we pray: ◆ For refugees and noncombatants, we pray: ◆ For all who are crushed between great powers, we pray: ◆ For all who have lost loved ones in war, we pray: ◆ For all who have lost their lives to violence, we pray: ◆

Our Father . . .

God of the sorrowing,
the horrors of war bring suffering
to the innocent and the guilty.
Cleanse us from the hatred
that leads to war
and the violence that brings death.
May we live always
as citizens of your kingdom,
with Prince of Peace as our ruler
forever and ever. Amen.

✠ *Let us see, O LORD, your mercy.*
Give us your saving help.

✙ *Let us see, O LORD, your mercy.*
Give us your saving help.

PSALM 85 *page 417*

READING *2 Corinthians 12:7–10*

To keep me from being too elated, a thorn was given me in the flesh, a messenger of Satan to torment me, to keep me from being too elated. Three times I appealed to the Lord about this, that it would leave me, but he said to me, "My grace is sufficient for you, for power is made perfect in weakness." So, I will boast all the more gladly of my weaknesses, so that the power of Christ may dwell in me. Therefore I am content with weaknesses, insults, hardships, persecutions, and calamities for the sake of Christ; for whenever I am weak, then I am strong.

REFLECTION

This last Sunday reading from Second Corinthians sounds a familiar Pauline theme: God's power revealed in weakness. Biblical scholars and even psychologists have tried to guess what Paul's "thorn in the flesh" might have been, but what is most important is Paul's own response. If God's power is most fully revealed in the cross, then our own sufferings and even failures can also be moments in which God's power is made perfect in us. For us Christians, sickness, disability, and injury, while difficult, can be opportunities to open ourselves more fully to God's powerful work.

PRAYERS *others may be added*

Strong by the power of Christ, we pray:

◆ Revive us, O God our helper!

That the baptized may boast only in their Savior, we pray: ◆ *That the powerful may find in the crucified Christ an image of power in the service of others, we pray:* ◆ *That those who suffer insult and hardship may find comfort in Christ's suffering, we pray:* ◆ *That the power of God may be made perfect in the sick, injured, and downtrodden, we pray:* ◆ *That the grace of God may fill the sorrowful with peace and hope, we pray:* ◆ *That our weakness may reveal the power of Christ crucified, we pray:* ◆

Our Father . . .

God of the cross,
your power is revealed in weakness
for you confound the wisdom
    of the world.
Open our eyes to your presence
in the suffering of the world,
that we may join ourselves
to the cross of Christ,
in which the fullness
of your power shines forth.
We ask this through the same
    Jesus Christ,
who lives and reigns with you,
in the unity of the Holy Spirit,
one God of all. Amen.

✙ *Let us see, O LORD, your mercy.*
Give us your saving help.

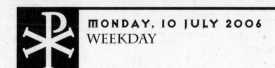
✚ *Let us see, O LORD, your mercy.*
Give us your saving help.

PSALM 85   *page 417*

READING   *2 Kings 24:8a, 9–10, 12–14*

Jehoiachin was eighteen years old when he began to reign; he reigned three months in Jerusalem. He did what was evil in the sight of the LORD. At that time the servants of King Nebuchadnezzar of Babylon came up to Jerusalem, and the city was besieged. King Jehoiachin of Judah gave himself up to the king of Babylon, himself, his mother, his servants, his officers, and his palace officials. The king of Babylon took him prisoner in the eighth year of his reign. He carried off all the treasures of the house of the LORD, and the treasures of the king's house; he cut in pieces all the vessels of gold in the temple of the LORD, which King Solomon of Israel had made, all this as the LORD had foretold. He carried away all Jerusalem, all the officials, all the warriors, ten thousand captives, all the artisans and the smiths; no one remained, except the poorest people of the land.

REFLECTION

The first fall of Jerusalem and exile of its elite to Babylon was only the beginning of Judah's suffering. As is so often the case, those least able to fend for themselves were left behind, while the land was stripped of wealth. Those in exile lived more or less as guests—hostages—of Nebuchadnezzar, and the "poorest of the land" were left with
nothing. Is it any different in our own age? In war-torn Africa especially, it is poor noncombatants—women, children, the elderly—who suffer most.

PRAYERS   *others may be added*

Saddened by the suffering of God's people, we pray:

◆ Revive us, O God our helper!

That nations may set aside the desire for power and control, we pray: ◆ *That civil wars and terrorism may come to an end, we pray:* ◆ *That nationalism may give way to unity among peoples and cultures, we pray:* ◆ *That racism and cultural superiority may be cast aside, we pray:* ◆ *That apathy to the suffering of the poor and defenseless may be overcome, we pray:* ◆

Our Father . . .

Father of all,
you do not desire our suffering
but call us instead to full human life.
Bless us with the vision
of who we are to be:
May we reject all
that leads to our destruction,
embracing the life
you offer in Jesus Christ,
who lives and reigns
forever and ever. Amen.

✚ *Let us see, O LORD, your mercy.*
Give us your saving help.

✦ *Let us see, O Lᴏʀᴅ, your mercy.*
   Give us your saving help.

Pꜱᴀʟᴍ 85   *page 417*

Rᴇᴀᴅɪɴɢ   2 Kings 24:17, 20b;
                        25:1b, 2–4a, 5

The king of Babylon made Mattaniah,
Jehoiachin's uncle, king in his place,
and changed his name to Zedekiah.
Zedekiah rebelled against the king of
Babylon. King Nebuchadnezzar of
Babylon came with all his army against
Jerusalem, and laid siege to it. So the
city was besieged until the eleventh
year of King Zedekiah. On the ninth
day of the fourth month the famine
became so severe in the city that there
was no food for the people of the land.
Then a breach was made in the city
wall; the king with all the soldiers fled
by night. But the army of the
Chaldeans pursued the king, and over-
took him in the plains of Jericho; all
his army was scattered, deserting him.

Rᴇꜰʟᴇᴄᴛɪᴏɴ   *U.S. bishops*

Violence and war are very much present in
the history of the People of God, [who] is
often seen as the one who leads the
Hebrews in battle, protects them from their
enemies, makes them victorious over other
armies . . . No one can deny the presence
of such images in the Old Testament nor
their powerful influence upon the articula-
tion of this people's understanding of the
involvement of God in their history. . . .
But this image was not the only image, and
it was gradually transformed, particularly
after the experience of exile, when God
was no longer identified with military vic-
tory and might.

Pʀᴀʏᴇʀꜱ   *others may be added*

Turning away from pride and hope for
glory, we pray:

◆ Revive us, O God our helper!

That bishops and pastors may always
speak out for the sake of the defenseless,
we pray: ◆ That civil leaders may seek
first the good of their people, we pray: ◆
That cities plagued by violence may know
reconciliation and peace, we pray: ◆
That those suffering famine and poverty
may find relief, we pray: ◆ That we may
seek an end to violence in our homes and
communities, we pray: ◆

Our Father . . .

Source of peace,
too often we choose
the path of violence,
worshiping at the altar
   of national pride.
Bless us with solidarity,
that we may recognize all people
   as your children,
adopted in Jesus Christ,
who lives and reigns
forever and ever. Amen.

✦ *Let us see, O Lᴏʀᴅ, your mercy.*
   Give us your saving help.

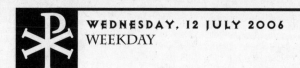
✚ *Let us see, O LORD, your mercy.*
Give us your saving help.

PSALM 85 *page 417*

READING *2 Kings 25:8–12*

In the fifth month, on the seventh day of the month—which was the nineteenth year of King Nebuchadnezzar, king of Babylon—Nebuzaradan, the captain of the bodyguard, a servant of the king of Babylon, came to Jerusalem. He burned the house of the LORD, the king's house, and all the houses of Jerusalem; every great house he burned down. All the army of the Chaldeans who were with the captain of the guard broke down the walls around Jerusalem. Nebuzaradan the captain of the guard carried into exile the rest of the people who were left in the city and the deserters who had defected to the king of Babylon—all the rest of the population. But the captain of the guard left some of the poorest people of the land to be vine-dressers and tillers of the soil.

REFLECTION

So ends the history of ancient Israel. Jerusalem and the temple were destroyed and the Israelites made unclean in a foreign land. But there was hope as well; the exile forced the Jewish people to rethink their faith. Exile became a time of renewal, a preparation for a return. Hope remained for the Israelites, as it does for us today, even in our worst times.

PRAYERS *others may be added*

Longing for the coming of the heavenly Jerusalem, we pray:

◆ Revive us, O God our helper!

For those unable to practice their faith, we pray: ◆ *For religious communities whose places of worship have been destroyed or vandalized, we pray:* ◆ *For countries decimated by civil war, we pray:* ◆ *For cities destroyed by inequality and crime, we pray:* ◆ *For all who suffer the destruction of their homes and livelihoods, we pray:* ◆

Our Father . . .

Hope of Israel,
though Jerusalem lay in ruins
you did not abandon your people
but accompanied them into exile
to prepare a way for their return.
Be with us in our times of exile
and show us the way to restoration:
May we always know
    your faithful presence,
through Christ our Lord. Amen.

✚ *Let us see, O LORD, your mercy.*
Give us your saving help.

✚ *Let us see, O LORD, your mercy.*
  Give us your saving help.

PSALM 85   page 417

READING   *Lamentations 1:1–3*

How lonely sits the city
    that once was full of people!
How like a widow she has become,
    she that was great
        among the nations!
She that was a princess
        among the provinces
    has become a vassal.
She weeps bitterly in the night,
    with tears on her cheeks;
among all her lovers
    she has no one to comfort her;
all her friends have dealt
        treacherously with her,
    they have become her enemies.
Judah has gone into exile
        with suffering
    and hard servitude;
she lives now among the nations,
    and finds no resting place;
her pursuers have all overtaken her
    in the midst of her distress.

REFLECTION

*The beautiful poetry of Lamentations
expresses the great sorrow of Israel after
the destruction of Jerusalem. Christians
often use it on Good Friday and Holy
Saturday as a meditation on Christ's death.
Its sorrow speaks to us in our own times of
desolation and exile; indeed, it is a comfort that such a deep expression of sorrow
is present within the inspired word of God.*

PRAYERS   *others may be added*

*Hopeful even in the face of disaster,
we pray:*

◆ Revive us, O God our helper!

*For communities overcome by grief,
we pray:* ◆ *For lands decimated by war
and lawlessness, we pray:* ◆ *For cities
burdened by inequality, we pray:* ◆
*For those exiled from their homelands,
we pray:* ◆ *For all who feel abandoned
by God, we pray:* ◆ *For those who feel
betrayed by their friends, we pray:* ◆

Our Father . . .

Faithful God of Israel,
though your footstool was destroyed
and your people dispersed,
you were with them in their sorrow.
Abide with us in times of difficulty
and comfort us in our sadness,
that we may praise you
through Jesus Christ
who lives and reigns forever and ever.
Amen.

✚ *Let us see, O LORD, your mercy.*
  Give us your saving help.

✚ *Let us see, O LORD, your mercy.*
Give us your saving help.

PSALM 85 *page 417*

READING *Lamentations 1:5–6, 8*

Her foes have become the masters,
    her enemies prosper,
because the LORD has made her suffer
    for the multitude of her
        transgressions;
her children have gone away,
    captives before the foe.
From daughter Zion has departed
    all her majesty.
Her princes have become like stags
    that find no pasture;
they fled without strength
    before the pursuer.
Jerusalem sinned grievously,
    so she has become a mockery;
all who honored her despise her,
    for they have seen her nakedness;
she herself groans,
    and turns her face away.

REFLECTION *Robert Schreiter*

Suffering is the human struggle with and against pain. It is the experience of the breakdown of our systems of meaning and our stories about ourselves, and the struggle to restore those senses of safety and selfhood. Suffering in itself is neither noble nor redeeming. . . . Suffering only becomes redemptive or ennobling when we struggle against these corroding powers and rebuild ourselves in spite of the pain we are experiencing.

PRAYERS *others may be added*

Acknowledging the nakedness of our sin, we pray:

◆ Revive us, O God, our helper!

That God's people may boldly confess their sinfulness, we pray: ◆ *That nations may turn aside from the pursuit of glory, we pray:* ◆ *That the enemies of justice may not triumph over God's children, we pray:* ◆ *That those who have suffered injustice may be restored, we pray:* ◆ *That those who have grown in sorrow may find comfort, we pray:* ◆ *That we may turn aside from our transgressions, we pray:* ◆

Our Father . . .

Comfort of Jerusalem,
we have relied on earthly glory
but it has deserted us.
Cover our nakedness with your
    loving-kindness:
May we seek your eternal help,
for you live and reign
    forever and ever. Amen.

✚ *Let us see, O LORD, your mercy.*
Give us your saving help.

✚ *Let us see, O LORD, your mercy.*
Give us your saving help.

PSALM 85 page 417

READING Lamentations 2:11–13

My eyes are spent with weeping;
 my stomach churns;
my bile is poured out on the ground
 because of the destruction
  of my people,
because infants and babes faint
 in the streets of the city.
They cry to their mothers,
 "Where is bread and wine?"
as they faint like the wounded
 in the streets of the city,
as their life is poured out
 on their mothers' bosom.
What can I say for you,
  to what compare you,
 O daughter Jerusalem?
To what can I liken you,
  that I may comfort you,
 O virgin daughter Zion?
For vast as the sea is your ruin;
 who can heal you?

REFLECTION

It may be hard for many of us to imagine Israel's exile; the closest modern equivalent may be the current occupation of Tibet and the dispersal of many of the country's people. Yet we know or can imagine the psychological experience of exile: the teenage runaway exiled from home; the mentally ill person who experiences alienation in his or her own self; the person exiled from their faith, or an experience of rejection. Such exile is equally painful, yet equally open to the healing power of God.

PRAYERS others may be added

Seeking comfort and solace,
we pray:

◆ Revive us, O God our helper!

For parents who must watch their children suffer, we pray: ◆ For children ailing from hunger and disease, we pray: ◆ For the sick, who long for relief, we pray: ◆ For those who undergo the desolation of depression, we pray: ◆ For those who mourn the loss of loved ones, we pray: ◆

Our Father . . .

Source of healing,
our wounds have become
too much to bear
and sorrow overwhelms us.
Anoint us with your healing love
and plant within us the seed of hope:
May we know again the joy
of your love in Christ,
who lives and reigns forever and ever.
Amen.

✚ *Let us see, O LORD, your mercy.*
Give us your saving help.

✠ *Let us see, O LORD, your mercy.*
   Give us your saving help.

PSALM 85   *page 417*

READING   *Ephesians 1:3–10*

Blessed be the God and Father of our Lord Jesus Christ, who has blessed us in Christ with every spiritual blessing in the heavenly places, just as he chose us in Christ before the foundation of the world to be holy and blameless before him in love. He destined us for adoption as his children through Jesus Christ, according to the good pleasure of his will, to the praise of his glorious grace that he freely bestowed on us in the Beloved. In him we have redemption through his blood, the forgiveness of our trespasses, according to the riches of his grace that he lavished on us. With all wisdom and insight he has made known to us the mystery of his will, according to his good pleasure that he set forth in Christ, as a plan for the fullness of time, to gather up all things in him, things in heaven and things on earth.

REFLECTION

The writer of Ephesians highlights the absolute graciousness of God. Even before Creation, we were destined in Christ for glory. Nothing we have done warrants such an honor; it is pure gift—God's choice rather than ours.

PRAYERS   *others may be added*

Chosen in Christ before the world's foundation, we cry out:

◆ Revive us, O God our helper!

That the Church may boldly proclaim God's desire that all be saved, we cry out: ◆ *That God's people may give thanks for the gifts bestowed on them in Christ, we cry out:* ◆ *That the poor may know their dignity as God's beloved children, we cry out:* ◆ *That the dead who set their hope in Christ may live forever in God's presence, we cry out:* ◆ *That we may rejoice in the glory we have inherited in Christ, we cry out:* ◆

Our Father . . .

Blessed are you,
our God and Father,
for in Christ you have revealed
the fullness of wisdom.
Make us holy and blameless
    before you,
that we may know redemption
and be gathered up into the glory
of the fullness of creation,
where Christ lives and reigns with you,
in the unity of the Holy Spirit,
one God,
forever and ever. Amen.

✠ *Let us see, O LORD, your mercy.*
   Give us your saving help.

✝ *Let us see, O LORD, your mercy.*
Give us your saving help.

PSALM 85 — page 417

READING — Jeremiah 2:4–7

Hear the word of the LORD, O house of Jacob, and all the families of the house of Israel. Thus says the LORD:
What wrong did your ancestors
    find in me
    that they went far from me,
and went after worthless things, and
    became worthless themselves?
They did not say, "Where is the LORD
    who brought us up from the land
        of Egypt,
who led us in the wilderness,
    in a land of deserts and pits,
in a land of drought and deep darkness,
    in a land that no one passes through,
    where no one lives?"
I brought you into a plentiful land
    to eat its fruits and its good things.
But when you entered you defiled
    my land,
    and made my heritage
        an abomination.

REFLECTION

Like other prophets, the prophet Jeremiah proclaimed a message of repentance and renewal to Judah in the last days before its defeat. Yet the prophet's writings are also filled with words of hope that encouraged the people while exiled in Babylon. God would not abandon them in a foreign land, but would again deliver them as at the time of the Exodus from Egypt.

PRAYERS — *others may be added*

Remembering all God has done for us, we pray:

◆ Revive us, O God our helper!

For all who proclaim God's work of liberation, we pray: ◆ For all who dwell today in Palestine and Israel, we pray: ◆ For all who flee oppression and injustice, we pray: ◆ For all who feel worthless and forgotten, we pray: ◆ For all who seek restoration and renewal, we pray: ◆ For all who remember God's marvelous deeds, we pray: ◆

Our Father . . .

God of deliverance,
you never abandon your people
or forget your promises.
Remind us of your saving deeds:
May we never forget
what you have done in Jesus Christ,
who lives and reigns
forever and ever. Amen.

✝ *Let us see, O LORD, your mercy.*
Give us your saving help.

✙ *Let us see, O LORD, your mercy.*
Give us your saving help.

PSALM 85 $\qquad$ *page 417*

READING $\qquad$ *Jeremiah 3:12–14*

Go, and proclaim these words toward
the north, and say:
Return, faithless Israel, says the
LORD.
I will not look on you in anger,
for I am merciful, says the LORD;
I will not be angry forever.
Only acknowledge your guilt,
that you have rebelled against the
LORD your God,
and scattered your favors among
strangers under every green tree,
and have not obeyed my voice,
says the LORD.
Return, O faithless children, says the
LORD,
for I am your master;
I will take you, one from a city and
two from a family,
and I will bring you to Zion.

REFLECTION

Truth-telling has a power of its own; it's
the only thing God asks of the Israelites,
that they "acknowledge guilt." Countries
such as post-apartheid South Africa and
Guatemala after its devastating civil war
set up truth commissions just for this
purpose—not to assign blame or punish
offenders. Somehow, acknowledging wrongs
and wounds, describing them truthfully
in all their ugliness, is the beginning of
reconciliation, although it is pain enough
in itself.

PRAYERS

Returning to God with contrite hearts,
we pray:

◆ Revive us, O God our helper!

That God's people may be a source
of mercy for those burdened by guilt,
we pray: ◆ *That the world may be spared*
God's anger but know his divine love,
we pray: ◆ *That the truth may bring*
freedom and reconciliation to all people,
we pray: ◆ *That those who have turned*
away from God may hear him calling
them to conversion, we pray: ◆ *That we*
may confess our faithlessness, returning
to God with all our hearts, we pray: ◆

Our Father . . .

Compassionate God,
your anger lasts but a moment,
but your mercy is everlasting.
Give us courage to confess
our failings,
that we may return to you
with clean hearts,
embracing the salvation you offer
in Jesus,
who lives and reigns with you
in the unity of the Holy Spirit,
God forever and ever. Amen.

✙ *Let us see, O LORD, your mercy.*
Give us your saving help.

✦ *Let us see, O LORD, your mercy.*
Give us your saving help.

PSALM 85   *page 417*

READING   *Jeremiah 3:15–18*

I will give you shepherds after my own heart, who will feed you with knowledge and understanding. And when you have multiplied and increased in the land, in those days, says the LORD, they shall no longer say, "The ark of the covenant of the LORD." It shall not come to mind, or be remembered, or missed; nor shall another one be made. At that time Jerusalem shall be called the throne of the LORD, and all nations shall gather to it, to the presence of the LORD in Jerusalem, and they shall no longer stubbornly follow their own evil will. In those days the house of Judah shall join the house of Israel, and together they shall come from the land of the north to the land that I gave your ancestors for a heritage.

REFLECTION

The prophet offers a vision of unity. Instead of the division caused by the ancient kings of Israel, when ten tribes formed the kingdom of Samaria with two forming the kingdom of Judah, Jeremiah imagines a day when new shepherds will restore the ancient unity of the tribes. Now, we hope for the day when our own leaders—both religious and civil—will make the unity of people their first priority.

PRAYERS   *others may be added*

Seeking the unity of humankind,
we pray:

◆ Revive us, O God our helper!

That the baptized may work together for reconciliation among Christians, we pray: ◆ That all people of faith may grow in understanding, we pray: ◆ That the world's races and cultures may seek peace and unity, we pray: ◆ That the prophetic vision may unite poor and rich, powerful and powerless, we pray: ◆ That we may shepherd those entrusted to us with love and care, we pray: ◆

Our Father . . .

Shepherd of Israel,
in the prophet's vision
you promise a new day
when all your people
will live as one.
Inspire us with hope:
May we seek the world
in which all your children
live as one family.
This we ask in Jesus' name. Amen.

✦ *Let us see, O LORD, your mercy.*
Give us your saving help.

✦ *Let us see, O LORD, your mercy.*
Give us your saving help.

PSALM 85   page 417

READING   *Jeremiah 18:1–6*

The word that came to Jeremiah from the LORD: "Come, go down to the potter's house, and there I will let you hear my words." So I went down to the potter's house, and there he was working at his wheel. The vessel he was making of clay was spoiled in the potter's hand, and he reworked it into another vessel, as seemed good to him. Then the word of the LORD came to me: Can I not do with you, O house of Israel, just as this potter has done? says the LORD. Just like the clay in the potter's hand, so are you in my hand, O house of Israel.

REFLECTION   *Pope John Paul II*

With loving regard, the divine Artist passes on to the human artist a spark of his own surpassing wisdom, calling [human beings] to share in his creative power. Obviously, this is a sharing which leaves intact the infinite distance between the Creator and the creature, as Cardinal Nicholas of Cusa made clear: "Creative art, which it is the soul's good fortune to entertain, is not to be identified with that essential art which is God himself, but is only a communication of it and a share in it."

PRAYERS   *others may be added*

Shaped by the hands of the Divine Potter, we pray:

◆ Revive us, O God our helper!

For catechists and all who form God's people in their faith, we pray: ◆
For parents and all who nurture God's children, we pray: ◆ *For educators, and all who foster wisdom, we pray:* ◆
For artisans, craftspeople and all who embody the creativity of God, we pray: ◆
For all creatures, shaped by the skill of the heavenly artist, we pray: ◆

Our Father . . .

Loving Creator,
you form us in your own image
and repair us when we are warped
    by sin.
Gently mold us by your will
and cast us into beautiful vessels
    of your Spirit,
that we may testify
to your creative skill
and glorify you in our beauty.
We ask this in the name
    of Jesus Christ,
perfected in obedience to you,
who lives and reigns forever and ever.
Amen.

✦ *Let us see, O LORD, your mercy.*
Give us your saving help.

✦ *Let us see, O LORD, your mercy.*
   Give us your saving help.

PSALM 85
page 417

READING
Jeremiah 30:1–3, 8–9

The word that came to Jeremiah from the LORD: Thus says the LORD, the God of Israel: Write in a book all the words that I have spoken to you. For the days are surely coming, says the LORD, when I will restore the fortunes of my people, Israel and Judah, says the LORD, and I will bring them back to the land that I gave to their ancestors and they shall take possession of it. On that day, says the LORD of hosts, I will break the yoke from off his neck, and I will burst his bonds, and strangers shall no more make a servant of him. But they shall serve the LORD their God and David their king, whom I will raise up for them.

REFLECTION

For the people of Judah, both before and during the exile, Jeremiah's words spoke of the restoration of Israel as a nation. His words also eventually came to mean the realization of God's rule on earth—the kingdom Jesus preached. While it is easy to relegate that kingdom to a time that will come only after death, the two interpretations should be held in tension: God's reign has everything to do with the here and now, but it also lies beyond our present reality.

PRAYERS
others may be added

Hopeful of the fulfillment of God's promises, we pray:

◆ Revive us, O God our helper!

That the Church may always proclaim God's message of liberation and hope, we pray: ◆ That God may raise up wise and just rulers for all nations, we pray: ◆ That God's people may labor to break the yoke of poverty and oppression, we pray: ◆ That refugees may return to their homes in peace, we pray: ◆ That we may trust in the faithfulness of God, we pray: ◆

Our Father . . .

Faithful God,
in Jesus you restore to life
all who trust in your mercy,
breaking the bonds of sin and death.
Create us anew as your holy people
that we may be gathered
    into your harvest
and take possession of the land
    you promise,
where Jesus Christ lives and reigns
forever and ever. Amen.

✦ *Let us see, O LORD, your mercy.*
   Give us your saving help.

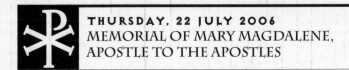
✝ *Alleluia! Christ is risen!*
Christ is risen indeed!
Alleluia! Alleluia!

PSALM 34 *page 412*

READING *Song of Solomon 3:1–4*

Upon my bed at night
I sought him whom my soul loves;
I sought him, but found him not;
 I called him, but he gave
  no answer.
"I will rise now and go about the city,
 in the streets and in the squares;
I will seek him whom my soul loves."
 I sought him, but found him not.
The sentinels found me,
 as they went about in the city.
"Have you seen him
  whom my soul loves?"
Scarcely had I passed them,
 when I found him
  whom my soul loves.
I held him, and would not let him go
 until I brought him into my
  mother's house,
and into the chamber of her
  that conceived me.

REFLECTION *Rosemary Ruether*

It is Jesus' women friends who remain faithful to him through his crucifixion and burial. They, especially his closest friend Mary Magdalene, are the first witnesses of the resurrection. Jewish law regarded women as incapable of acting as responsible witnesses. To make women the first witnesses of the resurrection was to make them the original source of credibility of the Christian faith.

PRAYERS *others may be added*

With longing for the Beloved,
we pray:

◆ Turn toward us, Lord of life!

For all women who serve the Church as ministers, we pray: ◆ *For religious women, who embrace lives of poverty, chastity, and obedience for the sake of God's reign, we pray:* ◆ *For those who suffer discrimination because of their gender, we pray:* ◆ *For all who look to Mary Magdalene as patron and teacher, we pray:* ◆ *For all who seek with passion the Lover of their souls, we pray:* ◆

Our Father . . .

God of apostles,
your servant Mary Magdalene
was first to behold the Risen One,
and first to proclaim Christ's Good
 News,
for she sought him
whom her soul loved
 above all else.
Fill us with desire
for the Beloved One,
that we may serve Christ faithfully
as we await the wedding feast.
We ask this through Jesus Christ,
the Lover of our souls,
now and forever. Amen.

✝ *Alleluia! Christ is risen!*
Christ is risen indeed!
Alleluia! Alleluia!

✦ *Let us see, O LORD, your mercy.*
Give us your saving help.

PSALM 85 *page 417*

READING *Ephesians 2:13–18*

In Christ Jesus you who once were far off have been brought near by the blood of Christ. For he is our peace; in his flesh he has made both groups into one and has broken down the dividing wall, that is, the hostility between us. He has abolished the law with its commandments and ordinances, that he might create in himself one new humanity in place of the two, thus making peace, and might reconcile both groups to God in one body through the cross, thus putting to death that hostility through it. So he came and proclaimed peace to you who were far off and peace to those who were near; for through him both of us have access in one Spirit to the Father.

REFLECTION

The author of Ephesians describes the unity Christ brings to Jews and Gentiles; though at one time excluded from the covenant, in Christ non-Jews now have a share in God's promise. This unity extends also beyond the bounds of any one culture or people or even religion. This unity is universal, the meaning of the word "catholic." The Second Vatican Council puts it this way: "All are called to this catholic unity of the people of God, which prefigures and promotes universal peace. And to it belong, or are related in different ways: the catholic faithful, others who believe in Christ, and finally all of humankind, called by God's grace to salvation" (Lumen gentium, *13*).

PRAYERS *others may be added*

Seeking the unity of all people,
we pray:

◆ Revive us, O God our helper!

For the unity of the Christian household, we pray: ◆ *For unity among the spiritual children of Abraham, we pray:* ◆ *For unity among all people of faith, we pray:* ◆ *For unity among earth's nations, we pray:* ◆ *For unity among poor and rich, we pray:* ◆ *For unity among sick and well, we pray:* ◆ *For unity among living and dead, we pray:* ◆

Our Father . . .

God of all creation,
in Christ you gather humanity
as one body, one family,
rich in varied gifts.
Strengthen the bonds of charity
that unite nations and peoples.
May peace replace hostility
and unity overcome division
to the glory of your name,
one God, Father, Son and Holy Spirit,
both now and forever. Amen.

✦ *Let us see, O LORD, your mercy.*
Give us your saving help.

✝ *Let us see, O LORD, your mercy.*
Give us your saving help.

PSALM 85   *page 417*

READING   *Jeremiah 30:18–22*

Thus says the LORD:
I am going to restore the fortunes
    of the tents of Jacob,
  and have compassion
    on his dwellings;
the city shall be rebuilt upon its mound,
    and the citadel set on its rightful site.
Out of them shall come thanksgiving,
    and the sound of merrymakers.
I will make them many,
    and they shall not be few;
  I will make them honored,
    and they shall not be disdained.
Their children shall be as of old,
  their congregation shall be
    established before me;
  and I will punish all
    who oppress them.
Their prince shall be one of their own,
  their ruler shall come
    from their midst;
I will bring him near,
    and he shall approach me,
for who would otherwise dare
    to approach me? says the LORD.
And you shall be my people,
  and I will be your God.

REFLECTION

Jeremiah's vision is an exile's dream: the
destroyed city restored, its temple rebuilt;
the forgotten people remembered, their
oppressors cast down; a new ruler, near
to God. Such a vision would give hope to
many in our own day, exiled by war or
natural disaster, poverty or oppression.
How different would the world be if all of
us shared the prophet's vision, if all of
us sought to bring it to fullness?

PRAYERS   *others may be added*

Inspired by the prophet's vision,
we pray:

◆ Revive us, O God our helper!

That the baptized may strive for the
kingdom Jesus announced, we pray: ◆
That all people of faith may seek
the restoration of exiles, we pray: ◆
That nations together may bring an
end to war and oppression, we pray: ◆
That world leaders may draw near
to the God of all the earth, we pray: ◆
That the sorrowful may find joy in the
God of life, we pray: ◆ *That we may*
take part in God's work of restoration,
we pray: ◆

Our Father . . .

God of our future,
you promise relief for the weary
and restoration to those cast down.
Make us your people,
that we may sing in thanksgiving
and enjoy the fullness
of your promise in Jesus Christ,
who is Lord forever and ever. Amen.

✝ *Let us see, O LORD, your mercy.*
Give us your saving help.

✛ *Alleluia! Christ is risen!*
Christ is risen indeed!
Alleluia! Alleluia!

PSALM 34 *page 412*

READING *Matthew 20:20–28*

Then the mother of the sons of Zebedee came to him with her sons, and kneeling before him, she asked a favor of him. And he said to her, "What do you want?" She said to him, "Declare that these two sons of mine will sit, one at your right hand and one at your left, in your kingdom." But Jesus answered, "You do not know what you are asking. Are you able to drink the cup that I am about to drink?" They said to him, "We are able." He said to them, "You will indeed drink my cup, but to sit at my right hand and at my left, this is not mine to grant, but it is for those for whom it has been prepared by my Father."

When the ten heard it, they were angry with the two brothers. But Jesus called them to him and said, "You know that the rulers of the Gentiles lord it over them, and their great ones are tyrants over them. It will not be so among you; but whoever wishes to be great among you must be your servant, and whoever wishes to be first among you must be your slave; just as the Son of Man came not to be served but to serve, and to give his life a ransom for many."

REFLECTION

Jesus makes clear what it means to follow him: Anyone who wants to share his glory must share his cup of suffering. Beyond this, anyone who wants to exercise leadership in the community of disciples must become the servant of all.

PRAYERS *others may be added*

Joining the holy apostles, we pray:

◆ Turn to us, Lord of life!

For the pope, patriarchs, and bishops: May they be servants of all, we pray: ◆ For pastors and all ministers: May they pour themselves out in service to God's people, we pray: ◆ For elected officials, judges, and civil authorities: May they seek only the well-being of those they serve, we pray: ◆ For all those sent to announce the Good News: May they embrace the cross they proclaim, we pray: ◆

Our Father . . .

God of the apostles,
those who follow your Son
will share his suffering
yet you raise them to eternal life.
Give us courage to embrace
apostolic service to one another:
May we proclaim by our good works
the life you offer in Jesus Christ,
in whose name we pray. Amen.

✛ *Alleluia! Christ is risen!*
Christ is risen indeed!
Alleluia! Alleluia!

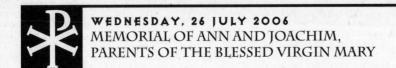
✠ *Let us see, O LORD, your mercy.*
   Give us your saving help.

PSALM 85   *page 417*

READING   *Jeremiah 31:1–5*

At that time, says the LORD, I will be
the God of all the families of Israel,
and they shall be my people.
Thus says the LORD:
The people who survived the sword
   found grace in the wilderness;
when Israel sought for rest,
   the LORD appeared to him
      from far away.
I have loved you with an
      everlasting love;
   therefore I have continued
      my faithfulness to you.
Again I will build you,
   and you shall be built,
   O virgin Israel!
Again you shall take
   your tambourines,
   and go forth in the dance
      of the merrymakers.
Again you shall plant vineyards
   on the mountains of Samaria;
the planters shall plant,
   and shall enjoy the fruit.

REFLECTION   *Pope John Paul II*

*Elderly people help us to see human
affairs with greater wisdom, because life's
vicissitudes have brought them knowledge
and maturity. They are the guardians of
our collective memory, and thus the privi-
leged interpreters of that body of ideals
and common values which support and
guide life in society. To exclude the elderly*
*is, in a sense, to deny the past, in which
the present is firmly rooted, in the name of
a modernity without memory. Precisely
because of their mature experience, the
elderly are able to offer young people precious advice and guidance.*

PRAYERS   *others may be added*

   *Joining grandparents and all elders,
   we pray:*

◆ Revive us, O God our helper!

*For parents and grandparents, aunts and
uncles, we pray: ◆ For spiritual mentors
who have nurtured and guided us through
life's journey, we pray: ◆ For spouses
and friends, and all those committed
to one another in love, we pray: ◆
For childcare workers and all who care
for children, we pray: ◆ For all who
make present God's maternal love and
fatherly care, we pray: ◆*

Our Father . . .

God of our ancestors,
in Ann and Joachim you provided
loving parents for the Virgin Mary
and grandparents for the Savior.
Bless our parents and grandparents;
fill them with joy and holiness.
May all the love and care
they have given us
return to them in abundance.
We ask this in the name of Jesus,
grandson of Joachim and Ann,
your Son and Mary's,
now and forever. Amen.

✠ *Let us see, O LORD, your mercy.*
   Give us your saving help.

✛ *Let us see, O LORD, your mercy.*
Give us your saving help.

PSALM 85   page 417

READING   Jeremiah 31:8–10

See, I am going to bring them
    from the land of the north,
  and gather them from the farthest
    parts of the earth,
among them the blind and the lame,
  those with child
    and those in labor, together;
  a great company,
    they shall return here.
With weeping they shall come,
  and with consolations
    I will lead them back,
I will let them walk by brooks
    of water,
  in a straight path in which
    they shall not stumble;
for I have become a father to Israel,
  and Ephraim is my firstborn.
Hear the word of the LORD, O nations,
  and declare it in the coastlands
    far away;
say, "He who scattered Israel
    will gather him,
and will keep him as a shepherd
    a flock."

REFLECTION

*We Christians sometimes imagine that
Jesus' descriptions of God as "father" and
"shepherd" were original to him, but actually they show just how steeped Jesus was
in his own Jewish tradition. While he may
have expanded upon them—teaching us to
call God "Abba," and describing himself
as the "Good Shepherd"—his religious
imagination came straight from the Hebrew
prophets. Rather than revealing two different gods—a "god of wrath" and a "god of
love"—the two Testaments really flow
from one to the other.*

PRAYERS   *others may be added*

*Praising God, who shepherds us,
we pray:*

◆ Revive us, O God our helper!

*That God may provide loving and gentle
shepherds for the Church, we pray:* ◆
*That the world's people may recognize
one another as God's children, we pray:* ◆
*That God may console the world's
sorrow, we pray:* ◆ *That persons with
disabilities may take their place in Church
and society, we pray:* ◆ *That God may
gather all people into one community
of love, we pray:* ◆

Our Father . . .

Shepherd of Israel,
you gather all creation into one flock,
uniting all races and languages.
Give us vision to recognize
  one another
as brothers and sisters,
adopted children of God,
that together we may praise you
  through Jesus Christ,
who lives and reigns
forever and ever. Amen.

✛ *Let us see, O LORD, your mercy.*
Give us your saving help.

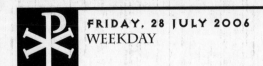
✚ *Let us see, O LORD, your mercy.*
Give us your saving help.

PSALM 85 *page 417*

READING *Jeremiah 31:31–34*

The days are surely coming, says the LORD, when I will make a new covenant with the house of Israel and the house of Judah. It will not be like the covenant that I made with their ancestors when I took them by the hand to bring them out of the land of Egypt—a covenant that they broke, though I was their husband, says the LORD. But this is the covenant that I will make with the house of Israel after those days, says the LORD: I will put my law within them, and I will write it on their hearts; and I will be their God, and they shall be my people. No longer shall they teach one another, or say to each other, "Know the LORD," for they shall all know me, from the least of them to the greatest, says the LORD; for I will forgive their iniquity, and remember their sin no more.

REFLECTION *Second Vatican Council*

Deep within their consciences men and women discover a law which they have not laid upon themselves and which they must obey. Its voice, ever calling them to love, to do what is good and to avoid evil, tells them inwardly at the right moment: do this, and shun that, for they have in their hearts a law inscribed by God. Their dignity rests in observing this law, and by it they will be judged. Their conscience is people's most secret core—their sanctuary.

Within this sanctuary they are alone with God and his voice echoes in their depths.

PRAYERS *others may be added*

Embracing the new covenant offered in Christ, we pray:

◆ Revive us, O God our helper!

That the people of God, from least to greatest, may proclaim their knowledge of God, we pray: ◆ *That God may write the law of love on the hearts of all people, we pray:* ◆ *That forgiveness may overcome the hunger for revenge, we pray:* ◆ *That God's compassion for the poor may take root among the disciples of Jesus, we pray:* ◆ *That God may forgive our iniquities, embracing us in Christ as daughters and sons, we pray:* ◆

Our Father . . .

God of the covenant,
though we turn from you,
you draw us back,
inscribing your law within our hearts.
Plant deep within us love for you,
that from least to greatest
we may grow in love of you
    and one another
through our Savior Jesus Christ,
in whose name we pray. Amen.

✚ *Let us see, O LORD, your mercy.*
Give us your saving help.

✠ *Alleluia! Christ is risen!*
Christ is risen indeed!
Alleluia! Alleluia!

PSALM 34 page 412

READING John 11:19–27

Many of the Jews had come to Martha and Mary to console them about their brother. When Martha heard that Jesus was coming, she went and met him, while Mary stayed at home. Martha said to Jesus, "Lord, if you had been here, my brother would not have died. But even now I know that God will give you whatever you ask of him." Jesus said to her, "Your brother will rise again." Martha said to him, "I know that he will rise again in the res-urrection on the last day." Jesus said to her, "I am the resurrection and the life. Those who believe in me, even though they die, will live, and everyone who lives and believes in me will never die. Do you believe this?" She said to him, "Yes, Lord, I believe that you are the Messiah, the Son of God, the one com-ing into the world."

REFLECTION

Today we commemorate Martha of Bethany, along with her sister Mary and brother Lazarus. We usually remember Martha as the busy sister in Luke's Gospel (10:38– 42), but here she is the model disciple, professing the fullness of faith in Jesus as both Messiah and Son of God. Beyond this, she professes her faith in a time of great sorrow, trusting in the power of Jesus. Her character would have been a great *comfort to the early Johannine Christians, who may themselves have been facing death because of their belief in Jesus.*

PRAYERS others may be added

Inspired by Martha's faith, we pray:

◆ Turn to us, Lord of life!

For those who believe in Jesus as the Messiah and Son of God, we pray: ◆ *For those who seek the One coming into the world, we pray:* ◆ *For those who dare ask for their heart's desire, we pray:* ◆ *For those who trust in God in times of sorrow, we pray:* ◆ *For those who mourn their beloved dead, we pray:* ◆ *For those who await the fullness of resurrection, we pray:* ◆

Our Father . . .

God of hope,
in Martha you give us
a model of trust in sorrow.
Renew our faith in your Son.
May our belief sustain us
in times of sadness,
that on the day of salvation
we may behold the same Jesus Christ,
the resurrection and the life,
who lives and reigns with you
in the unity of the Holy Spirit,
God forever and ever. Amen.

✠ *Alleluia! Christ is risen!*
Christ is risen indeed!
Alleluia! Alleluia!

✚ *I will wait for the L*ORD,
  for God will hear my cry.

PSALM 40 *page 413*

READING *John 6:1–9*

After this Jesus went to the other side of the Sea of Galilee, also called the Sea of Tiberias. A large crowd kept following him, because they saw the signs that he was doing for the sick. Jesus went up the mountain and sat down there with his disciples. Now the Passover, the festival of the Jews, was near. When he looked up and saw a large crowd coming toward him, Jesus said to Philip, "Where are we to buy bread for these people to eat?" He said this to test him, for he himself knew what he was going to do. Philip answered him, "Six months' wages would not buy enough bread for each of them to get a little." One of his disciples, Andrew, Simon Peter's brother, said to him, "There is a boy here who has five barley loaves and two fish. But what are they among so many people?"

REFLECTION

Generally during Year B of the Lectionary cycle (this year), the Gospel for Sunday Mass is from Mark. Beginning today and continuing for the next four Sundays, however, the Church proclaims the bread of life discourse from the Gospel of John (John chapter 6), which begins with John's account of the feeding of the multitude. Because of the importance and richness of this part of scripture, for the next several weeks, *our reading of the Sunday Gospel will often continue on Monday.*

PRAYERS *others may be added*

Trusting in God for our daily bread, we pray:

◆ Deliver us, O God.

For disciples, attending to the words of the Teacher, we pray: ◆ *For inquirers, looking for the presence of God, we pray:* ◆ *For the crowds, hoping for signs of deliverance, we pray:* ◆ *For the hungry, seeking to fill their need, we pray:* ◆ *For the sick, awaiting a healing touch, we pray:* ◆ *For all of us, feasting on the Bread of Heaven, we pray:* ◆

Our Father . . .

Bread for the poor,
in Jesus Christ you satisfy
the hunger of the multitudes.
By our sharing in the living bread,
may we become what we receive,
the body of Christ,
blessed, broken, and given
for the sake of the world.
We ask this in the name of Jesus,
the Bread of life,
who lives and reigns with you,
in the unity of the Holy Spirit,
one God, forever and ever. Amen.

✚ *I will wait for the L*ORD,
  for God will hear my cry.

✠ *I will wait for the LORD,*
for God will hear my cry.

PSALM 40   *page 413*

READING   *John 6:10–15*

Jesus said, "Make the people sit down." Now there was a great deal of grass in the place; so they sat down, about five thousand in all. Then Jesus took the loaves, and when he had given thanks, he distributed them to those who were seated; so also the fish, as much as they wanted. When they were satisfied, he told his disciples, "Gather up the fragments left over, so that nothing may be lost." So they gathered them up, and from the fragments of the five barley loaves, left by those who had eaten, they filled twelve baskets. When the people saw the sign that he had done, they began to say, "This is indeed the prophet who is to come into the world."

When Jesus realized that they were about to come and take him by force to make him king, he withdrew again to the mountain by himself.

REFLECTION

The Gospel of John has no account of Jesus "instituting" the Eucharist. Today's passage is the only place in John's Gospel where Jesus blesses bread and shares it with those around him. As a symbol of what our Eucharist should be, however, this passage has no match. Here, everyone is welcome; here, everyone is satisfied; here, there is abundance left over.

PRAYERS   *others may be added*

Ready to share what we have in thanksgiving, we pray:

◆ Deliver us, O God.

That the celebration of the Eucharist may enliven the Church to serve the hungry, we pray: ◆ *That catechumens may grow in their desire to partake of the Body and Blood of Christ, we pray:* ◆ *That Christians may overcome the divisions that prevent them from gathering at one table, we pray:* ◆ *That the world's hungry may receive their just share of the creation's bounty, we pray:* ◆ *That we may invite all people to the Church's table, we pray:* ◆

Our Father . . .

Provident God,
you fed Israel with manna
    in the desert
and even now you feed us
with the living bread of your Son.
May our sharing in the Eucharist
inspire us to greater service
of the hungry and poor,
that what we have received
    from your hand
we may generously offer
to all the world.
We ask this in the name of Jesus,
the Manna from heaven,
who lives and reigns
forever and ever. Amen.

✠ *I will wait for the LORD,*
for God will hear my cry.

✜ *I will wait for the LORD,*
for God will hear my cry.

PSALM 40 *page 413*

READING *Job 1:1–5*

There was once a man in the land of Uz whose name was Job. That man was blameless and upright, one who feared God and turned away from evil. There were born to him seven sons and three daughters. He had seven thousand sheep, three thousand camels, five hundred yoke of oxen, five hundred donkeys, and very many servants; so that this man was the greatest of all the people of the east. His sons used to go and hold feasts in one another's houses in turn; and they would send and invite their three sisters to eat and drink with them. And when the feast days had run their course, Job would send and sanctify them, and he would rise early in the morning and offer burnt offerings according to the number of them all; for Job said, "It may be that my children have sinned, and cursed God in their hearts." This is what Job always did.

REFLECTION

The Book of Job comes from the wisdom tradition of the Old Testament, collectively known in the Jewish tradition as "Writings." This book is a fable about a righteous man who suffers great calamity despite his innocence. In a series of dialogues with his friends and finally with God, Job explores the meaning of faith in the midst of suffering, wavering throughout between despair and trust. Job's author leaves no stone unturned—the book has more than 40 chapters! Interestingly enough, Job and his friends are not Jews; the author deals with human suffering outside the bounds of the Hebrew covenant. In this way the author faces the mystery of human suffering on its broadest level.

PRAYERS *others may be added*

Opening ourselves to divine wisdom, we pray:

◆ Deliver us, O God.

For those who offer a pleasing sacrifice to God, we pray: ◆ *For those who seek in scripture answers to life's questions, we pray:* ◆ *For those who celebrate God's mercy with family and friends, we pray:* ◆ *For parents who guard the well-being of their children, we pray:* ◆ *For all who seek to live in righteousness before God, we pray:* ◆

Our Father . . .

Source of insight,
in sacred scripture
you guide us in right paths.
Open us to wisdom's instruction,
that we may grow in faithfulness
to the way of salvation
and come to your heavenly
dwelling place,
for you alone are God,
now and forever. Amen.

✜ *I will wait for the LORD,*
for God will hear my cry.

✦ *I will wait for the LORD,*
  for God will hear my cry.

PSALM 40   *page 413*

READING   *Job 1:6–12*

One day the heavenly beings came to present themselves before the LORD, and Satan also came among them. The LORD said to Satan, "Where have you come from?" Satan answered the LORD, "From going to and fro on the earth, and from walking up and down on it." The LORD said to Satan, "Have you considered my servant Job? There is no one like him on the earth, a blameless and upright man who fears God and turns away from evil." Then Satan answered the LORD, "Does Job fear God for nothing? Have you not put a fence around him and his house and all that he has, on every side? You have blessed the work of his hands, and his possessions have increased in the land. But stretch out your hand now, and touch all that he has, and he will curse you to your face." The LORD said to Satan, "Very well, all that he has is in your power; only do not stretch out your hand against him!" So Satan went out from the presence of the LORD.

REFLECTION

Job's author characterizes God as an ancient Near Eastern monarch, with servants who keep on eye on things in the realm. Satan, meaning simply "adversary" rather than "the devil," takes the role of prosecutor in the ancient court. His question cuts to the heart of the divine-human relationship: Do we serve God purely out of love or because we expect something in return? Satan cynically argues the latter, while God seems more positive about Job's intentions; God even calls attention to "my servant Job," bestowing a title of high honor. In the end, the LORD and Satan make a bet, with God expressing confidence that Job will prove faithful.

PRAYERS   *others may be added*

  Seeking to praise God with pure
  hearts, we pray:

◆ Deliver us, O God.

For true worship offered in thanksgiving, we pray: ◆ *For faith cleansed of idolatry and self-interest, we pray:* ◆ *For courage to turn from evil ways, we pray:* ◆*For confidence in God's faithfulness, we pray:* ◆ *For defenders against adversaries, we pray:* ◆ *For blameless and upright lives, we pray:* ◆

Our Father . . .

Faithful God,
though adversaries surround us
you speak on our behalf,
for you have made us your own.
Keep our worship faithful
and our piety beyond reproach,
that we may love you alone,
praising you always
through our Savior Jesus Christ,
who is Lord forever and ever. Amen.

✦ *I will wait for the LORD,*
  for God will hear my cry.

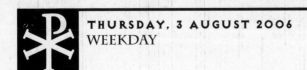
✦ *I will wait for the* LORD,
 for God will hear my cry.

PSALM 40   *page 413*

READING   *Job 1:13–22*

One day when his sons and daughters were eating and drinking wine in the eldest brother's house, a messenger came to Job and said, "The oxen were plowing and the donkeys were feeding beside them, and the Sabeans fell on them and carried them off, and killed the servants with the edge of the sword; I alone have escaped to tell you." While he was still speaking, another came and said, "The fire of God fell from heaven and burned up the sheep and the servants, and consumed them; I alone have escaped to tell you." While he was still speaking, another came and said, "The Chaldeans formed three columns, made a raid on the camels and carried them off, and killed the servants with the edge of the sword; I alone have escaped to tell you." While he was still speaking, another came and said, "Your sons and daughters were eating and drinking wine in their eldest brother's house, and suddenly a great wind came across the desert, struck the four corners of the house, and it fell on the young people, and they are dead; I alone have escaped to tell you."

Then Job arose, tore his robe, shaved his head, and fell on the ground and worshiped. He said, "Naked I came from my mother's womb, and naked shall I return there; the LORD gave, and the LORD has taken away; blessed be the name of the LORD."

In all this Job did not sin or charge God with wrong-doing.

REFLECTION

Today Judaism keep Tisha B'av, the "day of destruction" commemorating the capture of the Jerusalem temple, first by the Babylonians, then by the Romans. It is such communal suffering, continuing all the way to the Holocaust, that has inspired Jewish writers—including the author of Job—to reflect on the question of why we suffer.

PRAYERS   *others may be added*

 In sorrow, we pray:

◆ Deliver us, O God.

For lands ravaged by war, we pray: ◆
For victims of accidents and calamities, we pray: ◆ *For communities destroyed by natural disaster, we pray:* ◆ *For parents who mourn the loss of children, we pray:* ◆ *For all who suffer pain, trouble, and fear, we pray:* ◆

Our Father . . .

God of mystery,
we call out to you,
for sorrow plagues us.
Raise us from sorrow
and comfort us from fear,
that we may trust in you
and find hope in one another.
This we ask in Jesus' name. Amen.

✦ *I will wait for the* LORD,
 for God will hear my cry.

✝ *I will wait for the LORD,*
for God will hear my cry.

PSALM 40 *page 413*

READING *Job 2:1–6*

One day the heavenly beings came to present themselves before the LORD, and Satan also came among them to present himself before the LORD. The LORD said to Satan, "Where have you come from?" Satan answered the LORD, "From going to and fro on the earth, and from walking up and down on it." The LORD said to Satan, "Have you considered my servant Job? There is no one like him on the earth, a blameless and upright man who fears God and turns away from evil. He still persists in his integrity, although you incited me against him, to destroy him for no reason." Then Satan answered the LORD, "Skin for skin! All that people have they will give to save their lives. But stretch out your hand now and touch his bone and his flesh, and he will curse you to your face." The LORD said to Satan, "Very well, he is in your power; only spare his life."

REFLECTION

As if the loss of Job's material goods and family weren't enough, Satan convinces the LORD to allow Job's health to be taken away as well. It seems that Job is to be put to the severest of tests—to face the deterioration of his body and his hope. Even if we have never experienced the destruction of war or natural disaster, the terror of bombings or economic upheaval, illness manages to touch everyone eventually. At such times we cannot deny our own mortality.

PRAYERS *others may be added*

Open to finding God even in illness, we pray:

◆ Deliver us, O God.

For Church ministers who visit the sick, we pray: ◆ *For doctors, nurses, and health care professionals, we pray:* ◆ *For those with chronic illnesses and disabilities, we pray:* ◆ *For those with terminal illness and those near death, we pray:* ◆ *For those who keep vigil with the dying, we pray:* ◆ *For all who are faced with mortality, we pray:* ◆

Our Father . . .

Source of healing,
the specter of illness
brings fear and sorrow,
for death looms ever nearer.
Be with us in our anxiety,
and comfort us in illness:
May we trust in your saving help
and have confidence
in your promise of life,
for you live and reign
forever and ever. Amen.

✝ *I will wait for the LORD,*
for God will hear my cry.

✛ *I will wait for the LORD,*
for God will hear my cry.

PSALM 40   page 413

READING   Job 2:7–13

So Satan went out from the presence of the LORD, and inflicted loathsome sores on Job from the sole of his foot to the crown of his head. Job took a potsherd with which to scrape himself, and sat among the ashes.

Then his wife said to him, "Do you still persist in your integrity? Curse God, and die." But he said to her, "You speak as any foolish woman would speak. Shall we receive the good at the hand of God, and not receive the bad?" In all this Job did not sin with his lips.

Now when Job's three friends heard of all these troubles that had come upon him, each of them set out from his home—Eliphaz the Temanite, Bildad the Shuhite, and Zophar the Naamathite. They met together to go and console and comfort him. When they saw him from a distance, they did not recognize him, and they raised their voices and wept aloud; they tore their robes and threw dust in the air upon their heads. They sat with him on the ground seven days and seven nights, and no one spoke a word to him, for they saw that his suffering was very great.

REFLECTION   Gregory the Great

The truly patient person is he who is exhausted by adversity, yet is not deflected from the rightness of his hope. . . . The difference between the just and the unjust heart is seen in this, that the just utters praise of almighty God even in adversity. He is not shattered with his possessions, he does not tumble with the fall of his external reputation, but shows by his greater strength without possessions what he was like when he had them.

PRAYERS   *others may be added*

Upholding in prayer those touched by sorrow, we pray:

◆ Deliver us, O God.

That the disciples of Jesus may accompany one another in joy and sorrow, we pray: ◆ That governments may provide for the needs of the chronically ill, we pray: ◆ That the sick may find comfort in the company of friends, we pray: ◆ That the prayers of the sick may bring healing and hope, we pray: ◆

Our Father . . .

Source of friendship,
you do not abandon us in troubled
    times
but accompany us with your presence.
Fill us with compassion
for the sick and sorrowful:
May your healing touch
reach them through us,
that together we may praise you
through Jesus Christ,
who is Lord forever and ever. Amen.

✛ *I will wait for the LORD,*
for God will hear my cry.

✦ *Alleluia! Christ is risen!*
Christ is risen indeed!
Alleluia! Alleluia!

PSALM 34 *page 412*

READING *Daniel 7:9–10a, 13–14*

As I watched, thrones were set in place, and an Ancient One took his throne, his clothing was white as snow, and the hair of his head like pure wool; his throne was fiery flames, and its wheels were burning fire. A stream of fire issued and flowed out from his presence. A thousand thousands served him, and ten thousand times ten thousand stood attending him. As I watched in the night visions, I saw one like a human being coming with the clouds of heaven. And he came to the Ancient One and was presented before him. To him was given dominion and glory and kingship, that all peoples, nations, and languages should serve him. His dominion is an everlasting dominion that shall not pass away, and his kingship is one that shall never be destroyed.

REFLECTION

In addition to being the Feast of the Transfiguration, today is also the anniversary of the atomic bombing of Hiroshima. We remember two "transfigurations" today: one in which creation, in the body of Jesus, radiated God's glory, and one in which humanity was terribly disfigured with a weapon of war. This reality calls us to turn from the heavenly vision of Daniel to our earthly reality recognizing that God's rule over creation in Christ is not yet complete. We who have been given a vision of the glory to come must now carry that vision to a world disfigured by violence, injustice, poverty, and hate.

PRAYERS *others may be added*

Awestruck by God's glory, we pray:

◆ Turn to us, Lord of life!

That the baptized may carry within them the hope of the Resurrection, we pray: ◆
That governments may forsake weapons of mass destruction for the transfiguring power of peace, we pray: ◆ *That the glory of God shining in the poor may draw others to their service, we pray:* ◆
That the dead may live forever in glory among the prophets and saints of God, we pray: ◆ *That we may always be attentive to the voice of God's Beloved One speaking in our hearts, we pray:* ◆

Our Father . . .

Ancient One,
in Jesus you give us a foretaste
of the glory we will share.
Open our hearts to the One
given glory and dominion,
that we may be like lamps
shining in the darkness
until Christ's eternal day dawns,
for he lives and reigns with you,
in the unity of the Holy Spirit,
one God forever and ever. Amen.

✦ *Alleluia! Christ is risen!*
Christ is risen indeed!
Alleluia! Alleluia!

✝ *I will wait for the LORD,*
for God will hear my cry.

PSALM 40   *page 413*

READING   *John 6:24–29*

So when the crowd saw that neither Jesus nor his disciples were there, they themselves got into the boats and went to Capernaum looking for Jesus. When they found him on the other side of the sea, they said to him, "Rabbi, when did you come here?" Jesus answered them, "Very truly, I tell you, you are looking for me, not because you saw signs, but because you ate your fill of the loaves. Do not work for the food that perishes, but for the food that endures for eternal life, which the Son of Man will give you. For it is on him that God the Father has set his seal." Then they said to him, "What must we do to perform the works of God?" Jesus answered them, "This is the work of God, that you believe in him whom he has sent."

REFLECTION

Though yesterday's readings for the feast of the Transfiguration replaced Sunday's reading, we continue today with John's bread of life discourse (John 6). At the end of last Sunday's Gospel (John 6:10–15), Jesus withdrew to the mountain so the people wouldn't make him king. In the meantime, his disciples crossed the Sea of Tiberias and were met by Jesus himself, walking on the water. Today, the crowd realizes that Jesus is gone and seeks him out. Having filled their bodies with food,
Jesus now seeks to draw them—and us— beyond the physical to the deeper meaning of the food he offers.

PRAYERS   *others may be added*

With faith in the one sent by God, we pray:

◆ Deliver us, O God.

That the Church may generously offer the food of life eternal, we pray: ◆ *That catechumens may feast on the living bread of God's word, we pray:* ◆ *That the world's people may seek the wisdom from above, we pray:* ◆ *That the poor may have not only their fill of earthly food but of heavenly wisdom as well, we pray:* ◆ *That our faith in Christ may nourish us on our pilgrim journey, we pray:* ◆

Our Father . . .

Jesus, Bread of life,
you offer yourself
as food for soul and body.
Increase our hunger
for the bread that endures
and the cup that sustains.
May we take our place
at eternity's table,
for you live and reign
forever and ever. Amen.

✝ *I will wait for the LORD,*
for God will hear my cry.

✦ *I will wait for the LORD,*
  for God will hear my cry.

PSALM 40 *page 413*

READING *John 6:30–35*

So they said to him, "What sign are you going to give us then, so that we may see it and believe you? What work are you performing? Our ancestors ate the manna in the wilderness; as it is written, 'He gave them bread from heaven to eat.'" Then Jesus said to them, "Very truly, I tell you, it was not Moses who gave you the bread from heaven, but it is my Father who gives you the true bread from heaven. For the bread of God is that which comes down from heaven and gives life to the world." They said to him, "Sir, give us this bread always." Jesus said to them, "I am the bread of life. Whoever comes to me will never be hungry, and whoever believes in me will never be thirsty."

REFLECTION *Thomas Aquinas*

O precious and wonderful banquet, health-giving and full of all sweetness! What could be more precious than this banquet, in which no longer as under the law the flesh of calves and goats is eaten, but Christ the true God is set before us that we may receive him? . . . Of all the sacraments none is more health-giving, for by it sins are washed away, virtues are increased, and the soul is fed with an abundance of spiritual gifts.

PRAYERS *others may be added*

Fed by a loving God, we pray:

◆ Deliver us, O God.

That the baptized may faithfully offer praise and thanksgiving for their life in Christ, we pray: ◆ *That the desire to share the Eucharistic banquet may grow in the hearts of catechumens, we pray:* ◆ *That the world's people may share in the bread of heaven, we pray:* ◆ *That the celebration of the Eucharist may impel all Christians to feed the hungry, we pray:* ◆ *That our sharing in the bread of life may increase our faith in the one sent by God, we pray:* ◆

Our Father . . .

Bounteous God,
in every age you nourish your people
with living bread from heaven.
Increase our faith in Jesus,
the manna for our journey,
that we may become what we receive,
bread broken for the world,
and wine poured out in compassion.
This we ask in Jesus' name. Amen.

✦ *I will wait for the LORD,*
  for God will hear my cry.

✛ *I will wait for the LORD,*
for God will hear my cry.

PSALM 40   *page 413*

READING   *Job 3:1–3, 11–13, 16–19*

After this Job opened his mouth and
cursed the day of his birth. Job said:
"Let the day perish in which I
    was born,
  and the night that said,
  'A man-child is conceived.'
"Why did I not die at birth,
  come forth from the womb
    and expire?
Why were there knees to receive me,
  or breasts for me to suck?
Now I would be lying down and quiet;
  I would be asleep; then I would be
    at rest.
Or why was I not buried like a
    stillborn child,
  like an infant that never sees
    the light?
There the wicked cease
    from troubling,
  and there the weary are at rest.
There the prisoners are
    at ease together;
  they do not hear the voice
    of the taskmaster.
The small and the great are there,
  and the slaves are free
    from their masters."

REFLECTION

Job's words are full of anguish, and he
echoes the cries of many who are beaten
down by depression and grief. At such times
we are forced to ask whether life is really
worth such suffering. Tragic stories of
abused and neglected children, the desper-
ately poor and starving, the tortured and
brutalized, force us to ask even greater
questions: What kind of God allows such
horrors? Despite our faith in Christ's ulti-
mate victory over suffering, at times we
must sit in silence before the terrible mys-
tery of evil.

PRAYERS   *others may be added*

   Seeking understanding, we pray:

◆ *Deliver us, O God.*

That the Church may proclaim God's
reign in the face of tevil, we pray: ◆
That Church ministers may reach out to
the brokenhearted, we pray: ◆ *That the*
depressed and grieving may have faithful
companions, we pray: ◆ *That those*
contemplating suicide may find hope,
we pray: ◆ *That our hope in Christ may*
overcome despair, we pray: ◆

Our Father . . .

Source of hope,
despite our faith
despair sets in,
and we long for death's silence.
Be with us when courage fails
and fear extinguishes hope,
that we may trust in your care
and remain faithful in your service,
for you alone are God
forever and ever. Amen.

✛ *I will wait for the LORD,*
for God will hear my cry.

✝ *Alleluia! Christ is risen!*
Christ is risen indeed!
Alleluia! Alleluia!

PSALM 34   *page 412*

READING   *2 Corinthians 9:6–10*

The point is this: the one who sows sparingly will also reap sparingly, and the one who sows bountifully will also reap bountifully. Each of you must give as you have made up your mind, not reluctantly or under compulsion, for God loves a cheerful giver. And God is able to provide you with every blessing in abundance, so that by always having enough of everything, you may share abundantly in every good work. As it is written, "He scatters abroad, he gives to the poor; his righteousness endures forever." He who supplies seed to the sower and bread for food will supply and multiply your seed for sowing and increase the harvest of your righteousness.

REFLECTION

Saint Lawrence was a third-century deacon martyred under the Emperor Valerian. At the time deacons were charged with distributing the Church's wealth to those in need; when he captured Lawrence the emperor thought he had also captured the Church's wealth. When the emperor demanded the treasure, Lawrence brought him the poor—Christ's treasure. For that the emperor had him tortured and roasted on a gridiron. However, even in death Lawrence praised Christ. A liturgical antiphon for today proclaims, "When I was

asked I acknowledged you to be Lord. Now that I am roasted, I give you thanks."

PRAYERS   *others may be added*

Offering all we have, we pray:

◆ Turn to us, Lord of life!

That God's people may have an abundance of good works, we pray: ◆
That deacons may faithfully see to the needs of Christ's poor, we pray: ◆
That earthly wealth may become heavenly treasure in service to the world's poor, we pray: ◆ *That the hungry may benefit from the generous service of Jesus' disciples, we pray:* ◆ *That the example of Lawrence may inspire us to courageous witness to the Gospel, we pray:* ◆

Our Father . . .

God of deacons and martyrs,
your servant Lawrence cheerfully
   and bravely
accepted the martyr's crown.
Through his intercession,
make us faithful servants of all people,
that our good works may multiply,
producing a rich harvest
   of righteousness.
We ask this in the name of Jesus,
first among martyrs and servant of all,
who lives and reigns
forever and ever. Amen.

✝ *Alleluia! Christ is risen!*
Christ is risen indeed!
Alleluia! Alleluia!

✦ *I will wait for the LORD,*
for God will hear my cry.

PSALM 40   *page 413*

READING   *Job 3:20–26*

Job continued,
"Why is light given to one in misery,
   and life to the bitter in soul,
who long for death, but it does
     not come,
   and dig for it more than
     for hidden treasures;
who rejoice exceedingly,
   and are glad when they find
     the grave?
Why is light given to one who cannot
     see the way,
   whom God has fenced in?
For my sighing comes like my bread,
   and my groanings are poured out
     like water.
Truly the thing that I fear comes
     upon me,
   and what I dread befalls me.
I am not at ease, nor am I quiet;
   I have no rest; but trouble comes."

REFLECTION   *Second Vatican Council*

It is when faced with the mystery of death that the enigma of the human condition is most evident. People are tormented not only by pain and by the gradual diminution of their bodily powers but also, and even more, by the dread of forever ceasing to be. But a deep instinct leads them rightly to shrink from and to reject the utter ruin and total loss of their personality. Because they bear in themselves the seed of eternity, which cannot be reduced to mere matter, they rebel against death.

PRAYERS   *others may be added*

  Rebelling against death's power,
  we pray:

◆ Deliver us, O God.

For those for whom life is bitter,
we pray: ◆ *For those overcome by misery,*
we pray: ◆ *For those who battle against*
death, we pray: ◆ *For those exhausted*
by illness and pain, we pray: ◆ *For those*
filled with dread, we pray: ◆ *For those*
who have lost hope, we pray: ◆

Our Father . . .

Living God,
with you death has no place,
for you promise life eternal.
Refresh those overcome
by pain, fear and despair,
and give them new hope
in your eternal promise,
that Christ's victory over death
may come to fulfillment
and all may enjoy eternal light,
through the same Christ our Savior.
Amen.

✦ *I will wait for the LORD,*
for God will hear my cry.

✚ *I will wait for the LORD,*
for God will hear my cry.

PSALM 40 *page 413*

READING *Job 4:1–9*

Then Eliphaz the Temanite answered:
"If one ventures a word with you,
    will you be offended?
    But who can keep from speaking?
See, you have instructed many;
    you have strengthened
        the weak hands.
Your words have supported
        those who were stumbling,
    and you have made firm
        the feeble knees.
But now it has come to you,
    and you are impatient;
    it touches you,
        and you are dismayed.
Is not your fear of God
    your confidence,
    and the integrity of your ways
        your hope?
"Think now, who that was innocent
    ever perished?
    Or where were the upright cut off?
As I have seen, those who
    plow iniquity
    and sow trouble reap the same.
By the breath of God they perish,
    and by the blast of his anger
        they are consumed."

REFLECTION

Eliphaz offers a standard answer for why
people suffer: It is punishment for sin. Job
has argued that he is innocent; he has
examined his conscience and found nothing
wrong. His life contradicts Eliphaz's easy
answer. As we know, there are many inno-
cents in the world who suffer; the pain of
children is most obvious, but there are
many others who suffer through no fault of
their own. Job's author will simply not
permit an easy answer.

PRAYERS *others may be added*

Seeking wisdom, we pray:

◆ Deliver us, O God.

For those persecuted for their faith,
we pray: ◆ *For those driven from*
home by war and violence, we pray: ◆
For those enduring discrimination because
of race, creed, or way of life we pray: ◆
For children suffering in disease and
poverty, we pray: ◆ *For families who lack*
sufficient food and clean water, we pray: ◆
For victims of hurricanes, earthquakes,
and drought, we pray: ◆

Our Father . . .

We cry out to you,
O God of power and might,
for the innocent suffer
and the sinless perish.
Sustain us in suffering;
give us hope in pain.
May we trust in your care
and so find restoration.
We ask this in the name of Jesus,
crucified yet risen,
Lord forever and ever. Amen.

✚ *I will wait for the LORD,*
for God will hear my cry.

✛ *I will wait for the LORD,*
 for God will hear my cry.

PSALM 40   *page 413*

READING   *John 6:44–51*

"No one can come to me unless drawn by the Father who sent me; and I will raise that person up on the last day. It is written in the prophets, 'And they shall all be taught by God.' Everyone who has heard and learned from the Father comes to me. Not that anyone has seen the Father except the one who is from God; he has seen the Father. Very truly, I tell you, whoever believes has eternal life. I am the bread of life. Your ancestors ate the manna in the wilderness, and they died. This is the bread that comes down from heaven, so that one may eat of it and not die. I am the living bread that came down from heaven. Whoever eats of this bread will live forever; and the bread that I will give for the life of the world is my flesh."

REFLECTION   *Augustine of Hippo*

You are there on the table; you are there in the chalice. You are this body with us, for, collectively, we are this body. We drink of the same chalice because we live the same life.

PRAYERS   *others may be added*

Sustained by the Bread of Heaven, we pray:

◆ Deliver us, O God.

For the Church of God, entrusted with heavenly food for the life of the world, we pray: ◆ *For leaders of nations, charged with caring for the hungry and poor, we pray:* ◆ *For those who lack faith, sought by God in love and care, we pray:* ◆ *For the dead, fed forever at the wedding banquet of the Lamb, we pray:* ◆ *For us, commissioned to offer ourselves for all people, we pray:* ◆

Our Father . . .

Heavenly Teacher,
in Christ you offer wisdom and life,
nourishment for spirit and body.
Open our hearts to embrace
the one sent from heaven,
that through Christ we may draw
    nearer to you
and so receive the gift of life eternal
through the same Jesus Christ,
who lives and reigns forever and ever.
Amen.

✛ *I will wait for the LORD,*
 for God will hear my cry.

✚ *I will wait for the LORD,*
   for God will hear my cry.

PSALM 40   *page 413*

READING   *Job 4:12–19*

Eliphaz continued,
"Now a word came stealing to me,
   my ear received the whisper of it.
Amid thoughts from visions
      of the night,
   when deep sleep falls on mortals,
dread came upon me, and trembling,
   which made all my bones shake.
A spirit glided past my face;
   the hair of my flesh bristled.
It stood still,
   but I could not discern
      its appearance.
A form was before my eyes;
   there was silence, then I heard
      a voice:
'Can mortals be righteous before God?
   Can human beings be pure before
      their Maker?
Even in his servants he puts no trust,
   and his angels he charges with error;
how much more those who live in
      houses of clay,
   whose foundation is in the dust,
   who are crushed like a moth.'"

REFLECTION

*Today we remember Saint Maximilian
Kolbe, a Polish Franciscan priest who was
martyred at Auschwitz because of his
opposition to the Nazis during World War
II. He volunteered to take the place of a
Jewish man who was slated to be executed
because of another prisoner's escape.*

*Maximilian's example, along with count-
less other victims of the Holocaust, mirrors
that of Job, who remained faithful despite
the seeming triumph of evil. As Maximilian
demonstrated, and as we believe, evil has no
true power; ultimately, it is only an illusion.*

PRAYERS   *others may be added*

*Urged forward by the communion
of saints, we pray:*

◆ Deliver us, O God.

*For faithful witnesses to Christ's victory,
we pray: ◆ For those who denounce
injustice and hatred, we pray: ◆ For those
seduced by prejudice and desire for
power, we pray: ◆ For victims of
persecution and genocide, we pray: ◆
For those who accept the suffering of
others, we pray: ◆ For those who oppose
evil in all its forms, we pray: ◆*

Our Father . . .

God of witness,
your servant Maximilian
opposed evil to its face
and won the martyr's crown.
Fill us with his courage:
May our witness to Christ
overcome the sham of evil
and bring forth your dominion
of peace, justice and love,
for Christ is Lord
forever and ever. Amen.

✚ *I will wait for the LORD,*
   for God will hear my cry.

✝ *Alleluia! Christ is risen!*
Christ is risen indeed!
Alleluia! Alleluia!

PSALM 66 *page 415*

READING *1 Corinthians 15:20–27*

But in fact Christ has been raised from the dead, the first fruits of those who have died. For since death came through a human being, the resurrection of the dead has also come through a human being; for as all die in Adam, so all will be made alive in Christ. But each in his own order: Christ the first fruits, then at his coming those who belong to Christ. Then comes the end, when he hands over the kingdom to God the Father, after he has destroyed every ruler and every authority and power. For he must reign until he has put all his enemies under his feet. The last enemy to be destroyed is death. For "God has put all things in subjection under his feet." But when it says, "All things are put in subjection," it is plain that this does not include the one who put all things in subjection under him.

REFLECTION

Today's reading highlights Christ's undoing of the sin of Adam. Some early Fathers of the Church, including Ephrem of Syria and Irenaeus of Lyons, argued that Mary undid the sin of Eve by her obedience to God's eternal Word. Because of this, she is first to hear that Word, first among disciples, and, as we celebrate today, first to share Christ's risen glory.

PRAYERS *others may be added*

With Mary as a model for our faith, we cry out:

◆ Pray for us, holy Mother of God.

For all God's people, heirs of Christ's resurrection, we pray: ◆ *For all women, made in the image and likeness of God, we pray:* ◆ *For mothers, nurturers of the image of God in their children, we pray:* ◆ *For the deceased, sharing with Mary, Christ's glory, we pray:* ◆ *For all of us, with Mary, disciples of Jesus, her Son, we pray:* ◆

Our Father . . .

God of holiness,
the Virgin Mary embraced
the gift of your Word
and now shares his glory.
Through her intercession,
may we embrace and obey
your Word of life
that we may come to share life
with Mary and all the saints
in the heavenly Jerusalem.
We ask this in the name
    of Jesus Christ,
son of Mary and of God,
who lives and reigns with you,
in the unity of the Holy Spirit,
one God, forever and ever. Amen.

✝ *Alleluia! Christ is risen!*
Christ is risen indeed!
Alleluia! Alleluia!

✦ *I will wait for the LORD,*
for God will hear my cry.

PSALM 40 page 413

READING Job 5:8–16

Eliphaz continued,
"As for me, I would seek God,
and to God I would commit
my cause.
He does great things
and unsearchable,
marvelous things without number.
He gives rain on the earth
and sends waters on the fields;
he sets on high those who are lowly,
and those who mourn are lifted
to safety.
He frustrates the devices of the crafty,
so that their hands achieve
no success.
He takes the wise in their
own craftiness;
and the schemes of the wily
are brought to a quick end.
They meet with darkness
in the daytime,
and grope at noonday as
in the night.
But he saves the needy
from the sword of their mouth,
from the hand of the mighty.
So the poor have hope,
and injustice shuts its mouth.

REFLECTION

Eliphaz expresses profound trust in divine
judgment and justice, naming God as both
sustainer and judge. In doing so, he pro-
fesses unwavering faith in God's fairness
and reinforces his argument that Job must
have done something to warrant the cata-
strophe he suffered. But, as we know from
the beginning of the story, Eliphaz is wrong.

PRAYERS others may be added

Praising God, who works marvels
without number, we pray:

◆ Deliver us, O God.

For success in the search for God,
we pray: ◆ *For deliverance of the weak*
from the hands of the mighty, we pray: ◆
For the lifting up of those who mourn,
we pray: ◆ *For a quick end to the schemes*
of the wily, we pray: ◆ *For abundant rain*
on farmers' fields, we pray: ◆ *For hope*
among the poor and downtrodden,
we pray: ◆

Our Father . . .

Marvelous God,
you send rain upon the earth
and water the fields,
always attentive to the work
of your hands.
Fill us with faith
in your provident care,
that we may trust always in you,
who thwart the crafty
and lift up the poor,
unto the endless ages of ages. Amen.

✦ *I will wait for the LORD,*
for God will hear my cry.

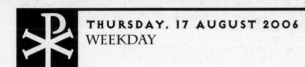
✦ *I will wait for the LORD,*
for God will hear my cry.

PSALM 40 — page 413

READING — Job 5:17–18, 21–22, 25–27

Eliphaz continued,
"How happy is the one
whom God reproves;
therefore do not despise the
discipline of the Almighty.
For he wounds, but he binds up;
he strikes, but his hands heal.
You shall be hidden from the scourge
of the tongue,
and shall not fear destruction
when it comes.
At destruction and famine you
shall laugh,
and shall not fear the wild animals
of the earth.
You shall know that your descendants
will be many,
and your offspring like the grass
of the earth.
You shall come to your grave
in ripe old age,
as a shock of grain comes up
to the threshing floor
in its season.
See, we have searched this out;
it is true.
Hear, and know it for yourself."

REFLECTION — Pope John Paul II

*In order to perceive the true answer to the
"why" of suffering, we must look to the
revelation of divine love, the ultimate
source of the meaning of everything that
exists. Love is also the richest source of
the meaning of suffering, which always
remains a mystery: we are conscious of the
insufficiency and inadequacy of our expla-
nations. Christ causes us to enter into the
mystery and to discover the "why" of suffering, as far as we are capable of grasping the sublimity of divine love.*

PRAYERS — others may be added

*Seeking our answers in God's love,
we pray:*

◆ Deliver us, O God.

*That the baptized may reach out to
comfort the sick, we pray: ◆ That those
who search for answers may find
God's presence, we pray: ◆ That those
overcome with sorrow may at last find
joy, we pray: ◆ That the power of God's
love may raise the dead to life, we pray: ◆
That we may face trials and difficulties
with confidence in God's presence,
we pray: ◆*

Our Father . . .

God of mystery,
you never abandon us
but always bear us up
in your provident care.
Strengthen us in difficulty,
that we may never despair
of your love,
but find in you life eternal
through Jesus Christ,
who lives and reigns
forever and ever. Amen.

✦ *I will wait for the LORD,*
for God will hear my cry.

✠ *I will wait for the LORD,*
for God will hear my cry.

PSALM 40 · *page 413*

READING · *Job 9:1–8*

Then Job answered:
"Indeed I know that this is so;
 but how can a mortal be just
 before God?
If one wished to contend with him,
 one could not answer him once
 in a thousand.
He is wise in heart, and mighty
 in strength
—who has resisted him, and
 succeeded?—
he who removes mountains,
 and they do not know it,
 when he overturns them
 in his anger;
who shakes the earth out of its place,
 and its pillars tremble;
who commands the sun,
 and it does not rise;
 who seals up the stars;
who alone stretched out the heavens
and trampled the waves of the Sea."

REFLECTION

Today we celebrate the memorial of Saint Jane Frances de Chantal, a woman who experienced many of Job's sorrows. As a young mother of 28 with four children, Jane lost her husband in a hunting accident. Like Job, she was overwhelmed with grief but eventually found her way through her sorrow through the help of Saint Francis de Sales. Their spiritual friendship is recorded in the letters they exchanged,
and Jane Frances eventually founded a new religious community.

PRAYERS · *others may be added*

Inspired by holy women, we pray:

◆ Deliver us, O God.

For all women, married and single, widowed and religious, we pray: ◆
For mothers, grandmothers, and aunts, we pray: ◆ *For those who reach out to the poor and hungry, we pray:* ◆
For those grieving the loss of loved ones, we pray: ◆ *For those who pray for joy in times of sorrow, we pray:* ◆ *For those who accompany one another in lives of faith, we pray:* ◆

Our Father . . .

God of holy women,
your servant Jane
sought you in grief,
and you gave her the joy
of a spiritual companion and friend.
Show us your presence
in the company of others,
that we may find strength
in difficult times
and share our joy
in your blessings.
This we ask through Jesus Christ,
who accompanies us on the Way,
and who lives and reigns
forever and ever. Amen.

✠ *I will wait for the LORD,*
for God will hear my cry.

✝ *I will wait for the LORD,*
for God will hear my cry.

PSALM 40 *page 413*

READING *Job 9:11–12, 14–16, 19–20*

Job continued,
"Look, God passes by me,
   and I do not see him;
he moves on, but I do not
      perceive him.
He snatches away; who can stop him?
   Who will say to him,
      'What are you doing?'
How then can I answer him,
   choosing my words with him?
Though I am innocent,
      I cannot answer him;
   I must appeal for mercy
      to my accuser.
If I summoned him and he
      answered me,
   I do not believe that he would
      listen to my voice.
If it is a contest of strength,
      he is the strong one!
   If it is a matter of justice,
      who can summon him?
Though I am innocent, my own
      mouth would condemn me;
   though I am blameless, he would
      prove me perverse."

REFLECTION

Job does not dispute Eliphaz's assertion
that no one can be justified before God,
and he professes God's ultimate power
over heaven and earth. This is the God
who "stretched out the heavens and tram-
pled the waves of the Sea," who, in other
words, gave order to the formless void in
Creation's first moments. Faced with the
chaos of his own situation and the threat
of the ultimate chaos of death, Job pro-
fesses faith in a God of order, a God whose
actions make sense, even if Job and his
friends cannot discern it.

PRAYERS *others may be added*

   With wonder at God's power,
   we pray:

◆ Deliver us, O God.

That the baptized may seek justice
before God, we pray: ◆ That the chaos
of war may not overcome earth's nations,
we pray: ◆ That the integrity of God's
creation may be respected and maintained,
we pray: ◆ That all people may see God's
hand in the rising sun and the starry
night, we pray: ◆ That we may rely on
the wise heart and mighty strength
of our faithful God, we pray: ◆

Our Father . . .

Mighty God,
who can contend with you?
Who can know your ways?
Give us your heart's wisdom,
and show us your mighty strength,
that in the morning sun
and nighttime's glory
we may see your wondrous hand
and so praise you
with all creation
now and forevermore. Amen.

✝ *I will wait for the LORD,*
for God will hear my cry.

✚ *I will wait for the LORD,*
  for God will hear my cry.

PSALM 40   *page 413*

READING   *John 6:52–58*

The Jews then disputed among themselves, saying, "How can this man give us his flesh to eat?" So Jesus said to them, "Very truly, I tell you, unless you eat the flesh of the Son of Man and drink his blood, you have no life in you. Those who eat my flesh and drink my blood have eternal life, and I will raise them up on the last day; for my flesh is true food and my blood is true drink. Those who eat my flesh and drink my blood abide in me, and I in them. Just as the living Father sent me, and I live because of the Father, so whoever eats me will live because of me. This is the bread that came down from heaven, not like that which your ancestors ate, and they died. But the one who eats this bread will live forever."

REFLECTION   *Augustine of Hippo*

There feeding the angels, here on earth a hungry child; there unfailing Bread with perfect powers, here, along with speechless children, needing the nourishment of milk; there doing good, here suffering evil; there never dying, here rising after death and bestowing eternal life on mortals. God became one of us so that we might become God.

PRAYERS   *others may be added*

Nourished by the Bread of Life,
we pray:

◆ Deliver us, O God.

That the baptized may find sustenance in Christ's body and blood, we pray: ◆
That Christians of all denominations may one day share the living bread at one table, we pray: ◆ *That the hungry may find relief in the service of all who share in the true food and drink of the Eucharistic feast, we pray:* ◆ *That our sharing in the Eucharist may propel us to works of justice, we pray:* ◆ *That the dead may share in the eternal feast of the Lamb of God, we pray:* ◆

Our Father . . .

Living Father,
in Jesus you give us food
for life eternal
and drink for everlasting joy.
Fill us with your own life:
May our sharing in the Eucharist
make visible in us
the presence of the Bread of Life,
Jesus Christ, who lives and reigns,
  with you,
in the unity of the Holy Spirit,
one God, now and forever. Amen.

✚ *I will wait for the LORD,*
  for God will hear my cry.

✝ *I will wait for the LORD,*
for God will hear my cry.

PSALM 40   *page 413*

READING   *Job 19:21–27*

Job said,
"Have pity on me, have pity on me,
    O you my friends,
  for the hand of God has touched me!
Why do you, like God, pursue me,
  never satisfied with my flesh?
"O that my words were written down!
    O that they were inscribed
    in a book!
O that with an iron pen and with lead
  they were engraved
    on a rock forever!
For I know that my Redeemer lives,
  and that at the last he will stand
    upon the earth;
and after my skin has been
    thus destroyed,
  then in my flesh I shall see God,
whom I shall see on my side,
  and my eyes shall behold,
    and not another.
  My heart faints within me!

REFLECTION

Job is certain that his death is at hand, but
he still appeals to a future in which he
might be vindicated before God. Even
reduced to mere physical existence—and
a tenuous one at that—Job has hope that
after his death he will behold God with his
own eyes. Since belief in an afterlife or
resurrection didn't really arise among the
Israelites until just before the time of
Jesus, the author portrays Job as making
a great leap of faith. Job is confident
that the living God, the Vindicator and
Redeemer, will reveal himself.

PRAYERS   *others may be added*

With hope greater than despair,
we pray:

◆ Deliver us, O God.

That the baptized may cling to faith
in the Redeemer even in harrowing times,
we pray: ◆ *That those contemplating*
suicide may not be overcome by despair,
we pray: ◆ *That those reduced to mere*
survival may find full human life,
we pray: ◆ *That those nearing death may*
find comfort and confidence, we pray: ◆
That we may never lose hope in God's
saving power, we pray: ◆

Our Father . . .

Living God,
Redeemer of the accused,
Savior of the innocent,
hear the cries of those burdened
with sorrow and despair.
Rise up and save them!
Give the hope of life
to those gripped by death,
that they may behold you
with their own eyes,
and give you due praise
forever and ever. Amen.

✝ *I will wait for the LORD,*
for God will hear my cry.

✦ *I will wait for the LORD,*
for God will hear my cry.

PSALM 40 *page 413*

READING *Job 38:1–11*

Then the LORD answered Job out of
the whirlwind:
"Who is this that darkens counsel
    by words without knowledge?
Gird up your loins like a man,
  I will question you, and you shall
    declare to me.
"Where were you when I laid
    the foundation of the earth?
  Tell me, if you have understanding.
Who determined its measurements—
    surely you know!
  Or who stretched the line upon it?
On what were its bases sunk,
  or who laid its cornerstone
when the morning stars sang together
  and all the heavenly beings
    shouted for joy?
"Or who shut in the sea with doors
  when it burst out from the womb?—
when I made the clouds its garment,
  and thick darkness its
    swaddling band,
and prescribed bounds for it,
  and set bars and doors,
and said, 'Thus far shall you come,
  and no farther,
  and here shall your proud waves
    be stopped'?"

REFLECTION

We have passed over much of the dialogue
between Job and his friends; their entire
conversation is worth reading, both for its
literary beauty and its struggle with diffi-
cult questions. After much conversation,
the LORD finally answers Job "out of the
whirlwind." In four chapters, God engages
Job with no small amount of sarcasm.
To question after question Job must remain
in awe-filled silence, as God leads him
deeper and deeper into divine mystery.

PRAYERS *others may be added*

  Dumbstruck with wonder, we pray:

◆ Deliver us, O God.

In the majestic song of heavenly beings,
we pray: ◆ *In the marvels of earth's*
foundations, we pray: ◆ *In the wondrous*
dance of the nighttime stars, we pray: ◆
In the clouds that robe the sky in beauty,
we pray: ◆ *In the sea's proud waves,*
we pray: ◆ *In the height and depth and*
wonder of creation's glory, we pray: ◆

Our Father . . .

O eternal One,
it is you who set the bounds of the sea,
and gave the heavenly beings
their song of praise,
you who clothed the sky
with clouds and darkness:
Reveal to us your beauty,
and show us your wondrous power,
that we may shout for joy
with saints and angels
and worship forever before you,
for you alone are God
now and forever. Amen.

✦ *I will wait for the LORD,*
for God will hear my cry.

✝ *I will wait for the LORD,*
for God will hear my cry.

PSALM 40 *page 413*

READING *Job 38:12–13, 16–21*

The LORD answered Job,
"Have you commanded the morning
    since your days began,
  and caused the dawn to know
    its place,
so that it might take hold of the skirts
    of the earth,
  and the wicked be shaken out of it?
"Have you entered into the springs
    of the sea,
  or walked in the recesses
    of the deep?
Have the gates of death been revealed
    to you,
  or have you seen the gates
    of deep darkness?
Have you comprehended the expanse
    of the earth?
  Declare, if you know all this.
"Where is the way to the dwelling
    of light,
  and where is the place of darkness,
that you may take it to its territory
  and that you may discern
    the paths to its home?
Surely you know, for you were
    born then,
  and the number of your days
    is great!"

REFLECTION

God's speech cuts to the heart. God's self-revelation to Job is an indication of God's great desire to be in relationship with human beings. The New Revised Standard Version of the Bible's introduction to the book of Job puts it marvelously: "The LORD cares for Job so much that he reveals himself personally and shares with him the vision of cosmic responsibilities. A God who confesses his burdens to a human being is a God who is profoundly involved in human destiny."

PRAYERS *others may be added*

Accepting divine correction,
we pray:

◆ Deliver us, O God.

That God may reveal to us dawn's morning glory, we pray: ◆ *That God may show us light's dwelling place, we pray:* ◆ *That God may accompany us through the deep darkness, we pray:* ◆ *That we may behold earth's wondrous expanse, we pray:* ◆ *That God may show the dead eternal paths, we pray:* ◆

Our Father . . .

God of all time,
your days are without number
and your wisdom without end.
Reveal to us the dwelling of light,
and show us the glory
of the deep darkness,
that we may discern at last
your majestic design
and so give you thanks,
you who live and reign
forever and ever. Amen.

✝ *I will wait for the LORD,*
for God will hear my cry.

✝ *Alleluia! Christ is risen!*
Christ is risen indeed!
Alleluia, alleluia!

PSALM 34   *page 412*

READING   *Revelation 21:9b–14*

Then the angel said to me, "Come, I will show you the bride, the wife of the Lamb." And in the spirit he carried me away to a great, high mountain and showed me the holy city Jerusalem coming down out of heaven from God. It has the glory of God and a radiance like a very rare jewel, like jasper, clear as crystal. It has a great, high wall with twelve gates, and at the gates twelve angels, and on the gates are inscribed the names of the twelve tribes of the Israelites; on the east three gates, on the north three gates, on the south three gates, and on the west three gates. And the wall of the city has twelve foundations, and on them are the twelve names of the twelve apostles of the Lamb.

REFLECTION   *John Henry Newman*

We have the history of Saint Bartholomew and the other apostles to recall us to ourselves, and to assure us that we need not give up our usual manner of life, in order to serve God; that the most humble and quietest station is acceptable to him, if improved duly—nay affords means for maturing the highest Christian character, even that of an apostle. Bartholomew read the scriptures and prayed to God, and thus was trained at length to give up his life for Christ, when he demanded it.

PRAYERS   *others may be added*

Resting on a firm foundation,
we pray:

◆ Turn to us, Lord of life!

That the people of God may be a shining sign of God's coming glory, we pray: ◆
That the Church may have worthy successors to the apostles, we pray: ◆
That people of every nation, language, and way of life may be welcomed into the heavenly city, we pray: ◆ *That the earthly Jerusalem may at last find peace, we pray:* ◆ *That we may one day behold the glory of God's new and eternal city, we pray:* ◆

Our Father . . .

Light of the heavenly city,
on the pillars of the apostles
you build up your Church,
as we await the coming of your Son.
Fill us with hope
in this time of trial,
that we may at last join
the company of the apostles
in the eternal Jerusalem,
where Christ the Lamb
reigns forever and ever. Amen.

✝ *Alleluia! Christ is risen!*
Christ is risen indeed!
Alleluia, alleluia!

✝ *I will wait for the LORD,*
for God will hear my cry.

PSALM 40 page 413

READING Job 42:1–6

Then Job answered the LORD:
"I know that you can do all things,
and that no purpose of yours
can be thwarted.
'Who is this that hides counsel
without knowledge?'
Therefore I have uttered
what I did not understand,
things too wonderful for me,
which I did not know.
'Hear, and I will speak;
I will question you,
and you declare to me.'
I had heard of you by the hearing
of the ear,
but now my eye sees you;
therefore I despise myself,
and repent in dust and ashes."

REFLECTION

God answered Job's prayer with an imma-
nent experience of divine presence. After
the great privilege of being led by God into
the depths of creation and into the divine
heart, Job can only confess God's great-
ness. What Job had heard about God, he
has now experienced firsthand. Job has
become a friend of God, and he now
knows the true meaning of humility—
acknowledging that one is but a creature
before God without beginning or end.

PRAYERS *others may be added*

With humility before God's majesty,
we pray:

◆ Deliver us, O God.

That God's people may model true
friendship with God for all the world,
we pray: ◆ *That those who seek God may*
experience divine presence, we pray: ◆
That those who speak without knowledge
may find humility, we pray: ◆ *That the*
dead may behold God's face with their
own eyes, we pray: ◆ *That we may*
discover for ourselves the God about
whom we have heard so much, we pray: ◆

Our Father . . .

God of majesty,
your thoughts are wonderful,
and before you we are but dust
and ashes.
Give us true humility before you,
that we may become your true friends,
knowing your ways
and walking in them,
and finding eternal favor
in your loving gaze,
for you live and reign
forever and ever. Amen.

✝ *I will wait for the LORD,*
for God will hear my cry.

✦ *I will wait for the LORD,*
for God will hear my cry.

PSALM 40   *page 413*

READING   *Job 42:12–17*

And the LORD restored the fortunes of Job when he had prayed for his friends; and the LORD gave Job twice as much as he had before. The LORD blessed the latter days of Job more than his beginning; and he had fourteen thousand sheep, six thousand camels, a thousand yoke of oxen, and a thousand donkeys. He also had seven sons and three daughters. He named the first Jemimah, the second Keziah, and the third Keren-happuch. In all the land there were no women so beautiful as Job's daughters; and their father gave them an inheritance along with their brothers. After this Job lived one hundred and forty years, and saw his children, and his children's children, four generations. And Job died, old and full of days.

REFLECTION

Job's story seems to end well enough: His fortunes are restored; new children are born to him. Yet this "happy ending" perhaps leaves us unsatisfied. What of all the human suffering that goes unresolved? Where is the "happy ending" for the great multitudes of hungry and forgotten? We Christians find the answer in Jesus' ultimate triumph over death in the Resurrection, yet we must still reflect upon, and face in our own lives, the mystery of the cross.

PRAYERS   *others may be added*

Trusting in our generous God,
we pray:

◆ Deliver us, O God.

For long lives blessed with God's favor, we pray: ◆ For bodies full of vigor and health into old age, we pray: ◆ For joy in children and in children's children, we pray: ◆ For a sufficient share of earth's bounty, we pray: ◆ For lives filled with the beauty of friendship and the joy of family life, we pray: ◆ For a happy death after many full days, we pray: ◆

Our Father . . .

Blessed are you,
LORD God of all good gifts,
for you fill creation
with your abundance.
Give us the joy of a full life,
the comfort of family,
and freedom from anxiety.
May we never fail to share
your many blessings
with all our brothers and sisters.
This we ask in Jesus' name. Amen.

✦ *I will wait for the LORD,*
for God will hear my cry.

✠ *We praise you, O God our savior,*
   for you fill us with your blessings.

PSALM 90   *page 420*

READING   *John 6:60–64, 66–69*

When many of Jesus' disciples heard him, they said, "This teaching is difficult; who can accept it?" But Jesus, being aware that his disciples were complaining about it, said to them, "Does this offend you? Then what if you were to see the Son of Man ascending to where he was before? It is the spirit that gives life; the flesh is useless. The words that I have spoken to you are spirit and life. But among you there are some who do not believe." For Jesus knew from the first who were the ones that did not believe, and who was the one that would betray him.

Because of this many of his disciples turned back and no longer went about with him. So Jesus asked the twelve, "Do you also wish to go away?" Simon Peter answered him, "Lord, to whom can we go? You have the words of eternal life. We have come to believe and know that you are the Holy One of God."

REFLECTION

This final passage from the bread of life discourse from John's Gospel highlights the heart of discipleship: faith. The community to which John's Gospel was addressed was struggling with the defection of some members and the persecution of those who remained; this passage assures them that Jesus himself knew some would abandon faith in him. Peter's words are our response as well. Even in the face of others' unbelief or even persecution, we place our trust in God's Holy One, whose words are spirit and life.

PRAYERS   *others may be added*

Finding in Jesus spirit and life,
we pray:

◆ Let your favor be upon us.

For the Church, enlivened by Christ's spirit of life, we pray: ◆ For catechumens, attentive to the teachings of God's Holy One, we pray: ◆ For the nations, longing for words of life and hope, we pray: ◆ For those seeking faith, struggling against doubt, we pray: ◆ For us, faithful to the path of God's Holy One, we pray: ◆

Our Father . . .

Source of life,
the words of the Holy One
are spirit and life,
sustaining us on our journey.
Open our hearts to your wisdom,
that confusion may give way to faith
and unbelief to trust.
We ask this in the name of Jesus,
the Bread of Life,
who is Lord with you,
in the unity of the Holy Spirit,
one God, forever and ever. Amen.

✠ *We praise you, O God our savior,*
   for you fill us with your blessings.

✝ *We praise you, O God our savior,*
   for you fill us with your blessings.

PSALM 90   page 420

READING   *Proverbs 3:27–30*

Do not withhold good from those
    to whom it is due,
  when it is in your power to do it.
Do not say to your neighbor,
    "Go, and come again,
  tomorrow I will give it"—
    when you have it with you.
Do not plan harm
    against your neighbor
who lives trustingly beside you.
Do not quarrel with anyone
    without cause,
  when no harm has been done
    to you.
Do not envy the violent
  and do not choose any
    of their ways;
for the perverse are an abomination
    to the LORD,
  but the upright are
    in his confidence.
The Lord's curse is on the house
    of the wicked,
  but he blesses the abode
    of the righteous.
Toward the scorners he is scornful,
  but to the humble he shows favor.
The wise will inherit honor,
  but stubborn fools, disgrace.

REFLECTION

The Book of Proverbs is part of a body
of ancient Hebrew wisdom literature.
It was written to instruct young nobles in
righteousness and justice. Much of the
book, as in today's reading and those for
the rest of this week, consists of enduring
wisdom that can guide us today.

PRAYERS   *others may be added*

Docile to the wisdom of God,
we pray:

◆ Let your favor be upon us.

That Christian communities may
be sources of good to those in need,
we pray: ◆ *That the homes of Christians*
may be places of peace and righteousness,
we pray: ◆ *That civil leaders may be*
drawn from the humble and honorable,
we pray: ◆ *That neighbors may generously*
support one another, we pray: ◆ *That the*
poor and hungry may receive what is
justly due them, we pray: ◆ *That we may*
humbly accept the correction of the wise,
we pray: ◆

Our Father . . .

Blessed are you,
God of righteousness,
for you pour out your favor
on those who attend to your law.
Guide us in the ways of peace
  and humility,
that we may be counted
  among the righteous
upon whom you bestow honor.
Blessed are you, God of wisdom,
through your Word made flesh,
Jesus Christ, now and forever. Amen.

✝ *We praise you, O God our savior,*
   For you fill us with your blessings.

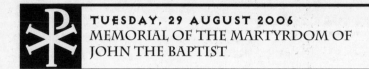
✠ *We praise you, O God our savior,*
for you fill us with your blessings.

PSALM 90 page 420

READING *Proverbs 21:1–4*

The king's heart is a stream of water
    in the hand of the LORD;
  he turns it wherever he wills.
All deeds are right in the sight
    of the doer,
  but the LORD weighs the heart.
To do righteousness and justice
  is more acceptable to the LORD
    than sacrifice.
Haughty eyes and a proud heart—
  the lamp of the wicked—are sin.

REFLECTION

Reflections on righteous kings may seem a
little out of date when so many nations
elect their leaders. Yet democracy makes
Proverbs' words all the more challenging.
Ancient kings inherited their positions or
won them through force of arms; they
alone were responsible for their behavior.
By choosing our leaders, we associate
ourselves with them and their actions, and
so we must ask ourselves: Do we choose
leaders who "do righteousness and jus-
tice" or those with "haughty eyes and a
proud heart"?

PRAYERS *others may be added*

With hearts open to the judgment of
God, we pray:

◆ Let your favor be upon us.

That the baptized may offer a fitting
sacrifice of justice and humility, we pray: ◆
That God may generously water the earth
with the river of divine wisdom, we pray: ◆
That the hearts and minds of rulers may
be open to the will of God, we pray: ◆
That pride and arrogance may be tempered
by humility and fear of the Lord,
we pray: ◆ *That the desires of our hearts*
may be pleasing in the sight of God,
we pray: ◆

Our Father . . .

God of the humble,
your eyes see to our depths,
revealing our motivations and desires.
Bless us with single-heartedness
  in the pursuit of wisdom
that we may serve you in purity
  and humility
offering the sacrifice you desire,
the sacrifice of obedience
  and righteousness
offered by Jesus Christ our Savior,
who lives and reigns forever and ever.
Amen.

✠ *We praise you, O God our savior,*
for you fill us with your blessings.

✣ *We praise you, O God our savior,*
for you fill us with your blessings.

PSALM 90 *page 420*

READING *Proverbs 21:5–8*

The plans of the diligent lead
   surely to abundance,
 but everyone who is hasty
   comes only to want.
The getting of treasures
   by a lying tongue
 is a fleeting vapor and a snare
   of death.
The violence of the wicked
   will sweep them away,
 because they refuse to do
   what is just.
The way of the guilty is crooked,
 but the conduct of the pure is right.

REFLECTION

The Book of Proverbs often offers rewards
for the righteous, arguing that following
the path of wisdom in life will lead to pros-
perity in this world. Unfortunately, we
know—as did the ancient Hebrew writers
(see the books of Ecclesiastes and Job)—
that injustice can indeed bring wealth to
some and suffering to many. Believing
people throughout the ages have asked the
same question: Why do the wicked pros-
per? The dissonance became so great for
many Jews that, in the last couple of cen-
turies before the coming of Christ, they
began to hope in an otherworldly inheri-
tance for the just—Resurrection.

PRAYERS *others may be added*

Seeking the reward of the righteous,
we pray:

◆ Let your favor be upon us.

That the people of God may diligently
observe the way of the righteous,
we pray: ◆ *That violence among nations*
may be swept away by the servants of
peace, we pray: ◆ *That those who seek*
gain through deceit may turn to the ways
of justice, we pray: ◆ *That the poor may*
receive an abundance of the good things
of the earth, we pray: ◆ *That patience*
and discernment may guide our actions,
we pray: ◆

Our Father . . .

God of rich and poor,
unjust and righteous alike,
you sweep away the profits
   of the deceitful
and cast from your presence
   the violent.
Steer us from the crooked path
   of the guilty,
and guide us on the path to peace
that together we may arrive at our
   final destination
to share in the abundance
   of your new creation,
where Jesus Christ lives and reigns
forever and ever. Amen.

✣ *We praise you, O God our savior,*
for you fill us with your blessings.

✛ *We praise you, O God our savior,*
   for you fill us with your blessings.

PSALM 90 — page 420

READING — *Proverbs 21:10–13*

The souls of the wicked desire evil;
   their neighbors find no mercy
      in their eyes.
When a scoffer is punished,
   the simple become wiser;
   when the wise are instructed,
      they increase in knowledge.
The Righteous One observes
   the house of the wicked;
   he casts the wicked down to ruin.
If you close your ear to the cry
   of the poor,
   you will cry out and not be heard.

REFLECTION

The writer of Proverbs points out that wickedness and righteousness are revealed in human relationships. It is our actions— rather than our religious or political beliefs—that reveal our true character. The wicked show no mercy; the righteous hear the cry of the poor. Virtue is not so much a matter of thinking or believing correctly, but of embodying belief in actions for others.

PRAYERS — *others may be added*

Putting our faith into action,
we pray:

♦ Let your favor be upon us.

That the baptized may embody Gospel justice in their parishes, schools, and places of work, we pray: ♦ *That people of faith may seek the just world envisioned in sacred texts and ritual actions, we pray:* ♦ *That political leaders may fulfill promises made to the poor and hungry, we pray:* ♦ *That human communities may shun wickedness, we pray:* ♦ *That the cry of the suffering may be heard and heeded, we pray:* ♦ *That we may put into practice the faith we profess, we pray:* ♦

Our Father . . .

Righteous One,
you lead us in justice
and guide us in wisdom.
Give us courage to embody
the values we profess,
that hypocrisy may have
   no place with us,
and we may be bright beacons
of knowledge and insight
to all the world.
In Jesus' name we pray. Amen.

✛ *We praise you, O God our savior,*
   for you fill us with your blessings.

✚ *We praise you, O God our savior,*
   for you fill us with your blessings.

PSALM 90   *page 420*

READING   *Proverbs 8:1, 4–8*

Does not wisdom call,
    and does not understanding
        raise her voice?
"To you, O people, I call,
    and my cry is to all that live.
O simple ones, learn prudence;
    acquire intelligence,
        you who lack it.
Hear, for I will speak noble things,
    and from my lips will come
        what is right;
for my mouth will utter truth;
    wickedness is an abomination
        to my lips.
All the words of my mouth
    are righteous;
    there is nothing twisted or crooked
        in them."

REFLECTION

Lady Wisdom is one of many feminine
images for God found in the Old Testa-
ment. Proverbs presents Wisdom as a
teacher and preacher, calling the children
of Israel away from ignorance and offer-
ing insight and intelligence. She is often
connected to the gift of the Torah to Israel,
and some scripture scholars and theolo-
gians believe that the tradition of Holy
Wisdom was adopted by the author of
John's Gospel and personified as God's
Logos, *the Word who takes flesh in Jesus*
of Nazareth—God and human.

PRAYERS   *others may be added*

Simple ones before God's wisdom,
we pray:

◆ Let your favor be upon us.

To fill the baptized with a spirit of
righteousness, we pray: ◆ *To open the*
ears of catechumens to wisdom's counsel,
we pray: ◆ *To straighten the paths of*
the wicked, we pray: ◆ *To give insight to*
the ignorant, we pray: ◆ *To teach prudence*
to the young, we pray: ◆ *To make us*
children of wisdom, we pray: ◆

Our Father . . .

God of insight,
deep in our hearts Holy Wisdom
    calls to us,
showing us the path of life.
Open our ears
that we may receive
insight and understanding
and become your friends
    and prophets,
praising you forever and ever. Amen.

✚ *We praise you, O God our savior,*
   or you fill us with your blessings.

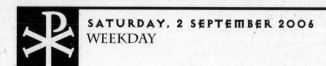
✠ *We praise you, O God our savior,*
For you fill us with your blessings.

PSALM 90 *page 420*

READING: *Proverbs 8:12–14, 17*

"I, wisdom, live with prudence,
and I attain knowledge
and discretion.
The fear of the LORD is hatred of evil.
Pride and arrogance and the way
of evil
and perverted speech I hate.
I have good advice and sound
wisdom;
I have insight, I have strength.
I love those who love me,
and those who seek me diligently
find me."

REFLECTION

The image of a woman sharing God's wisdom is an easy one to relate to. There are countless women in most people's lives in whom God's wisdom speaks. Mothers and grandmothers, aunts and teachers, sisters and women religious: The list goes on. God's wisdom speaks in many men as well, of course, but the image of Lady Wisdom is an opportunity for us to call to mind, pray for and thank her many sisters who have guided us on our way.

PRAYERS *others may be added*

Diligently seeking Holy Wisdom,
we pray:

◆ Let your favor be upon us.

That God's people may be bold witnesses of his wisdom revealed in Jesus, we pray: ◆ *That all who faithfully seek Holy Wisdom may find her, we pray:* ◆ *That God may pour out insight and prudence upon the world's leaders, we pray:* ◆ *That the ignorant and uneducated may receive a generous share of God's wisdom, we pray:* ◆ *That we may turn from pride and arrogance, loving wisdom above all else, we pray:* ◆

Our Father . . .

God of insight,
you love those who seek wisdom
and bless them with prudence
and understanding.
Instill in us your hatred of evil,
that we may live in the fear of God,
diligently searching for Lady Wisdom
and finding her in the words
of your Son, Jesus Christ,
who lives and reigns forever and ever.
Amen.

✠ *We praise you, O God our savior,*
for you fill us with your blessings.

✝ *We praise you, O God our savior,*
for you fill us with your blessings.

PSALM 90   *page 420*

READING   *James 1:17–18, 21b–22, 27*

Every generous act of giving, with every perfect gift, is from above, coming down from the Father of lights, with whom there is no variation or shadow due to change. In fulfillment of his own purpose he gave us birth by the word of truth, so that we would become a kind of first fruits of his creatures.

Therefore welcome with meekness the implanted word that has the power to save your souls. But be doers of the word, and not merely hearers who deceive themselves. Religion that is pure and undefiled before God, the Father, is this: to care for orphans and widows in their distress, and to keep oneself unstained by the world.

REFLECTION   *Second Vatican Council*

One of the gravest errors of our time is the dichotomy between the faith which many profess and their day-to-day conduct. As far back as the Old Testament, the prophets vehemently denounced this scandal, and in the New Testament Christ himself even more forcibly threatened it with severe punishment. Let there, then, be no such pernicious opposition between professional and social activity on the one hand and religious life on the other. Christians who shirk their temporal duties shirk their duties towards their neighbor, neglect God himself, and endanger their eternal salvation.

PRAYERS   *others may be added*

Attentively listening to God's word implanted within us, we pray:

◆ Let your favor be upon us.

That Church leaders may inspire God's people to dicipleship, we pray: ◆ *That political leaders may attentively listen to the needs of their people, we pray:* ◆ *That those charged with administering justice may be quick t o listen and slow to anger, we pray:* ◆ *That societies may rid themselves of the rank growth of injustice and inequality, we pray:* ◆ *That we may not be content with being merely hearers of God's word, we pray:* ◆

Our Father . . .

God of salvation,
you have planted
    your life-giving Word
in the depths of our hearts,
a word with the power to save us.
Open us to the voice of Christ
speaking deep within us
that we may put into action
your perfect law of liberty.
We ask this through Jesus Christ,
    our generous giver,
who lives and reigns with you,
in the unity of the Holy Spirit,
one God, forever and ever. Amen.

✝ *We praise you, O God our savior,*
for you fill us with your blessings.

✛ *We praise you, O God our savior,*
for you fill us with your blessings.

PSALM 90   *page 420*

READING   *Proverbs 8:22–26*

Thus says the Wisdom of God:
"The LORD created me at the
       beginning of his work,
    the first of his acts of long ago.
Ages ago I was set up,
    at the first, before the beginning
       of the earth.
When there were no depths
       I was brought forth,
    when there were no springs
       abounding with water.
Before the mountains
       had been shaped,
    before the hills,
       I was brought forth—
when he had not yet made earth
       and fields,
    or the world's first bits of soil."

REFLECTION

Many see in this passage the first inklings
of the Christian doctrine of the Trinity.
God, the supreme Creator of all things,
was not alone at the earth's beginnings but
was accompanied by Holy Wisdom. Later
Christians further developed this belief
that Wisdom is the Word of God, made
flesh in Jesus of Nazareth.

PRAYERS   *others may be added*

Attending carefully to God's ancient
wisdom, we pray:

◆ Let your favor be upon us.

That God's people may proclaim the
wisdom that was with God from the
beginning, we pray: ◆ *That the mountains*
and springs of the earth may reveal
the presence and action of their Creator,
we pray: ◆ *That earth's water and soil,*
hills and fields, may be honored and
cared for, we pray: ◆ *That we may attend*
to the voice of wisdom speaking in those
who have gone before us, we pray: ◆
That we may discover the wisdom of God
in the words and actions of one another,
we pray: ◆

Our Father . . .

Source of creation,
before even the first
speck of dust came into being
you set up your wisdom
as a gift to your people.
Inspire us to seek
    your wisdom revealed
in the mountains and streams,
in the hills and the sea,
that we may praise and thank you
through Jesus Christ forever and ever.
Amen.

✛ *We praise you, O God our savior,*
for you fill us with your blessings.

✦ *We praise you, O God our savior,*
for you fill us with your blessings.

PSALM 90 *page 420*

READING *Proverbs 8:27–31*

"When God established the heavens,
I was there,
when he drew a circle on the face
of the deep,
when he made firm the skies above,
when he established the fountains
of the deep,
when he assigned to the sea its limit,
so that the waters might not
transgress his command,
when he marked out the foundations
of the earth,
then I was beside him,
like a master worker;
and I was daily his delight,
rejoicing before him always,
rejoicing in his inhabited world
and delighting in the human race."

REFLECTION

Mother Teresa of Calcutta, whose death in
1997 we remember today, certainly embod-
ied Holy Wisdom's "delight in the human
race." She found it especially in the aban-
doned and forgotten: the lepers of India,
the orphans of Haiti, and those all over the
world suffering with AIDS. Her example
reminds us the God's beauty is often found
in unexpected places, among people who
may frighten us because they remind us of
our own weakness and mortality. Yet in them
we will surely find Jesus, Holy Wisdom
made flesh.

PRAYERS *others may be added*

As people in whom Holy Wisdom
delights, we pray:

◆ Let your favor be upon us.

That the people of God might find joy in
one another, we pray: ◆ *That all cultures*
and races may delight in one another's
beauty and genius, we pray: ◆ *That all*
people may be awestruck before the
fountains and foundations of the earth,
we pray: ◆ *That artisans and builders*
may rejoice in being master workers with
God, we pray: ◆ *That with Lady Wisdom*
we might always rejoice before our God
of creation, we pray: ◆

Our Father . . .

God of joy and delight,
you formed the earth
and all its creatures
and fashioned women and men
    in your image,
and called us very good.
Complete in us the work of creation,
that your glory may shine in our lives
and bring you joy in your creation.
This we ask in Jesus' name. Amen.

✦ *We praise you, O God our savior,*
For you fill us with your blessings.

✠ *We praise you, O God our savior,*
for you fill us with your blessings.

PSALM 90 *page 420*

READING *Proverbs 8:32–36*

"And now, my children, listen to me:
    happy are those who keep my ways.
Hear instruction and be wise,
    and do not neglect it.
Happy is the one who listens to me,
    watching daily at my gates,
    waiting beside my doors.
For whoever finds me finds life
    and obtains favor from the LORD;
but those who miss me
      injure themselves;
    all who hate me love death."

REFLECTION *Elizabeth Johnson, CSJ*

The biblical depiction of Wisdom is itself consistently female, casting her as sister, mother, female beloved, chef and hostess, preacher judge, liberator, establisher of justice, and a myriad of other female roles wherein she symbolizes transcendent power ordering and delighting in the world. She pervades the world, both nature and human beings, interacting with them all to lure them along the right path to life.

PRAYERS *others may be added*

Children of Wisdom, keeping her ways, we pray:

◆ Let your favor be upon us.

For all who walk in the path of righteousness, we pray: ◆ *For all who listen with an open ear, we pray:* ◆ *For all who seek the instruction of the wise, we pray:* ◆ *For all who ignore the gift of instruction, we pray:* ◆ *For all who suffer ignorance or lack of any kind, we pray:* ◆ *For all who seek God in the ignored and broken of the world, we pray:* ◆ *For all who keep watch for the presence of God, we pray:* ◆

Our Father . . .

We seek you,
O Heavenly Wisdom,
for you show us the path of life.
Give us your favor:
May our ears welcome your message
and our hearts embrace your love,
that we may keep your ways
and so find everlasting life.
This we ask in Jesus' name. Amen.

✠ *We praise you, O God our savior,*
for you fill us with your blessings.

✤ *We praise you, O God our savior,*
for you fill us with your blessings.

PSALM 90 *page 420*

READING *Proverbs 9:1–6*

Wisdom has built her house,
    she has hewn her seven pillars.
She has slaughtered her animals,
        she has mixed her wine,
    she has also set her table.
She has sent out her servant girls,
        she calls
    from the highest places
        in the town,
"You that are simple, turn in here!"
    To those without sense she says,
"Come, eat of my bread
    and drink of the wine
        I have mixed.
Lay aside immaturity, and live,
    and walk in the way of insight."

REFLECTION

In both the Old Testament and the teachings of Jesus, food and wisdom go hand in hand; their union finds its most profound expression for us in our Eucharistic celebrations. As a Church, we gather to hear God's word in scripture and then gather around the altar—the Church's table—to offer earthly food—bread and wine—which becomes for us Christ's Body and Blood, real food for eternal life. Our family tables prepare us for our Church's, and our Church's table sends us back out to our family's. The offering of food becomes the currency for sharing in God's wisdom leading to life eternal.

PRAYERS *others may be added*

Gathering at Wisdom's table,
we pray:

◆ Let your favor be upon us.

That the table of the Church may be a source of the Wisdom's nourishment, we pray: ◆ *That world leaders may eat the bread of insight and drink deeply from the cup of wisdom, we pray:* ◆ *That the simple and educated, saint and sinner, may be welcomed to Wisdom's feast, we pray:* ◆ *That the hungry may receive not only bread for their bodies but food for their spirits, we pray:* ◆ *That we may be nourished by Wisdom's bread and fortified by her wine, we pray:* ◆

Our Father . . .

Sustainer of body and soul,
your eternal Word nourishes us
with food for life eternal.
May the tables of our homes
and the altars of our Churches
be sources of both holy food
    and holy wisdom,
that we may walk faithfully on the
    path of discipleship
and come to the eternal banquet
where Christ is host forever and ever.
Amen.

✤ *We praise you, O God our savior,*
for you fill us with your blessings.

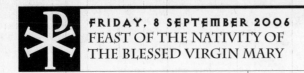
✦ *Alleluia!*
The Word of God dwells among us!
God is one with humankind!

PSALM 96 *page 421*

READING *Micah 5:1–4*

Now you are walled around
    with a wall;
  siege is laid against us;
with a rod they strike the ruler of Israel
    upon the cheek.
But you, O Bethlehem of Ephrathah,
    who are one of the little clans
      of Judah,
from you shall come forth for me
    one who is to rule in Israel,
whose origin is from of old,
    from ancient days.
Therefore he shall give them up
    until the time
    when she who is in labor
    has brought forth;
then the rest of his kindred shall return
    to the people of Israel.
And he shall stand and feed his flock
    in the strength of the LORD,
  in the majesty of the name
    of the LORD his God.
And they shall live secure,
    for now he shall be great
to the ends of the earth.

REFLECTION *Pope John Paul II*

With the "fiat" of the Annunciation, Mary agreed to serve the divine will, and Wisdom made his dwelling in her bosom, making her an exemplary disciple. The Virgin was blessed not so much for having nursed the Son of God but rather for having nourished herself with the health-giving milk of the word of God.

PRAYERS *others may be added*

Joining the Mother of God in her song of praise, we pray:

◆ Word of God, abide with us.

That God's people may proclaim their faith in Mary's son, we pray: ◆ That the baptized may find joy in Mary's example, we pray: ◆ That the lowly may find hope in humble Mary, we pray: ◆ That the poor of God's flock may be nourished with love, we pray: ◆ That the dead may behold the majesty of our God, we pray: ◆ That we may witness the coming of Israel's ancient ruler, we pray: ◆

Our Father . . .

God of joy,
the birth of Mary of Nazareth
marked the beginning
of a new era of grace,
for through her your Word
took flesh and lived among us.
Inspire us by her example
to open ourselves more fully
    to your saving grace,
that we may live
as brothers and sisters
of the Sun of Justice, Jesus Christ,
who is Lord forever and ever. Amen.

✦ *Alleluia!*
The Word of God dwells among us!
God is one with humankind!

✝ *We praise you, O God our savior,*
for you fill us with your blessings.

PSALM 90 *page 420*

READING *Ecclesiastes 1:2–7*

Vanity of vanities, says the Teacher,
  vanity of vanities! All is vanity.
What do people gain from all the toil
  at which they toil under the sun?
A generation goes,
    and a generation comes,
  but the earth remains forever.
The sun rises and the sun goes down,
  and hurries to the place
    where it rises.
The wind blows to the south,
  and goes around to the north;
round and round goes the wind,
  and on its circuits the wind returns.
All streams run to the sea,
  but the sea is not full;
to the place where the streams flow,
  there they continue to flow.

REFLECTION

The colonization of the Americas was filled with shame, from the subjugation of the native peoples to the enslavement of Africans. Unfortunately the Church was not always on the side of the poor; Saint Peter Claver and others like him were exceptions. A Spanish Jesuit and missionary, Peter Claver worked on behalf of the slaves in what is today Colombia. Although he never denounced slavery as such, his care for the physical and spiritual needs of slaves and his support for their legal protection proclaimed their rights as human beings. He was a shining light in a dark time.

PRAYERS *others may be added*

Joining with all the saints of God, we pray:

◆ Let your favor be upon us.

For those who serve the oppressed and defenseless, we pray: ◆ *For those who suffer injustice and prejudice, we pray:* ◆ *For those whose rights are ignored by the law, we pray:* ◆ *For those who work to end slavery in all its forms, we pray:* ◆ *For those who defend the human rights of others, we pray:* ◆ *For those who challenge unjust systems by their words and actions, we pray:* ◆

Our Father . . .

God of liberation,
your son Peter Claver served
those degraded by slavery.
Inspire us by his example
that we may work tirelessly
on behalf of those
who make visible in their bodies
the suffering of Jesus,
who was crucified but raised up
to live and reign
forever and ever. Amen.

✝ *We praise you, O God our savior,*
for you fill us with your blessings.

✦ *We praise you, O God our savior,*
for you fill us with your blessings.

PSALM 90 — page 420

READING — James 2:1–5

My brothers and sisters, do you with your acts of favoritism really believe in our glorious Lord Jesus Christ? For if a person with gold rings and in fine clothes comes into your assembly, and if a poor person in dirty clothes also comes in, and if you take notice of the one wearing the fine clothes and say, "Have a seat here, please," while to the one who is poor you say, "Stand there," or, "Sit at my feet," have you not made distinctions among yourselves, and become judges with evil thoughts? Listen, my beloved brothers and sisters. Has not God chosen the poor in the world to be rich in faith and to be heirs of the kingdom he has promised to those who love him?

REFLECTION — U.S. bishops

Though in the Gospels and in the New Testament as a whole the offer of salvation is extended to all peoples, Jesus takes the side of those most in need, physically and spiritually. The example of Jesus poses a number of challenges to the contemporary Church. It imposes a prophetic mandate to speak for those who have no one to speak for them, to be a defender of the defenseless, who in biblical terms are the poor. It also demands a compassionate vision that enables the Church to see things from the side of the poor and powerless and to assess lifestyle, policies, and social institutions in terms of their impact on the poor.

PRAYERS — others may be added

Choosing with God the side of the poor, we pray:

◆ Let your favor be upon us.

That the Church may proclaim and live God's option for the poor, we pray: ◆
That local Church communities may welcome rich and poor alike, we pray: ◆
That nations may seek first the good of their weakest citizens, we pray: ◆ *That the wealthy and powerful may seek Christ among the humble, we pray:* ◆ *That the glorious Christ may be recognized in the sufferings of poor and sick, we pray:* ◆
That we may not be deceived by fame or reputation, we pray: ◆

Our Father . . .

God of truth,
you warn us against
    making distinctions
among your children
but call us instead to recognize you
in the poorest of our brothers
    and sisters.
Guard us against the deceptions
of wealth and fame,
that we may truly be a people
in whom all find welcome.
We ask this in the name of Jesus,
who lives and reigns with you,
in the unity of the Holy Spirit,
one God, forever and ever. Amen.

✦ *We praise you, O God our savior,*
for you fill us with your blessings.

✦ *We praise you, O God our savior,*
for you fill us with your blessings.

PSALM 90   *page 420*

READING   *Ecclesiastes 1:8–11*

All things are wearisome;
   more than one can express;
the eye is not satisfied with seeing,
   or the ear filled with hearing.
What has been is what will be,
   and what has been done
      is what will be done;
there is nothing new under the sun.
Is there a thing of which it is said,
   "See, this is new"?
It has already been,
   in the ages before us.
The people of long ago
      are not remembered,
   nor will there be any remembrance
of people yet to come
   by those who come after them.

REFLECTION

The Book of Ecclesiastes embodies the negative side of Old Testament wisdom literature. It takes a somber view of life, recognizing that much of human existence is toil and that no one can escape death. It is an accurate description of many peoples' lives; haven't we all experienced powerlessness in the face of illness and death? While we Christians cling to hope, we do not deny that life can be full of futility, grief, and suffering.

PRAYERS   *others may be added*

Wearied by futility and sadness,
we pray:

◆ Let your favor be upon us.

That the Church may be a source of hope for those who despair, we pray: ◆ *That the dead may be remembered and celebrated, we pray:* ◆ *That those bound by inhumane living and working conditions may be lifted up by God's people, we pray:* ◆ *That those suffering from depression or mental illness may be healed, we pray:* ◆ *That we may have faith in the God who makes all things new, we pray:* ◆

Our Father . . .

God of the ages,
in our sorrow and despair
we cry to you,
for our fear overwhelms us.
Instill in us hope in your promise
That we may not give ourselves
   to hopelessness
but place our trust in your kindness,
for you promise to make
   all things new.
We ask this in Jesus' name. Amen.

✦ *We praise you, O God our savior,*
for you fill us with your blessings.

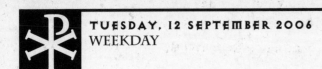
✠ *We praise you, O God our savior,*
  for you fill us with your blessings.

PSALM 90 *page 420*

READING *Ecclesiastes 3:1–4*

For everything there is a season,
    and a time for every matter
      under heaven:
a time to be born, and a time to die;
a time to plant, and a time to pluck up
    what is planted;
a time to kill, and a time to heal;
a time to break down, and a time
    to build up;
a time to weep, and a time to laugh;
a time to mourn, and a time to dance.

REFLECTION

There is a profound truthfulness to the Teacher's words: He unflinchingly describes the ebb and flow of human life, both the good and the bad. It is as if the writer counsels us to live in the moment, to acknowledge both joy and sorrow, birth and death, sowing and reaping. All are part of the cycle of life; perhaps all have something to teach us. For Christians, however, there is another aspect to the list. With the Incarnation of the Word of God, each of these moments contains within it the possibility of revelation, for each of these moments has, in Jesus, been taken up into the life of God.

PRAYERS *others may be added*

Crying out to God in all times and places, we pray:

◆ Let your favor be upon us.

For those giving birth and those being born, we pray: ◆ *For those nearing death, we pray:* ◆ *For those who plant and those who reap, we pray:* ◆ *For those who build and those who tear down, we pray:* ◆ *For those who weep and mourn, we pray:* ◆ *For those who laugh, dance and rejoice, we pray:* ◆

Our Father . . .

God of our journey,
you are present with us
in each stage of life,
walking with us from birth to death.
Make us aware of your
    faithful presence,
that we may praise and thank you
in times of weeping and laughing,
birthing and dying, planting
    and reaping,
until at last the cycle is complete
in your heavenly dwelling place,
where Jesus Christ lives and reigns
forever and ever. Amen.

✠ *We praise you, O God our savior,*
  for you fill us with your blessings.

✠ *We praise you, O God our savior,*
for you fill us with your blessings.

PSALM 90 — page 420

READING — *Ecclesiastes 3:5–8*

There is a time to throw away stones,
and a time to gather stones
together;
a time to embrace, and a time
to refrain from embracing;
a time to seek, and a time to lose;
a time to keep, and a time
to throw away;
a time to tear, and a time to sew;
a time to keep silence, and a time
to speak;
a time to love, and a time to hate;
a time for war, and a time for peace.

REFLECTION — *John Chrysostom*

When people receive a dear friend in their homes, is it not obvious that everything is a pleasure for them, and that they run about in all directions, sparing no effort to please their guest, even if it means spending all they have? Well, Christ is our guest, so let us show him that we are really happy, and do nothing to displease him. Let us decorate the house he has come to as a sign of our joy. Let us put before him the kind of food he likes best to show our delight. What is this food? He tells us himself: "My food is to do the will of him who sent me." Let us feed him when he is hungry, and give him a drink when he is thirsty. If you offer him a cup of cold water he will accept it because he loves you. However small a loved one's gifts may be, they have great value in the eyes of a friend.

PRAYERS — *others may be added*

Guided through every time and season
by great saints and preachers, we pray:

◆ Let your favor be upon us.

For holy bishops, who guide and protect Christ's flock, we pray: ◆ *For eloquent preachers, who break open God's word and reveal the mind of Christ, we pray:* ◆ *For dedicated priests, who lead Christian assemblies in God's praise, we pray:* ◆ *For inspired ministers, who call forth the many gifts of God's people, we pray:* ◆ *For wise teachers, who impart heavenly knowledge to those who would hear them, we pray:* ◆

Our Father . . .

God of wisdom,
in Bishop John you give us
a worthy guide and teacher.
Through your servant's intercession
open our hearts to know your word,
that we may be filled with the Spirit
and share the mind of Christ,
who is Lord forever and ever. Amen.

✠ *We praise you, O God our savior,*
for you fill us with your blessings.

✜ *Holy is God, holy and strong!*
Holy immortal One,
have mercy on us!

PSALM 34   *page 412*

READING   *John 3:13–17*

Jesus said to Nicodemus, "No one has ascended into heaven except the one who descended from heaven, the Son of Man. And just as Moses lifted up the serpent in the wilderness, so must the Son of Man be lifted up, that whoever believes in him may have eternal life.

"For God so loved the world that he gave his only Son, so that everyone who believes in him may not perish but may have eternal life.

"Indeed, God did not send the Son into the world to condemn the world, but in order that the world might be saved through him."

REFLECTION

"The triumph of the cross" probably sounded to first-century ears the way "the triumph of the electric chair" would in our own. Today's feast is a celebration of the kind of divine foolishness Paul talks about in First Corinthians—a stumbling block to some, yet the source of salvation. In Jesus' crucifixion, our God of reversal has transformed a symbol of brutal tyranny and oppression into a sign of divine power. Even at its most horrible, human evil is overturned by divine righteousness; the one executed unjustly is transformed into the radiant sun of justice and glory.

PRAYERS   *others may be added*

Rejoicing in the triumph of Christ's cross, we pray:

◆ Turn to us, Lord of life!

That the Church may boldly proclaim the cross as the source of salvation, we pray: ◆ *That the baptized may take up the cross in their lives of discipleship, we pray:* ◆ *That catechumens may embrace Jesus' example of humility, we pray:* ◆ *That the world's people may know God's love offered in the gift of the Son, we pray:* ◆ *That Jesus' disciples may recognize the triumphant Crucified One in the broken, abused, and forgotten, we pray:* ◆ *That through the cross we might all come to inherit eternal life, we pray:* ◆

Our Father . . .

God of glory,
the cross shines as a sign
of Jesus' obedience to your will
and a symbol of your love
   for the world.
Bless us who find salvation
in the cross of Christ:
May we always recognize his glory
in the weak, suffering,
   and condemned of the world.
We ask this through Christ,
   crucified and exalted,
who lives and reigns
forever and ever. Amen.

✜ *Holy is God, holy and strong!*
Holy immortal One,
have mercy on us!

✝ *We praise you, O God our savior,*
for you fill us with your blessings.

PSALM 90 *page 420*

READING *Ecclesiastes 11:9—12:1*

Rejoice, young man, while you are young, and let your heart cheer you in the days of your youth. Follow the inclination of your heart and the desire of your eyes, but know that for all these things God will bring you into judgment. Banish anxiety from your mind, and put away pain from your body; for youth and the dawn of life are vanity. Remember your creator in the days of your youth, before the days of trouble come.

REFLECTION

Today's memorial is the companion observance to the feast of the Holy Cross and was formerly known as the Seven Sorrows of Mary. In our prayer today, we might list the "seven sorrows" of our own time, which are much the same as those suffered by Mary and her contemporaries: torture and execution of loved ones, hunger, homelessness, and poverty, war and terrorism. By our fasting and remembrance, we join ourselves to those who suffer now and hopefully hasten the day when suffering will be transformed in glory.

PRAYERS *others may be added*

In solidarity with those wrapped in sorrow, we pray:

◆ Let your favor be upon us.

For churches beaten down by repression and persecution, we pray: ◆ *For mothers who mourn the deaths of children, we pray:* ◆ *For victims of torture, oppression, and violence, we pray:* ◆ *For the disappeared and political prisoners, we pray:* ◆ *For those who suffer pain and face death alone, we pray:* ◆ *For all who carry the marks of suffering on their bodies or in their hearts, we pray:* ◆

Our Father . . .

Fountain of compassion,
you hear the prayers of the sorrowful
for you care for us
as a mother cares for her children.
Sustain us in times of sorrow
and comfort us in our grief.
May our faith in you bring us hope
and give us strength in sadness.
We make our prayer
    through Jesus Christ,
son of Mary and your Son,
who is Lord forever and ever. Amen.

✝ *We praise you, O God our savior,*
for you fill us with your blessings.

✛ *We praise you, O God our savior,*
For you fill us with your blessings.

PSALM 90 *page 420*

READING *Ecclesiastes 12:1b–8*

The years draw near when you will say, "I have no pleasure in them"; before the sun and the light and the moon and the stars are darkened and the clouds return with the rain; in the day when the guards of the house tremble, and the strong men are bent, and the women who grind cease working because they are few, and those who look through the windows see dimly; when the doors on the street are shut, and the sound of the grinding is low, and one rises up at the sound of a bird, and all the daughters of song are brought low; when one is afraid of heights, and terrors are in the road; the almond tree blossoms, the grasshopper drags itself along and desire fails; because all must go to their eternal home, and the mourners will go about the streets; before the silver cord is snapped, and the golden bowl is broken, and the pitcher is broken at the fountain, and the wheel broken at the cistern, and the dust returns to the earth as it was, and the breath returns to God who gave it. Vanity of vanities, says the Teacher; all is vanity.

REFLECTION

For the Teacher, the greatest vanity is death, for it is as inevitable as the rising of the sun. His somber words are a healthy reminder that what we have we hold on loan; even our breath belongs to God, and to God it will return. But in Christ we believe that God's living spirit will return to us, never to leave us again.

PRAYERS *others may be added*

Facing death in hope, we pray:

◆ Let your favor be upon us.

That God's people may comfort the dying, we pray: ◆ *That the mourning may be upheld in prayer, we pray:* ◆ *That the elderly may be cared for and supported, we pray:* ◆ *That the troubled and depressed may not lose hope, we pray:* ◆ *That we may embrace death as the path to life, we pray:* ◆

Our Father . . .

God of the living and the dead,
death awaits all of us,
rich and poor alike,
Not even your Anointed One
     could escape it,
yet in your power you raised him
     to life.
Give us hope as death draws near
as you await us on the other side
     of death's door
in the new and eternal creation
where death has been conquered
and Christ presides at the
     wedding feast
forever and ever. Amen.

✛ *We praise you, O God our savior,*
for you fill us with your blessings.

✝ *We praise you, O God our savior,*
For you fill us with your blessings.

PSALM 90 *page 420*

READING *James 2:14–18*

What good is it, my brothers and sisters, if you say you have faith but do not have works? Can faith save you? If a brother or sister is naked and lacks daily food, and one of you says to them, "Go in peace; keep warm and eat your fill," and yet you do not supply their bodily needs, what is the good of that? So faith by itself, if it has no works, is dead. But someone will say, "You have faith and I have works." Show me your faith apart from your works, and I by my works will show you my faith.

REFLECTION

The author of James leaves little wiggle room for believers: If we claim faith in Jesus, it should show in the way we live. In other words, if we have to actually tell anyone we are Christian, we must not be doing a very good job of it! If we wonder why so few are attracted to Christianity, perhaps we must ask ourselves if our example of Gospel living—or lack thereof—might be keeping people away.

PRAYERS *others may be added*

Showing faith in our works,
we pray:

◆ Let your favor be upon us.

That the baptized may proclaim the Gospel in deeds of justice and mercy, we pray: ◆ *That all people of faith may focus on the care of the needy, we pray:* ◆ *That empty words may give way to true service in the name of God, we pray:* ◆ *That the hungry and naked may find comfort in the community of believers, we pray:* ◆ *That we may embody the kingdom Jesus proclaimed, we pray:* ◆

Our Father . . .

God of the poor,
you are deaf to empty words
but welcome lives made rich
in works of justice and love.
Give us deeds to match our faith:
May our lives proclaim
your great work in Jesus Christ,
who lives and reigns with you,
in the unity of the Holy Spirit,
one God, forever and ever. Amen.

✝ *We praise you, O God our savior,*
for you fill us with your blessings.

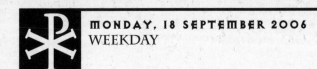
✣ *We praise you, O God our savior,*
  For you fill us with your blessings.

PSALM 90 *page 420*

READING *Galatians 1:1–5*

Paul an apostle—sent neither by human commission nor from human authorities, but through Jesus Christ and God the Father, who raised him from the dead—and all the members of God's family who are with me, To the Churches of Galatia: Grace to you and peace from God our Father and the Lord Jesus Christ, who gave himself for our sins to set us free from the present evil age, according to the will of our God and Father, to whom be the glory forever and ever. Amen.

REFLECTION

Paul's letter to the Galatians opens beautifully with invocations of peace and grace. Yet there is also a hint of controversy; Paul's declaration that he was sent "neither by human commission nor from human authorities" telegraphs Paul's need to answer criticism he faces from some members of the Galatian church. Its inclusion is a reminder to us that, although we treasure Paul's letters as scripture, they were written originally to deal with issues facing the ancient churches.

PRAYERS *others may be added*

Glorifying God through Jesus the Christ, we pray:

◆ Let your favor be upon us.

For the Church, the family of God, sent to proclaim the Good News, we pray: ◆ *For the many churches of the world, living in the grace of our Savior Jesus Christ, we pray:* ◆ *For all the baptized, journeying with one another in this present age, we pray:* ◆ *For all people, called to deeper relationship with the God of creation, we pray:* ◆ *For the dead, invited to share the eternal glory of Christ, we pray:* ◆

Our Father . . .

Praise to you,
God of glory and wonder,
for you support us in grace
as we await redemption.
Strengthen us as we seek
to live in harmony,
that we may grow in love
  as your family,
offering praise and thanksgiving
  through Jesus Christ,
your Son and our brother,
who lives and reigns with you
in the unity of the Holy Spirit,
God forever and ever. Amen.

✣ *We praise you, O God our savior,*
  for you fill us with your blessings.

✚ *We praise you, O God our savior,*
  For you fill us with your blessings.

PSALM 90   *page 420*

READING   *Galatians 1:6–8, 10–12*

I am astonished that you are so quickly deserting the one who called you in the grace of Christ and are turning to a different gospel—not that there is another gospel, but there are some who are confusing you and want to pervert the gospel of Christ. But even if we or an angel from heaven should proclaim to you a gospel contrary to what we proclaimed to you, let that one be accursed! Am I now seeking human approval, or God's approval? Or am I trying to please people? If I were still pleasing people, I would not be a servant of Christ. For I want you to know, brothers and sisters, that the gospel that was proclaimed by me is not of human origin; for I did not receive it from a human source, nor was I taught it, but I received it through a revelation of Jesus Christ.

REFLECTION

Paul writes to the Galatians concerned about "another gospel" that has been preached to them, specifically one that insisted that Gentiles first become Jews before becoming Christians. Before making his argument, though, Paul establishes his credibility as an apostle by sharing the story of his persecution of the Church, his conversion and the mission given him by Christ. His story, like our own, is really a proclamation of the Gospel: The grace of

Christ overcomes even our worst sins. Like Paul, we must offer our stories, both to encourage others and to praise God.

PRAYERS   *others may be added*

Faithful to Gospel we have received, we pray:

◆ Let your favor be upon us.

That we may never twist the Gospel to our own ends, we pray: ◆ *That we may shun the message of deceptive teachers, we pray:* ◆ *That we may not be fooled by mere human wisdom, we pray:* ◆ *That we may avoid the hunger for human favor, we pray:* ◆ *That we may remain clear-headed and faithful to the Gospel, we pray:* ◆

Our Father . . .

God of truth,
in Jesus you offer the Word of life,
yet we often listen to other voices.
Open our ears to hear your message
and our hearts to discern
    your presence,
that we may never be led astray
    by false gospels
but always remain faithful to you.
We ask this in the name
    of Jesus Christ,
your Word of life and truth,
who lives and reigns forever and ever.
Amen.

✚ *We praise you, O God our savior,*
  for you fill us with your blessings.

✠ *We praise you, O God our savior,*
For you fill us with your blessings.

PSALM 90 *page 420*

READING *Galatians 1:13–17*

You have heard, no doubt, of my earlier life in Judaism. I was violently persecuting the church of God and was trying to destroy it. I advanced in Judaism beyond many among my people of the same age, for I was far more zealous for the traditions of my ancestors. But when God, who had set me apart before I was born and called me through his grace, was pleased to reveal his Son to me, so that I might proclaim him among the Gentiles, I did not confer with any human being, nor did I go up to Jerusalem to those who were already apostles before me, but I went away at once into Arabia, and afterwards I returned to Damascus.

REFLECTION

Paul quickly explains his assertion that he was not sent by any human authority— God called him before birth, he claims— while also establishing his credentials as a Jew. Paul is setting the Galatians up: By proclaiming his expertise in both Judaism and in the Gospel, Paul is preparing to win the Galatians to his way of thinking.

PRAYERS *others may be added*

Called to proclaim Jesus Christ to all people, we pray:

◆ Let your favor be upon us.

That God may reveal the Son to all God's people, we pray: ◆ *That Christian communities may support and uphold one another, we pray:* ◆ *That the Gospel of Christ may be proclaimed to all the nations, we pray:* ◆ *That the Jewish people may be zealous in the traditions of their ancestors, we pray:* ◆ *That we may testify to God's power in our lives, we pray:* ◆

Our Father . . .

God of revelation,
you chose the apostle Paul
to proclaim Christ to the Gentiles,
filling him with grace
as a preacher and teacher.
Give us the courage to proclaim
    as he did
your marvelous work in our lives,
that with him and all the saints
we may praise you forever and ever.
Amen.

✠ *We praise you, O God our savior,*
for you fill us with your blessings.

✝ *Alleluia! Christ is risen!*
Christ is risen indeed!
Alleluia, alleluia!

PSALM 34 — page 412

READING — Matthew 9:9–13

As Jesus was walking along, he saw a man called Matthew sitting at the tax booth; and he said to him, "Follow me." And he got up and followed him. And as he sat at dinner in the house, many tax collectors and sinners came and were sitting with him and his disciples. When the Pharisees saw this, they said to his disciples, "Why does your teacher eat with tax collectors and sinners?" But when he heard this, he said, "Those who are well have no need of a physician, but those who are sick. Go and learn what this means, 'I desire mercy, not sacrifice.' For I have come to call not the righteous but sinners."

REFLECTION

There is an unnerving willingness on the part of Christians in the public forum to separate sinner from saint, excluding the "sinner" from fellowship and worship. Oddly enough, the only obvious requirement in the Gospels for eating with Jesus was that one be a sinner, and it seems that he favored the ones who knew they were sinners over the ones who had conveniently forgotten that they were.

PRAYERS — *others may be added*

Sinners embraced by God's mercy, we pray:

◆ Turn toward us, Lord of life.

That the baptized may welcome sinner and saint alike, we pray: ◆ *That the Church's ministers may generously offer God's boundless mercy in Christ, we pray:* ◆ *That the Eucharistic table may join rich and poor, every race and way of life, as one family, we pray:* ◆ *That sinners may know God's healing love, we pray:* ◆ *That we may turn away from self-righteousness and judgment, we pray:* ◆

Our Father . . .

God of the lost,
you desire mercy before sacrifice,
compassion rather than judgment.
Heal us of the self-righteousness
that afflicts our hearts,
and give us a desire
to seek the lost,
that we may welcome
those in need of your mercy,
recognizing in them
our own wounds and sin.
We ask this through the one
who welcomed sinners
    and ate with them,
for Christ lives and reigns
forever and ever. Amen.

✝ *Alleluia! Christ is risen!*
Christ is risen indeed!
Alleluia, alleluia!

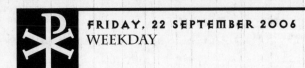

✝ *We praise you, O God our savior,*
  For you fill us with your blessings.

PSALM 90 *page 420*

READING *Galatians 2:1–2, 7–10*

After fourteen years I went up again to Jerusalem with Barnabas, taking Titus along with me. I went up in response to a revelation. Then I laid before them (though only in a private meeting with the acknowledged leaders) the gospel that I proclaim among the Gentiles, in order to make sure that I was not running, or had not run, in vain. On the contrary, when they saw that I had been entrusted with the gospel for the uncircumcised, just as Peter had been entrusted with the gospel for the circumcised (for he who worked through Peter making him an apostle to the circumcised also worked through me in sending me to the Gentiles), and when James and Cephas and John, who were acknowledged pillars, recognized the grace that had been given to me, they gave to Barnabas and me the right hand of fellowship, agreeing that we should go to the Gentiles and they to the circumcised. They asked only one thing, that we remember the poor, which was actually what I was eager to do.

REFLECTION

It's hard to miss the rivalry that must have existed between Paul and the leaders of the Jerusalem community. It seems that from the beginning to our own day, the desire to be "the greatest"—apostle, teacher, leader—is a constant temptation. Perhaps that's why the Jesus was so insistent that the greatest should be the one that serves everyone else.

PRAYERS *others may be added*

United in our proclamation of the Gospel, we pray:

◆ Let your favor be upon us.

That all Christians may grow in fellowship and cooperation, we pray: ◆ *That God's people may avoid competition and controversy, we pray:* ◆ *That all entrusted with proclaiming the Gospel may do so faithfully, we pray:* ◆ *That the poor may be remembered by Jesus' disciples, we pray:* ◆ *That we may always seek unity with our sisters and brothers, we pray:* ◆

Our Father . . .

Source of unity,
you call us all to work together
in proclaiming the one
    Gospel of Christ.
Remove from us the divisions
caused by pride and jealousy
that we may be servants
    of one another,
supporting each other
    in our common task
and so together building up
    your kingdom,
where Jesus is Lord forever and ever.
Amen.

✝ *We praise you, O God our savior,*
  for you fill us with your blessings.

✝ *We praise you, O God our savior,*
For you fill us with your blessings.

PSALM 90 *page 420*

READING *Galatians 2:11–14*

But when Cephas came to Antioch, I opposed him to his face, because he stood self-condemned; for until certain people came from James, he used to eat with the Gentiles. But after they came, he drew back and kept himself separate for fear of the circumcision faction. And the other Jews joined him in this hypocrisy, so that even Barnabas was led astray by their hypocrisy. But when I saw that they were not acting consistently with the truth of the gospel, I said to Cephas before them all, "If you, though a Jew, live like a Gentile and not like a Jew, how can you compel the Gentiles to live like Jews?"

REFLECTION

Today is Rosh Hashanah ("Head of the Year"), the new year on the Jewish calendar. Rosh Hashanah begins the "Days of Awe," a period of ten days in which Jews examine the past year, confess their sins to God, and ask forgiveness. These days culminate in Yom Kippur, the Day of Atonement and the holiest day of the year for Jews. We who are Christians do well to join the children of Abraham and Sarah, Isaac and Rebekah, Jacob and Leah and Rachel, in their prayers for mercy and reconciliation.

PRAYERS *others may be added*

Joining Israel in its prayers,
we cry out:

◆ Let your favor be upon us.

That the people of God may examine themselves, rooting out prejudice and fear, we cry out: ◆ *That the Jewish people remain faithful to the covenant, seeking God in fasting and prayer, we cry out:* ◆ *That the children of Abraham may seek unity, joining one another in the quest for peace and justice, we cry out:* ◆ *That all people may seek righteousness, pursuing together the way of salvation, we cry out:* ◆ *That together we may pray for the reconciliation of the world, uniting our voices with all people of good will, we cry out:* ◆

Our Father . . .

Blessed are you, God of Israel,
for your love endures forever.
Hear us as we pray
   with the Chosen People.
Cleanse the earth of injustice
and fill all people with righteousness.
May all the children of Abraham
   and Sarah,
and all the people of the earth,
one day rejoice together
in the heavenly Jerusalem.
Blessed are you, God of Israel,
for your love endures forever. Amen.

✝ *We praise you, O God our savior,*
for you fill us with your blessings.

✠ *We praise you, O God our savior,*
For you fill us with your blessings.

PSALM 90 *page 420*

READING *James 3:16—4:3*

Where there is envy and selfish ambition, there will also be disorder and wickedness of every kind. But the wisdom from above is first pure, then peaceable, gentle, willing to yield, full of mercy and good fruits, without a trace of partiality or hypocrisy. And a harvest of righteousness is sown in peace for those who make peace.

Those conflicts and disputes among you, where do they come from? Do they not come from your cravings that are at war within you? You want something and do not have it; so you commit murder. And you covet something and cannot obtain it; so you engage in disputes and conflicts. You do not have, because you do not ask. You ask and do not receive, because you ask wrongly, in order to spend what you get on your pleasures.

REFLECTION

The epistle's author warns his readers about the dangers of envy and ambition, especially within the community of faith. The household of God is no place to seek power or honor, although history shows us that many churches have been corrupted by those who see authority, wealth and prestige. Today's passage is a reminder to all God's people—individually and as a community—to continual reform. Only with vigilance and constant self-examination

can the Church be the symbol and means of salvation we are is called to be.

PRAYERS *others may be added*

Seeking to bear a harvest of righteousness, we pray:

◆ *Let your favor be upon us.*

That the works of God's people may be done with gentleness born of wisdom, we pray: ◆ *That the earthly wisdom of power and domination may yield to the spiritual discipline of mercy and peace, we pray:* ◆ *That a harvest of peace may sprout in places torn by war, we pray:* ◆ *That wisdom and understanding may shine in our works, we pray:* ◆

Our Father . . .

Gentle Wisdom from on high,
you enliven your people
with purity and gentleness,
righteousness and mercy.
Free us from selfish ambition
and the devilish wisdom
of envy and greed,
that we may bear
the good fruits of righteousness,
a harvest of peace sown in peace.
We ask this through the Source
of peace, Jesus Christ,
who is Lord with you,
in the unity of the Holy Spirit,
one God, now and forever. Amen.

✠ *We praise you, O God our savior,*
for you fill us with your blessings.

✝ *We praise you, O God our savior,*
For you fill us with your blessings.

PSALM 90 *page 420*

READING *Galatians 3:1–5*

You foolish Galatians! Who has bewitched you? It was before your eyes that Jesus Christ was publicly exhibited as crucified! The only thing I want to learn from you is this: Did you receive the Spirit by doing the works of the law or by believing what you heard? Are you so foolish? Having started with the Spirit, are you now ending with the flesh? Did you experience so much for nothing?—if it really was for nothing. Well then, does God supply you with the Spirit and work miracles among you by your doing the works of the law, or by your believing what you heard?

REFLECTION

The controversy Paul alludes to has troubled Christians throughout the centuries. How are we saved, by faith or by works? Paul argued about it with the Judaizers, Augustine argued with the Pelagians, and Martin Luther with some Roman Catholics during the Protestant Reformation. Each time the Church declared: We are saved by faith in Jesus Christ. In other words, the Church is the community of those who have believed, not those who have "earned" their way to glory.

PRAYERS *others may be added*

Embracing the Spirit of faith,
we pray:

◆ Deliver your people.

That the Church may proclaim the salvation offered to those who believe in Jesus, we pray: ◆ *That the baptized may trust in God's saving grace, we pray:* ◆ *That God may pour out upon us an abundance of the Spirit, we pray:* ◆ *That our belief may bear fruit in works of justice, we pray:* ◆ *That we may set aside earthly foolishness for divine wisdom, we pray:* ◆

Our Father . . .

God of the cross,
in Jesus Christ crucified
you have reconciled the world
    to yourself,
offering the gift of salvation
to those who believe.
Pour out upon us your Spirit of faith
that we may accept your generous
    offer of grace,
receiving in abundance what
we could never achieve on our own.
This we ask through the same
    Jesus Christ,
the hand you stretch out to sinners,
who lives and reigns forever and ever.
Amen.

✝ *We praise you, O God our savior,*
for you fill us with your blessings.

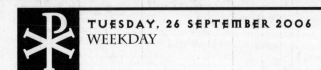
✙ *We praise you, O God our savior,*
For you fill us with your blessings.

PSALM 90 page 420

READING Galatians 3:23–29

Now before faith came, we were imprisoned and guarded under the law until faith would be revealed. Therefore the law was our disciplinarian until Christ came, so that we might be justified by faith. But now that faith has come, we are no longer subject to a disciplinarian, for in Christ Jesus you are all children of God through faith. As many of you as were baptized into Christ have clothed yourselves with Christ. There is no longer Jew or Greek, there is no longer slave or free, there is no longer male and female; for all of you are one in Christ Jesus. And if you belong to Christ, then you are Abraham's offspring, heirs according to the promise.

REFLECTION

In today's passage, Paul is responding to some missionaries who had convinced the Gentile Galatians to observe some precepts of the Jewish law, notably circumcision and some festivals. Paul rejects this completely, arguing that accepting circumcision means accepting the entire law. Because Christ has taken the burden of the law of Moses on himself, there is no need for Christians to observe it. Instead, we share in the blessing of Abraham, who believed long before there was any law.

PRAYERS others may be added

Heirs through faith of God's promise of salvation, we pray:

◆ Deliver your people.

That God's people may proclaim the blessing offered in the sacrifice of Christ, we pray: ◆ That all who claim Abraham as their ancestor in faith may live in peace with one another, we pray: ◆ That all nations may be blessed through the faith of God's people, we pray: ◆ That the those who seek it may find the blessing of faith, we pray: ◆ That our faith may bring us the Spirit of promise, we pray: ◆

Our Father . . .

God of spirit and life,
your Son Jesus Christ
became a curse for us
that we might be freed from slavery
    to sin.
Give us faith to recognize the gift
you offer in Christ's cross
that with Abraham and all people
    of faith
we may embrace your generous grace
and so come to inherit the glory
Christ shares with you,
in the unity of the Holy Spirit,
now and forever. Amen.

✙ *We praise you, O God our savior,*
For you fill us with your blessings.

✦ *We praise you, O God our savior,*
For you fill us with your blessings.

PSALM 90 *page 420*

READING *Galatians 4:21–26*

Tell me, you who desire to be subject to the law, will you not listen to the law? For it is written that Abraham had two sons, one by a slave woman and the other by a free woman. One, the child of the slave, was born according to the flesh; the other, the child of the free woman, was born through the promise. Now this is an allegory: these women are two covenants. One woman, in fact, is Hagar, from Mount Sinai, bearing children for slavery. Now Hagar is Mount Sinai in Arabia and corresponds to the present Jerusalem, for she is in slavery with her children. But the other woman corresponds to the Jerusalem above; she is free, and she is our mother.

REFLECTION *Vincent DePaul*

The service of the poor is to be preferred to all else, and to be performed without delay. If, at a time set aside for prayer, medicine or help has to be brought to some poor man, go and do what has to be done with an easy mind, offering it up to God as a prayer. Do not be put out by uneasiness or a sense of sin because of prayers interrupted by the service of the poor: for God is not neglected if prayers are put aside, if God's work is interrupted in order that another such work may be completed.

PRAYERS *others may be added*

Children of the heavenly Jerusalem,
we pray:

◆ Let your favor be upon us.

That the Church may proclaim the freedom offered to God's daughters and sons: ◆ That the baptized may offer the gift of the new covenant to all who desire it: ◆ That the present Jerusalem and all places torn by conflict may embrace God's peace: ◆ That those bound by disbelief and fear may receive the gift of faith: ◆ That we may live as citizens of the city yet to come: ◆

Our Father . . .

God of freedom,
in the waters of baptism
we were born anew
as your daughters and sons,
children of the heavenly Jerusalem.
Give us courage to embrace
the freedom you offer in Christ,
accepting the salvation won
    by his cross,
for he is Lord forever and ever. Amen.

✦ *We praise you, O God our savior,*
for you fill us with your blessings.

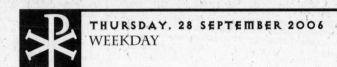
✛ *We praise you, O God our savior,*
  For you fill us with your blessings.

PSALM 90 *page 420*

READING *Galatians 4:28—5:1*

Now you, my friends, are children of the promise, like Isaac. But just as at that time the child who was born according to the flesh persecuted the child who was born according to the Spirit, so it is now also. But what does the scripture say? "Drive out the slave and her child; for the child of the slave will not share the inheritance with the child of the free woman." So then, friends, we are children, not of the slave but of the free woman. For freedom Christ has set us free. Stand firm, therefore, and do not submit again to a yoke of slavery.

REFLECTION

Paul employs an allegory to make his point, contrasting the child of the slave woman Hagar, Abraham's "child of the flesh," with the child of Sarah, "the child of the promise." While Paul's logic may not make as much sense to us today, his mention of the two women directs us to their spiritual descendants. Hagar is believed by Muslims to be the ancestral mother of Islam through her son Ishmael. Sarah is the spiritual mother of Judaism through her son Isaac. Both religious families are celebrating important festivals: Muslims began the month-long Ramadan fast with the crescent moon at the beginning of this week; Jews began the Days of Awe with Rosh Hashanah last Saturday.

PRAYERS *others may be added*

Joining the children of Hagar and Sarah, we pray:

◆ Let your favor be upon us.

That Jews, Muslims, and Christians may grow in mutual understanding and affection, we pray: ◆ *That peace may come at last to the homeland of Moses, Jesus, and Mohammed, we pray:* ◆ *That prejudice and violence driven by religion may have no place among the children of Sarah and Hagar, we pray:* ◆ *That the people of the Book may work together to bring about greater justice, we pray:* ◆ *That we may join all people of faith in prayers for peace and unity, we pray:* ◆

Our Father . . .

God of our mothers,
through Hagar and Sarah
you drew forth people
to praise your name.
Fill our hearts with love
for our spiritual family:
May all your children
enjoy the promise
you made to our ancestors,
for you live and reign
forever and ever. Amen.

✛ *We praise you, O God our savior,*
  for you fill us with your blessings.

✦ *Alleluia! Christ is risen!*
Christ is risen indeed!
Alleluia, alleluia!

PSALM 34   page 412

READING   *Revelation 12:7, 9ac–12*

And war broke out in heaven; Michael
and his angels fought against the
dragon. The great dragon was thrown
down, that ancient serpent, who is
called the Devil and Satan, and his
angels were thrown down with him.
    Then I heard a loud voice
    in heaven, proclaiming,
"Now have come the salvation
    and the power
    and the kingdom of our God
    and the authority of his Messiah,
for the accuser of our comrades
    has been thrown down,
    who accuses them day and night
    before our God.
But they have conquered him
    by the blood of the Lamb
    and by the word of their testimony,
for they did not cling to life
    even in the face of death.
Rejoice then, you heavens
    and those who dwell in them!
But woe to the earth and the sea,
    for the devil has come down to you
    with great wrath,
because he knows that his time
    is short!"

REFLECTION

*Today we commemorate the three angels
named in scripture. Saint Michael, the con-
queror of Satan, is associated with the*
*story above. Saint Raphael accompanied
Tobias on his journey, posing as Tobias'
relative. (See the book of Tobit.) Saint
Gabriel we know as the angelic messenger
who foretold the births of both John the
Baptist and Jesus. (See Luke 1:1–45.)*

PRAYERS   *others may be added*

Joining the heavenly hymn, we pray:

◆ Let all your works praise you!

*That the baptized may join the angelic
hosts in praising God through the Lamb,
we pray:* ◆ *That God may protect all
people from the snares of the Evil One,
we pray:* ◆ *That our heavenly relatives
may accompany travelers and refugees,
we pray:* ◆ *That the lowly may hear
the good news of salvation, we pray:* ◆
*That we may proclaim with the angels
the power of God and the authority
of the Messiah, we pray:* ◆

Our Father . . .

God of hosts,
your angels serve before your throne
joyfully singing of your glory.
Encourage us with the presence
of our angelic kin,
that when our journey is ended
we may join them in praising you
through Jesus Christ the Lamb,
unto the endless ages of ages. Amen.

✦ *Alleluia! Christ is risen!*
Christ is risen indeed!
Alleluia, alleluia!

✦ *We praise you, O God our savior,*
For you fill us with your blessings.

PSALM 90 *page 420*

READING *Galatians 5:18–25*

But if you are led by the Spirit, you are not subject to the law. Now the works of the flesh are obvious: fornication, impurity, licentiousness, idolatry, sorcery, enmities, strife, jealousy, anger, quarrels, dissensions, factions, envy, drunkenness, carousing, and things like these. I am warning you, as I warned you before: those who do such things will not inherit the kingdom of God. By contrast, the fruit of the Spirit is love, joy, peace, patience, kindness, generosity, faithfulness, gentleness, and self-control. There is no law against such things. And those who belong to Christ Jesus have crucified the flesh with its passions and desires. If we live by the Spirit, let us also be guided by the Spirit.

REFLECTION

Lest anyone think that Paul advocates an "anything goes" approach to the freedom of God's children, Paul points out that life in Christ does have ethical demands. We are not to be dominated by lust or jealousy but are to seek virtue in all that we do, using our freedom in Christ for the service of others, for the sake of building up the Church and the reign of God.

PRAYERS *others may be added*

Guided by the Spirit of life, we pray:

◆ Let your favor be upon us.

To protect us from envy, jealousy, and anger, we pray: ◆ *To prevent enmities, strife, quarrels, and factions, we pray:* ◆ *To keep us from impurity, idolatry, and licentiousness, we pray:* ◆ *To give us love, patience, and kindness, we pray:* ◆ *To fill us with faithfulness and generosity, we pray:* ◆ *To grant us joy and peace, we pray:* ◆

Our Father . . .

Source of our joy,
you guide us in the life of the Spirit,
freeing us from dissension
    and idolatry.
Give us strength to live
    as your children,
embracing the love, joy, and peace
    you offer,
that we may be a sign to others
of the life you offer in Jesus Christ,
who lives and reigns with you,
in the unity of the Holy Spirit,
one God, forever and ever. Amen.

✦ *We praise you, O God our savior,*
for you fill us with your blessings.

✚ *Great are the works of the LORD!*
God's justice stands firm forever!

PSALM 111   *page 424*

READING   *James 5:1–6*

Come now, you rich people, weep and wail for the miseries that are coming to you. Your riches have rotted, and your clothes are moth-eaten. Your gold and silver have rusted, and their rust will be evidence against you, and it will eat your flesh like fire. You have laid up treasure for the last days. Listen! The wages of the laborers who mowed your fields, which you kept back by fraud, cry out, and the cries of the harvesters have reached the ears of the Lord of hosts. You have lived on the earth in luxury and in pleasure; you have fattened your hearts in a day of slaughter. You have condemned and murdered the righteous one, who does not resist you.

REFLECTION

James' author has hard words for the wealthy, and many who read them may protest. Haven't the rich earned what they have through hard work? Don't we have a right to gather wealth? Catholic social teaching defends the right to private property, but it also reminds us that such rights have limits. No one has a right to great wealth while the vast majority of people are destitute. The goods of creation are ultimately held in common and must serve the needs of all people, not just the chosen, lucky, or even hard-working few.

PRAYERS   *others may be added*

Preparing for God's coming day of judgment, we pray:

◆ Show us your faithfulness.

For those who seek economic and social justice, we pray: ◆ *For factory and farm owners, managers and stockholders, we pray:* ◆ *For day laborers and migrant farm workers, we pray:* ◆ *For the working poor, their families and children, we pray:* ◆ *For labor unions, their members and leaders, we pray:* ◆ *For all who seek to live as disciples in the marketplace, we pray:* ◆

Our Father . . .

God of judgment,
the unpaid wages of the day laborer
cry out for your justice,
and the apathy of the powerful
kindles your anger.
Stir in us the desire for justice:
May we always seek to promote
fair treatment and just wages
for all who labor,
and so be counted among
   the righteous
on the day of judgment.
We ask this through Jesus Christ,
   our redeemer,
who lives and reigns with you,
in the unity of the Holy Spirit,
one God, forever and ever. Amen.

✚ *Great are the works of the LORD!*
God's justice stands firm forever!

✦ *Great are the works of the LORD!*
God's justice stands firm forever!

PSALM 111   *page 424*

READING   *Philippians 1:1–5*

Paul and Timothy, servants of Christ Jesus,

To all the saints in Christ Jesus who are in Philippi, with the bishops and deacons:

Grace to you and peace from God our Father and the Lord Jesus Christ.

I thank my God every time I remember you, constantly praying with joy in every one of my prayers for all of you, because of your sharing in the gospel from the first day until now.

REFLECTION

Today we commemorate the guardian angels, whom we believe to be our special protectors. Angels have been quite popular of late, inspiring books and posters, television shows and movies. In our tradition they are quite imposing: wrestling Jacob (Genesis), announcing births (Luke), or bringing destruction (Revelation). In a way, they represent the constant presence and power of God among us. The Jewish Talmud puts it this way: "Every blade of grass has its angel that bends over it and whispers, 'Grow, grow.'"

PRAYERS   *others may be added*

Shielded by the presence of our angelic guardians, we pray:

◆ Deliver your people.

That the Church may trust in God's protective presence, we pray: ◆ *That the messengers of God may dissuade nations from violence, we pray:* ◆ *That runaways may be led to safety, we pray:* ◆ *That the light of God's presence may console those who live in the shadow of death, we pray:* ◆ *That we may be messengers of God's presence to the defenseless and abused, we pray:* ◆

Our Father . . .

Provident God,
in the guardian angels
you protect us with tender care.
Shield us from all evil
and protect the defenseless from harm,
that we may safely reach
our heavenly resting place,
guided by angelic messengers
and holy companions.
We ask this in the name of Jesus,
who lives and reigns
forever and ever. Amen.

✦ *Great are the works of the LORD!*
God's justice stands firm forever!

✝ *Great are the works of the LORD!*
God's justice stands firm forever!

PSALM 111 *page 424*

READING *Philippians 1:6–11*

I am confident of this, that the one who began a good work among you will bring it to completion by the day of Jesus Christ. It is right for me to think this way about all of you, because you hold me in your heart, for all of you share in God's grace with me, both in my imprisonment and in the defense and confirmation of the gospel. For God is my witness, how I long for all of you with the compassion of Christ Jesus. And this is my prayer, that your love may overflow more and more with knowledge and full insight to help you to determine what is best, so that in the day of Christ you may be pure and blameless, having produced the harvest of righteousness that comes through Jesus Christ for the glory and praise of God.

REFLECTION

We continue reading from Paul's letters in the coming weeks; yesterday we began the letter to the Philippians. The church in Philippi was the first founded by Paul in Europe, and he had a special affection for these believers. The Philippians seem to have been suffering hardship, and much of the letter is spent encouraging them to faithfulness, especially as Paul himself is imprisoned by the Romans. Paul's consistent theme is that we must rejoice in Christ, no matter what our current situation.

PRAYERS *others may be added*

Sharing together God's grace,
we pray:

◆ Deliver your people.

That Christ may bring to completion the good work begun in the Church, we pray: ◆ That love may overflow in Christian communities, we pray: ◆ That world leaders may be filled with knowledge of what is best for their people, we pray: ◆ That the dead may be gathered into the harvest of righteousness, we pray: ◆ That we may be found blameless on the day of Christ, we pray: ◆

Our Father . . .

Praise and glory to you,
strong and faithful God,
for you sustain us
in witness to the Gospel.
Fill us with knowledge
of what is best,
and give us your compassion,
that our love may overflow
and our strength endure
until the day of Jesus Christ,
who is Lord forever and ever. Amen.

✝ *Great are the works of the LORD!*
God's justice stands firm forever!

✚ *Great are the works of the LORD!*
God's justice stands firm forever!

PSALM 111 page 424

READING Philippians 1:12–18a

I want you to know, beloved that what has happened to me has actually helped to spread the gospel, so that it has become known throughout the whole imperial guard and to everyone else that my imprisonment is for Christ; and most of the brothers and sisters, having been made confident in the Lord by my imprisonment, dare to speak the word with greater boldness and without fear.

Some proclaim Christ from envy and rivalry, but others from goodwill. These proclaim Christ out of love, knowing that I have been put here for the defense of the gospel; the others proclaim Christ out of selfish ambition, not sincerely but intending to increase my suffering in my imprisonment. What does it matter? Just this, that Christ is proclaimed in every way, whether out of false motives or true; and in that I rejoice.

REFLECTION

Paul's words reflect some of the rivalry between himself and other preachers on the missionary circuit, suggesting that at least some of them were using his imprisonment to increase their stature. Others have been strengthened by Paul's example and have preached even more boldly. Either way, Paul asserts, Christ is proclaimed, and people come to faith. Paul

even rejoices in the fact that the pagan guards acknowledge that his imprisonment is for Christ's sake.

PRAYERS others may be added

Rejoicing whenever Christ is proclaimed, we pray:

◆ Deliver your people.

That ministers and preachers may proclaim the Gospel out of love, we pray: ◆
That the baptized may be encouraged by the example of those persecuted for their faith, we pray: ◆ *That rivalry and jealousy may find no place in God's household, we pray:* ◆ *That the imprisoned may find cause for hope, faith and joy, we pray:* ◆ *That our lives of faith may proclaim Christ crucified and risen, we pray:* ◆

Our Father . . .

We rejoice in you,
strong and faithful God,
for even when we suffer
Christ is proclaimed.
Cast out our fear,
and fill us with boldness,
that we may proclaim with love
the good news of salvation
and inherit at last
the eternal joy of the saints,
who worship around your throne
to the endless ages of ages. Amen.

✚ *Great are the works of the LORD!*
God's justice stands firm forever!

✠ *Great are the works of the LORD!*
  God's justice stands firm forever!

PSALM 111 page 424

READING *Philippians 1:18b–26*

Yes, and I will continue to rejoice, for I know that through your prayers and the help of the Spirit of Jesus Christ this will turn out for my deliverance. It is my eager expectation and hope that I will not be put to shame in any way, but that by my speaking with all bold-ness, Christ will be exalted now as always in my body, whether by life or by death. For to me, living is Christ and dying is gain. If I am to live in the flesh, that means fruitful labor for me; and I do not know which I prefer. I am hard pressed between the two: my desire is to depart and be with Christ, for that is far better; but to remain in the flesh is more necessary for you. Since I am convinced of this, I know that I will remain and continue with all of you for your progress and joy in faith, so that I may share abundantly in your boasting in Christ Jesus when I come to you again.

REFLECTION

Paul further explains why he is able to rejoice even in his difficulty; whether he dies or lives, it is a win-win situation! If he dies for Christ, he will inherit glory with Christ. If he lives for Christ, he will con-tinue to do the good work of proclaiming the Gospel. Though he is ready to die, he wants also to continue to support and encourage the Philippians in their progress.

Either way, he is able to surrender himself to God's will and so able to serve in any circumstance; no matter what, Paul will not be put to shame.

PRAYERS *others may be added*

Eager to be with Christ, yet eager to serve, we pray:

◆ Deliver your people.

For those who pray for the salvation of others, we pray: ◆ For those who support the Church's progress in faith, we pray: ◆ For those imprisoned for their faith, we pray: ◆ For those who exalt Christ in both life and death, we pray: ◆ For those who labor for a fruitful harvest, we pray: ◆ For the sick and the dying, we pray: ◆ For all who boast in Christ Jesus, we pray: ◆

Our Father . . .

Exalted One,
for us who believe,
life is Christ Jesus,
and dying is gain,
for we know we will share
our Savior's eternal glory.
Grant that in life and in death
we may boast in Christ alone
and so find favor
on the day of Christ's return,
for Jesus is Lord
now and forever. Amen.

✠ *Great are the works of the LORD!*
  God's justice stands firm forever!

✠ *Great are the works of the LORD!*
God's justice stands firm forever!

PSALM 111   *page 424*

READING   *Philippians 2:1–4*

If then there is any encouragement in Christ, any consolation from love, any sharing in the Spirit, any compassion and sympathy, make my joy complete: be of the same mind, having the same love, being in full accord and of one mind. Do nothing from selfish ambition or conceit, but in humility regard others as better than yourselves. Let each of you look not to your own interests, but to the interests of others.

REFLECTION

Tomorrow begins the celebration of Sukkot in the Jewish community, the joyful festival of the harvest. During this time, Jews commemorate their wandering in the desert, when they built sukkot *or "booths," temporary dwellings for travelers. Harvesters also built* sukkot *in the fields so that they could work late into the night and begin early in the morning. The Sukkot festival also commemorates ancestors, who, beginning with Sarah and Abraham, are said to visit each* sukkah *during the festival. It is also believed that the Messiah will come during Sukkot to gather the chosen people into God's eternal* sukkah.

PRAYERS   *others may be added*

Rejoicing in God's enduring presence, we pray:

◆ Deliver your people.

That the Church may find joy in God's word, we pray: ◆ *That the Jewish people may always celebrate the gift of the covenant, we pray:* ◆ *That Jews and Christians together may give thanks for God's saving work, we pray:* ◆ *That people of faith may invite all nations to share the joy of belief, we pray:* ◆ *That faithfulness to God's word may bear fruit in justice and mercy for those in need, we pray:* ◆ *That we may offer the pleasing sacrifice of humility, concord, and compassion, we pray:* ◆

Our Father . . .

Blessed are you,
God of everlasting joy,
for you make your dwelling
    among us.
Open us to receive your presence,
that in the fullness of time
you may gather us into
the harvest of salvation.
Blessed are you,
God ever-faithful,
now and forever. Amen.

✠ *Great are the works of the LORD!*
God's justice stands firm forever!

✚ *Great are the works of the LORD!*
God's justice stands firm forever!

PSALM 111   *page 424*

READING   *Philippians 2:6–11*

Though he was in the form of God, Christ did not regard equality with God as something to be exploited, but emptied himself, taking the form of a slave, being born in human likeness. And being found in human form, he humbled himself and became obedient to the point of death—even death on a cross. Therefore God also highly exalted him and gave him the name that is above every name, so that at the name of Jesus every knee should bend, in heaven and on earth and under the earth, and every tongue should confess that Jesus Christ is Lord, to the glory of God the Father.

REFLECTION

Today's passage is proclaimed on the feast of the Holy Cross (September 14) and explains why we Christians should not seek our own glory but should submit to one another. Christ set aside his rightful glory to become one of us for our sake. If Christ himself did not seek his own glory then we should do the same, working out our salvation in fear and trembling before so great a mystery.

PRAYERS   *others may be added*

Emptying ourselves for the sake of the world, we pray:

◆ Deliver your people.

That the baptized may seek only the glory of Christ, we pray: ◆ *That people of faith may glorify God in all that they do, we pray:* ◆ *That world leaders may humble themselves in service to their people, we pray:* ◆ *That those poured out in suffering may find relief, we pray:* ◆ *That we may embody the generosity of the one who gave everything for our sakes, we pray:* ◆

Our Father . . .

God of wondrous power,
your Son emptied himself
to become the servant of all.
Fill us with your generosity,
that we may offer ourselves
for the sake of all the world
to the glory of your name,
for you live and reign
forever and ever. Amen.

✚ *Great are the works of the LORD!*
God's justice stands firm forever!

✜ *Great are the works of the LORD!*
God's justice stands firm forever!

PSALM 111 *page 424*

READING *Hebrews 2:9–11*

Though for a little while Jesus was made lower than the angels, he is now crowned with glory and honor because of the suffering of death, so that by the grace of God he might taste death for everyone. It was fitting that God, for whom and through whom all things exist, in bringing many children to glory, should make the pioneer of their salvation perfect through sufferings. For the one who sanctifies and those who are sanctified all have one Father. For this reason Jesus is not ashamed to call them brothers and sisters.

REFLECTION

Today the second reading for Sunday Mass begins drawing from the letter to the Hebrews, a somewhat difficult text that is rich in imagery. Scripture scholars suggest that Hebrews is best understood as a homily, an exhortation to faith in Christ preached to a community whose hope in Christ was fading. As today's passage indicates, the letter's constant message is one of trust in Christ, who has made us God's children.

PRAYERS *others may be added*

Made holy in Christ, we pray:

◆ Deliver your people.

That the baptized may live always in God's grace, we pray: ◆ *That God may draw all nations to eternal glory, we pray:* ◆ *That Christ's example may strengthen the suffering, we pray:* ◆ *That those who have tasted death may find eternal life in Christ, we pray:* ◆ *That we may live always in holiness as God's children, we pray:* ◆

Our Father . . .

God of grace,
in Christ's saving death
you give us lasting life
and crown us with glory and honor.
Give us courage to follow Christ,
the pioneer of our faith,
that he may not be ashamed
to call us brothers and sisters,
children of one Father,
for Christ lives and reigns with you,
in the unity of the Holy Spirit,
one God, now and forever. Amen.

✜ *Great are the works of the LORD!*
God's justice stands firm forever!

✙ *Great are the works of the LORD!*
God's justice stands firm forever!

PSALM 111   page 424

READING   *Philippians 2:12–18*

Therefore, my beloved, just as you have always obeyed me, not only in my presence, but much more now in my absence, work out your own salvation with fear and trembling; for it is God who is at work in you, enabling you both to will and to work for his good pleasure.

Do all things without murmuring and arguing, so that you may be blameless and innocent, children of God without blemish in the midst of a crooked and perverse generation, in which you shine like stars in the world. It is by your holding fast to the word of life that I can boast on the day of Christ that I did not run in vain or labor in vain. But even if I am being poured out as a libation over the sacrifice and the offering of your faith, I am glad and rejoice with all of you—and in the same way you also must be glad and rejoice with me.

REFLECTION

Being "stars in the world" is a high calling and a daunting one! We know how often we fail to be "blameless and innocent," and so, indeed, we work out our salvation in fear and trembling. Yet, as Paul so often points out, it is God that saves us by our faith. We may struggle to live out our high calling, but in the end God assures the victory.

PRAYERS   *others may be added*

Holding fast to the word of life,
we pray:

◆ Deliver your people.

That the baptized may shine like stars in lives of justice and love, we pray: ◆
That inquirers and catechumens may ponder deeply the living Word, we pray: ◆
That people of faith may approach the divine mystery in fear and trembling, we pray: ◆ *That those poured out in sickness may find cause for joy, we pray:* ◆
That we may set aside murmuring and arguing for holy and blameless lives, we pray: ◆

Our Father . . .

Divine Artisan,
in Christ you give us
the Word of life,
and through him you make us
your new and holy creation.
Continue in us your good work,
and give us the will to serve you,
that we may be your children,
shining like stars on earth,
holy and blameless
for the day of salvation,
when Christ the Lord
will reign forever and ever. Amen.

✙ *Great are the works of the LORD!*
God's justice stands firm forever!

✠ *Great are the works of the LORD!*
God's justice stands firm forever!

PSALM 111 — page 424

READING — *Philippians 2:19–28*

I hope in the Lord Jesus to send Timothy to you soon, so that I may be cheered by news of you. I have no one like him who will be genuinely concerned for your welfare. All of them are seeking their own interests, not those of Jesus Christ. But Timothy's worth you know, how like a son with a father he has served with me in the work of the gospel. I hope therefore to send him as soon as I see how things go with me; and I trust in the Lord that I will also come soon.

Still, I think it necessary to send to you Epaphroditus—my brother and co-worker and fellow soldier, your messenger and minister to my need; for he has been longing for all of you, and has been distressed because you heard that he was ill. He was indeed so ill that he nearly died. But God had mercy on him, and not only on him but on me also, so that I would not have one sorrow after another. I am the more eager to send him, therefore, in order that you may rejoice at seeing him again, and that I may be less anxious.

REFLECTION

Paul gives us a glimpse into how the early churches kept in touch. Apostles like Paul had companions—Timothy and Epaphroditus in this case—who carried messages and checked in on the local communities.

Often the reports of these messengers—often that something was wrong—elicited a written response from Paul, which is why he seems to be correcting people so often!

PRAYERS — *others may be added*

Held together by bonds of charity,
we pray:

◆ Deliver your people.

For those who build up communities of faith, we pray: ◆ *For those who work together in service of the Gospel, we pray:* ◆ *For those who encourage communication, we pray:* ◆ *For those who bring joy to the sorrowful, we pray:* ◆ *For those who show concern for the sick, we pray:* ◆ *For those who rejoice in the return of friends, we pray:* ◆

Our Father . . .

God of friendship,
you give us companions
on the way of discipleship.
Encourage us as we follow
the path of salvation,
that together we may reach
the new and eternal Jerusalem,
where Christ lives and reigns
forever and ever. Amen.

✠ *Great are the works of the LORD!*
God's justice stands firm forever!

✝ *Great are the works of the LORD!*
God's justice stands firm forever!

PSALM 111   page 424

READING   Philippians 3:2–9

Beware of the dogs, beware of the evil workers, beware of those who mutilate the flesh! For it is we who are the circumcision, who worship in the Spirit of God and boast in Christ Jesus and have no confidence in the flesh—even though I, too, have reason for confidence in the flesh.

If anyone else has reason to be confident in the flesh, I have more: circumcised on the eighth day, a member of the people of Israel, of the tribe of Benjamin, a Hebrew born of Hebrews; as to the law, a Pharisee; as to zeal, a persecutor of the church; as to righteousness under the law, blameless.

Yet whatever gains I had, these I have come to regard as loss because of Christ. More than that, I regard everything as loss because of the surpassing value of knowing Christ Jesus my Lord. For his sake I have suffered the loss of all things, and I regard them as rubbish, in order that I may gain Christ and be found in him, not having a righteousness of my own that comes from the law, but one that comes through faith in Christ, the righteousness from God based on faith.

REFLECTION

We must be wary of Paul's harsh words about "circumcision" and the "dogs" who promote it; even great saints had their uncharitable moments! Such passages must be kept in their historical context. As he does in other places (Galatians 5:6, for example), Paul opposes those Christians who insisted that Gentiles first accept the Mosaic law before Baptism. Paul asserts that obedience to the law is not necessary for disciples.

PRAYERS   others may be added

Made righteous in Christ, we pray:

♦ Deliver your people.

That the baptized may trust in Christ's saving work, we pray: ♦ That religious leaders may not impose unnecessary burdens on the faithful, we pray: ♦ That name-calling and acrimony may have no place among God's people, we pray: ♦ That nations and people may resolve disputes in charity and mutual respect, we pray: ♦ That we know the surpassing value of life in Christ Jesus, we pray: ♦

Our Father . . .

God of salvation,
in Christ you extend
your gracious offer of life.
Give us true righteousness,
that we may rely not on ourselves
but on your grace alone,
regarding all else as rubbish
for the gift we have received
in Jesus your Son,
in whose name we pray. Amen.

✝ *Great are the works of the LORD!*
God's justice stands firm forever!

✛ *Great are the works of the LORD!*
God's justice stands firm forever!

PSALM 111   page 424

READING   *Philippians 3:10–16*

I want to know Christ and the power of his resurrection and the sharing of his sufferings by becoming like him in his death, if somehow I may attain the resurrection from the dead.

Not that I have already obtained this or have already reached the goal; but I press on to make it my own, because Christ Jesus has made me his own. Beloved, I do not consider that I have made it my own; but this one thing I do: forgetting what lies behind and straining forward to what lies ahead, I press on toward the goal for the prize of the heavenly call of God in Christ Jesus. Let those of us then who are mature be of the same mind; and if you think differently about anything, this too God will reveal to you. Only let us hold fast to what we have attained.

REFLECTION   *John Chrysostom*

When we suffer anything for Christ's sake, we should do so not only with courage, but even with joy. If we have to go hungry, let us be glad as if we were at a banquet. If we are insulted, let us be elated as though we had been showered with praises. If we lose all we possess, let us consider ourselves the gainers. If we provide for the poor, let us regard ourselves as the recipients. Anyone who does not give in this way will find it difficult to give at all. So when you wish to distribute alms, do not think only of what you are giving away; think rather of what you are gaining, for your gain will exceed your loss.

PRAYERS   *others may be added*

Pressing toward our heavenly goal, we pray:

◆ Deliver your people.

That God's people may strain forward toward the fullness of God's reign, we pray: ◆ *That the baptized may be of the same mind and heart in their proclamation of the Good News, we pray:* ◆ *That catechumens may grow toward maturity in Christ Jesus, we pray:* ◆ *That those who share Christ's suffering in illness may hope in the Resurrection, we pray:* ◆ *That the faithful dead may attain life eternal, we pray:* ◆

Our Father . . .

God of life,
in Christ you bestow
   a heavenly calling,
inviting us to pass
through the cross to life.
Give us strength in our struggle,
that we may press on
toward our glorious goal
and so be welcomed at last
into the heavenly city
and share the prize of the saints
unto the endless ages of ages. Amen.

✛ *Great are the works of the LORD!*
God's justice stands firm forever!

✚ *Great are the works of the LORD!*
God's justice stands firm forever!

PSALM 111 *page 424*

READING *Philippians 3:17—4:1*

Brothers and sisters, join in imitating me, and observe those who live according to the example you have in us. For many live as enemies of the cross of Christ; I have often told you of them, and now I tell you even with tears. Their end is destruction; their god is the belly; and their glory is in their shame; their minds are set on earthly things. But our citizenship is in heaven, and it is from there that we are expecting a Savior, the Lord Jesus Christ. He will transform the body of our humiliation that it may be conformed to the body of his glory, by the power that also enables him to make all things subject to himself. Therefore, my brothers and sisters, whom I love and long for, my joy and crown, stand firm in the Lord in this way, my beloved.

REFLECTION

Catholics in the United States used to be regarded with suspicion because some Americans believed that a Catholic's first allegiance was to the pope. This subsided after the election of John F. Kennedy to the presidency, but perhaps the detractors had an inkling of what faith is really about. As Paul asserts, the first allegiance of all the baptized—Catholic, Protestant, Orthodox, and so on—is to God's reign, where we have our true citizenship and our true ruler. It is a fine line we walk, but our commitment to Christ must come first.

PRAYERS *others may be added*

Standing firm in the Lord, we pray:

◆ Deliver your people.

That God's people may live in faithfulness to their heavenly home, we pray: ◆ *That catechumens may find good examples of Christian living as they journey toward Baptism, we pray:* ◆ *That the nations may not worship the false gods of wealth and earthly glory, we pray:* ◆ *That the justice of the heavenly city may overcome earthly oppression, we pray:* ◆ *That we may await with joy the coming of our heavenly Savior, we pray:* ◆

Our Father . . .

Divine Ruler,
our citizenship is from heaven,
where Christ our Savior
reigns in everlasting glory.
Write upon our hearts
the law of the world to come,
that during our earthly sojourn
we may live as your children
and so at last take our place
in the eternal city,
through the same Christ our Lord.
Amen.

✚ *Great are the works of the LORD!*
God's justice stands firm forever!

✛ *Great are the works of the LORD!*
   God's justice stands firm forever!

PSALM 111 *page 424*

READING *Philippians 4:2–9*

I urge Euodia and I urge Syntyche to be of the same mind in the Lord. Yes, and I ask you also, my loyal companion, help these women, for they have struggled beside me in the work of the gospel, together with Clement and the rest of my co-workers, whose names are in the book of life.

Rejoice in the Lord always; again I will say, Rejoice. Let your gentleness be known to everyone. The Lord is near. Do not worry about anything, but in everything by prayer and supplication with thanksgiving let your requests be made known to God. And the peace of God, which surpasses all understanding, will guard your hearts and your minds in Christ Jesus.

Finally, beloved, whatever is true, whatever is honorable, whatever is just, whatever is pure, whatever is pleasing, whatever is commendable, if there is any excellence and if there is anything worthy of praise, think about these things. Keep on doing the things that you have learned and received and heard and seen in me, and the God of peace will be with you.

REFLECTION

Paul's advice to the Christians in Philippi boils down to "Keep on going." His gentle encouragement is certainly appropriate for us, deep in Ordinary Time. His words can renew our strength any time we feel discouraged. His advice is simple: Don't worry; pray; remember what you've been taught; live what you've learned. Like all good wisdom, it's practical advice for practical people seeking to live the Gospel.

PRAYERS *others may be added*

Offering prayer and thanksgiving, we pray:

◆ Deliver your people.

That the Church may announce the peace beyond understanding, we pray: ◆ *That the people of the world may seek only what is honorable, just and commendable, we pray:* ◆ *That youth may be encouraged to be excellent in the ways of God, we pray:* ◆ *That the anxious and depressed may find peace in God, we pray:* ◆ *That we may persevere in all that we have heard and seen, we pray:* ◆

Our Father . . .

God of peace,
with praise and thanksgiving
we offer supplications to you,
confident of your presence among us.
Confirm in us
all that is honorable and pure,
commendable and worthy of praise,
that we may persevere
in all we have been taught,
offering praise to you
through Jesus Christ,
now and forever. Amen.

✛ *Great are the works of the LORD!*
   God's justice stands firm forever!

✤ *Great are the works of the LORD!*
God's justice stands firm forever!

PSALM 111 *page 424*

READING *Hebrews 4:12–13*

The word of God is living and active, sharper than any two-edged sword, piercing until it divides soul from spirit, joints from marrow; it is able to judge the thoughts and intentions of the heart. And before him no creature is hidden, but all are naked and laid bare to the eyes of the one to whom we must render an account.

REFLECTION *Symeon the New Theologian*

The word of God is like a two-edged sword, cutting off and separating the soul from all bodily desire and sensation. More than that, it is like a blazing fire, because it stirs up zeal in our souls, and makes us disregard all the sorrows of life, consider every trial we encounter a joy, and desire and embrace death, so fearful to others, as life and the means of attaining life.

PRAYERS *others may be added*

Ready to give an account of our lives, we pray:

◆ Deliver your people.

For all who proclaim the two-edged sword of God's word, we pray: ◆ For all who hold fast to their faith in God's Son, we pray: ◆ For all who seek grace in time of need, we pray: ◆ For all who are tested by weakness, we pray: ◆ For all who are faced with temptation, we pray: ◆ For all who rely on Christ, the judge of heaven and earth, we pray: ◆

Our Father . . .

Throne of grace,
your living Word judges our hearts
and lays them bare before you,
yet in Christ we have a high priest
who knows our weakness.
By our faith in your Son
bless us with mercy and grace,
that on the day of salvation
we may be found blameless
    before you
and so enter the heavenly city,
where the same Jesus Christ
lives and reigns with you,
in the unity of the Holy Spirit,
one God, forever and ever. Amen

✤ *Great are the works of the LORD!*
God's justice stands firm forever!

✢ *Great are the works of the* L<small>ORD</small>!
  God's justice stands firm forever!

PSALM 111   *page 424*

READING   *Philippians 4:10–14*

I rejoice in the Lord greatly that now
at last you have revived your concern
for me; indeed, you were concerned
for me, but had no opportunity to show
it. Not that I am referring to being in
need; for I have learned to be content
with whatever I have. I know what it is
to have little, and I know what it is to
have plenty. In any and all circumstances I have learned the secret of
being well-fed and of going hungry,
of having plenty and of being in need.
I can do all things through him who
strengthens me. In any case, it was
kind of you to share my distress.

REFLECTION

*Throughout his ministry, Paul experienced
hardship; he spent the end of his life in
prison awaiting execution. He takes comfort in the Philippians' concern for him
and also in the confidence that he is faithful to God. No doubt we too experience
difficult times and look to the presence of
Christ to strengthen us, whether we find
that presence in friends and family or in
the prayer of our hearts.*

PRAYERS   *others may be added*

*Strengthened by Christ, in whom we
can bear all things, we pray:*

◆ Deliver your people.

*That God's people may support one
another through good times and bad,
we pray:* ◆ *That wealthy Christian
communities may see to the needs
of poorer ones, we pray:* ◆ *That the
imprisoned may be accompanied
in prayer and love, we pray:* ◆ *That the
sick may find concern and help in the
community of faith, we pray:* ◆ *That we
may always find hope in the presence
of Christ, we pray:* ◆

Our Father . . .

God of comfort,
you are with us
when we are hungry
and when we are full,
in joy and in sadness.
Strengthen us in Christ,
that in every circumstance
we may praise you through him,
for Christ lives and reigns
forever and ever. Amen.

✢ *Great are the works of the* L<small>ORD</small>!
  God's justice stands firm forever!

✚ *Great are the works of the LORD!*
God's justice stands firm forever!

PSALM 111 page 424

READING Philippians 4:15–23

You Philippians indeed know that in the early days of the gospel, when I left Macedonia, no church shared with me in the matter of giving and receiving, except you alone. For even when I was in Thessalonica, you sent me help for my needs more than once. Not that I seek the gift, but I seek the profit that accumulates to your account. I have been paid in full and have more than enough; I am fully satisfied, now that I have received from Epaphroditus the gifts you sent, a fragrant offering, a sacrifice acceptable and pleasing to God. And my God will fully satisfy every need of yours according to his riches in glory in Christ Jesus. To our God and Father be glory forever and ever. Amen.

Greet every saint in Christ Jesus. The friends who are with me greet you. All the saints greet you, especially those of the emperor's household.

The grace of the Lord Jesus Christ be with your spirit.

REFLECTION

Paul closes his message to the Philippians with words of thanks for their generosity to him in his need. When others abandoned him, the church at Philippi sent Epaphroditus with gifts; Epaphroditus ended up risking his life in doing so, falling ill during his time with Paul and nearly dying (see 10 October). We must seek out ways to continue this ministry of support and encouragement today. The needs of fellow disciples remind us that the Christian life is never something one can do alone.

PRAYERS others may be added

Bearing one another up in need,
we pray:

◆ Deliver your people.

That the baptized may foster the work of missionaries and those who serve the poor, we pray: ◆ *That parishes may reach out to members isolated by sickness or imprisonment, we pray:* ◆ *That wealthy and poor communities may share their many gifts, we pray:* ◆ *That earth's nations may generously respond to those struck by famine and disaster, we pray:* ◆ *That we may be messengers of comfort and aid to those in need, we pray:* ◆

Our Father . . .

Gracious God,
you bless your people
with many good gifts,
and command us to share
what we have received.
Fill us with concern
for the needs of others,
that like the ancient Philippians
we too may offer aid and comfort
to the exhausted and forgotten,
for in serving them
we serve Christ your Son,
who is Lord forever and ever. Amen.

✚ *Great are the works of the LORD!*
God's justice stands firm forever!

✦ *Alleluia! Christ is risen!*
Christ is risen indeed!
Alleluia, alleluia!

PSALM 34 page 412

READING Luke 10:1–2a, 5–9

After this the Lord appointed seventy others and sent them on ahead of him in pairs to every town and place where he himself intended to go. He said to them, "Whatever house you enter, first say, 'Peace to this house!' And if anyone is there who shares in peace, your peace will rest on that person; but if not, it will return to you. Remain in the same house, eating and drinking whatever they provide, for the laborer deserves to be paid. Do not move about from house to house. Whenever you enter a town and its people welcome you, eat what is set before you; cure the sick who are there, and say to them, 'The kingdom of God has come near to you.'"

REFLECTION

This passage summarizes well the task of the disciple: to be messengers of peace, to cure the sick, and to announce the kingdom of God. We don't do our work in first-century Palestine, of course, but we are no less sent out together to continue the work begun in Jesus. Whether we serve as caregivers, preachers, advocates for social justice, parents, teachers, writers, health care workers—the list goes on—we are entrusted with a great task that will be brought to completion through the grace of God.

PRAYERS others may be added

Sent and gathered into the harvest of salvation, we pray:

◆ Turn to us, Lord of life!

For those sent to proclaim the Gospel to all nations, we pray: ◆ For those who offer hospitality to God's servants, we pray: ◆ For those who live and share the peace of God, we pray: ◆ For those who heal the sick, we pray: ◆ For those whose homes are places of welcome, we pray: ◆ For those who await the coming of God's reign, we pray: ◆

Our Father . . .

God of the harvest,
your Anointed One sends us forth
to proclaim the Gospel to all people.
By the power of your Spirit
make us good servants of your reign,
proclaiming and sharing
the peace you promise,
offering your compassion and healing
   to the sick,
and announcing to all people
that the kingdom of heaven
   has come near.
This we ask in the name of Jesus,
who lives and reigns
forever and ever. Amen.

✦ *Alleluia! Christ is risen!*
Christ is risen indeed!
Alleluia, alleluia!

✦ *Great are the works of the LORD!*
God's justice stands firm forever!

PSALM 111 *page 424*

READING *Ephesians 1:1–2, 11–14*

Paul, an apostle of Christ Jesus by the will of God, To the saints who are in Ephesus and are faithful in Christ Jesus: Grace to you and peace from God our Father and the Lord Jesus Christ.

In Christ we have obtained an inheritance, having been destined according to the purpose of him who accomplishes all things according to his counsel and will, so that we, who were the first to set our hope on Christ, might live for the praise of his glory. In him you also, when you had heard the word of truth, the Gospel of your salvation, and had believed in him, were marked with the seal of the promised Holy Spirit; this is the pledge of our inheritance toward redemption as God's own people, to the praise of his glory.

REFLECTION

Although probably not written by Paul himself, the letter to the Ephesians builds upon Pauline theology, developing especially the concepts of the Church as the Body of Christ and the Bride of Christ. While Paul himself was more concerned with the experiences and problems of local churches, the author of Ephesians thinks of the Church in more expansive, even cosmic, terms. In this way, Ephesians challenges us to see the Church as a great communion of peoples and cultures joined together with Christ as head.

PRAYERS *others may be added*

A community of faith, heirs of God's glory, we pray:

◆ Deliver your people.

That God's people may generously share their inheritance of grace, we pray: ◆ That those marked with the seal of the Holy Spirit may hope in Christ alone, we pray: ◆ That the world may receive and embrace God's word of truth, we pray: ◆ That the peace of Christ may calm conflicts among nations, we pray: ◆ That we may offer praise and thanksgiving as we await the fullness of our heavenly inheritance, we pray: ◆

Our Father . . .

God of glory,
you have elected us in Christ
to receive the inheritance
promised to all who believe.
Strengthen within us
the gift of your Spirit
that we may praise you
in this present age,
awaiting in hope the age to come,
when we will be revealed
    as your children,
joint heirs with Jesus Christ,
who lives and reigns
forever and ever. Amen.

✦ *Great are the works of the LORD!*
God's justice stands firm forever!

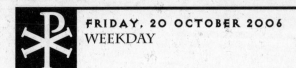

✦ *Great are the works of the LORD!*
God's justice stands firm forever!

PSALM 111   *page 424*

READING   *Ephesians 1:15–19*

I have heard of your faith in the Lord Jesus and your love toward all the saints, and for this reason I do not cease to give thanks for you as I remember you in my prayers. I pray that the God of our Lord Jesus Christ, the Father of glory, may give you a spirit of wisdom and revelation as you come to know him, so that, with the eyes of your heart enlightened, you may know what is the hope to which he has called you, what are the riches of his glorious inheritance among the saints, and what is the immeasurable greatness of his power for us who believe, according to the working of his great power.

REFLECTION   *Romano Guardini*

You have placed the honor of your will in my hands. Each word of your revelations says that you respect and trust me, that you give me dignity and responsibility. Teach me to understand that. Give me that holy maturity that is capable of receiving the light you grant and of assuming the responsibility that you entrust. Keep my heart awake that at all times it may be before you, and let what I do become one with the command and the obedience to which you have called me.

PRAYERS   *others may be added*

Remembering the whole Church before God, we pray:

◆ Deliver your people.

That the disciples of Jesus may grow in love and unity, we pray: ◆ *That the Spirit of wisdom may enlighten the leaders of the Church, we pray:* ◆ *That the Spirit of revelation may inspire preachers and theologians, we pray:* ◆ *That the poor may have hope in the glorious inheritance of God's holy ones, we pray:* ◆ *That we may reveal the power of God in works of justice and reconciliation, we pray:* ◆

Our Father . . .

Father of glory,
you give us a Spirit
of wisdom and revelation,
enlightening our hearts
to know you better.
Increase in us your gift of hope,
that we may have confidence
    in your power
and grow in love and unity
as we await the revelation
your Son and our Lord,
who lives and reigns
forever and ever. Amen.

✦ *Great are the works of the LORD!*
God's justice stands firm forever!

✝ *Great are the works of the LORD!*
  God's justice stands firm forever!

PSALM 111 *page 424*

READING *Ephesians 2:4–10*

But God, who is rich in mercy, out of the great love with which he loved us even when we were dead through our trespasses, made us alive together with Christ—by grace you have been saved—and raised us up with him and seated us with him in the heavenly places in Christ Jesus, so that in the ages to come he might show the immeasurable riches of his grace in kindness toward us in Christ Jesus. For by grace you have been saved through faith, and this is not your own doing; it is the gift of God—not the result of works, so that no one may boast. For we are what he has made us, created in Christ Jesus for good works, which God prepared beforehand to be our way of life.

REFLECTION

Unlike Paul, the author of Ephesians argues that the Christian has already been taken up with Christ into glory; we have already been saved and glorified by God's grace. Ephesians' author stresses that our salvation is a gift from God, but he also reminds us that we are saved for a purpose: good works. Our salvation and re-creation requires us to live as God's glorified children, showing forth God's kindness and mercy in all that we do. In this age, we are the kindness and mercy of God.

PRAYERS *others may be added*

Saved by the great mercy of God,
we pray:

◆ Deliver your people.

That the Church may be a sign of God's kindness to the world, we pray: ◆
That the baptized may reveal the grace of God within them by their works of mercy, we pray: ◆ *That all creation may be renewed in Christ, we pray:* ◆ *That the world's people may turn away from the death of violence and prejudice, we pray:* ◆
That we may embrace the way of life created for us in Christ Jesus, we pray: ◆

Our Father . . .

God rich in mercy,
in Christ you have made us
    a new creation,
filled with grace
revealed in good works.
Renew in us the faith
we embraced in baptism
that we may be a sign
    of your kindness
to all those in need.
We ask this in the name of Jesus,
in whom we have been reborn
    as your children,
and who lives and reigns
forever and ever. Amen.

✝ *Great are the works of the LORD!*
  God's justice stands firm forever!

✦ *Great are the works of the LORD!*
God's justice stands firm forever!

PSALM 111 page 424

READING *Hebrews 4:14–16*

Since we have a great high priest who has passed through the heavens, Jesus, the Son of God, let us hold fast to our confession. For we do not have a high priest who is unable to sympathize with our weaknesses, but we have one who in every respect has been tested as we are, yet without sin. Let us therefore approach the throne of grace with boldness, so that we may receive mercy and find grace to help in time of need.

REFLECTION

Last Sunday's reading from Hebrews presented the image of God's Word as a sharp sword, judging us by a high standard. Today's reading offers the image of Christ as our high priest, who sympathizes with our weakness. Both images are true, of course: The same Christ who is judge of creation is the source of mercy for those in need. In spite of our mixed motives and divided hearts, we can approach the throne of grace boldly.

PRAYERS *others may be added*

With confidence in Christ the high priest, we pray:

◆ Deliver your people.

From the power of temptation, we pray: ◆
From the weakness of sin, we pray: ◆
From the pain of our suffering, we pray: ◆
From the tears of our sorrow, we pray: ◆
From the sleep of apathy, we pray: ◆
From the refusal to show mercy,
we pray: ◆

Our Father . . .

Throne of grace,
alone we are lost,
but in Christ we are set free
    from our weakness.
Pour out your mercy upon us,
that we may confess
our faith in your Son,
offering the mercy
we have received in him
to all who seek it.
We ask this through
our great high priest, Jesus Christ,
who lives and reigns with you,
in the unity of the Holy Spirit,
one God, now and forever. Amen.

✦ *Great are the works of the LORD!*
God's justice stands firm forever!

✦ *Great are the works of the LORD!*
God's justice stands firm forever!

PSALM 111 *page 424*

READING *Ephesians 3:1–6*

This is the reason that I Paul am a prisoner for Christ Jesus for the sake of you Gentiles—for surely you have already heard of the commission of God's grace that was given me for you, and how the mystery was made known to me by revelation, as I wrote above in a few words, a reading of which will enable you to perceive my understanding of the mystery of Christ. In former generations this mystery was not made known to humankind, as it has now been revealed to his holy apostles and prophets by the Spirit: that is, the Gentiles have become fellow heirs, members of the same body, and sharers in the promise in Christ Jesus through the gospel.

REFLECTION *Second Vatican Council*

The Church of Christ acknowledges that in God's plan of salvation the beginnings of its faith and election are to be found in the patriarchs, Moses and the prophets. . . . On this account the Church cannot forget that it received the revelation of the Old Testament by way of that people with whom God in his inexpressible mercy established the ancient covenant. Nor can it forget that it draws nourishment from that good olive tree onto which the wild olive branches of the Gentiles have been grafted (see Romans 11:17–24).

PRAYERS *others may be added*

Fellow heirs with God's chosen people, members of one body, we pray:

◆ Deliver your people.

That the Church may embrace people of all races, languages, and cultures, we pray: ◆ *That Jews and Christians may grow in mutual respect and love, we pray:* ◆ *That the mystery of God's love may be revealed to all people, we pray:* ◆ *That the outcast and forgotten may know their inheritance among the holy ones, we pray:* ◆ *That we may live as sharers in the promise of Christ Jesus, we pray:* ◆

Our Father . . .

God of Israel,
in Christ you have grafted
    a new branch
upon the family of Abraham
    and Sarah,
offering your love to all humankind.
Inspire us with your generous love,
that we may invite and embrace
    all people
who seek you in truth.
This we ask in Jesus' name. Amen.

✦ *Great are the works of the LORD!*
God's justice stands firm forever!

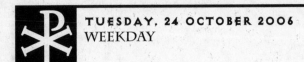
✚ *Great are the works of the LORD!*
God's justice stands firm forever!

PSALM 111 — page 424

READING — *Ephesians 3:7–12*

Of this gospel I have become a servant according to the gift of God's grace that was given me by the working of his power. Although I am the very least of all the saints, this grace was given to me to bring to the Gentiles the news of the boundless riches of Christ, and to make everyone see what is the plan of the mystery hidden for ages in God who created all things; so that through the church the wisdom of God in its rich variety might now be made known to the rulers and authorities in the heavenly places. This was in accordance with the eternal purpose that he has carried out in Christ Jesus our Lord, in whom we have access to God in boldness and confidence through faith in him.

REFLECTION

The author of Ephesians argues that creation reveals God's wisdom and purpose. Like the letter's author, some theologians have embraced science as ways to explore the mystery of God. The Jesuit Pierre Teilhard de Chardin saw in the theory of evolution a way of describing God's continuing act of creation that would eventually lead to the consummation of the universe in what he called the "divine milieu," the final and ultimate marriage of God and creation.

PRAYERS — *others may be added*

Servants of God's wisdom, we pray:

◆ Deliver your people.

That the Church may be a herald of God's mystery hidden in creation, we pray: ◆
That teachers and catechists may lead children into the rich mystery of God, we pray: ◆ *That scientists may reveal the wisdom of God expressed in the universe, we pray:* ◆ *That God's eternal purpose for all creation may come to fulfillment, we pray:* ◆ *That we may approach the Most High in bold confidence of God's mercy, we pray:* ◆

Our Father . . .

Wondrous God of mystery,
in creation you reveal
your eternal purpose,
showing forth the rich variety
    of your wisdom.
Inspire us to seek you
in the richness of creation
that we may recognize
    your glory revealed
in the animals and plants,
the stars and atoms,
and in your image shining within us.
This we ask through
your rich Wisdom-made-flesh,
who lives and reigns
forever and ever. Amen.

✚ *Great are the works of the LORD!*
God's justice stands firm forever!

✛ *Great are the works of the LORD!*
God's justice stands firm forever!

PSALM 111   *page 424*

READING   *Ephesians 4:7, 11–16*

Each of us was given grace according to the measure of Christ's gift. The gifts he gave were that some would be apostles, some prophets, some evangelists, some pastors and teachers, to equip the saints for the work of ministry, for building up the body of Christ, until all of us come to the unity of the faith and of the knowledge of the Son of God, to maturity, to the measure of the full stature of Christ. We must no longer be children, tossed to and fro and blown about by every wind of doctrine, by people's trickery, by their craftiness in deceitful scheming. But speaking the truth in love, we must grow up in every way into him who is the head, into Christ, from whom the whole body, joined and knit together by every ligament with which it is equipped, as each part is working properly, promotes the body's growth in building itself up in love.

REFLECTION   *Second Vatican Council*

The apostolate of the laity is a sharing in the Church's saving mission. Through baptism and confirmation all are appointed to this apostolate by the Lord himself. . . . The laity, however, are given this special vocation: to make the Church present and fruitful in those places and circumstances where it is only through them that it can become the salt of the earth. Thus, all lay
people, through the gifts which they have received, are at once the witnesses and living instruments of the mission of the Church itself "according to the measure of Christ's gift" (Ephesians 4:7).

PRAYERS   *others may be added*

Building up Christ's body, we pray:

◆ Deliver your people.

For apostles and evangelists, who proclaim the Good News, we pray: ◆
For prophets, who call God's people to lives of justice, we pray: ◆ *For pastors and teachers, who maintain the unity of Christ's body, we pray:* ◆ *For catechists and other ministers, who offer the truth in love, we pray:* ◆ *For all the saints, who sustain each other in growth, we pray:* ◆

Our Father . . .

Source of all good gifts,
you bless your Church
    with abundant gifts,
making some pastors, other preachers,
still others prophets.
Strengthen within us
the grace you have given
that we may use what you offer
for the sake of Christ's body,
building up the Church in love
    and truth,
giving you praise and glory
through Jesus Christ,
now and forever. Amen.

✛ *Great are the works of the LORD!*
God's justice stands firm forever!

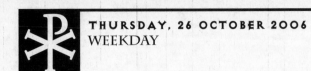
✤ *Great are the works of the LORD!*
  God's justice stands firm forever!

PSALM 111   *page 424*

READING   *Ephesians 4:17–24*

Now this I affirm and insist on in the Lord: you must no longer live as the Gentiles live, in the futility of their minds. They are darkened in their understanding, alienated from the life of God because of their ignorance and hardness of heart. They have lost all sensitivity and have abandoned themselves to licentiousness, greedy to practice every kind of impurity. That is not the way you learned Christ! For surely you have heard about him and were taught in him, as truth is in Jesus. You were taught to put away your former way of life, your old self, corrupt and deluded by its lusts, and to be renewed in the spirit of your minds, and to clothe yourselves with the new self, created according to the likeness of God in true righteousness and holiness.

REFLECTION   *Rite of Christian*
                           Initiation of Adults

You have been enlightened by Christ.
Walk always as children of the light
and keep the flame of faith alive
   in your hearts.
When the Lord comes, may you go out
   to meet him
with all the saints in the heavenly kingdom.

PRAYERS   *others may be added*

Clothed in garments of righteousness
and holiness, we pray:

◆ Deliver your people.

That the baptized may put away
their former selves to be renewed
in God's Spirit: ◆ *That those*
deluded by the promise of wealth
or power may embrace the path
of righteousness: ◆ *That enemies may*
turn away from hardness of heart and
seek reconciliation: ◆ *That those bound*
by the ignorance and fear of prejudice
may embrace the Spirit of truth: ◆

Our Father . . .

Holy God,
in Christ you remake us
   in righteousness,
freeing us from ignorance
   and delusion.
Confirm in us your gift
   of righteousness
so we may share more fully in the life
   you offer
and be renewed in spirit in mind,
made into the likeness of Christ
   our righteousness,
who lives and reigns forever and ever.
Amen.

✤ *Great are the works of the LORD!*
   God's justice stands firm forever!

✝ *Great are the works of the LORD!*
God's justice stands firm forever!

PSALM 111 *page 424*

READING *Ephesians 4:25–29, 31–32*

So then, putting away falsehood, let all of us speak the truth to our neighbors, for we are members of one another. Be angry but do not sin; do not let the sun go down on your anger, and do not make room for the devil. Thieves must give up stealing; rather let them labor and work honestly with their own hands, so as to have something to share with the needy. Let no evil talk come out of your mouths, but only what is useful for building up, as there is need, so that your words may give grace to those who hear. Put away from you all bitterness and wrath and anger and wrangling and slander, together with all malice, and be kind to one another, tenderhearted, forgiving one another, as God in Christ has forgiven you.

REFLECTION

The author of Ephesians offers a reminder that should guide all our actions: "You are members of one another." The things the passage counsels against—slander, bitterness, anger—all disrupt relationships in the Church. We are interconnected and intertwined; the sin of one affects the whole. In other words, our individual moral choices are not just about our spiritual and physical well-being; they affect the whole body, whether our family, our community, or our Church. We are in this together, both in sin and in salvation.

PRAYERS *others may be added*

Forgiving one another as we have been forgiven, we pray:

◆ Deliver your people.

From division among the disciples of Jesus, we pray: ◆ From violent anger in families, we pray: ◆ From slander and idle gossip, we pray: ◆ From falsehood and bitterness, we pray: ◆ From stealing and hoarding more than we need, we pray: ◆ From ignorance to the needs of the poor, we pray: ◆

Our Father . . .

God of grace and peace,
the wisdom of your word
guides us in ways
of gentleness and mercy.
Soothe the wounds of division
that bring us pain,
and cool the fire of our anger,
that we may seek peace
    above all else,
offering to one another
the kindness and compassion
you have extended to us
in Jesus your Son,
through whom we praise you
now and forever. Amen.

✝ *Great are the works of the LORD!*
God's justice stands firm forever!

✚ *Alleluia! Christ is risen!*
Christ is risen indeed!
Alleluia! Alleluia!

PSALM 34 *page 412*

READING *Luke 6:12–16*

Now during those days he went out to the mountain to pray; and he spent the night in prayer to God. And when day came, he called his disciples and chose twelve of them, whom he also named apostles: Simon, whom he named Peter, and his brother Andrew, and James, and John, and Philip, and Bartholomew, and Matthew, and Thomas, and James son of Alphaeus, and Simon, who was called the Zealot, and Judas son of James, and Judas Iscariot, who became a traitor.

REFLECTION *Eusebius of Emesa*

The apostles obeyed and their very shadows raised the sick, for Christ filled with his power those with whom he dwelt. They were not what they were before, what we all were, but were clothed with Christ. And as a bar of iron before heat is applied to it is cold, just like any other iron, but becomes glowing hot when placed in a fire, laying aside its natural coldness and burning with heat itself, so when mortal men and women are clothed with Jesus they perform the same works as he does.

PRAYERS *others may be added*

Built on the foundation of apostles and prophets, we pray:

◆ Deliver your people.

For all who are sent to preach the Good News, we pray: ◆ *For all who share the ministry of the apostles, we pray:* ◆ *For all called to service in the Church, we pray:* ◆ *For all who prepare candidates for ministry, we pray:* ◆ *For all who seek the will of God in prayer, we pray:* ◆ *For all who hear God's call to service in the depths of their hearts, we pray:* ◆

Our Father . . .

God of election,
in every time and place
you send your messengers
to proclaim the Good News
and be witnesses of the Resurrection.
Through the intercession
    of Simon and Jude
may we become more faithful heralds
    of the Gospel,
that all people may come to know
the salvation you offer
    in Jesus Christ,
who lives and reigns
forever and ever. Amen.

✚ *Alleluia! Christ is risen!*
Christ is risen indeed!
Alleluia! Alleluia!

✠ *Great are the works of the LORD!*
God's justice stands firm forever!

PSALM 111 *page 424*

READING *Hebrews 5:1–6*

Every high priest chosen from among mortals is put in charge of things pertaining to God on their behalf, to offer gifts and sacrifices for sins. He is able to deal gently with the ignorant and wayward, since he himself is subject to weakness; and because of this he must offer sacrifice for his own sins as well as for those of the people. And one does not presume to take this honor, but takes it only when called by God, just as Aaron was.

So also Christ did not glorify himself in becoming a high priest, but was appointed by the one who said to him, "You are my Son,
today I have begotten you";
as he says also in another place,
"You are a priest forever,
according to the order of
Melchizedek."

REFLECTION

The author of Hebrews offers a wonderful model—and reminder—for ministers today: Because they know their own weakness, they should be able "to deal gently with the ignorant and wayward." Indeed, it is sage advice for any Christian, especially when we are tempted to judge others harshly. The ministry entrusted to us is one of gentle grace, not fiery condemnation.

PRAYERS *others may be added*

Trusting in the one appointed by God, we pray:

◆ Deliver your people.

That the people of God may offer a fitting sacrifice of praise on behalf of the world, we pray: ◆ *That religious leaders may be gentle with the ignorant and wayward, we pray:* ◆ *That those called to ministry may seek only the honor of serving their sisters and brothers, we pray:* ◆ *That people of faith may avoid self-righteousness and rely on the mercy of God, we pray:* ◆ *That we may approach God mindful of our need for mercy, we pray:* ◆

Our Father . . .

God of mercy,
in the fullness of time
you sent your Only-begotten Son
as our great and eternal high priest.
May we who were called in baptism
to share Christ's eternal priesthood
fulfill our charge in works of mercy,
seeking out the ignorant
and wayward,
ever mindful of our own weakness
and need for your grace.
We make our prayer
through Jesus Christ,
who intercedes for us
at your right hand,
in the unity of the Holy Spirit,
one God, now and forever. Amen.

✠ *Great are the works of the LORD!*
God's justice stands firm forever!

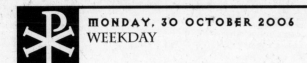
✦ *Great are the works of the LORD!*
God's justice stands firm forever!

PSALM 111 *page 424*

READING *Ephesians 6:10–11, 14–17*

Finally, be strong in the Lord and in the strength of his power. Put on the whole armor of God, so that you may be able to stand against the wiles of the devil. Stand therefore, and fasten the belt of truth around your waist, and put on the breastplate of righteousness. As shoes for your feet put on whatever will make you ready to proclaim the gospel of peace. With all of these, take the shield of faith, with which you will be able to quench all the flaming arrows of the evil one. Take the helmet of salvation, and the sword of the Spirit, which is the word of God.

REFLECTION

Many Protestant Christians observed yesterday as Reformation Sunday and tomorrow as Reformation Day, the anniversary of Martin Luther's posting of his 95 theses on the door of the cathedral in Wittenburg, Germany. While his act led unfortunately to the division of Christianity in Western Europe, it also sparked reform in the Roman Catholic Church, in the Council of Trent (1545–63). While our division remains, these days are a wonderful opportunity to pray for the unity of the whole people of God and for their continued reform.

PRAYERS *others may be added*

Clothing ourselves in the gifts of God, we pray:

◆ Deliver your people.

That the shield of faith may keep the baptized steadfast in holiness, we pray: ◆ *That the leaders of the Church may always be ready to proclaim the Gospel of peace, we pray:* ◆ *That the leaders of nations may be clothed in truth and righteousness, we pray:* ◆ *That the sword of the Spirit, the word of God, may cut through injustice and oppression, we pray:* ◆ *That God's presence may surround us with love and protection, we pray:* ◆

Our Father . . .

Strength of your people,
you surround us
with the armor of your power
and defend us
    as our shield of faith.
Clothe our weakness
with your many gifts;
place upon our feet
the shoes of apostleship:
May we always be ready
to proclaim the Gospel of peace
in a world torn by violence and fear.
Grant this through our Savior
    Jesus Christ,
who lives and reigns
forever and ever. Amen.

✦ *Great are the works of the LORD!*
God's justice stands firm forever!

✝ *Great are the works of the LORD!*
God's justice stands firm forever!

PSALM 111   *page 424*

READING   *Matthew 5:1–6*

When Jesus saw the crowds, he went up the mountain; and after he sat down, his disciples came to him. Then he began to speak, and taught them, saying:

> "Blessed are the poor in spirit, for theirs is the kingdom of heaven.
> "Blessed are those who mourn, for they will be comforted.
> "Blessed are the meek, for they will inherit the earth.
> "Blessed are those who hunger and thirst for righteousness, for they will be filled."

REFLECTION

Keeping vigil is an ancient tradition in the Church; assemblies used to anticipate the Lord's Day by gathering on Saturday night to read scripture, pray psalms, and greet the sunrise with joy as a sign of the Lord's Resurrection. Today the Church keeps vigil on the evenings before great feasts, including tomorrow's festival of All Saints, which is why we read part of the Gospel prescribed for Mass on All Saints Day. Today is also Reformation Day among Protestant churches; we keep vigil with them as we await the day when we shall gather as one people in the eternal communion of saints.

PRAYERS   *others may be added*

Seeking the blessedness of the saints, we pray:

◆ Deliver your people.

That the baptized may be poor in spirit and so inherit God's reign, we pray: ◆
That catechumens may humbly attend to the voice of the Teacher, we pray: ◆
That the nations may embrace meekness and so inherit the earth, we pray: ◆
That the sorrowful and grieving may find comfort, we pray: ◆ *That those who hunger for justice and thirst for righteousness may be filled, we pray:* ◆
That we may counted among those blessed by God, we pray: ◆

Our Father . . .

God of blessedness,
you call us to live in peace,
justice, and poverty of spirit.
Hear us as we keep vigil;
bless us in our search for holiness
that we may come to share
the glory of the saints
who worship at the throne
    of the Lamb.
We ask this in the name of Jesus
    the Christ,
who lives and reigns with you,
in the unity of the Holy Spirit,
one God, forever and ever. Amen.

✝ *Great are the works of the LORD!*
God's justice stands firm forever!

✚ *Alleluia! Christ is risen!*
Christ is risen indeed!
Alleluia, alleluia!

PSALM 66   page 415

READING   Matthew 5:7–12

"Blessed are the merciful, for they will receive mercy.

"Blessed are the pure in heart, for they will see God.

"Blessed are the peacemakers, for they will be called children of God.

"Blessed are those who are persecuted for righteousness' sake, for theirs is the kingdom of heaven.

"Blessed are you when people revile you and persecute you and utter all kinds of evil against you falsely on my account. Rejoice and be glad, for your reward is great in heaven, for in the same way they persecuted the prophets who were before you.

REFLECTION

All Saints Day is the feast of the heavenly Jerusalem, the holy city where the assembly of the redeemed is gathered forever. At one time, it was celebrated right after Easter, but its observance was eventually moved to November so that food would be plentiful for the crowds that filled Rome for the festival; thus today also became a harvest feast. In a sense, All Saints corresponds to the Jewish Sukkot festival, for today we celebrate the great harvest of the righteous into the city of God.

PRAYERS   *others may be added*

Surrounded by a cloud of witnesses, we cry out:

◆ Saints of God, pray for us!

Abraham and Sarah, patriarchs and matriarchs, we cry out: ◆ *Moses, Miriam, Elijah, all prophets of God, we cry out:* ◆ *Hannah, Ruth, Naomi, holy women of Israel, we cry out:* ◆ *Mary and Joseph, we cry out:* ◆ *Peter and Paul, Mary Magdalene, holy apostles, we cry out:* ◆ *Stephen, Agatha, holy martyrs, we cry out:* ◆ *Ambrose, Augustine, Catherine, Teresa, holy doctors of the Church, we cry out:* ◆ *Oscar Romero, Dorothy Day, Maura Clarke, Ita Ford, Dorothy Kazel, Jeanne Donovan, all holy men and women, we cry out:* ◆

Our Father . . .

Praise to you, God of all saints,
for your holy ones
show forth your salvation.
Fill us with their gifts
of courage and boldness,
wisdom and understanding,
compassion and hope.
May their examples inspire us
to lives of holiness
that we may join them in praising you,
through Jesus the Christ,
who lives and reigns with you,
in the unity of the Holy Spirit,
one God, forever and ever. Amen.

✚ *Alleluia! Christ is risen!*
Christ is risen indeed!
Alleluia, alleluia!

✝ *In you, O LORD, we take refuge:*
For you are our rock, our stronghold.

PSALM 71 *page 416*

READING *Luke 7:11–17*

Soon afterwards he went to a town called Nain, and his disciples and a large crowd went with him. As he approached the gate of the town, a man who had died was being carried out. He was his mother's only son, and she was a widow; and with her was a large crowd from the town. When the Lord saw her, he had compassion for her and said to her, "Do not weep." Then he came forward and touched the bier, and the bearers stood still. And he said, "Young man, I say to you, rise!" The dead man sat up and began to speak, and Jesus gave him to his mother. Fear seized all of them; and they glorified God, saying, "A great prophet has risen among us!" and "God has looked favorably on his people!" This word about him spread throughout Judea and all the surrounding country.

REFLECTION

November is a time of ingathering, of recalling the heavenly harvest at the end of time, of celebrating the saints and remembering the dead. It is also a time to consider the mystery of death, even to make preparations for it by revisiting wills and final directives, and making wishes known to loved one. This time spent with death does not have to be sorrowful; as today's passage reminds us, and as our faith confirms, the alienation of death is only temporary, for it gives way to new life.

PRAYERS *others may be added*

Confident in Jesus' promise of eternal life, we pray:

◆ Free us, who trust in you.

For departed ministers, who served the Church in life, we pray: ◆ For departed parents and grandparents, who showed us how to love, we pray: ◆ For departed teachers, who brought us understanding, we pray: ◆ For the forgotten dead, whose lives passed without mention, we pray: ◆ For those who died in violence or despair, we pray: ◆ For all who await the fullness of eternal life, we pray: ◆

Our Father . . .

God of life and promise,
you sent your Son
to lead us back to you.
In loving care embrace the dying,
and in mercy gather the dead
into your heavenly dwelling place.
May their prayers bear us up
to Paradise
when our earthly sojourn has ended.
We ask this in the name
of Jesus Christ,
who lives and reigns with you,
in the unity of the Holy Spirit,
one God, forever and ever. Amen.

✝ *In you, O LORD, we take refuge:*
For you are our rock, our stronghold.

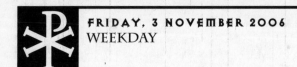

✠ *In you, O LORD, we take refuge:*
   For you are our rock, our stronghold.

PSALM 71 *page 416*

READING *Wisdom 3:1–3, 9*

The souls of the righteous are
    in the hands of God,
and no torment will ever touch them.
In the eyes of the foolish they seemed
    to have died
and their departure was thought
    to be a disaster,
and their going from us to be
    their destruction;
but they are at peace.
Those who trust in him
    will understand truth,
and the faithful will abide with him
    in love,
because grace and mercy are upon
    his holy ones,
and he watches over his elect.

REFLECTION

*For most of the next two weeks, keeping
November's focus on the heavenly harvest
of the dead, we will read from the scriptures used at funeral liturgies, passages
that acknowledge the pain and sorrow of
death while at the same time proclaiming
our hope in the life to come. Today's reading highlights our confident faith in the
face of death, even though we cannot see
what lies beyond.*

PRAYERS *others may be added*

*Confident of God's mercy to the holy
ones, we pray:*

◆ Free us, who trust in you.

*That God's loving gaze may comfort
the baptized, we pray:* ◆ *That those who
see in death disaster and destruction may
find hope, we pray:* ◆ *That those who
trust in God may share their confidence
with the anxious and fearful, we pray:* ◆
*That those who mourn the death of loved
ones may know God's peace, we pray:* ◆
*That God may shelter the dead with
loving hands, we pray:* ◆

Our Father . . .

Loving God,
you do not abandon
your righteous ones to destruction
but surround your beloved with peace.
Comfort those who mourn,
and give them confidence
in the life you promise,
that all your people
may declare their trust in you
whose mercy endures
    beyond the grave.
Grant this through Jesus Christ,
who has opened to us
the gates of heaven,
for he lives and reigns
forever and ever. Amen.

✠ *In you, O LORD, we take refuge:*
   For you are our rock, our stronghold.

✝ *In you, O LORD, we take refuge:*
For you are our rock, our stronghold.

PSALM 71   *page 416*

READING   *Wisdom 4:7–11, 13–14a*

But the righteous, though they die
    early, will be at rest.
For old age is not honored
    for length of time,
or measured by number of years;
but understanding is gray hair
    for anyone,
and a blameless life is ripe old age.
There were some who pleased God
    and were loved by him,
and while living among sinners
    were taken up.
They were caught up so that evil might
    not change their understanding
or guile deceive their souls.
Being perfected in a short time,
    they fulfilled long years;
for their souls were pleasing
    to the Lord.

REFLECTION

Though it may seem strange to us who believe in the resurrection, belief in an afterlife did not develop in Judaism until the last century or so before the birth of Jesus. Such belief was inspired primarily by reflection on the suffering and death of the innocent, and the apparent prosperity of the wicked: How could a just and loving God allow the wicked to prosper, while the innocent suffered and died? It is a question we must ask as children starve, countries are torn by war, and poverty crushes more than a billion people.

PRAYERS   *others may be added*

Seeking to be pleasing offerings to God, we pray:

◆ Free us, who trust in you.

That the baptized may be perfected by God's grace, we pray: ◆ *That the elderly may be supported and protected, we pray:* ◆ *That the wisdom of the young may be nurtured and embraced, we pray:* ◆ *That the dead may be found pleasing to God, we pray:* ◆ *That we may offer to God an acceptable sacrifice of blameless lives, we pray:* ◆

Our Father . . .

God of old and young,
true wisdom is not attained
    in length of years
but in seeking understanding.
Bless us as we continue
our journey to you
that our lives may be blameless
and pleasing before you,
fulfilling long years in your grace,
and coming at last into your presence
to praise you unto
the endless ages of ages. Amen.

✝ *In you, O LORD, we take refuge:*
For you are our rock, our stronghold.

✠ *In you, O LORD, we take refuge:*
For you are our rock, our stronghold.

PSALM 71   page 416

READING   *Hebrews 7:23–28*

The former priests were many in number, because they were prevented by death from continuing in office; but he holds his priesthood permanently, because he continues forever. Consequently he is able for all time to save those who approach God through him, since he always lives to make intercession for them. For it was fitting that we should have such a high priest, holy, blameless, undefiled, separated from sinners, and exalted above the heavens. Unlike the other high priests, he has no need to offer sacrifices day after day, first for his own sins, and then for those of the people; this he did once for all when he offered himself. For the law appoints as high priests those who are subject to weakness, but the word of the oath, which came later than the law, appoints a Son who has been made perfect forever.

REFLECTION

Scripture scholars suggest that Hebrews is directed to a Jewish Christian community whose members were contemplating a return to Jewish sacrificial practice. The preacher asserts that the perfect sacrifice of Christ has abolished the need for any further offerings. While this may seem far removed from our experience, we also are tempted to rely on certain "works" to justify ourselves. Hebrews reminds us,

however, that salvation is a gift, won and sustained forever by Christ, and not something that we can ever earn.

PRAYERS   *others may be added*

Relying on the One who is holy, blameless, and exalted above the heavens, we pray:

◆ Free us, who trust in you.

That the Church may always point the way to our eternal high priest, we pray: ◆ *That the people of God may unite themselves to Christ's prayer for the world, we pray:* ◆ *That the intercession of our great high priest may cleanse the world of all sin, we pray:* ◆ *That we may join ourselves to the one perfect sacrifice of Christ, we pray:* ◆ *That the dead may share Christ's exaltation in the reign of God, we pray:* ◆

Our Father . . .

God Most High,
we join ourselves to Jesus Christ
for through him you extend
your saving hand.
Hear the prayers we offer
through the One who offered
himself once for all,
that in the fullness of time
we might come to share
    his exaltation,
for Christ is Lord with you,
in the unity of the Holy Spirit,
one God, forever and ever. Amen.

✠ *In you, O LORD, we take refuge:*
For you are our rock, our stronghold.

✚ *In you, O LORD, we take refuge:*
For you are our rock, our stronghold.

PSALM 71 *page 416*

READING *Isaiah 25:6–9*

On this mountain the LORD of hosts
    will make for all peoples
  a feast of rich food, a feast of well-
    aged wines,
  of rich food filled with marrow,
    of well-aged wines strained clear.
And he will destroy on this mountain
  the shroud that is cast over
    all peoples,
  the sheet that is spread over
    all nations;
  he will swallow up death forever.
Then the Lord GOD will wipe away
    the tears from all faces,
  and the disgrace of his people he
    will take away from all the earth,
  for the LORD has spoken.
It will be said on that day,
  Lo, this is our God; we have
    waited for him, so that he
    might save us.
  This is the LORD for whom
    we have waited;
let us be glad and rejoice
    in his salvation.

REFLECTION

Any time we feel overwhelmed by death's shadow, Isaiah's rousing words have the power to restore. To destroy famine God spreads a great feast. To cast out sorrow God pours out rivers of rich wine. To overcome death itself, our God in Christ charges through the cross to save us. Indeed, such

is our God; even in sorrow, we rejoice and are glad!

PRAYERS

Trusting in God's salvation, we pray:

◆ Free us, who trust in you.

From the disgrace of sin, we pray: ◆
From the shroud of war and disease,
we pray: ◆ *From the blight of violence*
and murder, we pray: ◆ *From the death*
of poverty and starvation, we pray: ◆
From the tears of sorrow and mourning,
we pray: ◆ *From the pall of fear,*
we pray: ◆

Our Father . . .

God of promise,
at the end of time
you will free your people
from death's pall and sorrow's shroud,
wiping away all our tears.
Give us a vision of that future feast,
that we may praise you
as we await the day
when death itself will pass away,
and we will praise you
in endless songs of praise. Amen.

✚ *In you, O LORD, we take refuge:*
For you are our rock, our stronghold.

✝ *In you, O LORD, we take refuge:*
   For you are our rock, our stronghold.

PSALM 71   *page 416*

READING   *Lamentations 3:17–26*

My soul is bereft of peace;
   I have forgotten what happiness is;
so I say, "Gone is my glory,
   and all that I had hoped for
      from the LORD."
The thought of my affliction
      and my homelessness
   is wormwood and gall!
My soul continually thinks of it
   and is bowed down within me.
But this I call to mind,
   and therefore I have hope:
The steadfast love of the LORD
      never ceases,
   his mercies never come to an end;
they are new every morning;
   great is your faithfulness.
"The LORD is my portion,"
      says my soul,
   "therefore I will hope in him."
The LORD is good to those
      who wait for him,
   to the soul that seeks him.
It is good that one should wait quietly
   for the salvation of the LORD.

REFLECTION

The author of Lamentations expresses
what many feel in the depths of grief, even
forgetting what happiness is. The death of
a loved one may well feel like the loss of all
that one hoped for in life. Yet despite sad-
ness, there is the hope of faith, "new every
morning," and so even in sorrow we can

look forward in silent hope for the salva-
tion of God.

PRAYERS   *others may be added*

   Hopeful even in the silence of death,
   we pray:

◆ Free us, who trust in you.

For those among the baptized grieving
great loss, we pray: ◆ *For those among*
the nations who have forgotten happiness,
we pray: ◆ *For those among the suffering*
who can see no end to their affliction,
we pray: ◆ *For those among the dying*
who trust in God's mercy, we pray: ◆
For those among the dead who await
glory's morning, we pray: ◆

Our Father . . .

New every morning
is your faithfulness, O God,
and even in death
we hope in you alone.
Give us comfort in grief
and trust through our tears,
that we may never cease
   to praise you
as we await your salvation,
you who live and reign
forever and ever. Amen.

✝ *In you, O LORD, we take refuge:*
   For you are our rock, our stronghold.

✛ *In you, O LORD, we take refuge:*
For you are our rock, our stronghold.

PSALM 71 *page 416*

READING *Daniel 12:1–3*

At that time Michael, the great prince, the protector of your people, shall arise. There shall be a time of anguish, such as has never occurred since nations first came into existence. But at that time your people shall be delivered, everyone who is found written in the book. Many of those who sleep in the dust of the earth shall awake, some to everlasting life, and some to shame and everlasting contempt. Those who are wise shall shine like the brightness of the sky, and those who lead many to righteousness, like the stars forever and ever.

REFLECTION *Long Island epitaph*

This body sleeps in dust
Immortal joys await the host
In perfect beauty may it rise
When Gabriel's trumpet shakes the skies.

PRAYERS *others may be added*

Longing to be counted among the wise, we pray:

◆ Free us, who trust in you.

That the baptized may announce God's promise in the midst of suffering and strife, we pray: ◆ *That nations suffering disaster or unrest may be delivered and restored, we pray:* ◆ *That those who lead others to righteousness may shine like the stars for all the earth, we pray:* ◆ *That those who suffer the anguish of poverty and hunger may find comfort, we pray:* ◆ *That those who sleep in the dust may rise to everlasting glory, we pray:* ◆

Our Father . . .

God of the ages,
on your great day
the dead shall rise,
and the righteous and wise
shall shine with your glory.
Be with us in times
of anguish and trouble
that we may remain faithful
    through our trials
and be gathered up
into your eternal harvest
by the Son of Man and his angels,
for Christ is Lord
forever and ever. Amen.

✛ *In you, O LORD, we take refuge:*
For you are our rock, our stronghold.

✚ *In you, O LORD, we take refuge:*
For you are our rock, our stronghold.

PSALM 71 *page 416*

READING *1 Corinthians 3:9c–11, 16–17*

You are God's field, God's building. According to the grace of God given to me, like a skilled master builder I laid a foundation, and someone else is building on it. Each builder must choose with care how to build on it. For no one can lay any foundation other than the one that has been laid; that foundation is Jesus Christ.

Do you not know that you are God's temple and that God's Spirit dwells in you? If anyone destroys God's temple, God will destroy that person. For God's temple is holy, and you are that temple.

REFLECTION *Rite of Dedication*

Through his death and resurrection, Christ became the true and perfect temple of the New Covenant and gathered together a people to be his own. This holy people, made one as the Father, Son and Holy Spirit are one, is the Church, that is, the temple of God built of living stones, where the Father is worshipped in spirit and in truth. . . . Because the Church is a visible building, it stands as a special sign of the pilgrim Church on earth and reflects the Church dwelling heaven.

PRAYERS *others may be added*

Fashioned by God as a living temple of the Spirit, we pray:

◆ Free us, who trust in you.

For the people of God, living stones in a spiritual edifice, we pray: ◆ *For the diocese of Rome and its bishop, the pope, a visible sign and source of the unity of the Church, we pray:* ◆ *For communities of faith, local temples of the Holy Spirit, we pray:* ◆ *For those who build places of worship, creating houses of reverence for God, we pray:* ◆ *For spouses and parents, heads of the domestic Church, we pray:* ◆ *For all of us, built together on the foundation stone of Jesus Christ, we pray:* ◆

Our Father . . .

Master Builder,
you set us on the foundation of Christ,
ensuring that your household will
    stand firm.
Purify us of weakness and decay,
that we may stand solid and strong
as a sign of your presence in the world
and a precursor of your new creation,
where Christ lives and reigns
forever and ever. Amen.

✚ *In you, O LORD, we take refuge:*
For you are our rock, our stronghold.

✦ *In you, O LORD, we take refuge:*
For you are our rock, our stronghold.

PSALM 71   *page 416*

READING   *1 Corinthians 15:20–28*

Christ has been raised from the dead, the first fruits of those who have died. For since death came through a human being, the resurrection of the dead has also come through a human being; for as all die in Adam, so all will be made alive in Christ. But each in his own order: Christ the first fruits, then at his coming those who belong to Christ. Then comes the end, when he hands over the kingdom to God the Father, after he has destroyed every ruler and every authority and power. For he must reign until he has put all his enemies under his feet. The last enemy to be destroyed is death. For "God has put all things in subjection under his feet." But when it says, "All things are put in subjection," it is plain that this does not include the one who put all things in subjection under him. When all things are subjected to him, then the Son himself will also be subjected to the one who put all things in subjection under him, so that God may be all in all.

REFLECTION

Paul describes a reality that we experience profoundly when faced with sickness or death: This world is not yet as it should be; God is not yet "all in all," at least not in a way that we are yet able to recognize. No, we Christians live between the time of "first fruits," when Christ the divine harvester was himself born into resurrection's fullness, and the fullness of Christ's harvest, when living and dead together will be gathered into heavenly barns. We live in the meeting point between the old creation and the new—and sometimes it's difficult to be both in the "already" and the "not yet" of God's reign.

PRAYERS   *others may be added*

Looking for the day when God will be all and in all, we pray:

◆ Free us, who trust in you.

For all who see in Christ the first fruits of the heavenly harvest, we pray: ◆ *For all who mourn the loss of friends and family, we pray:* ◆ *For all who wait with longing for the fullness of justice, we pray:* ◆ *For all who suffer the agony of long illness and pain, we pray:* ◆ *For all who await the fullness of life in death's embrace, we pray:* ◆

Our Father . . .

God of the world to come,
we await with eagerness
the coming harvest of joy.
Give us strength to endure all things,
that we may at last
behold the dawn of that day
when even death shall surrender
and all shall be subject
to the Lord of the harvest
now and forever. Amen.

✦ *In you, O LORD, we take refuge:*
For you are our rock, our stronghold.

✤ *In you, O LORD, we take refuge:*
For you are our rock, our stronghold.

PSALM 71   *page 416*

READING   *1 Corinthians 15:51–57*

Listen, I will tell you a mystery! We will not all die, but we will all be changed, in a moment, in the twinkling of an eye, at the last trumpet. For the trumpet will sound, and the dead will be raised imperishable, and we will be changed. For this perishable body must put on imperishability, and this mortal body must put on immortality. When this perishable body puts on imperishability, and this mortal body puts on immortality, then the saying that is written will be fulfilled: "Death has been swallowed up in victory." "Where, O death, is your victory? Where, O death, is your sting?" The sting of death is sin, and the power of sin is the law. But thanks be to God, who gives us the victory through our Lord Jesus Christ.

REFLECTION

Paul writes to comfort and correct some in the Corinthian community. To one group, overcome with sorrow at the deaths of some members, Paul asserts that some of those remaining shall live to see Christ's return, along with the resurrection of their loved ones. To those who denied the resurrection altogether, Paul unabashedly proclaims Christ's victory, quoting two sayings known to the community that give us courage even today: "Where, O death, is your victory? Where, O death, is your sting?"

PRAYERS   *others may be added*

Confident of Christ's victory, we pray:

◆ Free us, who trust in you.

That the baptized may always share the mystery entrusted to them, we pray: ◆
That the dying may hope in God's promise of life in Christ, we pray: ◆
That those who mourn may not be overcome by sorrow and fear, we pray: ◆
That the dead may be restored on the day of salvation, we pray: ◆ *That we may behold the glory of Christ's Resurrection, we pray:* ◆

Our Father . . .

In the twinkling of an eye,
O God of wondrous power,
the trumpet will sound,
and you will restore the dead.
Make us confident in Christ's victory,
that we may shout with the blessed,
"Where, O death, is your victory?
Where, O death, is your sting?"
praising you without end
though the Living One,
who is Lord forever and ever. Amen.

✤ *In you, O LORD, we take refuge:*
For you are our rock, our stronghold.

✠ *In you, O LORD, we take refuge:*
For you are our rock, our stronghold.

PSALM 71   *page 416*

READING   *Hebrews 9:24–28*

Christ did not enter a sanctuary made by human hands, a mere copy of the true one, but he entered into heaven itself, now to appear in the presence of God on our behalf. Nor was it to offer himself again and again, as the high priest enters the Holy Place year after year with blood that is not his own; for then he would have had to suffer again and again since the foundation of the world. But as it is, he has appeared once for all at the end of the age to remove sin by the sacrifice of himself. And just as it is appointed for mortals to die once, and after that the judgment, so Christ, having been offered once to bear the sins of many, will appear a second time, not to deal with sin, but to save those who are eagerly waiting for him.

REFLECTION

Of all the words we use to describe Jesus' work, "sacrifice" can be the most troubling. Did God really require the brutal death of Jesus? Was bloodshed necessary for our salvation? Hebrews's preacher gives us the key to understanding Jesus' sacrifice: obedience (Hebrews 5:8). It was Christ's perfect obedience to God's will that won salvation. That obedience resulted in his death, of course, but Jesus' execution was the sinful human response to Jesus' life of obedience. Even in the face of death, Jesus was faithful to his mission, which is why the cross is the sign of our salvation.

PRAYERS   *others may be added*

Eagerly awaiting the return of the Mediator, we pray:

◆ Free us, who trust in you.

That the Church may point the way to the sanctuary not made by human hands, we pray: ◆ That the baptized may join themselves to Christ's sacrifice of praise, we pray: ◆ That the sins of war and injustice may be removed from the world by Christ's perfect intercession, we pray: ◆ That those who feel overwhelmed by guilt may trust in Christ's perfect offering, we pray: ◆ That we may live as children of the new age of salvation, we pray: ◆

Our Father . . .

Saving God,
your Anointed One ministers
   in your presence
pleading on our behalf.
By the work of our Mediator
pour out your loving kindness,
that we may be cleansed of our sin
and join Christ in his perfect praise,
the sacrifice of a humble heart
ready to do your will.
This we ask through Jesus Christ,
our great high priest,
Lord with you,
in the unity of the Holy Spirit,
one God, forever and ever. Amen.

✠ *In you, O LORD, we take refuge:*
For you are our rock, our stronghold.

✠ *In you, O LORD, we take refuge:*
  For you are our rock, our stronghold.

PSALM 71   *page 416*

READING   *2 Corinthians 4:14–18*

We know that the one who raised the Lord Jesus will raise us also with Jesus, and will bring us with you into his presence. Yes, everything is for your sake, so that grace, as it extends to more and more people, may increase thanksgiving, to the glory of God. So we do not lose heart. Even though our outer nature is wasting away, our inner nature is being renewed day by day. For this slight momentary affliction is preparing us for an eternal weight of glory beyond all measure, because we look not at what can be seen but at what cannot be seen; for what can be seen is temporary, but what cannot be seen is eternal.

REFLECTION

Praising God in times of trouble may seem a bit disingenuous; surely God wants the truth from us! We do not praise God at such times because there's some value in "sucking it up"; we praise God because we trust that God can transform our suffering. Just as God transformed Christ's cross into the tree of risen life, so our sickness, pain, and sorrow will, we believe, be gathered up into God's glory. We don't pretend to understand or try to explain away our suffering or anyone else's, but we do have hope in what we cannot yet see.

PRAYERS   *others may be added*

With hope in the promise of God, we pray:

◆ Free us, who trust in you.

That the baptized may speak of their faith with confidence and hope, we pray: ◆
That the grace of God may renew those preparing for baptism, we pray: ◆
That the world's people may join together in a chorus of thanksgiving to God, we pray: ◆ *That the sick may not lose heart but find comfort in God's presence, we pray:* ◆ *That those near death may trust in what they cannot yet see, we pray:* ◆
That present suffering may prepare us for the weight of glory to come, we pray: ◆

Our Father . . .

Faithful God,
though we suffer we trust in you
and come before you in thanksgiving.
Strengthen the hearts of the sick,
and give courage to the dying:
May we find in times of trial
your abiding presence
and so prepare to behold
the weight of your glory,
revealed in Jesus Christ,
in whose name we pray. Amen.

✠ *In you, O LORD, we take refuge:*
  For you are our rock, our stronghold.

✙ *In you, O LORD, we take refuge:*
For you are our rock, our stronghold.

PSALM 71 *page 416*

READING *2 Corinthians 5:1, 6–10*

We know that if the earthly tent we live in is destroyed, we have a building from God, a house not made with hands, eternal in the heavens. So we are always confident; even though we know that while we are at home in the body we are away from the Lord—for we walk by faith, not by sight. Yes, we do have confidence, and we would rather be away from the body and at home with the Lord. So whether we are at home or away, we make it our aim to please him. For all of us must appear before the judgment seat of Christ, so that each may receive recompense for what has been done in the body, whether good or evil.

REFLECTION

Paul seems to desire his own death, that he may be "at home with the Lord." Perhaps our own elderly parents or grandparents, or those we know who are terminally ill, have spoken also of a readiness for death. Neither Paul nor our loved ones are out of their minds or suicidal. Though Christianity affirms the goodness and infinite worth of earthly human life, it also has a positive outlook on death as the door to greater union with God in Christ. Though we may look upon death with trepidation, we can be confident in the dwelling we do not yet see. And so we can accompany those nearing death with compassion and faith.

PRAYERS *others may be added*

Walking by faith as we await the revelation of Christ, we pray:

◆ Free us, who trust in you.

That God's people may build up an inheritance of good works for eternal life, we pray: ◆ *That the world's people may find mercy and love on the day of judgment, we pray:* ◆ *That the dying may have confidence in the heavenly dwelling place that awaits them, we pray:* ◆ *That the dead may be received into glory when they approach Christ's judgment seat, we pray:* ◆ *That we may live with eyes of faith fixed on our home with God, we pray:* ◆

Our Father . . .

Eternal God,
we live as pilgrims
in our earthly tents,
longing for the day
when we will be united with you.
Fill us with faith
in what we cannot yet see,
that we may have confidence
    in the building
not made by humans hands
and so come at last
into our heavenly dwelling place,
living in glory with you,
where Christ is Lord
forever and ever. Amen.

✙ *In you, O LORD, we take refuge:*
For you are our rock, our stronghold.

✠ *In you, O LORD, we take refuge:*
For you are our rock, our stronghold.

PSALM 71   page 416

READING   *1 Thessalonians 4:13–18*

But we do not want you to be uninformed, brothers and sisters, about those who have died, so that you may not grieve as others do who have no hope. For since we believe that Jesus died and rose again, even so, through Jesus, God will bring with him those who have died. For this we declare to you by the word of the Lord, that we who are alive, who are left until the coming of the Lord, will by no means precede those who have died. For the Lord himself, with a cry of command, with the archangel's call and with the sound of God's trumpet, will descend from heaven, and the dead in Christ will rise first. Then we who are alive, who are left, will be caught up in the clouds together with them to meet the Lord in the air; and so we will be with the Lord forever. Therefore encourage one another with these words.

REFLECTION

Some early Christians believed that only those who were still living at the time of Jesus' second coming would share resurrection. The death of any Christian, then, was a cause of great grief. Paul corrects them, promising that the dead and the living will be reunited on the day of Christ's glory. This is the Christian hope in death: Though we grieve, in our depths we trust that God's promises will be fulfilled.

PRAYERS   *others may be added*

Comforting one another with words of hope, we pray:

◆ Free us, who trust in you.

That God's people may encourage one another in times of sorrow, we pray: ◆ That those who minister to the grieving may offer the hope of God's word, we pray: ◆ That those who mourn without hope may know the presence of the living God, we pray: ◆ That the dead may be revealed at the coming of our Savior Jesus Christ, we pray: ◆ That the absence of loved ones may increase our longing for eternal reunion with them, we pray: ◆

Our Father . . .

God of the living and the dead,
you sustain us in our sorrow
with the promise of eternal life.
Increase our hope
in the reunion to come,
that when our time on earth
    has ended
we may be reunited
with those who have preceded us,
caught up in the glory
of the risen Christ,
who lives and reigns
forever and ever. Amen.

✠ *In you, O LORD, we take refuge:*
For you are our rock, our stronghold.

✦ *In you, O LORD, we take refuge:*
For you are our rock, our stronghold.

PSALM 71 *page 416*

READING *2 Timothy 2:8–13*

Remember Jesus Christ, raised from the dead, a descendant of David—that is my gospel, for which I suffer hardship, even to the point of being chained like a criminal. But the word of God is not chained. Therefore I endure everything for the sake of the elect, so that they may also obtain the salvation that is in Christ Jesus, with eternal glory. The saying is sure: If we have died with him, we will also live with him; if we endure, we will also reign with him; if we deny him, he will also deny us; if we are faithless, he remains faithful—for he cannot deny himself.

REFLECTION

The writer of Second Timothy expresses the heart of our Christian faith: Through our sharing in Christ's paschal mystery— including the mystery of his death—we will come to the glory of resurrection. This is the mystery we celebrate in every Christian liturgy, from sacraments of initiation to liturgies of Christian funerals. In each celebration and through lives transformed by those celebrations, we are conformed more fully to the image of Christ, until as last, in eternity, we are recreated forever in him.

PRAYERS *others may be added*

Seeking ever greater transformation, we pray:

◆ Free us, who trust in you.

That celebrations of liturgy may proclaim the power of Christ's saving mystery, we pray: ◆ *That in the struggles of all people Christ may bring forth new life, we pray:* ◆ *That God's word may break chains of oppression and injustice, we pray:* ◆ *That the imprisoned may find reconciliation and encouragement, we pray:* ◆ *That we may live as witnesses to Christ in all that we do, we pray:* ◆

Our Father . . .

God of life eternal,
By the cross you have raised
all humanity to glory in Christ.
Reform us in his image,
that we may remain faithful
    to our call
and so reign with him
    in eternity,
for Christ is Lord
forever and ever. Amen.

✦ *In you, O LORD, we take refuge:*
For you are our rock, our stronghold.

✠ *In you, O LORD, we take refuge:*
   For you are our rock, our stronghold.

PSALM 71   *page 416*

READING   *John 12:23–26*

Jesus said to his disciples, "The hour has come for the Son of Man to be glorified. Very truly, I tell you, unless a grain of wheat falls into the earth and dies, it remains just a single grain; but if it dies, it bears much fruit. Those who love their life lose it, and those who hate their life in this world will keep it for eternal life. Whoever serves me must follow me, and where I am, there will my servant be also. Whoever serves me, the Father will honor."

REFLECTION   *John Chrysostom*

O seed by which the world was made, through which darkness was dispersed and the Church brought into being! In this seed hanging on the cross was such tremendous power that by a mere word, though bound itself, it snatched the thief from his cross and transported him to the joy of paradise. This seed, its side pierced by a spear, poured out for the thirsty an immortal drink. This mustard seed, taken down from the cross and planted in a garden, branched out over the whole world. This mustard seed sown in a garden sent its roots down to Hades, gathered together the souls that were there, and after three days raised them with itself to heaven.

PRAYERS   *others may be added*

Ready to give ourselves in service of the Gospel, we pray:

◆ Free us, who trust in you.

That the people of God may bear a great harvest of justice for all people, we pray: ◆ *That the baptized may be faithful followers of the Son of Man, we pray:* ◆ *That those who offer themselves in the service of others may receive the Father's honor, we pray:* ◆ *That those who sleep in the earth may be gathered into the eternal harvest, we pray:* ◆ *That we may seek only the glory of the cross, we pray:* ◆

Our Father . . .

Divine Sower,
as a grain of wheat
cast into the ground,
so the Son of Man was planted
to yield the harvest of life.
Give us courage to follow
where Christ has led,
that we may yield
the fruit of faithfulness,
a bounty of good works,
to the glory of your name,
for you live and reign
forever and ever. Amen.

✠ *In you, O LORD, we take refuge:*
   For you are our rock, our stronghold.

✝ *In you, O LORD, we take refuge:*
For you are our rock, our stronghold.

PSALM 71   *page 416*

READING   *John 14:1–6*

Jesus said to his disciples, "Do not let your hearts be troubled. Believe in God, believe also in me. In my Father's house there are many dwelling places. If it were not so, would I have told you that I go to prepare a place for you? And if I go and prepare a place for you, I will come again and will take you to myself, so that where I am, there you may be also. And you know the way to the place where I am going." Thomas said to him, "Lord, we do not know where you are going. How can we know the way?" Jesus said to him, "I am the way, and the truth, and the life. No one comes to the Father except through me."

REFLECTION

We leave the readings from the Masses for the Dead with a final assurance: Though we do not know where we are going—both in life and in death—Christ is our guide. If we keep our eyes fixed on Jesus' path, we can be confident that we will at last reach our heavenly dwelling place.

PRAYERS   *others may be added*

Finding comfort for our troubled hearts, we pray:

◆ Free us, who trust in you.

That God's people may follow Christ's way in hope, we pray: ◆ That all nations may find the path of salvation, we pray: ◆ That Christ's life and truth may renew the world in justice and peace, we pray: ◆ That those whose hearts are troubled may find comfort and hope, we pray: ◆ That the dead may be guided to heavenly glory, we pray: ◆ That we may trust in the one who is way, truth and life, we pray: ◆

Our Father . . .

Father of Jesus, God of all,
you have prepared a place
   for all people
in your heavenly household.
Guide us by Christ our way.
Enlighten us by Christ our truth.
Deliver us by Christ our life.
May we never lose hope
but live always in confidence,
secure in Jesus Christ,
Lord forever and ever. Amen.

✝ *In you, O LORD, we take refuge:*
For you are our rock, our stronghold.

✦ *In you, O LORD, we take refuge:*
For you are our rock, our stronghold.

PSALM 71   page 416

READING   Hebrews 10:11–14, 18

Every priest stands day after day at his service, offering again and again the same sacrifices that can never take away sins. But when Christ had offered for all time a single sacrifice for sins, "he sat down at the right hand of God," and since then has been waiting "until his enemies would be made a footstool for his feet." For by a single offering he has perfected for all time those who are sanctified. Where there is forgiveness of these, there is no longer any offering for sin.

REFLECTION

Though we speak often of God's mercy and forgiveness, many still fear that their own personal sin will prevent them from being admitted to eternal life. The constant sacrifices of the Jerusalem temple were expressions of this sense of unworthiness, but the author of Hebrews reminds us that our worry is unnecessary. Through his obedience Christ has brought us to God's right hand, where we find fullness of mercy. Our response is to live as those who have been forgiven.

PRAYERS   others may be added

Hoping in God's boundless mercy, we pray:

◆ Free us, who trust in you.

That God's people may offer Christ's sacrifice of obedience to God's will, we pray: ◆ That all Christians may offer the mercy they have received, we pray: ◆ That nations may be cleansed of all that is unjust, we pray: ◆ That those who feel overcome by sin may find God's mercy, we pray: ◆ That the dead may be gathered to God's right hand, we pray: ◆ That we may live as those whom God has forgiven, we pray: ◆

Our Father . . .

Source of compassion,
Boundless is your mercy,
for in Christ you have
restored us to you.
Help us to trust
in your promise of grace,
that we may bring
its reconciling power
to all in need of it.
We ask this through Jesus Christ,
who lives and reigns with you,
in the unity of the Holy Spirit,
one God, now and ever. Amen.

✦ *In you, O LORD, we take refuge:*
For you are our rock, our stronghold.

✤ *In you, O LORD, we take refuge:*
For you are our rock, our stronghold.

PSALM 71   *page 416*

READING   *Revelation 1:1–2, 4–6*

The revelation of Jesus Christ, which God gave him to show his servants what must soon take place; he made it known by sending his angel to his servant John, who testified to the word of God and to the testimony of Jesus Christ, even to all that he saw. John to the seven churches that are in Asia: Grace to you and peace from him who is and who was and who is to come, and from the seven spirits who are before his throne, and from Jesus Christ, the faithful witness, the first-born of the dead, and the ruler of the kings of the earth. To him who loves us and freed us from our sins by his blood, and made us to be a kingdom, priests serving his God and Father, to him be glory and dominion forever and ever. Amen.

REFLECTION

In these last two weeks of the liturgical year, we read from Revelation, which records the visions of a seer named John. Legend has it that he was the beloved disciple from John's Gospel, who as an old man exiled on the island of Patmos received visions of the age to come. Whoever he was, the seer offers both a message of challenge and hope, perhaps to communities experiencing persecution. Revelation's vision of our eternal future is especially appropriate in these late days of November before a new Advent, when we reflect on the final act of the paschal mystery, the parousia, the return of Christ in glory.

PRAYERS   *others may be added*

A nation of priests in Jesus Christ, we pray:

◆ Free us, who trust in you.

To offer you praise and thanksgiving through the Risen One, we pray: ◆
To welcome your day of judgment with joy, we pray: ◆ *To attend to the words of your prophets and apostles, we pray:* ◆
To accept the salvation you offer in the Savior, we pray: ◆ *To live in the love and freedom of God's children, we pray:* ◆
To welcome Christ Jesus when he comes in glory, we pray: ◆

Our Father . . .

God who is, who was,
and who is to come,
with eager anticipation
we await the fullness
of Christ's revelation.
Fill us with your grace
in this time of waiting
that we may faithfully serve you,
ready to greet your Holy One
when he returns in glory,
for Christ is Lord
forever and ever. Amen.

✤ *In you, O LORD, we take refuge:*
For you are our rock, our stronghold.

✚ *In you, O LORD, we take refuge:*
For you are our rock, our stronghold.

PSALM 71 — page 416

READING — *Revelation 2:1–5*

"To the angel of the church in Ephesus write: These are the words of him who holds the seven stars in his right hand, who walks among the seven golden lampstands:

"I know your works, your toil and your patient endurance. I know that you cannot tolerate evildoers; you have tested those who claim to be apostles but are not, and have found them to be false. I also know that you are enduring patiently and bearing up for the sake of my name, and that you have not grown weary. But I have this against you, that you have abandoned the love you had at first. Remember then from what you have fallen; repent, and do the works you did at first. If not, I will come to you and remove your lampstand from its place, unless you repent."

REFLECTION

The first part of Revelation is filled with warnings for the ancient Christian churches, calling them back to their original fervor. The church in Ephesus seems to have forgotten the love it first had; perhaps bickering and petty disputes fractured it, as they have in so many Christian communities. Indeed, we must always renew ourselves in love if we are to be signs of God's love for creation. If we fail in that, we fail in our baptismal mission.

PRAYERS — *others may be added*

Embracing Christ's words of support and correction, we pray:

◆ Free us, who trust in you.

That God's people may carefully discern the words and works of all who claim to speak in Christ's name, we pray: ◆
That those who have patiently suffered for Christ may be delivered, we pray: ◆
That countries and cities may not tolerate evil but cast out hatred in all its forms, we pray: ◆ *That the One who holds the stars in his hands may greet the dead on Judgment Day, we pray:* ◆ *That we may repent of stinginess and apathy and so share the love Christ has offered us, we pray:* ◆

Our Father . . .

God of heavenly glory,
in every time and place
your saints have patiently awaited
    Christ's return.
Renew in us the love
we inherited at baptism,
that it may bear fruit for eternal life
to be harvested on the day of glory,
when the One who holds
all creation in his hand
will reign unto the endless
    ages of ages. Amen.

✚ *In you, O LORD, we take refuge:*
For you are our rock, our stronghold.

✠ *In you, O LORD, we take refuge:*
For you are our rock, our stronghold.

PSALM 71   *page 416*

READING   *Revelation 3:1–6*

"And to the angel of the church in Sardis write: These are the words of him who has the seven spirits of God and the seven stars:

"I know your works; you have a name of being alive, but you are dead. Wake up, and strengthen what remains and is on the point of death, for I have not found your works perfect in the sight of my God. Remember then what you received and heard; obey it, and repent. If you do not wake up, I will come like a thief, and you will not know at what hour I will come to you. Yet you have still a few persons in Sardis who have not soiled their clothes; they will walk with me, dressed in white, for they are worthy. If you conquer, you will be clothed like them in white robes, and I will not blot your name out of the book of life; I will confess your name before my Father and before his angels. Let anyone who has an ear listen to what the Spirit is saying to the churches."

REFLECTION

Because so many of us were baptized as infants, perhaps we have forgotten the meaning of the "clothes" that God's messenger claims that the Sardisians have soiled. At our Baptism we were all clothed in the alb (meaning "white garment") as new creations in Christ. When we received it, the presider charged us to "bring it unstained to the judgment seat of our Lord Jesus Christ, so that you may have everlasting life" (RCIA, 229). Baptism carries great responsibilities; today's passage challenges us to keep them always in mind.

PRAYERS   *others may be added*

Seeking to bring our garments unstained to the wedding banquet, we pray:

◆ Free us, who trust in you.

From laziness in living the Gospel, we pray: ◆ *From apathy in doing good works, we pray:* ◆ *From the stains of injustice and sin, we pray:* ◆ *From closing our ears to the Spirit's message, we pray:* ◆ *From inattention to the word of God, we pray:* ◆ *From disobedience to God's will, we pray:* ◆ *From wandering from the path of discipleship, we pray:* ◆

Our Father . . .

God of holiness,
in Baptism we were
made clean by the blood of the Lamb.
Wake us from our apathy,
and keep us faithful
to the path of discipleship,
that on the day of salvation
we may take our place
among your saints in glory,
worshiping around your throne
forever and ever. Amen.

✠ *In you, O LORD, we take refuge:*
For you are our rock, our stronghold.

✛ *In you, O LORD, we take refuge:*
For you are our rock, our stronghold.

PSALM 71 — page 416

READING — *Colossians 3:12–17*

As God's chosen ones, holy and beloved, clothe yourselves with compassion, kindness, humility, meekness, and patience. Bear with one another and, if anyone has a complaint against another, forgive each other; just as the Lord has forgiven you, so you also must forgive. Above all, clothe yourselves with love, which binds everything together in perfect harmony. And let the peace of Christ rule in your hearts, to which indeed you were called in the one body. And be thankful. Let the word of Christ dwell in you richly; teach and admonish one another in all wisdom; and with gratitude in your hearts sing psalms, hymns, and spiritual songs to God. And whatever you do, in word or deed, do everything in the name of the Lord Jesus, giving thanks to God the Father through him.

REFLECTION

Colossians reminds us of the spiritual gifts we can never have enough of: compassion, kindness, humility, meekness, patience. While an abundance of food and drink and good company provides passing pleasure, the spiritual gifts of which the reading speaks offer lasting peace.

PRAYERS — *others may be added*

Blessing God for the goodness we have received, we cry out:

◆ Thanks be to God!

For communities of faith, we pray: ◆
For wisdom among our leaders,
we pray: ◆ *For peace in our land,*
we pray: ◆ *For parents and siblings,*
friends and neighbors, we pray: ◆
For an abundance of food and fellowship,
we pray: ◆ *For those who go without,*
we pray: ◆ *For comfort in times of*
sorrow, we pray: ◆ *For rich mercy and*
gentle kindness, we pray: ◆

Our Father . . .

We give you thanks,
God of creation,
for you fill our lives
with an abundance of gifts.
Open our eyes to see
your providence at work among us,
that we may in turn share
    with those in need
the abundance we have received.
We give you thanks, God of creation,
through Jesus Christ our Savior.
Amen.

✛ *In you, O LORD, we take refuge:*
For you are our rock, our stronghold.

✚ *In you, O LORD, we take refuge:*
   For you are our rock, our stronghold.

PSALM 71   *page 416*

READING   *Revelation 3:14–19*

"And to the angel of the church in Laodicea write: The words of the Amen, the faithful and true witness, the origin of God's creation:

"I know your works; you are neither cold nor hot. I wish that you were either cold or hot. So, because you are lukewarm, and neither cold nor hot, I am about to spit you out of my mouth. For you say, 'I am rich, I have prospered, and I need nothing.' You do not realize that you are wretched, pitiable, poor, blind, and naked. Therefore I counsel you to buy from me gold refined by fire so that you may be rich; and white robes to clothe you and to keep the shame of your nakedness from being seen; and salve to anoint your eyes so that you may see. I reprove and discipline those whom I love. Be earnest, therefore, and repent."

REFLECTION

It is easy to be deluded by wealth and security; at such times we are tempted to rest on our laurels and pat ourselves on the back. The heavenly messenger shatters the illusion of self-sufficiency; indeed, as long as any members of the Body are poor and naked, we are as well. And if we are unable to see and respond to those in need because of the protection of wealth, we suffer true blindness of the soul.

PRAYERS   *others may be added*

Earnest to repent, we pray:

◆ Free us, who trust in you.

That the Church may accept Christ's loving discipline, we pray: ◆ *That the baptized may be blazing signs of God's justice, we pray:* ◆ *That Jesus' disciples may be zealous in living the Gospel, we pray:* ◆ *That the world's people may seek eternal riches, we pray:* ◆ *That those blinded by worldly desires may accept Christ's healing salve, we pray:* ◆
That we may open the door to Christ when he appears in our sisters and brothers, we pray: ◆

Our Father . . .

Fire of the prophets,
in Jesus you call us
to single-hearted service,
that we may burn brightly
    with your glory.
Heal our divided hearts,
torn between this world
and the world to come.
Give us hearts filled with zeal for
    your reign,
that our lives may reveal
our commitment to Jesus Christ,
the Amen and true witness,
who lives and reigns
forever and ever. Amen.

✚ *In you, O LORD, we take refuge:*
   For you are our rock, our stronghold.

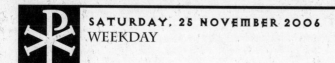

✠ *In you, O LORD, we take refuge:*
For you are our rock, our stronghold.

PSALM 71 *page 416*

READING *Revelation 4:1–4, 6a*

After this I looked, and there in heaven a door stood open! And the first voice, which I had heard speaking to me like a trumpet, said, "Come up here, and I will show you what must take place after this." At once I was in the spirit, and there in heaven stood a throne, with one seated on the throne! And the one seated there looks like jasper and carnelian, and around the throne is a rainbow that looks like an emerald. Around the throne are twenty-four thrones, and seated on the thrones are twenty-four elders, dressed in white robes, with golden crowns on their heads; and in front of the throne there is something like a sea of glass, like crystal.

REFLECTION

Of the seer's many visions, the poetic descriptions of God's dwelling place are perhaps most appealing—more inviting than the plagues and avenging angels that appear later, anyway! Revelation's symbols are meant to encourage us; the heavenly city is a place of great beauty, where a God of still greater beauty stands ready to welcome the holy ones.

PRAYERS *others may be added*

Longing for the glory of God's dwelling place, we pray:

◆ Free us, who trust in you.

That God's people may hope in the glory that awaits them, we pray: ◆ *That God's beauty may bring the world to faith, we pray:* ◆ *That God's Spirit may inspire the hopeless with a vision of what is yet to come, we pray:* ◆ *That the divine call may wake the dead to glory, we pray:* ◆ *That we may behold the heavenly city on the day of salvation, we pray:* ◆

Our Father . . .

Beautiful Ruler of heaven,
your glory outshines all things
for you are creation's source.
Fill us with wonder
before your glorious presence,
that we may recognize you
when we stand before you face to face.
We make our prayer
through the Savior,
who is seated in glory
at your right hand
now and forever. Amen.

✠ *In you, O LORD, we take refuge:*
For you are our rock, our stronghold.

✝ *In you, O LORD, we take refuge,*
for you are our rock, our stronghold.

PSALM 71 *page 416*

READING *John 18:33b–37*

Pilate asked Jesus, "Are you the King of the Jews?" Jesus answered, "Do you ask this on your own, or did others tell you about me?" Pilate replied, "I am not a Jew, am I? Your own nation and the chief priests have handed you over to me. What have you done?" Jesus answered, "My kingdom is not from this world. If my kingdom were from this world, my followers would be fighting to keep me from being handed over to the Jews. But as it is, my kingdom is not from here." Pilate asked him, "So you are a king?" Jesus answered, "You say that I am a king. For this I was born, and for this I came into the world, to testify to the truth. Everyone who belongs to the truth listens to my voice."

REFLECTION *John Chrysostom*

Do you not know that the cross symbolizes the kingdom? If you desire further proof, it lies in the fact that the cross did not leave Christ earthbound, but lifted him up and carried him back to heaven. We know this because at his glorious second coming the cross will be with him. He called it his glory to teach you how sacred it is. "When the Son of Man comes, the sun will be darkened and the moon will not give its light." Such a blaze of light will there be that even the brightest stars will be eclipsed. "Then the stars will fall, and the sign of the Son of Man will appear in heaven." So you see the power of the sign of the cross!

PRAYERS *others may be added*

Taking up the cross of Christ the King, we pray:

◆ Free us, who trust in you.

That the Church of Christ may proclaim the one who reigns from the cross, we pray: ◆ That the followers of Jesus may live as citizens of the world to come, we pray: ◆ That worldly power may give way to divine wisdom, we pray: ◆ That the rule of Christ may lift up the lowly and the poor, we pray: ◆ That we may live in faithfulness to the truth that comes from above, we pray: ◆

Our Father . . .

God of the beginning and the end,
soon and very soon
your Only-Begotten Son will return
to establish your reign
    of justice forever.
Hear us as we keep vigil
for Christ's coming:
Make of us a priestly people,
a royal gathering of your children.
May we live in this day
as citizens of the eternal future,
when Christ will be all in all,
for he lives and reigns with you,
in the unity of the Holy Spirit,
one God, forever and ever. Amen.

✝ *In you, O LORD, we take refuge,*
for you are our rock, our stronghold.

✠ *In you, O LORD, we take refuge:*
For you are our rock, our stronghold.

PSALM 71   *page 416*

READING   *Revelation 4:6b–8*

Around the throne, and on each side of the throne, are four living creatures, full of eyes in front and behind: the first living creature like a lion, the second living creature like an ox, the third living creature with a face like a human face, and the fourth living creature like a flying eagle. And the four living creatures, each of them with six wings, are full of eyes all around and inside. Day and night without ceasing they sing, "Holy, holy, holy, the Lord God the Almighty, who was and is and is to come."

REFLECTION

The strange creatures described in today's passage—described also in a passage from the prophet Ezekiel—were later interpreted to represent the four Gospel writers. Saint Matthew is represented by the creature with the human face, since he begins the Gospel with an account of Jesus' human ancestry. The lion creature represents Saint Mark, whose account begins in the wilderness. Since Saint Luke begins in the Jerusalem temple—a place of sacrifice—and with a birth in a place where farm animals lived, the ox is his symbol. Finally, Saint John, whose theology soars above all the others, is embodied in the flying eagle.

PRAYERS   *others may be added*

Joining the chorus of angels and saints, we pray:

◆ Free us, who trust in you.

That priests and presiders may lead God's people in giving thanks and praise to God, we pray: ◆ *That cantors and musicians may lead the baptized in joyful song, we pray:* ◆ *That all people of faith may join together in worship of the Creator, we pray:* ◆ *That all creation may praise God in beauty, we pray:* ◆ *That we may join the heavenly beings in praising God with lives of dedication and commitment, we pray:* ◆

Our Father . . .

God of heaven and earth,
a vast throng surrounds your throne,
voicing one mighty song of praise.
By the prayers of saints and angels,
fill us with thankful harmonies,
that we may one day
join the heavenly assembly,
who dances forever before you
led by Christ the choirmaster,
who is Lord forever and ever. Amen.

✠ *In you, O LORD, we take refuge:*
For you are our rock, our stronghold.

✙ *In you, O LORD, we take refuge:*
  For you are our rock, our stronghold.

PSALM 71   *page 416*

READING   *Revelation 5:6–10*

Then I saw between the throne and the four living creatures and among the elders a Lamb standing as if it had been slaughtered, having seven horns and seven eyes, which are the seven spirits of God sent out into all the earth. He went and took the scroll from the right hand of the one who was seated on the throne. When he had taken the scroll, the four living creatures and the twenty-four elders fell before the Lamb, each holding a harp and golden bowls full of incense, which are the prayers of the saints. They sing a new song: "You are worthy to take the scroll and to open its seals, for you were slaughtered and by your blood you ransomed for God saints from every tribe and language and people and nation; you have made them to be a kingdom and priests serving our God, and they will reign on earth."

REFLECTION   *Augustine of Hippo*

My dear brothers and sisters, sons and daughters, fruit of the true faith and holy seed of heaven, all you who have been born again in Christ and whose life is from above, listen to me; or rather, listen to the Holy Spirit saying through me: Sing to the Lord a new song. Look, you tell me, I am singing. Yes indeed, you are singing; you are singing clearly, I can hear you. But make sure that your life does not contradict your words. Sing with your voices, your hearts, your lips, and your lives: Sing to the Lord a new song.

PRAYERS   *others may be added*

Ransomed by the blood of the Lamb, we pray:

◆ Free us, who trust in you.

That God's people may declare Christ's saving death to all the world's people, we pray: ◆ *That the baptized may raise their voices in prayer, we pray:* ◆ *That people of every language, culture, and way of life may be gathered into God's reign, we pray:* ◆ *That those who have shared Christ's suffering may join him in glory, we pray:* ◆ *That our payers may rise like incense before God's throne, we pray:* ◆

Our Father . . .

Worthy are you,
Christ our Savior,
to open the scroll
and break its seals,
inaugurating on earth
the reign of our God.
Pour out upon us
    your Spirit,
that we might offer praise acceptable
    to the Eternal One,
now and forever. Amen.

✙ *In you, O LORD, we take refuge:*
  For you are our rock, our stronghold.

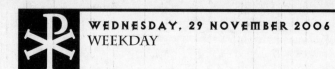
✛ *In you, O LORD, we take refuge:*
For you are our rock, our stronghold.

PSALM 71 *page 416*

READING *Revelation 14:1–3, 4b–5*

Then I looked, and there was the Lamb, standing on Mount Zion! And with him were one hundred forty-four thousand who had his name and his Father's name written on their foreheads. And I heard a voice from heaven like the sound of many waters and like the sound of loud thunder; the voice I heard was like the sound of harpists playing on their harps, and they sing a new song before the throne and before the four living creatures and before the elders. No one could learn that song except the one hundred forty-four thousand who have been redeemed from the earth. These follow the Lamb wherever he goes. They have been redeemed from humankind as first fruits for God and the Lamb, and in their mouth no lie was found; they are blameless.

REFLECTION

Some believe this passage refers to the number who will finally be redeemed. Yet, as the author points out, the 144,000 are merely the first fruits of redeemed humanity, the beginning of what will be an even greater multitude, for God desires the salvation of all people. The company of the saints is not an elite crowd but a countless multitude praising God in all the languages of creation.

PRAYERS *others may be added*

Hoping to be made blameless before God, we pray:

◆ Free us, who trust in you.

To follow Christ wherever he goes, we pray: ◆ *To learn the songs of those who praise you, we pray:* ◆ *To take our place in the heavenly chorus, we pray:* ◆ *To lead every people to the eternal banquet, we pray:* ◆ *To be gathered with the saints in the New Jerusalem, we pray:* ◆ *To found blameless on the day of judgment, we pray:* ◆

Our Father . . .

Mighty God,
you are worthy of praise
and all creation will someday
  sing of your glory.
Mark us with your holy name
and with the sign of the Lamb
that we may be counted
  among the righteous
singing before you on Mount Zion,
where the Christ the Lamb
lives and reigns now and forever.
Amen.

✛ *In you, O LORD, we take refuge:*
For you are our rock, our stronghold.

✠ *Alleluia! Christ is risen!*
Christ is risen indeed!
Alleluia! Alleluia!

PSALM 34   *page 412*

READING   *Romans 10:9–11,*
14–15, 17–18

If you confess with your lips that Jesus is Lord and believe in your heart that God raised him from the dead, you will be saved. For one believes with the heart and so is justified, and one confesses with the mouth and so is saved. The scripture says, "No one who believes in him will be put to shame." But how are they to call on one in whom they have not believed? And how are they to believe in one of whom they have never heard? And how are they to hear without someone to proclaim him? And how are they to proclaim him unless they are sent? As it is written, "How beautiful are the feet of those who bring good news!" So faith comes from what is heard, and what is heard comes through the word of Christ. But I ask, have they not heard? Indeed they have; for "Their voice has gone out to all the earth, and their words to the ends of the world."

REFLECTION

Having praised Christ as king of all creation—though one who reigns from the cross, and whose power lies not in military might but in forgiveness—we now honor one who proclaimed such a king. Like the messengers and pages of ancient rulers, the apostles were sent forth with a message, one so wonderful that even the feet of the bearer are beautiful!

PRAYERS   *others may be added*

Eager to be God's heralds, we pray:

◆ Turn to us, Lord of life!

That the apostles of our time may carry Christ's word to all nations, we pray: ◆ *That the disciples of Jesus may embrace and live his Gospel, we pray:* ◆ *That the power of Christ's Resurrection may prepare the world for its final glorious destiny, we pray:* ◆ *That those who hear the Good News may respond in faith, we pray:* ◆ *That our faith in Christ's Resurrection may give us hope in the fullness of his glory, we pray:* ◆

Our Father . . .

God of mission,
you send us out to proclaim the love
poured out in Christ's cross
and made alive in the Resurrection.
Make us heralds of the Savior,
and open the hearts of those
who do not yet believe,
that on the coming day of glory
all the earth may share
new life in Christ,
who is Lord forever and ever. Amen.

✠ *Alleluia! Christ is risen!*
Christ is risen indeed!
Alleluia! Alleluia!

✛ *In you, O LORD, we take refuge:*
  For you are our rock, our stronghold.

PSALM 71   page 416

READING   *Revelation 14:14–19*

Then I looked, and there was a white cloud, and seated on the cloud was one like the Son of Man, with a golden crown on his head, and a sharp sickle in his hand! Another angel came out of the temple, calling with a loud voice to the one who sat on the cloud, "Use your sickle and reap, for the hour to reap has come, because the harvest of the earth is fully ripe." So the one who sat on the cloud swung his sickle over the earth, and the earth was reaped. Then another angel came out of the temple in heaven, and he too had a sharp sickle. Then another angel came out from the altar, the angel who has authority over fire, and he called with a loud voice to him who had the sharp sickle, "Use your sharp sickle and gather the clusters of the vine of the earth, for its grapes are ripe." So the angel swung his sickle over the earth and gathered the vintage of the earth, and he threw it into the great wine press of the wrath of God.

REFLECTION

The image of harvest is often a comforting one, with grain bins full and grapes ready to be pressed into new wine. Revelation's vision is a bit more alarming; after all, it's us believers who are about to be "reaped." At the time of Revelation's writing, Christians were beginning to face the persecution that would dog them intermittently for almost three centuries. The seer in this passage looks forward to the day when the persecutors would get theirs! It may not be the most "Christian" of visions, but it's understandable!

PRAYERS   *others may be added*

Longing to be gathered into the eternal harvest, we pray:

◆ Free us, who trust in you.

That Christ may reap in the baptized a rich harvest of justice and mercy, we pray: ◆ *That the wine press of God's wrath may cleanse the world of war and violence, we pray:* ◆ *That the lowly and oppressed may be exalted on the coming day of God, we pray:* ◆ *That the harvester's sickle may slash the bonds of death, we pray:* ◆

Our Father . . .

God of fire,
the day is coming
when your angels will
gather the just into your barns.
Bless us with favor
in this time of growth,
that on harvest day
we may yield a hundred-fold
and produce a fine vintage
for the heavenly banquet,
where the Lord of the harvest
lives and reigns forever and ever.
Amen.

✛ *In you, O LORD, we take refuge:*
  For you are our rock, our stronghold.

✚ *In you, O LORD, we take refuge:*
  For you are our rock, our stronghold.

PSALM 71 *page 416*

READING *Revelation 22:1–5*

Then the angel showed me the river of the water of life, bright as crystal, flowing from the throne of God and of the Lamb through the middle of the street of the city. On either side of the river is the tree of life with its twelve kinds of fruit, producing its fruit each month; and the leaves of the tree are for the healing of the nations. Nothing accursed will be found there any more. But the throne of God and of the Lamb will be in it, and his servants will worship him; they will see his face, and his name will be on their foreheads. And there will be no more night; they need no light of lamp or sun, for the Lord God will be their light, and they will reign forever and ever.

REFLECTION

As the liturgical year comes to a close, we are treated with a vision of the age to come, one well worth carrying with us as the nights lengthen and winter's cold sets in. Then time will give way to eternity; sin's drought will give way to a river of mercy; war's wounds will be soothed with healing herbs; God's glory will light the heavenly city. Then at last we will behold the living God; at last we will know Christ's fullness; at last we will rejoice in the completion of God's reign.

PRAYERS *others may be added*

Trusting in the glorious future that awaits us, we pray:

◆ Free us, who trust in you.

That the Church may be a source of living water flowing out to refresh the world, we pray: ◆ *That the nations may be healed of the wounds of war and injustice, we pray:* ◆ *That God's light may cast out doubt and fear from among all people, we pray:* ◆ *That the sick may find comfort in the promise of life eternal, we pray:* ◆ *That we may return at last to the garden of paradise for all eternity, we pray:* ◆

Our Father . . .

Source of light and life,
a garden of paradise
awaits your holy ones—
a place of refreshment
and healing for eternity.
Fill us with hope
as we await that day
when all people will be gathered
into your new creation,
praising you together with the Lamb,
in the eternal light of your face,
forever and ever. Amen.

✚ *In you, O LORD, we take refuge:*
  For you are our rock, our stronghold.

✛ *Maranatha! Come, Lord Jesus!*

PSALM 85   *page 417*

READING   *Jeremiah 33:14–16*

The days are surely coming, says the LORD, when I will fulfill the promise I made to the house of Israel and the house of Judah. In those days and at that time I will cause a righteous Branch to spring up for David; and he shall execute justice and righteousness in the land. In those days Judah will be saved and Jerusalem will live in safety. And this is the name by which it will be called: "The LORD is our righteousness."

REFLECTION

As the liturgical year turns and begins once again, we come to the season of expectation, waiting, and hope. However, Advent begins, not in expectation for the birth of a baby, but for the return of our Messiah. Jeremiah describes the coming of an adult, one who will bring justice and righteousness to the land. Jeremiah's prophecy has themes similar to the Arthurian legends, both of which describe the coming of a ruler from the royal line. In the Christian imagination, that ruler, Christ, will come with divine glory, authority, and power.

PRAYERS   *others may be added*

Awaiting the return of the Just One, we cry out:

◆ Come quickly, Lord of glory!

To answer the prayers of God's hopeful people, we cry out: ◆ *To gather the house of Israel into the eternal Jerusalem, we cry out:* ◆ *To deliver the nations from fear and upheaval, we cry out:* ◆ *To bring justice and righteousness to the poor and outcast, we cry out:* ◆ *To fulfill our hope in the promise of God Most High, we pray:* ◆

Our Father . . .

God our deliverance,
you promise a righteous Branch,
a child of David's line,
to restore your people to peace.
Send us the Just One
with salvation in his hand,
that on the coming day
we may rise up with joy
    to praise you,
the LORD our righteousness,
one God, Father, Son,
and Holy Spirit, forever and ever.
Amen.

✛ *Maranatha! Come, Lord Jesus!*

✦ *Maranatha! Come, Lord Jesus!*

PSALM 85   *page 417*

READING   *Isaiah 2:2–4*

In days to come
   the mountain of the Lord's house
shall be established as the highest
      of the mountains,
   and shall be raised above the hills;
all the nations shall stream to it.
   Many peoples shall come and say,
"Come, let us go up to the mountain
      of the LORD,
   to the house of the God of Jacob;
that he may teach us his ways
   and that we may walk in his paths."
For out of Zion shall go forth
      instruction,
   and the word of the LORD
      from Jerusalem.
He shall judge between the nations,
   and shall arbitrate
      for many peoples;
they shall beat their swords
      into plowshares,
   and their spears into pruning hooks;
nation shall not lift up sword
      against nation,
   neither shall they learn war
      any more.

REFLECTION

Last Saturday was the anniversary of the murder of Maura Clarke, Ita Ford, Dorothy Kazel, and Jean Donovan—four women who worked to bring Isaiah's vision to reality among the poor of El Salvador. Although the students of war silenced them, their work for peace and right relationship surely continues to bear fruit, and our confidence in God's promised day of salvation assures us that, in Christ, these four holy martyrs will certainly triumph, along with the struggling poor they served.

PRAYERS   *others may be added*

With hearts open to the ways of our God, we cry out:

◆ Come quickly, Lord of glory!

To gather the Church on God's holy mountain, we cry out: ◆ *To bring all people into the one household of God, we cry out:* ◆ *To beat swords into plowshares and pruning hooks, we cry out:* ◆ *To wipe out hatred among nations, we cry out:* ◆ *To guide the feet of the weary on the path to rest, we cry out:* ◆ *To teach our hearts the ways of salvation, we cry out:* ◆

Our Father . . .

Just Judge of the nations,
the day of Christ's glory
will bring justice for the poor
and an end to violence.
Give us a foretaste of that day
as we long for its fullness
that even now we may labor
to bring its promise to life.
We ask this through Jesus Christ,
who is coming in glory. Amen.

✦ *Maranatha! Come, Lord Jesus!*

✦ *Maranatha! Come, Lord Jesus!*

PSALM 85 *page 417*

READING *Isaiah 4:2–3, 5–6*

On that day the branch of the LORD shall be beautiful and glorious, and the fruit of the land shall be the pride and glory of the survivors of Israel. Whoever is left in Zion and remains in Jerusalem will be called holy, everyone who has been recorded for life in Jerusalem. Then the LORD will create over the whole site of Mount Zion and over its places of assembly a cloud by day and smoke and the shining of a flaming fire by night. Indeed over all the glory there will be a canopy. It will serve as a pavilion, a shade by day from the heat, and a refuge and a shelter from the storm and rain.

REFLECTION

The readings from Isaiah for this first week of Advent give us a taste of what the fullness of God's reign might be like: the great multitude of humanity, gathered in peace, ruled in justice, and sheltered by God's radiant glory. While Advent is a time to wait and hope for that great day, it is also a time that calls us to a fearless evaluation of the world as it is. Isaiah gives us God's vision of what the world should be; we must commit ourselves to that vision and to making it a reality in both small and great ways, just as the holy women we remembered yesterday did.

PRAYERS *others may be added*

Longing for shelter of God's glory, we pray:

◆ Come quickly, Lord of glory!

That the Church may offer the shelter of God's compassion to all people, we pray: ◆ *That the nations may gather beneath God's canopy, we pray:* ◆ *That homeless people and refugees may find shade from heat and cold, and shelter from storm and rain, we pray:* ◆ *That the dead may behold God's shining glory in eternity, we pray:* ◆ *That we may be counted among the survivors of Israel, we pray:* ◆

Our Father . . .

Shelter of Israel,
your presence surrounds your people,
covering them with your protection.
Hear our cries for deliverance
in this time of expectation,
and strengthen us in our waiting
that we may be among those recorded
for life
and counted with your holy ones.
We ask this through our Savior
Jesus Christ,
whose coming we await. Amen.

✦ *Maranatha! Come, Lord Jesus!*

✤ *Maranatha! Come, Lord Jesus!*

PSALM 85 *page 417*

READING *Isaiah 30:19–21, 23–25a, 26*

Truly, O people in Zion, inhabitants of Jerusalem, you shall weep no more. God will surely be gracious to you at the sound of your cry; when he hears it, he will answer you. Though the Lord may give you the bread of adversity and the water of affliction, yet your Teacher will not hide himself any more, but your eyes shall see your Teacher. And when you turn to the right or when you turn to the left, your ears shall hear a word behind you, saying, "This is the way; walk in it."

He will give rain for the seed with which you sow the ground, and grain, the produce of the ground, which will be rich and plenteous. On that day your cattle will graze in broad pastures; and the oxen and donkeys that till the ground will eat silage, which has been winnowed with shovel and fork. On every lofty mountain and every high hill there will be brooks running with water. Moreover the light of the moon will be like the light of the sun, and the light of the sun will be sevenfold, like the light of seven days, on the day when the LORD binds up the injuries of his people, and heals the wounds inflicted by his blow.

REFLECTION

We are accompanied in our journey through Advent by many saints. Today we honor Saint Nicholas, a bishop of Myra (in modern Turkey) during the fourth century. Many legends surround his life and ministry—including that he fasted on Wednesdays and Fridays from birth! Many of the stories about him tell of his concern for the poor. Our modern folk character Santa Claus, whose lineage includes Saint Nicholas, would benefit from an infusion of Nicholas's service to those in need.

PRAYERS *others may be added*

The dominion of righteousness and justice approaches; in hope, we pray:

◆ Come quickly, Lord of glory!

For bishops who seek first the good of the poor, we pray: ◆ *For world leaders who guarantee justice for all, we pray:* ◆ *For judges who defend the rights of the unjustly accused, we pray:* ◆ *For teachers who guide children in right paths, we pray:* ◆ *For those who give comfort to the harried and weary, we pray:* ◆ *For all who serve the needy, we pray:* ◆

Our Father . . .

God of holy bishops,
your servant Nicholas
was an anchor for the needy
and a model of Christian virtue.
By his example and prayer
inspire us with concern for the poor
and love of justice,
that we may be a shelter for the weary
and hope for the oppressed.
This we ask in Jesus' name. Amen.

✤ *Maranatha! Come, Lord Jesus!*

✦ *Maranatha! Come, Lord Jesus!*

PSALM 85 *page 417*

READING *Isaiah 32:1–6*

See, a king will reign in righteousness,
  and princes will rule with justice.
Each will be like a hiding place
    from the wind,
  a covert from the tempest,
like streams of water in a dry place,
  like the shade of a great rock
    in a weary land.
Then the eyes of those who have sight
    will not be closed,
  and the ears of those who have
    hearing will listen.
The minds of the rash will have
    good judgment,
  and the tongues of stammerers will
    speak readily and distinctly.
A fool will no longer be called noble,
  nor a villain said to be honorable.
For fools speak folly,
  and their minds plot iniquity:
to practice ungodliness,
  to utter error concerning the LORD,
to leave the craving of the hungry
    unsatisfied,
  and to deprive the thirsty of drink.

REFLECTION

Isaiah's description of what rulers will be like in God's future might elicit a wry chuckle from us today. Where would we ever find leaders "like a hiding place from the wind" or "the shade of a great rock in a weary land"? Though we may despair of ever finding politicians who fit that bill, there is nothing to prevent us from showing these qualities in our own leadership, whether in our family, our workplace, our parish, or our local community.

PRAYERS *others may be added*

Living as streams of water in dry places, we pray:

◆ Come quickly, Lord of glory!

That God's people may be a shelter for the storm-tossed and weary, we pray: ◆
That Christian leaders open eyes and ears to the good news of God's justice, we pray: ◆ *That rulers and heads of state may serve in righteousness and justice, we pray:* ◆ *That the world's people may cast aside fools and villains, we pray:* ◆
That the craving of the hungry and thirsty be filled, we pray: ◆ *That we may speak readily and distinctly of the wisdom of God, we pray:* ◆

Our Father . . .

Your justice, O God,
flows as a stream
    in dry places,
and your righteousness shields us
    from life's storm.
Give us wisdom and right judgment,
that our stammering tongues
may speak your truth,
casting down fools and villains
and raising up the poor.
We ask this through the one
whose day draws near,
our Savior Jesus Christ,
now and forever. Amen.

✦ *Maranatha! Come, Lord Jesus!*

✦ *Maranatha! Come, Lord Jesus!*

PSALM 96 *page 421*

READING *Ephesians 1:3–6, 11–12*

Blessed be the God and Father of our Lord Jesus Christ, who has blessed us in Christ with every spiritual blessing in the heavenly places, just as he chose us in Christ before the foundation of the world to be holy and blameless before him in love. He destined us for adoption as his children through Jesus Christ, according to the good pleasure of his will, to the praise of his glorious grace that he freely bestowed on us in the Beloved. In Christ we have also obtained an inheritance, having been destined according to the purpose of him who accomplishes all things according to his counsel and will, so that we, who were the first to set our hope on Christ, might live for the praise of his glory.

REFLECTION

Today we celebrate the Immaculate Conception of the mother of Jesus. In doing so, we honor Mary as one uniquely favored by God, who from the first moment of her life was without sin. Mary did nothing to earn such an honor, but when the time came she embraced the mission it entailed: to be the mother of God's eternal Word-made-flesh. Like Mary, we have done nothing to merit the blessing we have received in Christ, but our blessing too has been given for the sake of the same mission: to bring forth in our lives the Son of God.

PRAYERS *others may be added*

Chosen in Christ before the world's foundation, we cry out:

◆ Pray for us, favored one!

That the Church may boldly proclaim God's desire that all be saved, we cry out: ◆ *That God's people may give thanks for the gifts bestowed on them in Christ, we cry out:* ◆ *That the poor may know their dignity as God's beloved children, we cry out:* ◆ *That the dead who set their hope in Christ may live forever in God's presence, we cry out:* ◆ *That we may rejoice in the glory we have inherited in Christ, we cry out:* ◆

Our Father . . .

Blessed are you,
God and Father of Jesus Christ.
From before time you chose
a daughter of Israel
to bear your eternal Word.
May Mary's example
of openness and humility,
courage and faith,
inspire us to become ever more open
to the grace you offer Jesus Christ,
Son of God and of Mary,
who lives and reigns with you,
in the unity of the Holy Spirit,
one God, forever and ever. Amen.

✦ *Maranatha! Come, Lord Jesus!*

✦   *Maranatha! Come, Lord Jesus!*

PSALM 85   *page 417*

READING   *Isaiah 32:16–20*

Then justice will dwell
        in the wilderness,
and righteousness abide
        in the fruitful field.
The effect of righteousness
        will be peace,
and the result of righteousness,
        quietness and trust forever.
My people will abide
        in a peaceful habitation,
in secure dwellings,
        and in quiet resting places.
The forest will disappear completely,
        and the city will be utterly laid low.
Happy will you be who sow
        beside every stream,
who let the ox and the donkey
        range freely.

REFLECTION

*The Advent image of a "messenger to pre-
pare the way" usually calls to mind John
the Baptist. Today, however, we remember
a latter-day messenger: Juan Diego or
Cuatitlatoatzin, who was canonized by
John Paul II in 2002. Juan Diego was a
poor Native American in sixteenth-century
Mexico who had a vision of the Mother of
God as an Aztec princess. Mary entrusted
Cuatitlatoatzin with a message to the
Spanish bishop of Mexico, and eventually
confirmed her message with a sign: her
image on Juan Diego's tilma. Since then,
Our Lady of Guadalupe has become a sign
of the justice Isaiah speaks of in today's*
*passage, the justice that Juan Diego her-
alded in his own time.*

PRAYERS   *others may be added*

*Ready to carry the message of peace,
we pray:*

◆ Come quickly, Lord of glory!

*To complete the Gospel's work in God's
people, we pray:* ◆ *To bring peaceful
habitation for every people, we pray:* ◆
*To bring an end to oppression and
genocide, we pray:* ◆ *To show forth your
glory in all races and cultures, we pray:* ◆
*To replace fear and envy with quiet
trust, we pray:* ◆ *To bring justice to
the wilderness and righteousness
to the fruitful field, we pray:* ◆

Our Father . . .

God of the conquered,
your servant Juan Diego
dared to speak your message
in places of power.
Give us his faithful courage:
May our lands be sown in justice
to bear the fruit of righteousness,
that all may share earth's bounty
to the glory of your name,
for you live and reign
forever and ever. Amen.

✦   *Maranatha! Come, Lord Jesus!*

✠ *Maranatha! Come, Lord Jesus!*

PSALM 85   *page 417*

READING   *Baruch 5:1–5, 9*

Take off the garment of your sorrow
    and affliction, O Jerusalem,
    and put on forever the beauty
      of the glory from God.
Put on the robe of the righteousness
    that comes from God;
    put on your head the diadem
      of the glory of the Everlasting;
for God will show your splendor
    everywhere under heaven.
For God will give you evermore
    the name,
    "Righteous Peace, Godly Glory."
Arise, O Jerusalem, stand
    upon the height;
    look toward the east,
and see your children gathered
    from west and east
    at the word of the Holy One,
    rejoicing that God has
      remembered them.
For God will lead Israel with joy,
    in the light of his glory,
    with the mercy and righteousness
      that come from him.

REFLECTION

The prophet Baruch, read only a few times during the liturgical year, offers stirring words of hope. The prophet addresses Israel's ancient exiles, and today's refugees, migrants, and other displaced persons would no doubt find comfort in such a promise. We can all look forward to the day when those driven from home will come streaming back at the call of the Most High.

PRAYERS   *others may be added*

    Confident that God remembers us,
    we pray:

◆ Come quickly, Lord of glory!

To robe your people in righteousness, we pray: ◆ *To rend the garments of sorrow and affliction, we pray:* ◆ *To lead the nations by the light of glory, we pray:* ◆ *To gather the poor from east and west, we pray:* ◆ *To restore children to parents, we pray:* ◆ *To rejoice in the beauty of God's glory, we pray:* ◆ *To crown us with the glory of the Everlasting, we pray:* ◆

Our Father . . .

God of everlasting beauty,
you promise a crown of justice
and a robe of righteousness.
Raise us to the heights,
that we may behold your children,
gathered from east and west,
journeying toward the holy city,
where Christ lives and reigns with you,
in the unity of the Holy Spirit,
one God, forever and ever. Amen.

✠ *Maranatha! Come, Lord Jesus!*

✝ *Maranatha! Come, Lord Jesus!*

PSALM 85 *page 417*

READING *Luke 1:5–10*

In the days of King Herod of Judea, there was a priest named Zechariah, who belonged to the priestly order of Abijah. His wife was a descendant of Aaron, and her name was Elizabeth. Both of them were righteous before God, living blamelessly according to all the commandments and regulations of the Lord. But they had no children, because Elizabeth was barren, and both were getting on in years.

Once when he was serving as priest before God and his section was on duty, he was chosen by lot, according to the custom of the priesthood, to enter the sanctuary of the Lord and offer incense. Now at the time of the incense offering, the whole assembly of the people was praying outside.

REFLECTION

Beginning today and for the next two weeks, we will read from the beginning of the Gospel of Luke, which describes the events that led up to the births of John the Baptist and Jesus. This may seem like an early turn toward Bethlehem in this second week of Advent, but Luke's early narratives are really a summary of his entire Gospel. Not only does the evangelist introduce the main characters—John the Baptist and Jesus—he introduces the themes of his account of the Good News: salvation for all, the raising up of the poor and hungry, and God's faithfulness to Israel.

PRAYERS *others may be added*

Seeking to live blamelessly before our God, we pray:

◆ Come quickly, Lord of glory!

To make of the Church a pleasing offering to God, we pray: ◆ *To instill righteousness in priests and ministers, we pray:* ◆ *To sanctify the rulers of the earth, we pray:* ◆ *To bring new life to those barren in spirit, we pray:* ◆ *To give hope to those getting on in years, we pray:* ◆ *To bless those who walk the path of justice, we pray:* ◆

Our Father . . .

Mighty God of Israel,
you are always faithful
to the chosen people
and raise up among them
holy and blameless women and men.
Fill us with the faithfulness
of Elizabeth and Zechariah,
that like them
we may witness the dawn of salvation
in Jesus the Christ,
who lives and reigns with you,
in the unity of the Holy Spirit,
one God, forever and ever. Amen.

✝ *Maranatha! Come, Lord Jesus!*

✦ *Maranatha! Come, Lord Jesus!*

PSALM 96   *page 421*

READING   *Revelation 12:1–6, 10ab*

A great portent appeared in heaven: a woman clothed with the sun, with the moon under her feet, and on her head a crown of twelve stars. She was pregnant and was crying out in birth pangs, in the agony of giving birth. Then another portent appeared in heaven: a great red dragon, with seven heads and ten horns, and seven diadems on his heads. His tail swept down a third of the stars of heaven and threw them to the earth. Then the dragon stood before the woman who was about to bear a child, so that he might devour her child as soon as it was born. And she gave birth to a son, a male child, who is to rule all the nations with a rod of iron. But her child was snatched away and taken to God and to his throne; and the woman fled into the wilderness, where she has a place prepared by God.

Then I heard a loud voice in heaven, proclaiming,

"Now have come the salvation
    and the power
  and the kingdom of our God
  and the authority of his Messiah."

REFLECTION

Today we commemorate the appearance of the Mother of God to Juan Diego, a poor Native American whose people had been conquered by Europeans and whose culture had been practically destroyed. Appearing as an Aztec princess, Mary brought a message of hope to a conquered people, as well as a warning to their conquerors: God chooses the side of the oppressed and casts down the powerful. It is the same message Mary of Nazareth proclaimed in both her words and her life.

PRAYERS   *others may be added*

Awaiting with joy for the coming of God among us, we pray:

◆ Come quickly, Lord of glory!

For the many races and peoples that make up the household of God, we pray: ◆ *For indigenous peoples throughout the world, we pray:* ◆ *For those who face cultural annihilation or genocide, we pray:* ◆ *For those oppressed by racism and prejudice, we pray:* ◆ *For those who promote equity and peace among nations, we pray:* ◆ *For those who labor for racial justice and unity among cultures, we pray:* ◆

Our Father . . .

God of glory,
you make the Virgin Mary
a sign to the nations,
clothed with the sun
and crowned with the stars.
May the image of Mary,
once lowly but now exalted,
lead us always to her Son,
    our Messiah,
who lives and reigns
forever and ever. Amen.

✦ *Maranatha! Come, Lord Jesus!*

✠ *Maranatha! Come, Lord Jesus!*

PSALM 85   *page 417*

READING   *Luke 1:11–17*

Then there appeared to Zechariah an angel of the Lord, standing at the right side of the altar of incense. When Zechariah saw him, he was terrified; and fear overwhelmed him. But the angel said to him, "Do not be afraid, Zechariah, for your prayer has been heard. Your wife Elizabeth will bear you a son, and you will name him John. You will have joy and gladness, and many will rejoice at his birth, for he will be great in the sight of the Lord. He must never drink wine or strong drink; even before his birth he will be filled with the Holy Spirit. He will turn many of the people of Israel to the Lord their God. With the spirit and power of Elijah he will go before him, to turn the hearts of parents to their children, and the disobedient to the wisdom of the righteous, to make ready a people prepared for the Lord."

REFLECTION

At the center of the ancient Jewish religion, in the Holy of Holies itself, the angel of God addresses Zechariah the priest, one of the faithful remnants of Israel, one who, with his wife, had lived "blamelessly according to all the commandments and regulations of the Lord." And the child promised by the angel stands in a line of great Hebrew prophets: Samuel, also promised to a barren couple, and Elijah, the prophet who was expected to precede

the Messiah. From conception, John the Baptist is the forerunner who prepares the way of the Lord.

PRAYERS   *others may be added*

Struck with wonder by God's promises, we pray:

◆ Come quickly, Lord of glory!

That God's people may prepare themselves to receive the Promised One, we pray: ◆ *That the disobedient may attend to the wisdom of the righteous, we pray:* ◆ *That those burdened by grief or sorrow may know joy and gladness, we pray:* ◆ *That the fearful may be heartened by the Good News, we pray:* ◆ *That we, like John, may be filled with the Holy Spirit of Jesus, we pray:* ◆

Our Father . . .

God of prophets,
when the time was right
you raised up a new Elijah
to prepare the way of salvation.
Give us fiery servants
of the Gospel
that Christ may find ready hearts
when he returns in glory,
for Christ is Lord forever and ever.
Amen.

✠ *Maranatha! Come, Lord Jesus!*

✦ *Maranatha! Come, Lord Jesus!*

PSALM 85   page 417

READING   Luke 1:18–25

Zechariah said to the angel, "How will I know that this is so? For I am an old man, and my wife is getting on in years." The angel replied, "I am Gabriel. I stand in the presence of God, and I have been sent to speak to you and to bring you this good news. But now, because you did not believe my words, which will be fulfilled in their time, you will become mute, unable to speak, until the day these things occur."

Meanwhile the people were waiting for Zechariah, and wondered at his delay in the sanctuary. When he did come out, he could not speak to them, and they realized that he had seen a vision in the sanctuary. He kept motioning to them and remained unable to speak. When his time of service was ended, he went to his home.

After those days his wife Elizabeth conceived, and for five months she remained in seclusion. She said, "This is what the Lord has done for me when he looked favorably on me and took away the disgrace I have endured among my people."

REFLECTION

Gabriel's harsh response to Zechariah's apparently reasonable question may seem puzzling. Perhaps Zechariah was asking for a sign and so the angel gave him one, though probably not the one he was hoping for! On the other hand, he could simply have been dumbstruck (literally) by the news. Or the Gospel writer could have added it to heighten the drama, which comes to a climax when Zechariah's tongue is eventually set free and he utters his first words.

PRAYERS   others may be added

Confident of God's promises,
we pray:

◆ Come quickly, Lord of glory!

To bring to fullness the prophets' vision, we pray: ◆ *To deliver good news of salvation, we pray:* ◆ *To loosen tongues for the praise of God, we pray:* ◆ *To give the nations a sign of hope, we pray:* ◆ *To vindicate those considered disgraced, we pray:* ◆ *To open our eyes to the vision of God's reign, we pray:* ◆

Our Father . . .

We are struck dumb
by your promise, O God,
for with you
all things are possible.
Open our eyes
to the signs of your glory,
and loose our tongues
to tell of your wonders,
that all people may welcome
the day of salvation,
when Christ shall reign
forever and ever. Amen.

✦ *Maranatha! Come, Lord Jesus!*

✝ *Maranatha! Come, Lord Jesus!*

PSALM 85 — page 417

READING — *Luke 1:26–33*

In the sixth month the angel Gabriel was sent by God to a town in Galilee called Nazareth, to a virgin engaged to a man whose name was Joseph, of the house of David. The virgin's name was Mary. And he came to her and said, "Greetings, favored one! The Lord is with you." But she was much perplexed by his words and pondered what sort of greeting this might be. The angel said to her, "Do not be afraid, Mary, for you have found favor with God. And now, you will conceive in your womb and bear a son, and you will name him Jesus. He will be great, and will be called the Son of the Most High, and the Lord God will give to him the throne of his ancestor David. He will reign over the house of Jacob forever, and of his kingdom there will be no end."

REFLECTION

Unlike the announcement of John the Baptist's birth, the annunciation to Mary takes place in Nazareth, far away from Jerusalem and the center of Jewish religious life. Jesus' origins foreshadow his ministry: God's salvation comes from an unexpected place, from the middle of nowhere, and many missed Jesus because he wasn't the Messiah they expected. He was neither priest nor warrior nor king, at least not in the usual ways. We do well to pay attention, for God surely still seeks us in places, at times, and in people we may not expect.

PRAYERS — *others may be added*

Rejoicing in God's favor, we cry out:

◆ Come quickly, Lord of glory!

To bring deliverance to your faithful ones, we cry out: ◆ *To bring divine favor to the silent and forgotten, we cry out:* ◆ *To bring the dawn of justice for the poor, we cry out:* ◆ *To bring freedom from fear and worry, we cry out:* ◆ *To bring fulfillment to God's promise to David, we cry out:* ◆ *To bring salvation to all who trust in you, we cry out:* ◆

Our Father . . .

God of boundless grace,
you poured out your favor
on a daughter of Israel
and through her
gave the world a Savior.
Favor us with your presence
that we may bear your Son
to all we meet.
We ask this through the same Christ,
Son of God and of Mary,
who lives and reigns
forever and ever. Amen.

✝ *Maranatha! Come, Lord Jesus!*

✚ *Maranatha! Come, Lord Jesus!*

PSALM 85   *page 417*

READING   *Luke 1:34–38*

Mary said to the angel, "How can this be, since I am a virgin?" The angel said to her, "The Holy Spirit will come upon you, and the power of the Most High will overshadow you; therefore the child to be born will be holy; he will be called Son of God. And now, your relative Elizabeth in her old age has also conceived a son; and this is the sixth month for her who was said to be barren. For nothing will be impossible with God." Then Mary said, "Here am I, the servant of the Lord; let it be with me according to your word." Then the angel departed from her.

REFLECTION   *Germanus*

Hail Mary, full of grace . . . Hail, dove, you who bring to us the fruit of the olive, and announce a preserver and harbor of safety from the spiritual deluge; whose wings, covered with silver, and the hinder parts of her back with the paleness of gold, shine with the brightness of the most holy and enlightening Spirit. . . . Hail, O most holy building, spotless and pure palace of God, the most high King, adorned with the magnificence of God the King himself, receiving all with hospitality and refreshing them with mystical delights, wherein is that couch of the mystical Spouse, not made with hands, gleaming with every beauty; in which the Word, wishing to recall the wandering human race, himself espoused flesh, that he might reconcile to his Father those who, of their own will, had banished themselves from him.

PRAYERS   *others may be added*

Servants of God, disciples with Mary, we pray:

◆ Come quickly, Lord of glory!

That God's people may faithfully embrace their mission, we pray: ◆ *That Church ministers may be willing bearers of God's word, we pray:* ◆ *That all Christians may trust that nothing is impossible with God, we pray:* ◆ *That all people may open themselves to God's creative Spirit, we pray:* ◆ *That we may be faithful disciples of the Son of the Most High, we pray:* ◆

Our Father . . .

We rejoice in your love,
God of wondrous power,
for nothing is impossible with you.
Overshadow us with the power
   of your Spirit
that we, like Mary, may be vessels
   of your grace,
holy children of a holy mother,
and brothers and sisters of our Savior,
who is Lord forever and ever. Amen.

✚ *Maranatha! Come, Lord Jesus!*

✦ *Come, O Holy Wisdom of God!*
Teach us the way of salvation!

PSALM 89 page 419

READING Zephaniah 3:14–18

Sing aloud, O daughter Zion;
   shout, O Israel!
Rejoice and exult with all your heart,
   O daughter Jerusalem!
The LORD has taken away
     the judgments against you,
   he has turned away your enemies.
The king of Israel, the LORD,
     is in your midst;
   you shall fear disaster no more.
On that day it shall be said
     to Jerusalem:
Do not fear, O Zion;
   do not let your hands grow weak.
The LORD, your God, is
     in your midst,
   a warrior who gives victory;
he will rejoice over you with gladness,
   he will renew you in his love;
he will exult over you
     with loud singing
   as on a day of festival.
I will remove disaster from you,
   so that you will not bear reproach
     for it.

REFLECTION

As we approach the end of Advent two
"countdowns" to Christmas begin. The first,
Las Posadas, *or "inns," is a novena (nine-*
day devotion) that recalls the pilgrimage of
Mary and Joseph to Bethlehem; it began
yesterday. Today, we begin a second count-
down to Christmas—the O Antiphons,

short antiphons proclaimed before the
Magnificat *during Vespers. They draw on*
imagery from the Old Testament to name
Jesus and are used from December 17 to 23.

PRAYERS *others may be added*

Longing for the peace of the Messiah,
we pray:

◆ Come, O holy Wisdom of God!

To rejoice with your spouse, the Church,
we pray: ◆ *To renew your covenant*
with the Chosen People, we pray: ◆
To draw back in love those who have
turned away from you, we pray: ◆
To remove disaster from among the
nations, we pray: ◆ *To strengthen*
the hands of those burdened by labor,
we pray: ◆ *To cast out sorrow with a*
festive song, we pray: ◆ *To make your*
dwelling place among us, we pray: ◆

Our Father . . .

Faithful God,
we long for the coming
of the Promised One
and the peace he will bring.
Send to us the Desire of nations,
the Prince of Peace,
that we may rejoice and exult
with all our hearts
and praise you forever
through the same Jesus Christ,
who is Lord with you,
in the unity of the Holy Spirit,
one God, forever and ever. Amen.

✦ *Come, O Holy Wisdom of God!*
Teach us the way of salvation!

✦ *Come, O Adonai, O Lord of Israel!*
Come to rule your people
with justice!

PSALM 89 *page 419*

READING *Luke 1:39–45*

In those days Mary set out and went with haste to a Judean town in the hill country, where she entered the house of Zechariah and greeted Elizabeth. When Elizabeth heard Mary's greeting, the child leaped in her womb. And Elizabeth was filled with the Holy Spirit and exclaimed with a loud cry, "Blessed are you among women, and blessed is the fruit of your womb. And why has this happened to me, that the mother of my Lord comes to me? For as soon as I heard the sound of your greeting, the child in my womb leaped for joy. And blessed is she who believed that there would be a fulfillment of what was spoken to her by the Lord."

REFLECTION *John Chrysostom*

You see, O beloved, how new and wonderful is this mystery. The prophet John is not yet born, and he speaks by leapings; he does not yet appear, and he utters threats; he may not yet cry out, and by his acts he is heard; he does not yet draw the breath of life, and he preaches God; he does not yet behold the light, and he points out the sun; he is not yet brought forth, and he hastens to be the forerunner. For, in the presence of the Lord, he cannot bear to be restrained.

PRAYERS *others may be added*

Blessed with hope in Christ's coming,
we pray:

◆ Come, O Adonai, O Lord of Israel!

That God's people may have confidence in the fulfillment of God's promises, we pray: ◆ *That the baptized may greet one another as bearers of Christ's presence, we pray:* ◆ *That women and their children may be assured of medical care and protection, we pray:* ◆ *That travelers and pilgrims may be protected from harm, we pray:* ◆ *That we may be favored by the presence of God, we pray:* ◆

Our Father . . .

Blessed are you, faithful God,
for your word always bears fruit
and you never fail to bring about
what you promise.
Fill us with the insight of Elizabeth,
that we may recognize
the presence of your Anointed One
and so share her joy as well.
We ask this through the Promised One,
Jesus Christ, who lives and reigns
forever and ever. Amen.

✦ *Come, O Adonai, O Lord of Israel!*
Come to rule your people
with justice!

✦ *Come, O Flower of Jesse!*
Come and refresh us with the
fragrance of your glory!

PSALM 89   *page 419*

READING   *Luke 1:46–50*

And Mary said,
"My soul magnifies the Lord,
  and my spirit rejoices in God
    my Savior,
for he has looked with favor
    on the lowliness of his servant.
  Surely, from now on all
    generations will call me blessed;
for the Mighty One has done
    great things for me,
  and holy is his name.
His mercy is for those who fear him
  from generation to generation."

REFLECTION

Today we begin reading the Magnificat, *Mary's great hymn of praise for all that God has done for her and for the chosen people. Her song echoes the praise of many daughters of Israel before her, especially Hannah, the mother of Samuel (see 1 Samuel 2:1–11). But Mary not only summarizes the "great things" God has done in the past, she also anticipates what her child will bring—food for the hungry, the casting down of the powerful. And so her song begins with great joy and thanksgiving: Her soul "magnifies"—extols, gives thanks, rejoices in—the mighty God of Israel. Generation upon generation of Christians have echoed her words of praise, and every day at sunset the Church sings the* Magnificat *at Vespers.*

PRAYERS   *others may be added*

Rejoicing in the mighty deeds of God, we pray:

◆ Come, O Flower of Jesse!

To bring joy to the hearts of the baptized, we pray: ◆ *To give words of blessing to those who seek you, we pray:* ◆ *To show the nations your mighty deeds, we pray:* ◆ *To show favor to the lowliest of your servants, we pray:* ◆ *To shower mercy on the poor and disenfranchised, we pray:* ◆ *To pour out your Spirit on all who fear you, we pray:* ◆ *To favor us with knowledge of you, we pray:* ◆

Our Father . . .

We praise you, mighty God,
for you choose the lowly
to reveal your power and wisdom.
Shower your favor upon us:
May our souls reflect your glory
that from one generation to the next,
your servants may praise
  your mighty deeds,
for you live and reign
forever and ever. Amen.

✦ *Come, O Flower of Jesse!*
Come and refresh us with the
fragrance of your glory!

✠ *Come, O Key of David!*
Come and restore your people!

PSALM 89 *page 419*

READING *Luke 1:51–56*

"God has shown strength with his arm;
    he has scattered the proud
        in the thoughts of their hearts.
He has brought down the powerful
        from their thrones,
    and lifted up the lowly;
he has filled the hungry
        with good things,
    and sent the rich away empty.
He has helped his servant Israel,
    in remembrance of his mercy,
according to the promise he made
        to our ancestors,
    to Abraham and to his descendants
        forever."
And Mary remained with Elizabeth about three months and then returned to her home.

REFLECTION

Though we tend to think of Mary only in her role as mother—of Jesus, of God, of the Church—in Luke she is also a prophet. Like the women prophets of ancient Israel— Miriam at the Exodus, Deborah during the time of the judges, Huldah at the time of King Saul—Mary announces what God has done and has yet to do. Unlike the quiet, contemplative images of Mary that fill churches and museums, Luke's Mary shouts aloud in praise.

PRAYERS *others may be added*

Longing for the justice of God's reign, we pray:

◆ Come, O Key of David!

To help, with your mercy, the servant Church, we pray: ◆ To fill the hearts of the baptized with praise, we pray: ◆ To lift up the downtrodden and abused, we pray: ◆ To defend the powerless with your mighty arm, we pray: ◆ To fill the hungry with your abundance, we pray: ◆ To scatter the proud, and humble the powerful, we pray: ◆ To fulfill your promise of life to our ancestors, we pray: ◆

Our Father . . .

Faithful God,
we long for the day of your power
when the lost and forsaken,
the humble and the hungry,
will gather in the holy city.
Fill us with hope as we await
the fullness of your power.
May we prepare for its coming
by feeding the hungry,
lifting up the poor,
and casting pride from our hearts.
We ask this in the name of Jesus,
the Promised One,
who lives and reigns
forever and ever. Amen.

✠ *Come, O Key of David!*
Come and restore your people!

✦ *Come, O radiant Dawn!*
  Come and brighten our hearts
      with your love!

PSALM 89 *page 419*

READING *Luke 1:57–66*

Now the time came for Elizabeth to give birth, and she bore a son. Her neighbors and relatives heard that the Lord had shown his great mercy to her, and they rejoiced with her.

On the eighth day they came to circumcise the child, and they were going to name him Zechariah after his father. But his mother said, "No; he is to be called John." They said to her, "None of your relatives has this name." Then they began motioning to his father to find out what name he wanted to give him. He asked for a writing tablet and wrote, "His name is John." And all of them were amazed. Immediately his mouth was opened and his tongue freed, and he began to speak, praising God. Fear came over all their neighbors, and all these things were talked about throughout the entire hill country of Judea. All who heard them pondered them and said, "What then will this child become?" For, indeed, the hand of the Lord was with him.

REFLECTION *Ambrose of Milan*

Elizabeth brought forth a son, and her neighbors rejoiced with her. The birth of saints brings joy to very many, since it is a benefit to all; for justice is a virtue for all. And so, in the birth of a just man, a token of his future life is foreshown, and the grace of the virtue to come is expressed by the prophetic joy of the neighbors.

PRAYERS *others may be added*

Rejoicing with all the saints at the birth of the Forerunner, we pray:

◆ Come, O Dawn!

That the Church may remain faithful to the Gospel, we pray: ◆ *That God's people may rejoice in the fulfillment of God's promises, we pray:* ◆ *That the people of the world may be amazed by the great works of God, we pray:* ◆ *That pregnant women may have safe deliveries and the support of their neighbors:* ◆ *That our tongues may be free to praise God, we pray:* ◆

Our Father . . .

God of Israel,
your servants Elizabeth
    and Zechariah
were faithful to your message
and raised their son
to be the faithful herald of your own.
By their holy example
may we too be faithful to you
that we, like them, may witness
your mighty works
and sing your praise
forever and ever. Amen.

✦ *Come, O radiant Dawn!*
  Come and brighten our hearts
      with your love!

✝ *Come, O Desire of nations!*
Come and bring us peace!

PSALM 89 *page 419*

READING *Luke 1:67–75*

Then John's father Zechariah was
filled with the Holy Spirit and spoke
this prophecy:
"Blessed be the Lord God of Israel,
  for he has looked favorably
    on his people and redeemed them.
He has raised up a mighty savior
    for us
  in the house of his servant David,
as he spoke through the mouth
    of his holy prophets from of old,
  that we would be saved from our
    enemies and from the hand
    of all who hate us.
Thus he has shown the mercy
    promised to our ancestors,
  and has remembered
    his holy covenant,
the oath that he swore
    to our ancestor Abraham,
  to grant us that we, being rescued
    from the hands of our enemies,
might serve him without fear,
    in holiness and righteousness
  before him all our days."

REFLECTION

Like Mary's song, Zechariah's Benedictus
is an unbridled song of praise to the God
of Israel. Although proclaimed at John's
birth, Zechariah prophesies about Jesus,
the "mighty savior" and "Key" (in Wednes-
day's O Antiphon) of King David's house.
However, Zechariah's words are not about

the birth of a baby. Both Mary's and
Zechariah's hymns are about all that God
has done through Christ. This should
say something about our celebration of
Christmas: We don't celebrate a birthday;
we celebrate the coming of Christ and all
it means — the whole paschal mystery —
foreshadowed in the Christmas story.

PRAYERS *others may be added*

Blessing God always, we pray:

◆ Come, O Desire of nations!

To bring favor on your holy people,
we pray: ◆ *To fill the baptized with*
holiness and righteousness, we pray: ◆
To show your faithfulness to servant
Israel, we pray: ◆ *To fulfill the words of*
the holy prophets, we pray: ◆ *To bring*
salvation to the needy and hope to the
exiled, we pray: ◆ *To inspire us to serve*
you, we pray: ◆

Our Father . . .

Blessed are you, Lord God of Israel,
for you have redeemed us
through a mighty Savior.
Continue to show us your favor
that we may faithfully serve you
in holiness and righteousness
and be counted among your
    chosen people.
We ask this through the Key of David,
Jesus Christ, who lives and reigns
forever and ever. Amen.

✝ *Come, O Desire of nations!*
Come and bring us peace!

✦ *Come, Emmanuel, God-with-us!*
Come and make your dwelling
among us!

PSALM 89 page 419

READING Luke 1:76–80

"And you, child, will be called the
prophet of the Most High;
for you will go before the Lord
to prepare his ways,
to give knowledge of salvation
to his people
by the forgiveness of their sins.
By the tender mercy of our God,
the dawn from on high will break
upon us,
to give light to those who sit
in darkness and in the shadow
of death,
to guide our feet into the way
of peace."

The child grew and became strong
in spirit, and he was in the wilderness
until the day he appeared publicly
to Israel.

REFLECTION

Today, one of the shortest days of the year,
our scripture passage speaks of the "dawn
from on high." By happy coincidence,
today is also the last day of Hanukkah, the
Jewish festival of light. Together Christians
and Jews can celebrate with confidence
that, even when we fear that darkness may
triumph, when night seems to have the
upper hand over the day, the light of God's
glory never dies away.

PRAYERS others may be added

Awaiting the light of God's tender
mercy, we pray:

◆ Come, O Emmanuel, God-with-us!

To strengthen the spirits of the baptized,
we pray: ◆ To enlighten the minds of all
people, we pray: ◆ To warm the bodies
of the cold and homeless, we pray: ◆
To melt hearts frozen by depression and
anxiety, we pray: ◆ To shine on those
in darkness and the shadow of death,
we pray: ◆ To restore the earth to life
and freshness, we pray: ◆ To show
us the way of peace, we pray: ◆

Our Father . . .

God of shining glory,
in these darkest days
we await the coming
of the Light of the world.
Give us courage in this time
of twilight
to keep vigil for the one
who will restore sight to the blind
and lead us all in the way
of salvation,
Emmanuel, God-with-us,
who lives and reigns with you,
in the unity of the Holy Spirit,
one God, forever and ever. Amen.

✦ *Come, Emmanuel, God-with-us!*
Come and make your dwelling
among us!

✦ *Come, beloved Bridegroom,*
heaven's eternal spring!
Come speak to us your
eternal Word.

PSALM 89   *page 419*

READING   *Micah 5:2–5a*

But you, O Bethlehem of Ephrathah,
   who are one of the little clans
      of Judah,
from you shall come forth for me
   one who is to rule in Israel,
whose origin is from of old,
   from ancient days.
Therefore he shall give them up
    until the time
   when she who is in labor
    has brought forth;
then the rest of his kindred shall return
   to the people of Israel.
And he shall stand and feed his flock
    in the strength of the LORD,
   in the majesty of the name
    of the LORD his God.
And they shall live secure, for now
    he shall be great
   to the ends of the earth;
and he shall be the one of peace.

REFLECTION

At last we stand at the threshold of Christ-mas, and today's reading sounds a famil-iar theme: From out of nowhere, from "one of the little clans of Judah," will come a ruler who will finally bring peace. In this long night of war and in security, we wait in hope for Christ's new birth in each one of us, for it is in us that the promise of peace must first bear fruit.

Though we may long for Christ to sud-denly appear and set things right, we know that Christ cannot come in fullness until we have opened wide the door.

PRAYERS   *others may be added*

Ready to give birth to the Just One,
we pray:

◆ Come, O Bridegroom!

That God's people may celebrate
Christ's birth in works of peace, we pray: ◆
That the nations may make ready for the
return of the Ancient of Days, we pray: ◆
That war and violence may at last be
overcome, we pray: ◆ *That the labor*
of the downtrodden may give birth to
a new day of freedom and joy, we pray: ◆
That the majesty of God's name may
transform creation in power, we pray: ◆

Our Father . . .

Hear our cry,
O Ancient of Days,
and come dwell among us.
Make your home in our hearts;
adorn them with peace and mercy.
May all your children
live secure at last,
lovingly tended
   by their shepherd and spouse,
our Savior Jesus Christ,
who lives and reigns with you,
in the unity of the Holy Spirit,
one God, forever and ever. Amen.

✦ *Come, beloved Bridegroom,*
heaven's eternal spring!
Come speak to us your
eternal Word.

✢ *Alleluia!*
The Word of God dwells among us!
God is one with humankind!

PSALM 96   *page 421*

READING   *Isaiah 9:2–3, 6–7*

The people who walked in darkness
   have seen a great light;
those who lived in a land
    of deep darkness—
   on them light has shined.
You have multiplied the nation,
   you have increased its joy;
they rejoice before you
   as with joy at the harvest,
   as people exult
    when dividing plunder.
For a child has been born for us,
   a son given to us;
authority rests upon his shoulders;
   and he is named
Wonderful Counselor, Mighty God,
   Everlasting Father, Prince of Peace.
His authority shall grow continually,
   and there shall be endless peace
for the throne of David
    and his kingdom.
   He will establish and uphold it
with justice and with righteousness
   from this time onward
    and forevermore.
The zeal of the LORD of hosts
   will do this.

REFLECTION   *Sedatus of Béziers*

Those who lived before the incarnation
approached their noble task differently
from those who lived after it, but even so
Christ was born to all who lived to one
and the same faith. Yet what is more amaz-
ing is that Christ continues to be born to
us today. Daily he allows himself to be
brought forth by every believing soul.

PRAYERS   *others may be added*

   Turning with joy to greet God who
   loves us, we cry out:

◆ May all your works praise you!

For bringing joy to the baptized, we
cry out: ◆ *For shining brightly on a world*
touched by sin and sadness, we pray: ◆
For setting up the throne of peace and the
rule of justice, we pray: ◆ *For establishing*
righteousness forevermore, we pray: ◆
For making your dwelling among all
people, we pray: ◆

Our Father . . .

Shine on us, God of light,
and reveal to us your Beloved One,
the Wonderful Counselor,
the Prince of Peace.
As we keep the festival
of Christ's birth,
may your light shine through us
and bring joy and peace
to those shrouded by sorrow and fear.
We ask this through the Son
you have given,
our Savior Jesus Christ,
who lives and reigns with you,
in the unity of the Holy Spirit,
one God, now and forever. Amen.

✢ *Alleluia!*
The Word of God dwells among us!
God is one with humankind!

✚ *Alleluia!*
  The Word of God dwells among us!
  God is one with humankind!

PSALM 96 *page 421*

READING *Matthew 10:17–22*

Jesus said to his disciples: "See, I am sending you out like sheep into the midst of wolves; so be wise as serpents and innocent as doves. Beware of them, for they will hand you over to councils and flog you in their synagogues; and you will be dragged before governors and kings because of me, as a testimony to them and the Gentiles. When they hand you over, do not worry about how you are to speak or what you are to say; for what you are to say will be given to you at that time; for it is not you who speak, but the Spirit of your Father speaking through you. Brother will betray brother to death, and a father his child, and children will rise against parents and have them put to death; and you will be hated by all because of my name. But the one who endures to the end will be saved."

REFLECTION

The feast of Saint Stephen directs us quickly away from the idyllic scene at the manger. The birth of Jesus has consequences; the world he will announce threatens the status quo: religious, economic, and political. Many, Christians and members of other religious traditions alike, have given their lives in the service of God's reign, as the infant in the manger eventually did.

PRAYERS *others may be added*

Recognizing in the child of Bethlehem the fiery Messiah, we cry out:

◆ May all your works praise you!

For the witness of Stephen, the first martyr, we cry out: ◆ *For the service of deacons to the Church, we cry out:* ◆ *For the courage to profess boldly our faith in Christ, we cry out:* ◆ *For the wisdom to speak words of justice to the powerful, we cry out:* ◆ *For the strength to endure until the day of salvation, we cry out:* ◆ *For your presence with us in times of trial, we cry out:* ◆

Our Father . . .

God of mission,
you send us forth
as sheep among wolves
to share the fate of your Son.
Fill us with your Spirit,
that with courage and boldness
we may speak the word of truth
to the glory of your name.
We ask this through your Son
    Jesus Christ,
Child of Bethlehem
    and Suffering Servant,
who lives and reigns forever and ever.
Amen.

✚ *Alleluia!*
  The Word of God dwells among us!
  God is one with humankind!

✦ *Alleluia!*
The Word of God dwells among us!
God is one with humankind!

PSALM 96 *page 421*

READING *John 1:1–5, 10–12, 14*

In the beginning was the Word, and the Word was with God, and the Word was God. He was in the beginning with God. All things came into being through him, and without him not one thing came into being. What has come into being with him was life, and the life was the light of all people. The light shines in the darkness, and the darkness did not overcome it.

He was in the world, and the world came into being through him; yet the world did not know him. He came to what was his own, and his own people did not accept him. But to all who received him, who believed in his name, he gave power to become children of God.

And the Word became flesh and lived among us, and we have seen his glory, the glory as a of a father's only son, full of grace and truth.

REFLECTION *John Chrysostom*

How can I put this into words, how express it? This wonder fills me with amazement. The Ancient of Days becomes a child; he who sits upon the throne, high and exalted, is laid in a manger. He who has broken the bonds of sin is wrapped in swaddling bands, for this is his will. He wills opprobrium to become honor, disgrace to be clothed in glory, and the most outrageous
abuse to demonstrate the extent of his goodness.

PRAYERS *others may be added*

Rejoicing that the light has pierced our darkness, we pray:

◆ May all your works praise you!

For enlivening the Church with the light of grace and truth, we pray: ◆
For filling creation with the glory of your Only-begotten, we pray: ◆ *For inspiring prophets and judges, evangelists and poets, to give form and language to your Word, we pray:* ◆ *For overcoming the darkness of sorrow and sickness with the light of your healing, we pray:* ◆
For choosing us from the beginning as your beloved daughters and sons, we pray: ◆

Our Father . . .

Light of creation,
you pierce our darkness
with the glory of your Word
and exalt us by humbling yourself.
May we who have been showered
with grace and truth
shine in our world
as children of God.
We ask this in the name of Jesus,
your Word made flesh,
who lives and reigns
forever and ever. Amen.

✦ *Alleluia!*
The Word of God dwells among us!
God is one with humankind!

✠ *Alleluia!*
The Word of God dwells among us!
God is one with humankind!

PSALM 96 *page 421*

READING *Matthew 2:16–18*

When Herod saw that he had been tricked by the wise men, he was infuriated, and he sent and killed all the children in and around Bethlehem who were two years old or under, according to the time that he had learned from the wise men. Then was fulfilled what had been spoken through the prophet Jeremiah:

"A voice was heard in Ramah,
wailing and loud lamentation,
Rachel weeping for her children;
she refused to be consoled
because they are no more."

REFLECTION *Gabe Huck*

We take our Christmas with lots of sugar. And take it in a day. Though we've been baptized into his death, we have little time for or patience with how that death is told at Christmas, a death that confuses lament and praise forever. And no wonder we are careful to keep Christmas at an arm's length. . . .

Where is that mystery in our Christmastime, the mystery that is victorious cross? It is right there in the stories we tell, the carols we sing, the gifts we give and cards we write, the time we take to process through the dozen days from Christmas to Epiphany, the many ways we have to whisper to one another that the
days are numbered now for the world's business-as-usual.

PRAYERS *others may be added*

Recognizing the suffering of God's children today, we pray:

◆ Word of God, abide with us.

When the Church suffers persecution for the sake of Emmanuel, we pray: ◆
When rulers oppress the people entrusted to their care, we pray: ◆ *When refugees are forced to flee the terrors of war and natural disaster, we pray:* ◆ *When tribes and peoples suffer genocide, we pray:* ◆
When children are abused, neglected, or unloved, we pray: ◆ *When mothers and fathers mourn the death of a child, we pray:* ◆ *When we turn our faces from the suffering of the innocent, we pray:* ◆

Our Father . . .

God of Rachel,
the forces of greed and evil
sought to destroy the Child of justice
and even today oppose his reign.
Forgive us for the times
we have failed to protect
   the innocent:
May we who adore the Christ Child
seek him among the suffering
and innocent of the world.
We ask through Christ our Savior,
who lives and reigns
forever and ever. Amen.

✠ *Alleluia!*
The Word of God dwells among us!
God is one with humankind!

✤ *Alleluia!*
The Word of God dwells among us!
God is one with humankind!

PSALM 96 *page 421*

READING *1 John 2:7–11*

Beloved, I am writing you no new commandment, but an old commandment that you have had from the beginning; the old commandment is the word that you have heard. Yet I am writing you a new commandment that is true in him and in you, because the darkness is passing away and the true light is already shining. Whoever says, "I am in the light," while hating a brother or sister, is still in the darkness. Whoever loves a brother or sister lives in the light, and in such a person there is no cause for stumbling. But whoever hates another believer is in the darkness, walks in darkness, and does not know the way to go, because the darkness has brought on blindness.

REFLECTION

Throughout much of the Christmas season, the first readings for weekday Mass come from the First Letter of John, which offers a commentary on what it means to love God. Like the author of John's Gospel, the author of the epistle uses the images of light and darkness, sight and blindness, to describe those who truly love and those who do not.

PRAYERS *others may be added*

Rejoicing that Christ our light dwells among us, we pray:

◆ May all your works praise you!

That the Church may be a shining example of love of neighbor, we pray: ◆ That the world's people may leave the shroud of hatred and recognize one another as brothers and sisters, we pray: ◆ That those blinded by addiction may be healed by the light of God's presence, we pray: ◆ That the poor and oppressed may find new hope in the service of God's children, we pray: ◆ That we may carry Christ's love to all we meet, we pray: ◆

Our Father . . .

God of gentle glory,
you have pierced our darkness
with the radiance of love.
May we who celebrate
your love born at Christmas
live that love more fully in our
    bodies.
We ask this in the name of Jesus,
our light and our love,
who lives and reigns with you,
in the unity of the Holy Spirit,
one God, forever and ever. Amen.

✤ *Alleluia!*
The Word of God dwells among us!
God is one with humankind!

✦ *Alleluia!*
The Word of God dwells among us!
God is one with humankind!

PSALM 96   *page 421*

READING   *1 John 2:14–17*

Do not love the world or the things in the world. The love of the Father is not in those who love the world; for all that is in the world—the desire of the flesh, the desire of the eyes, the pride in riches—comes not from the Father but from the world. And the world and its desire are passing away, but those who do the will of God live forever.

Children, it is the last hour! As you have heard that antichrist is coming, so now many antichrists have come. From this we know that it is the last hour. They went out from us, but they did not belong to us; for if they had belonged to us, they would have remained with us. But by going out they made it plain that none of them belongs to us. But you have been anointed by the Holy One, and all of you have knowledge.

REFLECTION

The author of First John refers to some who "went out" from the community that produced the text—even calling them "antichrists"—indicating that disunity troubled Christians even at that early time. We, too, are part of a Church torn by disunity and even recrimination, a Church that sometimes fails to be a sign of the Good News brought by Mary's child. May this Christmas season be a time to renew our commitment to Christian unity and Christian charity.

PRAYERS   *others may be added*

Seeking to be faithful to God-with-us, we pray:

◆ May all your works praise you!

That all the baptized may seek Christian unity, drawing in rather than casting out, we pray: ◆ *That those who have left the practice of their faith may be welcomed and restored, we pray:* ◆ *That those who twist the Gospel message may turn and embrace the true knowledge of Christ, we pray:* ◆ *That those greedy for wealth may instead share what they have with those who go without, we pray:* ◆ *That we who have been anointed with God's love may grow in wisdom and knowledge, we pray:* ◆

Our Father . . .

God of truth,
you remind us of discipleship's
    challenge
and warn us of those
who would dissuade us
from following Christ's path.
Anoint us once more
with the gift of your Spirit,
that we may grow in knowledge and
    love of Christ,
who lives and reigns
forever and ever. Amen.

✦ *Alleluia!*
The Word of God dwells among us!
God is one with humankind!

SOURCES

Scripture quotations are from the *New Revised Standard Version of the Bible,* © 1989 Division of Christian Education of the National Council of Churches of Christ in the United States of America. Used with permission. All rights reserved.

Psalms are from *The Psalms: Grail Translation from the Hebrew,* Ladies of the Grail (England). Used by permission of GIA Publications, Inc., exclusive agent. All rights reserved.

Excerpts from the documents of the Second Vatican Council are from Austin Flannery, OP ed., *Vatican Council II: The Basic Sixteen Documents, A Completely Revised Translation in Inclusive Language* © 1996, Costello Publishing Company, Inc., Northport, N.Y. Used by permission. All rights reserved. No part of these excerpts may be reproduced, stored in a retrieval system, or transmitted in any form or by any means—electronic, mechanical, photocopying, recording, or otherwise—without express permission of Costello Publishing Company, Inc.

Excerpts from the English translation of *The Roman Missal* © 1973, International Committee on English in the Liturgy, Inc. (ICEL); excerpts from the English translation of *The Liturgy of the Hours* © 1974, ICEL; excerpts from the English translation of *Dedication of a Church and an Altar* © 1978, ICEL; excerpts from the English translation of *Rite of Christian Initiation of Adults* © 1985, ICEL. All rights reserved.

Excerpts from *Economic Justice for All* copyright © 1986, United Conference of Catholic Bishops, Washington, D.C. Used with permission. All rights reserved. No part of this work may be reproduced or transmitted in any form without the permission in writing from the copyright holder.

Excerpts from *The Challenge of Peace* copyright © 1986, United Conference of Catholic Bishops, Washington, D.C. Used with permission. All rights reserved. No part of this work may be reproduced or transmitted in any form without the permission in writing from the copyright holder.

English translation of the *Catechism of the Catholic Church* for the United States of America © 1994 USCC, Inc.—Libreria Editrice Vaticana.

Information about the saints and days of the year can be found in *Companion to the Calendar* by Mary Ellen Hynes (Chicago: LTP, 1993).

30 November 2005: From Sermo 43, 5–6, in *Tradition Day by Day,* ed. John Rotelle, OSA (Villanova, Pennsylvania: Augustinian Press, 1994; www.augustinian.org), page 211.

7 December 2005: Found in *Social Thought: Message of the Fathers of the Church 20,* page 173.

12 December 2005: Found in *A Sourcebook about Mary,* eds. J. Robert Baker and Barbara Budde (Chicago: LTP, 2002), page 80.

18 December 2005: From *The Prayers of Catherine of Siena,* translated and edited by Suzanne Noffke OP, 2d ed. © 2006. Used with permission.

25 January 2006: *Ut unum sint,* 8.

4 March 2006: From *Days of Devotion,* by Pope John XXIII. © 1967 The K.S. Giniger Company, Inc. Used by permission.

11 March 2006: *Roman Missal.*

17 March 2006: From *School Year, Church Year* (Chicago: LTP, 2001), page 215.

23 March 2006: Found in *A Reconciliation Sourcebook* (Chicago: LTP, 1997), page 127.

31 March 2006: *On the Good of Patience,* CCL 111A. 120, in *Divine Providence and Human Suffering,* page 108.

5 April 2006: Found in "Many Other Things" by Gabe Huck, in *Rite* 33:2 (February-March 2002), page 12.

6 April 2006: Found in "Many Other Things" by Gabe Huck.

11 April 2006: *Homilies on Ezekiel* II.4.20.

14 April 2006: From *The Lenten Tridion* translated from the original Greek by Mother Mary and Archimandrite Kallistos Ware. Published by Faber and Faber, 1978. Found in *A Triduum Sourcebook II* (Chicago: LTP, 1996), page 83.

15 April 2006: From *Easter in the Early Church,* selected, annotated and introduced by Raniero Cantalamessa, revised and augmented by the author. Newly translated from the sources and edited with further annotations by James M. Quigley, SJ, and Joseph T. Lienhard, SJ. Published by The Liturgical Press, Collegeville, Minnesota. Found in *A Triduum Sourcebook I* (Chicago: LTP, 1996), page 167.

29 April 2006: From *The Dialogues of Catherine of Siena on Divine Revelation,* chapter 167.

4 May 2006: From *The Liturgy of the Hours.*

6 May 2006: Office of Readings, December 26, cited in *A Christmas Sourcebook* (Chicago: LTP, 1984), page 73.

10 May 2006: From a letter to his brother Father Pamphile, November 1873, reproduced in *The Heart of Father Damien, 1840–1889,* by Vital Jourdan, SSCC, trans. Francis Larkin and Charles Davenport (Milwaukee: Bruce Publishing Company, 1955).

14 May 2006: *Lumen gentium,* 6.

15 May 2006: *Economic Justice for All,* 235.

16 May 2006: *Lumen gentium,* 16.

25 May 2006: Preface of Ascension I.

30 May 2006: From *Medieval Women's Visionary Literature,* Elizabeth Alvilda Petroff, ed. © 1986 Oxford University Press. Used with permission.

1 June 2006: From *Hildegard of Bingen: An Anthology,* trans. Robert Carver, ed. Fiona Bowie and Oliver Davies (London: Society for Promoting Christian Knowledge, 1990). Found in *The Book of Catholic Wisdom,* pages 5–6.

4 June 2006: From the preface for Pentecost Day, in *We Give You Thanks and Praise: The Ambrosian Eucharistic Prefaces,* trans. Alan Griffiths (Norwich: The Canterbury Press, 1999; and Franklin, Wis., Sheed and Ward, 2000), page 140.

8 June 2006: *Gaudium et spes,* 18.

18 June 2006: From *Lauda Sion (sequence for the solemnity of the Body and Blood of Christ)* copyright © 1964, United States Conference of Catholic Bishops, Washington, D.C. Used with permission. All rights reserved. No part of this work may be reproduced or transmitted in any form without the permission in writing of the copyright holder.

24 June 2006: From "Hymn for the Nativity of John the Baptist" in *The Hymns of the Roman Breviary and Missal.* Published by Brown and Nolan, Ltd., Dublin.

4 July 2006: "Signs of the Times," *America* 182:20 (June 3–10, 2000), 5.

11 July 2006: *The Challenge of Peace,* 31.

14 July 2006: *Reconciliation: Mission and Ministry in a Changing Social Order* by Robert J. Schreiter, CPPS, in The Boston Theological Institute Series, volume 3, 1992.

20 July 2006: *Letter to Artists,* 1.

22 July 2006: From *New Women, New Earth: Sexist Ideologies and Human Liberation* by Rosemary Radford Ruether. Published by Seabury Press, New York, 1977.

26 July 2006: *Letter to the Elderly,* 10.

28 July 2006: *Gaudium et spes,* 16.

5 August 2006: From "Moral Reflections on Job," found in *Divine Providence and Human Suffering: Message of the Fathers 17,* ed. James Walsh and P. G. Walsh (Wilmington: Michael Glazier, 1985), page 123.

8 August 2006: From a sermon of Thomas Aquinas, in *The Roman Breviary*, (New York: Benzinger Brothers, 1964), page 487.

11 August 2006: *Gaudium et spes,* 18.

13 August 2006: From "Commentaries on the Lord's Sermon on the Mount," *The Fathers of the Church* vol. 11 (New York: The Fathers of the Church, 1951), pages 322–23. Used with permission. The Catholic University of America Press, Washington, D.C.

17 August 2006: *Salvifici doloris,* 13.

20 August 2006: Found in *The Fathers of the Church* vol. 38 (New York: The Fathers of the Church, Inc., 1959), page 27. Used with permission. The Catholic University of America Press, Washington, D.C.

23 August 2006: *The New Oxford Annotated Bible, New Revised Standard Version.* Bruce Metzger and Herbert May, eds. © 1973, 1977, 1999, 2001, by Oxford University Press, Inc. Used by permission of Oxford University Press, Inc. Old Testament page 625.

24 August 2006: *Plain and Parochial Sermons II,* 336–37, in *Tradition Day by Day,* page 272.

3 September 2006: *Gaudium et spes,* 43.

6 September 2006: From *She Who Is* by Elizabeth Johnson, CSJ (New York: Crossroad, 1997), 87.

8 September 2006: Found in *A Sourcebook about Mary* (Chicago: LTP, 2002), page 99.

10 September 2006: *Economic Justice for All,* 52.

13 September 2006: *Hom. XX* on John's Gospel, in *Tradition Day by Day,* page 152.

27 September 2006: From *Letter 2546,* in *Tradition Day by Day,* page 309.

12 October 2006: *II Cor. Hom. 12, 4,* in *Tradition Day by Day,* page 325.

15 October 2006: *Cat. 1, 3:* SC 96, 299–305, in *Tradition Day by Day,* page 362.

20 October 2006: From *The Hodder Book of Christian Prayers,* compiled by Tony Castle. Published by Hodder and Stoughton Limited, 1986. Reprinted by permission Tony Castle.

23 October 2006: *Nostra aetate,* 4.

25 October 2006: *Lumen gentium,* 33.

26 October 2006: *Rite of Christian Initiation of Adults,* 230.

28 October 2006: *Or. 14, 7–8,* found in *Tradition Day by Day,* page 342.

8 November 2006: Found in *A Sourcebook about Christian Death* (Chicago: LTP, 1989), page 13.

9 November 2006: *Rite of Dedication of a Church and an Altar,* 1–2.

17 November 2006: *Hom. 7:* PG 64, 21–26.

26 November 2006: From *De cruce et latrone,* 3–4, in *Tradition Day by Day,* page 368.

28 November 2006: Sermon 34, 1–3, in *Tradition Day by Day,* page 138.

16 December 2006: From a homily of Saint Germanus, bishop, on the Presentation of the Mother of God, in *The Roman Breviary*, pages 745–46.

18 December 2006: From a sermon on Metaphrastes in July, in *The Roman Breviary,* page 934.

21 December 2006: From a homily of Saint Ambrose, Commentary on Luke, Book 2, chapter 1, in *The Roman Breviary*, page 903.

25 December 2006: *Revue Bénédictine* 88 (1978), 89–91, in *Tradition Day by Day,* page 409.

27 December 2006: *Hom. in natalem Christi diem:* PG 56, 388–89, in *Tradition Day by Day,* page 408.

28 December 2006: From *A Christmas Sourcebook,* Mary Ann Simcoe, ed. (Chicago: LTP, 1984), pages 79–80.

SCRIPTURAL INDEX

The following chart offers an overview of the scripture passages in *Daily Prayer 2006*. Use the chart to discover which books of the Bible are read during the year. Since the intercessions and closing prayer for each day often reflect the reading, you can also use the chart to help locate appropriate intercessions and prayers for various occasions.

1st Sunday of Advent • *Mark 13:33–37*

Monday • *Isaiah 35:1–4*

Tuesday • *Isaiah 35:5–7*

Wednesday, Andrew • *Matthew 4:18–22*

Thursday • *Matthew 35:8–10*

Friday • *Matthew 40:1–5*

Saturday • *Matthew 40:9–11*

2nd Sunday of Advent • *Mark 1:1–8*

Monday • *Isaiah 40:27–31*

Tuesday • *Isaiah 41:13–14a, 15–16*

Wednesday • *Isaiah 41:17–20*

Thursday, Immaculate Conception
• *Ephesians 1:3–6, 11–12*

Friday • *1 Samuel 1:1–6*

Saturday • *1 Samuel 9–11*

3rd Sunday of Advent
• *1 Thessalonians 5:16–24*

Monday, Guadalupe • *Zechariah 2:10–13*

Tuesday • *1 Samuel 1:12–18*

Wednesday • *1 Samuel 1:20–22*

Thursday • *1 Samuel 1:24–28*

Friday • *1 Samuel 2:1–5*

Saturday • *Proverbs 8:22, 27–31*

4th Sunday of Advent • *Luke 1:28–33, 38*

Monday • *Jeremiah 23:5–8*

Tuesday • *Isaiah 22:15, 19–23*

Wednesday • *Luke 1:39–45*

Thursday • *Zephaniah 3:14–18*

Friday • *Isaiah 7:10–14*

Saturday • *Song of Songs 2:8–13*

Sunday, Nativity of the Lord • *Luke 2:1–7*

Monday, Stephen • *Matthew 10:17–22*

Tuesday, John • *1 John 1:1–4*

Wednesday, Holy Innocents
• *Jeremiah 31:15–17*

Thursday • *Luke 2:22–28*

Friday, Holy Family • *Luke 2:28b–35*

Saturday • *Luke 2:36–40*

Sunday, Mary, Mother of God
• *Galatians 4:4–7*

Monday • *John 1:1–5*

Tuesday • *John 1:6–9*

Wednesday • *John 1:10–13*

Thursday • *John 1:14–18*

Friday • *John 1:19–23*

Saturday • *John 1:24–28*

Sunday, Epiphany of the Lord
• *Ephesians 3:2–3a, 5–6*

Monday, Baptism of the Lord • *Mark 1:4–11*

Tuesday • *Mark 1:14–20*

Wednesday • *Mark 1:21–28*

Thursday • *Mark 1:29–34*

Friday • *Mark 1:35–39*

Saturday • *Mark 1:40–45*

2nd Sunday in O.T.
• *1 Corinthians 6:13c–15a, 17–20*

Monday • *Romans 8:18–23*

Tuesday • *Mark 2:1–5*

Wednesday • *Mark 2:6–12*

Thursday • *Mark 2:13–17*

Friday • *Mark 2:18–22*

Saturday • *Mark 2:23–28*

3rd Sunday in O.T. • *1 Corinthians 7:29–31*

Monday • *Mark 3:1–6*

Tuesday • *Mark 3:13–19*

Wednesday, Conversion of Paul • *Acts 9:1–5*

Thursday • *Mark 3:31–35*

Friday • *Mark 4:1–9*

Saturday • *Mark 4:10–20*

4th Sunday in O.T. • *1 Corinthians 7:32–35*

Monday • *Mark 4:21–25*

Tuesday • *Mark 4:26–34*

Wednesday • *Mark 4:35–41*

Thursday, Presentation of the Lord
  • *Malachi 3:1–4*

Friday • *Mark 5:1–10*

Saturday • *Mark 5:11–20*

5th Sunday in O.T.
  • *1 Corinthians 9:16–19, 22–23*

Monday • *Mark 5:21–29*

Tuesday • *Mark 5:30–36*

Wednesday • *Mark 5:37–43*

Thursday • *Mark 6:7–13*

Friday • *Mark 6:34–44*

Saturday • *Mark 7:1–5*

6th Sunday in O.T.
  • *1 Corinthians 10:31—11:1*

Monday • *Mark 7:6–13*

Tuesday • *Mark 7:14–23*

Wednesday • *Mark 7:24–30*

Thursday • *Mark 7:31–37*

Friday • *Mark 8:22–26*

Saturday • *Mark 8:31–35*

7th Sunday in O.T. • *2 Corinthians 1:18–22*

Monday • *Mark 9:14–22*

Tuesday • *Mark 9:23–29*

Wednesday, Chair of Peter
  • *Matthew 16:13–19*

Thursday • *Mark 10:17–22*

Friday • *Mark 10:23–27*

Saturday • *Mark 10:28–31*

8th Sunday in O.T. • *2 Corinthians 3:1b–6*

Monday • *Mark 10:32–34*

Tuesday • *Mark 10:35–38, 41–45*

Ash Wednesday • *2 Corinthians 5:20—6:2*

Thursday • *Isaiah 58:1–4*

Friday • *Isaiah 58:6–9*

Saturday • *Isaiah 58:9–12*

1st Sunday of Lent • *Mark 1:12–15*

Monday • *Genesis 2:4–9*

Tuesday • *Genesis 2:15–20*

Wednesday • *Genesis 2:21–25*

Thursday • *Genesis 3:1–7*

Friday • *Genesis 3:8–13*

Saturday • *Genesis 3:14–19*

2nd Sunday of Lent • *Mark 9:2–10*

Monday • *Genesis 4:1–7*

Tuesday • *Genesis 4:8–15*

Wednesday • *Genesis 6:5–8, 9a–10*

Thursday • *Genesis 6:13–14, 17–22*

Friday • *Genesis 7:1, 11–16*

Saturday • *Genesis 7:17–23*

3rd Sunday of Lent • *John 2:13–21*

Monday, Joseph • *Luke 2:41–51a*

Tuesday • *Genesis 8:1–5*

Wednesday • *Genesis 8:6–12*

Thursday • *Genesis 8:13, 15–19*

Friday • *Genesis 9:8–16*

Saturday, Annunciation
  • *Isaiah 7:10–14; 8:10*

4th Sunday of Lent • *John 3:14–17*

Monday • *John 18:1–8*

Tuesday • *John 18:9–15*

Wednesday • *Genesis 21:1–7*

Thursday • *Genesis 22:1–3a, 4–6a, 7–8a*

Friday • *Genesis 22:9–14*

Saturday • *Genesis 22:15–19*

5th Sunday of Lent • *John 12:20–26*

Monday • *Deuteronomy 26:4–10*

Tuesday • *Deuteronomy 26:16–19*

Wednesday • *Deuteronomy 30:15–20*

Thursday • *Deuteronomy 19:1–4, 9–14*

Friday • *Deuteronomy 19:15–18*

Saturday • *Deuteronomy 4:1, 5–9*

Passion Sunday • *Mark 11:2–10*

Monday • *Isaiah 53:1–4*

Tuesday • *Isaiah 53:7–9*

Wednesday • *Isaiah 53:10b–12*

Holy Thursday • *John 13:3–9*

Good Friday • *Hebrews 4:14–16; 5:7–9*

Holy Saturday • *Romans 6:3–8*

Easter Sunday • *John 20:1–7*

Monday • *John 20:11–14*

Tuesday • *John 20:15–18*

Wednesday • *John 21:1–7*

Thursday • *John 21:8–14*

Friday • *John 21:15–18*

Saturday • *John 20:19–23*

Octave of Easter • *John 20:24–29*

Monday • *Acts 2:14a, 22–27*

Tuesday • *Mark 16:15–20*

Wednesday • *Acts 2:32–36*

Thursday • *Acts 2:37–42*

Friday • *Acts 2:43–47*

Saturday • *Acts 4:32–35*

3rd Sunday of Easter • *Luke 24:35–43*

Monday • *Acts 3:1–2a, 3–8*

Tuesday • *Acts 3:11–16*

Wednesday, Philip and James
   • *1 Corinthians 15:1–8*

Thursday • *Acts 6:8–9, 9–12*

Friday • *Acts 6:13–14; 7:1–2, 51–53*

Saturday • *Acts 7:54–58a, 59–60*

4th Sunday of Easter • *John 10:11–16*

Monday • *Acts 8:1b–8*

Tuesday • *Acts 8:9–13*

Wednesday • *Acts 8:14–19*

Thursday • *Acts 8:20–25*

Friday • *Acts 8:26–31*

Saturday • *Acts 8:32–35*

5th Sunday of Easter • *John 15:1–5, 7–8*

Monday • *Acts 8:36–40*

Tuesday • *Acts 10:1–8*

Wednesday • *Acts 10:9–15*

Thursday • *Acts 10:17–23*

Friday • *Acts 10:23, 25–26, 28–32*

Saturday • *Acts 10:34–35, 44–47*

6th Sunday of Easter • *John 15:9–15*

Monday • *Acts 15:1–5*

Tuesday • *Acts 15:6–11*

Wednesday • *Acts 15:22–25a, 28–29*

Thursday, Ascension
   • *Ephesians 4:1–7, 11–13*

Friday • *Genesis 11:1–4*

Saturday • *Genesis 11:5–9*

7th Sunday of Easter
   • *John 17:1b, 11b–14, 17–19*

Monday • *Ezekiel 37:1–6*

Tuesday, Visitation • *Zephaniah 3:14–18*

Wednesday • *Ezekiel 37:7–10*

Thursday • *Ezekiel 37:11–14*

Friday • *Joel 2:28–32*

Saturday • *Romans 8:14–17*

Pentecost • *Acts 2:1–11*

Monday • *1 Kings 17:1–6*

Tuesday • *1 Kings 17:7–12*

Wednesday • *1 Kings 17:13–16*

Thursday • *1 Kings 17:17–22*

Friday • *1 Kings 18:1, 17–20*

Saturday • *1 Kings 18:21–24*

Holy Trinity • *Deuteronomy 4:32–34, 39–40*

Monday • *1 Kings 18:25–29*

Tuesday • *1 Kings 18:25–29*

Wednesday • *1 Kings 18:30–35*

Thursday • *1 Kings 18:36–39*

Friday • *1 Kings 19:9–13a*

Saturday • *1 Kings 19:13b, 15b–16, 19–21*

Body and Blood • *Exodus 24:3–8*

Monday • *Isaiah 6:1–4*

Tuesday • *Isaiah 6:5–8*

Wednesday • *Isaiah 1:10–15*

Thursday • *Isaiah 1:16–20*

Friday, Sacred Heart • *Hosea 11:1, 3–4, 8c–9*

Saturday, Birth of John the Baptist
   • *Isaiah 49:1–6*

12th Sunday in O.T. • *2 Corinthians 5:14–17*

Monday • *Isaiah 26:7–9, 12*

Tuesday • *Isaiah 26:16–19*

Wednesday • *Micah 6:1–4*

Thursday, Peter and Paul • *John 21:15–19*

Friday • *Micah 6:6–8*

Saturday • *Micah 7:14–15, 18–20*

13th Sunday in O.T.
   • *2 Corinthians 8:7, 9, 13–15*

Monday, Thomas • *Ephesians 2:19–22*

Tuesday • *2 Kings 22:1a, 2–6*

Wednesday • *2 Kings 22:8, 10–13*

Thursday • *2 Kings 22:14–20a*

Friday • *2 Kings 23:1–3, 21–23*

Saturday • *2 Kings 23:26–30*

14th Sunday in O.T. • *2 Corinthians 12:7–10*

Monday • *2 Kings 24:8a, 9–14*

Tuesday • *2 Kings 24:17, 20b—25:6a*

Wednesday • *2 Kings 25:8–12*

Thursday • *Lamentations 1:1–4*

Friday • *Lamentations 1:5–8*

Saturday • *Lamentations 2:11–13*

15th Sunday in O.T. • *Ephesians 1:3–10*

Monday • *Jeremiah 2:4–7*

Tuesday • *Jeremiah 3:12–14*

Wednesday • *Jeremiah 3:15–18*

Thursday • *Jeremiah 18:1–6*

Friday • *Jeremiah 30:1–3, 8–9*

Saturday, Mary Magdalene
   • *Song of Songs 3:1–4*

16th Sunday in O.T. • *Ephesians 2:13–18*

Monday • *Jeremiah 30:18–22*

Tuesday, James • *Matthew 20:20–28*

Wednesday • *Jeremiah 31:1–5*

Thursday • *Jeremiah 31:7–10*

Friday • *Jeremiah 31:31–34*

Saturday, Martha • *John 11:19–27*

17th Sunday in O.T. • *John 6:1–9*

Monday • *John 6:10–14*

Tuesday • *Job 1:1–5*

Wednesday • *Job 1:6–12*

Thursday • *Job 1:13–22*

Friday • *Job 2:1–6*

Saturday • *Job 2:7–13*

18th Sunday in O.T. • *Daniel 7:9–10, 13–14*

Monday • *John 6:24–29*

Tuesday • *John 6:30–35*

Wednesday • *Job 3:1–3, 11–13, 16–19*

Thursday, Lawrence • *2 Corinthians 9:6–10*

Friday • *Job 3:20–26*

Saturday • *Job 4:1–9*

19th Sunday in O.T. • *John 6:44–51*

Monday • *Job 4:12–19*

Tuesday, Assumption
   • *1 Corinthians 15:20–27*

Wednesday • *Job 5:8–16*

Thursday • *Job 5:17–18, 21–22, 25–27*

Friday • *Job 9:1–8*

Saturday • *Job 9:11–12, 14–16, 19–20*

20th Sunday in O.T. • *John 6:52–58*

Monday • *Job 19:21–27*

Tuesday • *Job 38:1–11*

Wednesday • *Job 38:12–13, 16–21*

Thursday, Bartholomew
   • *Revelation 21:9b–14*

Friday • *Job 42:1–6*

Saturday • *Job 42:10, 12–17*

21st Sunday in O.T. • *John 6:60–64, 66–69*

Monday • *Proverbs 3:27–35*

Tuesday • *Proverbs 21:1–4*

Wednesday • *Proverbs 21:5–8*

Thursday • *Proverbs 21:10–13*

Friday • *Proverbs 8:1, 4–8*

Saturday • *Proverbs 8:12–14, 17*

22nd Sunday in O.T.
• *James 1:17–18, 21b–22, 27*

Monday • *Proverbs 8:22–26*

Tuesday • *Proverbs 8:27–31*

Wednesday • *Proverbs 8:32–36*

Thursday • *Proverbs 9:1–6*

Friday, Birth of Mary • *Micah 5:1–4*

Saturday • *Ecclesiastes 1:2–7*

23rd Sunday in O.T. • *James 2:1–5*

Monday • *Ecclesiastes 1:8–11*

Tuesday • *Ecclesiastes 3:1–4*

Wednesday • *Ecclesiastes 3:5–8*

Thursday, Exaltation of the Holy Cross
• *John 3:13–17*

Friday • *Ecclesiastes 11:9—12:1a*

Saturday • *Ecclesiastes 12:1b–8*

24th Sunday in O.T. • *James 2:14–18*

Monday • *Galatians 1:1–5*

Tuesday • *Galatians 1:6–8, 10–12*

Wednesday • *Galatians 1:13–20*

Thursday, Matthew • *Matthew 9:9–13*

Friday • *Galatians 2:1–2, 7–10*

Saturday • *Galatians 2:11–14*

25th Sunday in O.T. • *James 3:16—4:3*

Monday • *Galatians 3:1–5*

Tuesday • *Galatians 3:23–29*

Wednesday • *Galatians 4:21–26*

Thursday • *Galatians 4:28—5:1*

Friday, Michael, Gabriel, Raphael
• *Revelation 12:7, 9ac–12*

Saturday • *Galatians 5:18–25*

26th Sunday in O.T. • *James 5:1–6*

Monday • *Philippians 1:1–5*

Tuesday • *Philippians 1:6–11*

Wednesday • *Philippians 1:12–18a*

Thursday • *Philippians 1:18b–26*

Friday • *Philippians 2:1–4*

Saturday • *Philippians 2:6–11*

27th Sunday in O.T. • *Hebrews 2:9–11*

Monday • *Philippians 2:12–18*

Tuesday • *Philippians 2:19–28*

Wednesday • *Philippians 3:2–9*

Thursday • *Philippians 3:10–16*

Friday • *Philippians 3:17—4:1*

Saturday • *Philippians 4:4–9*

28th Sunday in O.T. • *Hebrews 4:12–13*

Monday • *Philippians 4:10–14*

Tuesday • *Philippians 4:15–23*

Wednesday, • *Luke 10:1–2a, 5–9*

Thursday • *Ephesians 1:1–2, 11–14*

Friday • *Ephesians 1:15–19*

Saturday • *Ephesians 2:4–10*

29th Sunday in O.T. • *Hebrews 4:14–16*

Monday • *Ephesians 3:1–6*

Tuesday • *Ephesians 3:7–12*

Wednesday • *Ephesians 4:7, 11–16*

Thursday • *Ephesians 4:17–24*

Friday • *Ephesians 4:25–32*

Saturday, Simon and Jude • *Luke 6:12–16*

30th Sunday in O.T. • *Hebrews 5:1–6*

Monday • *Ephesians 6:10–11, 14–17*

Tuesday • *Matthew 5:1–6*

Wednesday, All Saints • *Matthew 5:7–12*

Thursday, All Souls • *Luke 7:11–17*

Friday • *Wisdom 3:1–6, 9*

Saturday • *Wisdom 4:7–11, 13–14a*

31st Sunday in O.T. • *Hebrews 7:23–28*

Monday • *Isaiah 25:6, 7–9*

Tuesday • *Lamentations 3:17–26*

Wednesday • *Daniel 12:1–3*

Thursday, Dedication of the Lateran Basilica
• *1 Corinthians 3:9c–11, 16–17*

Friday • *1 Corinthians 15:20–28*

Saturday • *1 Corinthians 15:51–57*

32nd Sunday in O.T. • *Hebrews 9:24–28*

Monday • *2 Corinthians 4:14–18*

Tuesday • *2 Corinthians 5:1, 6–10*

Wednesday
• *1 Thessalonians 4:13–18*

Thursday • *2 Timothy 2:8–13*

Friday • *John 12:23–26*

Saturday • *John 14:1–6*

33rd Sunday in O.T. • *Hebrews 10:11–14, 18*

Monday • *Revelation 1:1–2, 4–6*

Tuesday • *Revelation 2:1–5*

Wednesday • *Revelation 3:1–6*

Thursday, Thanksgiving Day
• *Colossians 3:12–17*

Friday • *Revelation 3:14–20*

Saturday • *Revelation 4:1–6a*

34th Sunday in O.T. • *John 18:33b–37*

Monday • *Revelation 4:6b–11*

Tuesday • *Revelation 5:6–10*

Wednesday • *Revelation 14:1–3, 4b–5*

Thursday, Andrew
• *Romans 10:9–11, 14–15, 17–18*

Friday • *Revelation 14:14–19*

Saturday • *Revelation 22:1–7*

1st Sunday of Advent • *Jeremiah 33:14–16*

Monday • *Isaiah 2:2–4*

Tuesday • *Isaiah 4:2–3, 5–6*

Wednesday • *Isaiah 30:19–21, 23–25a, 26*

Thursday • *Isaiah 32:1–6*

Friday, Immaculate Conception
• *Ephesians 1:3–6, 11–12*

Saturday • *Isaiah 32:16–20*

2nd Sunday of Advent • *Baruch 5:1–4, 9*

Monday • *Luke 1:5–10*

Tuesday, Guadalupe
• *Revelation 12:1–6a, 10ab*

Wednesday • *Luke 1:11–17*

Thursday • *Luke 1:18–25*

Friday • *Luke 1:26–33*

Saturday • *Luke 1:34–38*

3rd Sunday of Advent • *Zephaniah 3:14–18*

Monday • *Luke 1:39–45*

Tuesday • *Luke 1:46–50*

Wednesday • *Luke 1:51–56*

Thursday • *Luke 1:57–66*

Friday • *Luke 1:67–75*

Saturday • *Luke 1:76–80*

4th Sunday of Advent • *Micah 5:2–5a*

Nativity of the Lord • *Isaiah 9:2–3, 6–7*

Tuesday, Stephen • *Matthew 10:17–22*

Wednesday, John • *John 1:1–5, 10–12*

Thursday, Holy Innocents • *Matthew 2:16–18*

Friday • *1 John 2:7–11*

Saturday • *1 John 2:14–17*

Holy Family • *1 John 3:1–2, 21–24*

PSALTER

PSALM 22:2-3, 13-22

My God, my God, why have you forsaken me?
You are far from my plea and the cry of my distress.
O my God, I call by day and you give no reply;
I call by night and I find no peace.

Many bulls have surrounded me,
fierce bulls of Bashan close me in.
Against me they open wide their jaws,
like lions, rending and roaring.

Like water I am poured out,
disjointed are all my bones.
My heart has become like wax,
it is melted within my breast.
Parched as burnt clay is my throat,
my tongue cleaves to my jaws.

Many dogs have surrounded me,
a band of the wicked beset me.
They tear holes in my hands and my feet
and lay me in the dust of death.

I can count every one of my bones.
These people stare at me and gloat;
they divide my clothing among them.
They cast lots for my robe.

O Lord, do not leave me alone,
my strength, make haste to help me!
Rescue my soul from the sword,
my life from the grip of these dogs.
Save my life from the jaws of these lions,
my soul from the horns of these oxen.

PSALM 25:1–14

To you, O LORD, I lift up my soul.
My God, I trust you, let me not be disappointed;
do not let my enemies triumph.
Those who hope in you shall not be disappointed,
but only those who wantonly break faith.

LORD, make me know your ways.
LORD, teach me your paths.
Make me walk in your truth, and teach me,
for you are God my savior.

In you I hope all the day long
because of your goodness, O LORD.
Remember your mercy, LORD,
and the love that you have shown from of old.
Do not remember the sins of my youth.
In your love remember me.

The LORD is good and upright,
showing the path to those who stray,
guiding the humble in the right path,
and teaching the way to the poor.

God's ways are steadfastness and truth
for those faithful to the covenant decrees.
LORD, for the sake of your name
forgive my guilt, for it is great.

Those who revere the LORD
will be shown the path they should choose.
Their souls will live in happiness
and their children shall possess the land.
The LORD's friendship is for the God-fearing;
and the covenant is revealed to them.

PSALM 27:1–5, 13–14

The LORD is my light and my help;
whom shall I fear?
The LORD is the stronghold of my life;
before whom shall I shrink?

When evildoers draw near
to devour my flesh,
it is they, my enemies and foes,
who stumble and fall.

Though an army encamp against me
my heart would not fear.
Though war break out against me
even then would I trust.

There is one thing I ask of the LORD,
for this I long,
to live in the house of the LORD,
all the days of my life,
to savor the sweetness of the LORD,
to behold his temple.

For God makes me safe in his tent
in the day of evil.
God hides me in the shelter of his tent,
on a rock I am secure.

I am sure I shall see the LORD's goodness
in the land of the living.
In the LORD, hold firm and take heart.
Hope in the LORD.

PSALM 34:2–15

I will bless the LORD at all times,
God's praise always on my lips;
in the LORD my soul shall make its boast.
The humble shall hear and be glad.

Glorify the LORD with me.
Together let us praise God's name.
I sought the LORD and was heard;
from all my terrors set free.

Look towards God and be radiant;
let your faces not be abashed.
When the poor cry out the LORD hears them
and rescues them from all their distress.

The angel of the LORD is encamped
around those who fear God, to rescue them.
Taste and see that the LORD is good.
They are happy who seek refuge in God.

Revere the LORD, you saints.
They lack nothing, who revere the LORD.
Strong lions suffer want and go hungry
but those who seek the LORD lack no blessing.

Come, children, and hear me
that I may teach you the fear of the LORD.
Who are those who long for life
and many days, to enjoy their prosperity?

Then keep your tongue from evil
and your lips from speaking deceit.
Turn aside from evil and do good;
seek and strive after peace.

PSALM 40:2-3, 6-9, 11-12

I waited, I waited for the LORD
who stooped down to me,
and heard my cry.

God drew me from the deadly pit,
from the miry clay,
and set my feet upon a rock
and made my footsteps firm.

How many, O LORD my God,
are the wonders and designs
that you have worked for us;
you have no equal.
Should I proclaim and speak of them,
they are more than I can tell!

You do not ask for sacrifice and offerings,
but an open ear.
You do not ask for holocaust and victim.
Instead, here am I.

In the scroll of the book it stands written
that I should do your will.
My God, I delight in your law
in the depth of my heart.

I have not hidden your justice in my heart
but declared your faithful help.
I have not hidden your love and your truth
from the great assembly.

O LORD, you will not withhold
your compassion from me.
Your merciful love and your truth
will always guard me.

PSALM 51:3-17

Have mercy on me, God, in your kindness.
In your compassion blot out my offense.
O wash me more and more from my guilt
and cleanse me from my sin.

My offenses truly I know them;
my sin is always before me.
Against you, you alone, have I sinned;
what is evil in your sight I have done.

That you may be justified when you give sentence
and be without reproach when you judge,
O see, in guilt I was born,
a sinner was I conceived.

Indeed you love truth in the heart;
then in the secret of my heart teach me wisdom.
O purify me, then I shall be clean;
O wash me, I shall be whiter than snow.

Make me hear rejoicing and gladness
that the bones you have crushed may revive.
From my sins turn away your face
and blot out all my guilt.

A pure heart create for me, O God,
put a steadfast spirit within me.
Do not cast me away from your presence,
nor deprive me of your holy spirit.

Give me again the joy of your help;
with a spirit of fervor sustain me,
that I may teach transgressors your ways
and sinners may return to you.

O rescue me, God, my helper,
and my tongue shall ring out your goodness.
O LORD, open my lips
and my mouth shall declare your praise.

PSALM 66:1–9

Cry out with joy to God, all the earth,
O sing to the glory of his name,
rendering glorious praise.
Say to God: "How tremendous your deeds!

Because of the greatness of your strength
your enemies cringe before you.
Before you all the earth shall bow,
shall sing to you, sing to your name!"

Come and see the works of God,
tremendous deeds for the people.
God turned the sea into dry land,
they passed through the river dry-shod.

Let our joy then be in the LORD,
who rules forever in power,
whose eyes keep watch over nations;
let rebels not lift themselves up.

O peoples, bless our God;
let the voice of God's praise resound,
of the God who gave life to our souls
and kept our feet from stumbling.

PSALM 71:5-6, 16-24

It is you, O LORD, who are my hope,
my trust, O LORD, since my youth.
On you I have leaned from my birth;
from my mother's womb you have been my help.
My hope has always been in you.

LORD, I will declare your mighty deeds,
proclaiming your justice, yours alone.
O God, you have taught me from my youth
and I proclaim your wonders still.

Now that I am old and gray-headed,
do not forsake me, God.
Let me tell of your power to all ages,
praise your strength and justice to the skies,
tell of you who have worked such wonders.
O God, who is like you?

You have burdened me with bitter troubles
but you will give me back my life.
You will raise me from the depths of the earth;
you will exalt me and console me again.

So I will give you thanks on the lyre
for your faithful love, my God.
To you will I sing with the harp,
to you, the Holy One of Israel.
When I sing to you my lips shall rejoice
and my soul, which you have redeemed.

And all the day long my tongue
shall tell the tale of your justice:
for they are put to shame and disgraced,
all those who seek to harm me.

PSALM 85:2-14

O LORD, you once favored your land
and revived the fortunes of Jacob,
you forgave the guilt of your people
and covered all their sins.
You averted all your rage,
you calmed the heat of your anger.

Revive us now, God, our helper!
Put an end to your grievance against us.
Will you be angry with us for ever,
will your anger never cease?

Will you not restore again our life
that your people may rejoice in you?
Let us see, O LORD, your mercy
and give us your saving help.

I will hear what the LORD has to say,
a voice that speaks of peace,
peace for his people and friends
and those who turn to God in their hearts.
Salvation is near for the God-fearing,
and his glory will dwell in our land.

Mercy and faithfulness have met;
justice and peace have embraced.
Faithfulness shall spring from the earth
and justice look down from heaven.

The LORD will make us prosper
and our earth shall yield its fruit.
Justice shall march in the forefront,
and peace shall follow the way.

PSALM 86:1–10

Turn your ear, O LORD, and give answer
for I am poor and needy.
Preserve my life, for I am faithful;
save the servant who trusts in you.

You are my God, have mercy on me, LORD,
for I cry to you all the day long.
Give joy to your servant, O LORD,
for to you I lift up my soul.

O LORD, you are good and forgiving,
full of love to all who call.
Give heed, O LORD, to my prayer
and attend to the sound of my voice.

In the day of distress I will call
and surely you will reply.
Among the gods there is none like you, O LORD,
nor work to compare with yours.

All the nations shall come to adore you
and glorify your name, O LORD,
for you are great and do marvelous deeds,
you who alone are God.

PSALM 89:2–17

I will sing for ever of your love, O LORD;
through all ages my mouth will proclaim your truth.
Of this I am sure, that your love lasts for ever,
that your truth is firmly established as the heavens.

"With my chosen one I have made a covenant;
I have sworn to David my servant:
I will establish your dynasty for ever
and set up your throne through all ages."

The heavens proclaim your wonders, O LORD;
the assembly of your holy ones proclaims your truth.
For who in the skies can compare with the LORD;
who is like the LORD among the children of God?

A God to be feared in the council of the holy ones,
great and dreadful, revered above all.
O LORD God of hosts, who is your equal?
You are mighty, O LORD, and truth is your garment.

It is you who rule the sea in its pride;
it is you who still the surging of its waves.
It is you who trod Rahab underfoot like a corpse,
scattering your foes with your mighty arm.

The heavens are yours, the world is yours.
It is you who founded the earth and all it holds;
it is you who created the North and the South.
Tabor and Hermon shout for joy at your name.

Yours is a mighty arm, O LORD;
your hand is strong, your right hand ready.
Justice and right are the pillars of your throne,
love and truth walk in your presence.

Happy the people who acclaim such a God,
who walk, O LORD, in the light of your face,
who find their joy every day in your name,
who make your justice the source of their bliss.

PSALM 90:1-6, 9-10, 12-17

O Lord, you have been our refuge
from one generation to the next.
Before the mountains were born
or the earth or the world brought forth,
you are God, without beginning or end.

You turn us back into dust
and say: "Go back, children of the earth."
To your eyes a thousand years
are like yesterday, come and gone,
no more than a watch in the night.

You sweep us away like a dream,
like grass which springs up in the morning.
In the morning it springs up and flowers;
by evening it withers and fades.

All our days pass away in your anger.
Our life is over like a sigh.
Our span is seventy years,
or eighty for those who are strong.

Make us know the shortness of our life
that we may gain wisdom of heart.
LORD, relent! Is your anger for ever?
Show pity to your servants.

In the morning, fill us with your love;
we shall exult and rejoice all our days.
Give us joy to balance our affliction
for the years when we knew misfortune.

Show forth your work to your servants;
let your glory shine on their children.
Let the favor of the Lord be upon us:
give success to the work of our hands.

PSALM 96:1-13

O sing a new song to the LORD,
sing to the LORD all the earth.
O sing to the LORD, bless his name.

Proclaim God's help day by day,
tell among the nations his glory
and his wonders among all the peoples.

The LORD is great and worthy of praise,
to be feared above all gods;
the gods of the heathens are naught.

It was the LORD who made the heavens.
His are majesty and honor and power
and splendor in the holy place.

Give the LORD, you families of people,
give the LORD glory and power;
give the LORD the glory of his name.

Bring an offering and enter God's courts,
worship the LORD in the temple.
O earth, stand in fear of the LORD.

Proclaim to the nations: "God is king."
The world was made firm in its place;
God will judge the people in fairness.

Let the heavens rejoice and earth be glad,
let the sea and all within it thunder praise,
let the land and all it bears rejoice,
all the trees of the wood shout for joy

at the presence of the LORD who comes,
who comes to rule the earth,
comes with justice to rule the world,
and to judge the peoples with truth.

PSALM 103:1–10, 13–14, 17–18

My soul, give thanks to the LORD,
all my being, bless God's holy name.
My soul, give thanks to the LORD
and never forget all God's blessings.

It is God who forgives all your guilt,
who heals every one of your ills,
who redeems your life from the grave,
who crowns you with love and compassion,
who fills your life with good things,
renewing your youth like an eagle's.

The LORD does deeds of justice,
gives judgment for all who are oppressed.
The LORD's ways were made known to Moses;
the LORD's deeds to Israel's children.

The LORD is compassion and love,
slow to anger and rich in mercy.
The LORD will not always chide,
will not be angry forever.
God does not treat us according to our sins
nor repay us according to our faults.

As parents have compassion on their children,
the LORD has pity on those who are God-fearing
for he knows of what we are made
and remembers that we are dust.

But the love of the LORD is everlasting
upon those who fear the LORD.
God's justice reaches out to children's children
when they keep his covenant in truth,
when they keep his will in their mind.

PSALM 104:1–2, 10–12, 16–21, 27–30

Bless the LORD, my soul!
LORD God, how great you are,
clothed in majesty and glory,
wrapped in light as in a robe!

You make springs gush forth in the valleys;
they flow in between the hills.
They give drink to all the beasts of the field;
the wild asses quench their thirst.
On their banks dwell the birds of heaven;
from the branches they sing their song.

The trees of the LORD drink their fill,
the cedars God planted on Lebanon;
there the birds build their nests;
on the treetop the stork has her home.
The goats find a home on the mountains
and rabbits hide in the rocks.

You made the moon to mark the months;
the sun knows the time for its setting.
When you spread the darkness it is night
and all the beasts of the forest creep forth.
The young lions roar for their prey
and ask their food from God.

All of these look to you
to give them their food in due season.
You give it, they gather it up;
you open your hand, they have their fill.

You hide your face, they are dismayed;
you take back your spirit, they die,
returning to the dust from which they came.
You send forth your spirit, they are created;
and you renew the face of the earth.

PSALM 111:1–10

Alleluia!

I will thank the LORD with all my heart
in the meeting of the just and their assembly.
Great are the works of the LORD,
to be pondered by all who love them.

Majestic and glorious God's work,
whose justice stands firm for ever.
God makes us remember these wonders.
The LORD is compassion and love.

God gives food to those who fear him;
keeps his covenant ever in mind;
shows mighty works to his people
by giving them the land of the nations.

God's works are justice and truth,
God's precepts are all of them sure,
standing firm for ever and ever;
they are made in uprightness and truth.

God has sent deliverance to his people
and established his covenant for ever.
Holy is God's name, to be feared.

To fear the LORD is the first stage of wisdom;
all who do so prove themselves wise.
God's praise shall last for ever!

Alleluia!